Endorsements

The performance of supply chain management determines the performance of the corporation itself. In retail and wholesale industries, the effectiveness of supply chain and logistics management holds the key to provide competitive advantage. This book addresses the core issues and helps the students and practitioners to take an integrated view of supply chain management areas for making decisions in a business. The book deals with global supply chain and performance management for developing a sustainable and competitive supply chain in a highly dynamic and unpredictable business environment, and discusses the subject taking many practical examples and cases to provide the key insights. I am happy to see that Dr Rajat Baisya, who has helped us in setting up our Indian operation, has written a book on this important subject which is expected to be extremely useful for the students, researchers and professionals. I am happy to recommend this book.

—Charles Wilson
Chief Executive Officer
Booker–Tesco PLC, UK

* * *

It is refreshing to see an interesting book on supply chain and logistics management by Professor Baisya, who has established himself as a management educator, corporate consultant and wonderful trainer, besides a writer of substance.

Supply chain management (SCM) is a coordinated system of managing the transportation and logistics activities in a manufacturing, wholesale or retail business. The primary purpose of SCM is to optimize efficiency in supply chain distribution activities. Traditionally, each supply chain member took a myopic view of its role in moving goods to the next stage. With an SCM approach, all chain members collaborate with the end goal of delivering the best value to consumers, keeping the holistic perspective.

This book on integrated supply chain and logistics management presents a fresh perspective. The book is an outcome of huge experiential base of Professor Baisya, who has worked with organizations such as Emami, Reckitt Benckiser (India) Ltd, Escorts Group, United Breweries Group and Parle Bisleri. Professor Baisya has innovatively combined his field research and corporate experience in giving a unique perspective on SCM and logistics. The book is a treatise on handling various issues in SCM and gives clarion call for understanding the basics with clarity. Professor Baisya's strong corporate foundation and his worldview make the unfolding simple in an otherwise complex territory of SCM.

The book has nine chapters. Starting with the issue why SCM is important for businesses for their survival, the book brings in many short real-life cases and helps in cost management in supply chain for competitive advantage. It has sections on benchmarking supply chain, sustainable SCM and decision criteria for resolving various key issues in managing complexity in distribution management. Various issues in distribution, warehousing and inventory are handled in a comprehensive manner. The book also highlights performance management issues in supply chain. Looking at the emerging global scenario, there is a chapter on 'Global Logistics Value Chain Management', which is highly contemporary and relevant to the theme of the book.

I am sure the book will provide a good companion to those who are in search of innovative and real-life practices, which will improve the bottom line.

—Dr S. G. Deshmukh
Director
Atal Bihari Vajpayee Indian Institute of Information Technology and Management, Gwalior

Integrated Supply Chain and Logistics Management

Integrated Supply Chain and Logistics Management

Rajat K. Baisya

*Professor and Head (Retired), Department of Management Studies,
Indian Institute of Technology Delhi*

SAGE | TEXTS

Los Angeles | London | New Delhi
Singapore | Washington DC | Melbourne

First published in 2020 by

SAGE | TEXTS

SAGE Publications India Pvt Ltd
B1/I-1 Mohan Cooperative Industrial Area
Mathura Road, New Delhi 110 044, India
www.sagepub.in

SAGE Publications Inc
2455 Teller Road
Thousand Oaks, California 91320, USA

SAGE Publications Ltd
1 Oliver's Yard, 55 City Road
London EC1Y 1SP, United Kingdom

SAGE Publications Asia-Pacific Pte Ltd
18 Cross Street #10-10/11/12
China Square Central
Singapore 048423

Published by Vivek Mehra for SAGE Publications India Pvt Ltd. Typeset in 10.5/12.5 pt Baskerville by AG Infographics, Delhi.

Library of Congress Cataloging-in-Publication Data Available

ISBN: 978-93-532-8665-1 (PB)

SAGE Team: Amit Kumar, Indrani Dutta, Vandana Gupta, Syeda Aina Rahat Ali and Kanika Mathur

This book is dedicated to the warm and sacred memory of my parents,
Rabindra Kumar Baishya and Vidyut Prava Baishya,
who have been a constant source of inspiration all through my life.

Contents

Detailed Contents

CHAPTER 6

CHAPTER 7

List of Figures

List of Tables

List of Abbreviations

ABC	Activity-based costing
AFACT	Asia Pacific Council for Trade Facilitation & Electronic Business
AGV	Automated Guided Vehicle
AI	Artificial intelligence
AMCS	Automatic milk collection system
APL	American President Lines
ASEAN	Association of Southeast Asian Nations
ASNs	Advanced shipment notifications
ASRS	Automated Storage and Retrieval System
B2B	Business-to-business
B2C	Business-to-consumer
BOD	Board of Directors
BOP	Bottom of the pyramid
BPCS	Business Planning Control System
BPR	Business process re-engineering
C&F	Carrying and forwarding
C&S	Carrying and selling
C+D	Connect+Develop
CAFE	Coffee and Farmer Equity Initiative
CAGR	Compound annual growth rate
CCTs	Commodity competence teams
CEO	Chief executive officer
CFO	Chief financial officer
CLM	Council of Logistics Management
CMI	Co-managed inventory
CMM	Capability Maturity Model
CMM-I	Integrated CMM
CONCOR	Container Corporation of India Ltd
CPFR	Collaborative planning, forecasting and replenishment
CSFs	Critical success factors
CSL	Cycle service level
CTO	Chief technology officer
C-TPAT	Customs Trade Partnership Against Terrorism
DCS	Dairy Cooperative Society
DSE	Delhi School of Economics
DTMS	Domestic Terminal Management System
EDI	Electronic data interchange

EDLP	Everyday low pricing
ELV	End-of-Life Vehicle
EOQ	Economic order quantity
ERAP	Emergency response assistance plan
ERP	Enterprise resource planning
ETMS	Export/Import Terminal Management System
EU	European Union
EXIM	Export–import
FCI	Food Corporation of India
FCL	Full Container Load
FCPA	Foreign Corrupt Practices Act
FIFO	First-in, first-out
FMC	Federal Maritime Commission
FMCG	Fast-moving consumer goods
FPY	First-pass yield
FTA	Free trade agreement
FTEs	Full-time equivalents
GCMMF	Gujarat Cooperative Milk Marketing Federation
GDSN	Global Data Synchronisation Network
GIS	Geographic Information Systems
GRN	Goods receipt note
GST	Goods and Services Tax
HRM	Human resource management
HUL	Hindustan Unilever Limited
IATA	International Air Transport Association
ICDs	Inland container depots
IDSN	Integrated demand–supply network
IMDG	International Maritime Dangerous Goods
IMI	International Maritime Institute
IMO	International Maritime Organization
IPD-CMM	CMM for Integrated Product and Process Development
IS	Information system
ISMS	Information security management system
IT	Information technology
JIT	Just-in-time
KPIs	Key performance indicators
LCL	Less than container load
LPI	Logistics Performance Index
LYC	Last year consumption
MAD	Mean absolute deviation
MAPE	Mean absolute percentage error
MLM	Multi-level marketing
MMT	Million metric tonnes
MNCs	Multinational corporations

MRP	Material requirements planning
MSC	Mediterranean Shipping Company
MSE	Mean squared error
NCPDM	National Council of Physical Distribution Management
NIIF	National Investment and Infrastructure Fund
OOCL	Orient Overseas Container Line
OSEM	Office of Safety and Emergency Management
OTC	Over-the-counter
P&G	Procter & Gamble
PCs	Personal computers
PDS	Public distribution system
POP	Point of Purchase
POS	Point of sale
QMMG	Quality Management Maturity Grid
R&D	Research and development
ROCI	Return on capital invested
ROI	Return on investment
ROPs	Reorder points
RORO	Roll-on/roll-off
S&OP	Sales and operations planning
SBU	Strategic business unit
SCC	Supply Chain Council
SCM	Supply chain management
SCOR	Supply Chain Operation Reference
SCPM	Supply chain performance management
SECH	Social Ethical Cultural and Health
SE-CMM	CMM for Systems Engineering
SKU	Stock-keeping unit
SOX	Sarbanes–Oxley Act of 2002
TDGR	Transportation of Dangerous Goods Act & Regulations
TLC	Total logistics cost
TLEs	Transaction learning experiments
TPL	Third-party logistics
TPOP	Time-phased order point
TQM	Total quality management
TRU	Thompson Rivers University
VMI	Vendor-managed inventory
VMS	Volvo Mobility Systems
VPPs	Value payable parcels
WACC	Weighted Average Capital Cost
WCO	World Customs Organization
WES	Winters' exponential smoothing
WIP	Work in progress/process
WMSs	Warehouse management systems
WTO	World Trade Organization

Foreword

Supply chain management (SCM) has evolved over the years from an initial concept of moving goods and services from a point of origin to a point of consumption to a highly interlinked and interdependent discipline to be managed for better performance. What was originally started in the early 1980s in the USA when global sourcing was the key imperative to respond to a highly competitive business environment has now evolved as a fully developed integrated discipline supported by technology.

Logistics is a very important function in business and offers considerable scope for improvement. One of the important areas in SCM is logistics issues within the supply chain itself, and therefore, it is better to manage logistics as an integrated function. In the current context, SCM covers everything from procurement to delivering the product to customers. Managing supply chain for performance, thus, also needs effective and efficient management of logistics functions.

This book has been designed to cover important issues of both SCM and logistics management to enable the readers and students of SCM and logistics management to take an integrated view. Starting with the issue why SCM is so important for businesses for their survival and global SCM issues, the book brings in many short real-life cases and helps in cost management in supply chain for competitive advantage. It has sections on benchmarking supply chain, sustainable SCM, decision criteria for manufacturing in-house vs out-house, key issues and managing complexity in distribution management. The book also deals with performance management issues in supply chain as well as transportation and global logistics value chain management.

The book helps you to design an effective development and management of a supply chain network which is an invaluable source of sustainable advantage in today's turbulent global marketplace, where demand is difficult to predict and supply chains need to be more flexible and customer-focused.

The book will be a valuable addition to the existing literature available for students and practitioners in SCM and operations. Some examples have been taken and discussed from global business operations and will be useful for students abroad. The book covers a wide range of subjects and topics with real-life cases to help students and practising managers to get key insights into SCM as we understand now.

I know Professor Rajat Baisya very well. He has served as a visiting professor at our institute, teaching international students of both supply chain and logistics management. He has served for three decades working with leading industries and also as an academician and researcher with global exposure and association. He is also a corporate trainer and consultant of global repute. He, thus, brings with him a unique mix of industry experience to provide practitioners perspective as well as academic rigour and discipline.

I am happy to recommend this book to students and faculty of supply chain and logistics management as well as of production and operations management. The book will also serve as a good reference book for practitioners in consulting and industry.

—**Professor Bojan Rosi**
Dean, Faculty of Logistics
University of Maribor
Slovenia

Preface

Supply Chain Management (SCM) has evolved as a full-grown discipline and a subject of specialization in education and research as well as an important function in business to be managed during last two decades. Business consultants are talking about the importance of effective and efficient management of supply chain function as an essential prerequisite for delivering company's bottom-line performance objective. To be cost-effective and competitive in the marketplace managing the procurement, production and distribution function as a closely coordinated function is the key imperative. Businesses now compete through better SCM practices. Supply chain, therefore, has to be market-driven and is synonymous with value chain.

Around the late 1980s and early 1990s, the process of globalization was witnessed in businesses all over the world and in response to that environment, most of the global players opted to source the products and services from places where these were the cheapest and best. Forces of globalization in subsequent years forced the companies to improve the SCM functions, and we have seen the era of global manufacturing and sourcing.

In today's highly competitive global marketplace, organizations are looking for avenues to create higher value for their customers and in that context, there is an increasing recognition that through efficient logistics and effective SCM, both cost reduction and enhancement of service delivery can be achieved. Through supply chain, firms thus aim to achieve both cost-effectiveness and improved customer satisfaction. Technology plays a vital role in managing supply chain and making it efficient and effective in all its operations, and as such, decisions in supply chain are now mostly based on information.

The book has been designed to cover both SCM and logistics function to enable students and practitioners to take an integrated view for logical decision-making. Logistics companies around the world are offering value-added extended service and becoming strategic partners for the manufacturers, marketers and organized retailers. Corporations with global presence have to bring in the incremental benefits to their business, forging these key alliances, and this is most important for the global retailers and wholesalers where profit comes only from better SCM and logistics management practices.

The book has nine chapters and deals with all key activities and issues of the supply chain and logistics functions of the business, including demand forecasting and inventory management, and then dealing with the complexities and challenges of warehousing and distribution as well as transportation. The book covers global logistics value chain management as well as performance management in supply chain and deals with topics such as performance management matrix and maturity models. The book also covers the benchmarking and sustainability issues in supply chain to remain relevant and competitive in business with case studies to drive key insights into sustainability issues in supply chain and how those can help in terms of increased value delivery. There are short cases and real-life issues that are discussed to provide key insights into the decision-making criteria.

Integration of areas such as procurement, processing and distribution is possible through proper management and control of supply chain operations. In developing countries like India, distribution is highly complex and it takes years for businesses to develop an efficient distribution function which is so vital for business performance. Global companies are even seen acquiring companies in India only to get access to and familiarize themselves with the complex and difficult tasks of setting up distribution functions as their key entry strategy into the Indian market. The book discusses these complexities and challenges.

The book is targeted towards both academics and practitioners of SCM. In academics, the book should be appropriate for the MBA students as well as engineering students interested or specializing in SCM and logistics management.

Rajat K. Baisya

Acknowledgements

This book has referenced a few cases which are based on some practical data collected and reported by researchers. These case studies have been suitably adopted to explain and discuss certain theories and/or methods which I duly acknowledge.

I also gratefully acknowledge the support from Mr Charles Wilson, CEO of Booker Tesco Plc., UK, and Professor S. G. Deshmukh, Director, ABV-IIITM, Gwalior, for their critical review of the contents of my book and also for writing the endorsements for the book.

A friend, colleague and contemporary Professor Bojan Rosi kindly wrote the foreword for the book, and I am very thankful to him for his support.

All through the writing of this book, my assistant Debkumar Maity was very helpful in terms of verifying certain facts and figures as well as extending help while editing the manuscript. I thank him for his assistance and dedication.

Often, when you work for a book, it takes up a lot of your time which sometimes inconveniences your family; same happened with mine too. However, they are also the happiest at the completion of this book, and I gratefully acknowledge the overwhelming support from all of them. I thank my wife Susmita for standing by me all through the way and sometimes taking more responsibilities towards the family than due. I express my affection towards my son Rishabh and daughter Deepshikha and appreciate their patience and help through this journey. Both my children are successful professionals in their own right and have often offered suggestions and constructive feedback, especially my son, who has keen interest in this subject.

Finally, my publisher SAGE has done a great job in terms of providing all support to release the book on time. Amit Kumar, Indrani Dutta and Vandana Gupta of SAGE were of tremendous help and all of them worked closely with me on this project all through. I thank them for their constant help.

There are many people who have helped in small and big ways, and it is not possible to mention all of them; however, I would like to say that I recognize and appreciate their help at every step and humbly acknowledge that this book would not have been possible without all their support.

Rajat K. Baisya

About the Author

Rajat K. Baisya is the Professor and Head (Retired), Department of Management Studies, Indian Institute of Technology Delhi. He is an award-winning, highly noted and distinguished management consultant, visionary, teacher and successful businessman.

During his long-standing career spanning over 48 years, he has held various senior positions in large multinational organizations and business schools of global ranking.

Professor Baisya has been the President and CEO of Emami Group, and Senior Vice President of Reckitt Benckiser, among many other very challenging positions. He has also served on the board of Rajasthan Electronics and Instruments Ltd, Booker India Pvt Ltd and North Eastern Development Finance Corporation Ltd.

Currently, he is engaged in various academic and consulting assignments and is associated with global business institutions such as University of Maribor, Slovenia; Northwestern Polytechnical University, Xian, China; and ENPC International Business School, Paris, France, as a visiting professor.

He is also actively working as the President of Project and Technology Management Foundation and Chief Editor of *International Journal of Project and Technology Management*, and serving on the editorial board of many national and international journals.

He is the Founder Chairman and Director of Strategic Consulting Group Pvt Ltd and Frontier Agro Industries Pvt Ltd. As a part of his latest project, he has launched India's first online stock exchange for consultants called Winning Sparrow (www.winningsparrow.com).

Professor Baisya believes in learning something new every day and always looks for the next challenge.

1

Understanding the Supply Chain: The Core Concepts

LEARNING OBJECTIVES

- Understand the core concepts of a supply chain in terms of its definition and what it covers
- Identify the impacts and implications of supply chain management on business performance
- Understand key challenges of supply chain management to overcome for delivering results
- Appreciate the role of an effective and efficient supply chain in creating a competitive advantage for the business

INTRODUCTION

Supply chain management (SCM) as a discipline has developed during the last two decades, although business consultants have been discussing about the importance of managing a supply chain efficiently as a prerequisite of delivering expected level of the performance of any business since the late 1980s. But it was only during the post-liberalization and globalization era that the importance of the SCM was recognized by business leaders all over the world. SCM as a function has gone through significant changes during the last two decades. In the course of time, the scope and limits of SCM got extended to become end-to-end SCM. Today, it covers a wide range of functions in business, starting from procurement to productions and operations, and warehousing to distribution. Earlier, focus of business was on marketing and finance, which were considered as the key functions responsible for the delivery of business performance, and then came an era where businesses were focusing on people with the thought that it is the people who deliver the result and, therefore, employee engagement and retention and talent development had taken all the attention of the business leaders. This may be uniformly true for all functions, and under Industry 4.0 environment, which we are now passing through, talent has always been seen by business leaders all over the world as the topmost driver for global manufacturing competitiveness (Global Manufacturing Competitiveness Index Report, 2018, by Deloitte). A supply chain in today's business covers almost all line functions and, therefore, attracts the attention of the business. If a supply chain function is not efficient and effective, businesses will not remain competitive in the marketplace, and even survival of the business itself will be threatened.

Since the concept of a supply chain was initially developed as an integrated function, a lot of development has taken place since then. Today, it is highly technology-driven. Procurement was once upon a time considered as a very mundane function and very little attention was given by businesses which subsequently was found to be a very important function offering considerable scope for cost reduction and competitive advantage.

The purchase function was initially managed by some low-key executives by inviting quotations and going through negotiations to get the best possible price for the item(s) to be procured. Purchase managers were trying to focus on getting the best possible price for key items required for manufacturing. It was much later that businesses realized that over 75% of the cost of the product is constituted by procured items or bought-out items, and therefore, if a company has to be cost competitive, a greater opportunity lies in managing the procurement function better, and thereafter, the procurement function improves, adding a lot of incremental value to the business. Today, the procurement function is highly developed and a lot of technologies, including e-auction, vendor-managed inventory (VMI) and so on, are used in addition to the concept of just-in-time (JIT) inventory as well as focused and preferred supplier zeroed on after carrying out vendor development and vendor rating based on predetermined criteria. Businesses even use third-party funding and bill discounting to reduce the procurement cost.

After making significant improvement in procurement functions, businesses start focusing on core activities. And we have seen that companies started shifting manufacturing facilities to the places where it was costing least and satisfying all quality criteria and also from the perspective of better customer service. We have seen that companies started focusing on what they knew better, and thus manufacturing operations were shifting to outside the business. During the early 1990s, almost 100% production was carried out in companies' own manufacturing plants, but by the end of that decade, almost 100% manufacturing was contracted out and businesses were only focusing on marketing, research and development (R&D) and business development activities. Today, most of the manufacturing has been outsourced to smaller companies to benefit from the lower logistics and inventory holding cost, and thus manufacturing operations are also spread over many locations and coming closer to customers' locations. Globally, manufacturing operations shifted to China, it being a low-cost mass production country. China emerged as a global supply source.

India lost out on the race to become the global manufacturing hub mostly because in terms of key global manufacturing competitiveness drivers, India lacks in many of those parameters, including infrastructure and legal and regulatory framework. These issues are discussed in detail in the book. Many businesses follow many innovative processes to improve upon the supply chain efficiency. For example, Benetton produces all T-shirts in white and prints them closer to the season when they can get more accurate estimate of demand of the colour of the garments required in a particular year, thereby reducing the inventory. Otherwise, excess and unsold stock may have to be rejected or disposed of as a discounted stock, losing out on profitability. Dell manufactures laptops on getting confirmed orders to reduce the inventory.

It has now been observed that manufacturing in a global location in say China and selling the end product globally have other ramifications and complexities. In this scenario, many a time input material has to come from many countries all over the world, wherever those are best and cheapest, say China, and then re-transported to the countries where it has to be sold, and that increases cost and complexity. Because of the distance between selling countries and production countries, inventory holding gets larger, blocking costly working capital. The transportation cost also becomes higher, and global corporations are carefully analysing the parameters to decide the best ways to manage a global supply chain with a clear objective of least cost and best service to the customers. These issues are changing the SCM processes now from the earlier established practices. Many items and product categories are now standardized and delivered to customers based on order received in knocked down conditions, and these are assembled at customers' premises. IKEA is a Swedish-founded multinational group that designs and sells ready-to-assemble furniture, kitchen appliances and home accessories, among other useful goods and occasionally home services. The IKEA model of furniture business is now practised and replicated by even domestic furniture manufacturers. International furniture manufacturers are also entering countries with franchise route to be cost competitive. They supply in bulk only the panels which are cut to size as per the customer's order and fabricated at the customer's location or wherever they want. The business model is changing only from competitiveness point of view. As competition is increasing, businesses are trying to become more and more innovative to improve upon value delivery and, therefore, on both benefits in terms of quality and functionality and cost, businesses are constantly improving. And SCM offers greatest opportunity for incremental value delivery.

The logistics which covers warehousing and transportation is increasingly becoming costlier and can form a significant part of the cost of the entire supply chain. In the USA, logistics cost is about 8% of the GDP, whereas in India, it is about 15%. There are significant opportunities for improving the logistics cost as well as managing warehousing better through the use of technology. Logistics cost is the new area that businesses are now concentrating after taking care of procurement and production or manufacturing. There are inbound and outbound logistics to be tackled and non-value-adding activities to be eliminated. Logistics, therefore, is an integral part of the supply chain now and needs special attention. From the considerations of logistics cost, we can see that some East European countries are also now emerging as preferred locations for cost-effective manufacturing for global players. Companies in East Europe are producing auto components and accessories for all leading brands of automobiles. For this reason, the logistics management has been emerging as an independent discipline to focus on R&D in this area, and in many institutions abroad, logistics is offered as a separate area for specialization.

In this book, we have taken an integrated view on SCM and logistics and, therefore, chapters have been designed accordingly, which offers greater scope to take an integrated view and derive the advantage of cost efficiency. Today's supply chain involves all parties, directly or indirectly working together in fulfilling the customer expectations. SCM, thus, requires ability to work together with people and organization both within and outside the business.

SCM AND BUSINESS PERFORMANCE

The length of the supply chain in manufacturing and marketing of products will depend on the type of products and also on the processes followed, which determine the number of intermediaries and partners as well as associates involved in the entire value chain. For typical fast-moving consumer goods (FMCG) such as food and household goods, it will involve the following stages:

- Customers
- Retailers
- Wholesalers and distributors
- Manufacturers
- Raw material, packaging material and other input material suppliers

Under each stage, as mentioned above, the supply chain is connected by the flow of products, funds and information, which happens in both directions and is managed by one of the stages or even by an intermediary. Accordingly, the design of the supply chain depends on customer needs and role played by the stages involved. The supply chain complexity increases with the number of intermediaries in each stage. For example, if a company has both in-house and out-house manufacturing facilities, then the input material suppliers are also required to supply materials and components to the contract manufacturers, who in turn also supply to both company and its distributors and wholesalers as per the model, and if they are located at different geographical locations, then the complexity takes a much bigger dimension to be managed. The complexity increases further if the suppliers are also located overseas and customers located in other countries outside the parent company's location. It can, thus, take an enormous proportion of challenges which we have discussed in other chapters. Simplified supply chain stages can be shown as given in Figure 1.1.

The discipline of SCM has evolved over several decades of managing the industrial production and distribution. Considerable amount of academic research leading to innovations as well as

FIGURE 1.1 Supply Chain Linkages and Stages

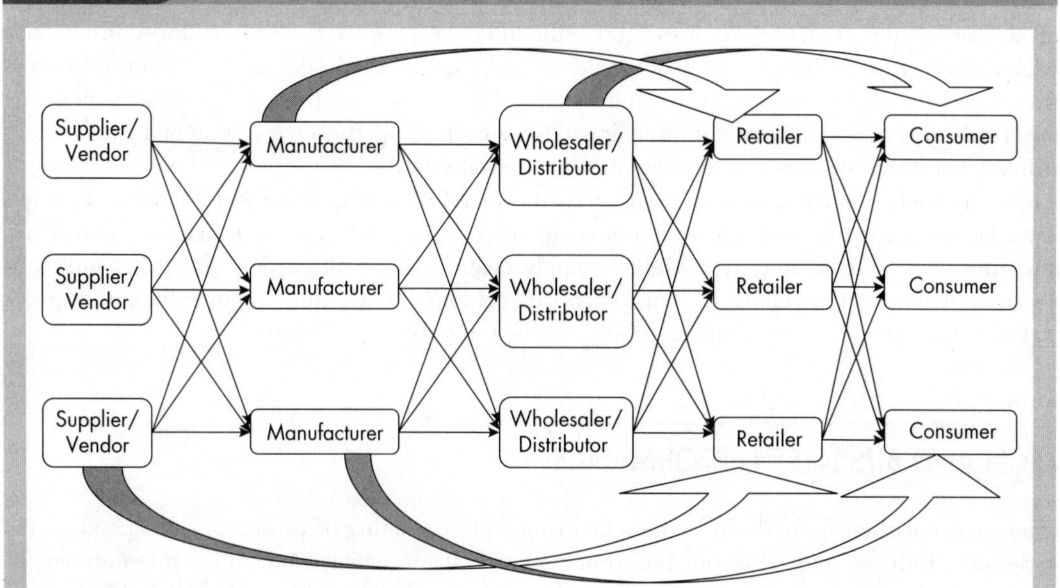

practitioners experience and experimentation have gone into the development of the SCM discipline and subject of study as we know it today (Chen and Paulraj 2004). These disciplines are operations management, industrial engineering as well as physical distribution. As can be understood that SCM involves multiple management functions, therefore, it is an interdisciplinary subject requiring knowledge of many other functions. Earlier, each of those functions was managed independently in silos, but now those have been integrated in one as integrated SCM. Each of these components of an integrated supply chain can be considered as a separate stream, which can be broadly classified as follows:

- Sourcing and procurement and supply chain
- Materials management
- Logistics and distribution management

The procurement function occupied a predominant position in the supply chain for the reason that it impacts both cash flow and profitability of the business and requires to be managed efficiently. If a company decides to manufacture all its products through third parties and also distributes the products to its independent distributors, then the whole supply chain will be a function of sourcing and procurement and delivery. Online retailers such as Amazon and Flipkart actually operate like that.

The materials management function includes demand forecasting, inventory management, warehousing, stock keeping and scheduling, as well as production planning and control. As over 60% of the manufactured cost is constituted by the bought-out items, materials management offers considerable scope of improvement in terms of route to cost reduction and, therefore, considered as very important. However, in relation to SCM, materials management can be regarded as flow of material into, through and out of the enterprise.

The logistics management function is actually derived from the military or defence logistics for managing military supply line. The Council of Logistics Management (CLM) defines it as that part of the SCM process that plans, implements and controls efficient and effective forward and backward flow and storage of goods and services as well as information from the point of origin to the point of consumption to meet the customers' requirement. The distribution function in businesses in that sense comes under logistics and is very important to be managed effectively to deliver the overall performance of the SCM functions. Logistics comes for both bringing the input materials inside the manufacturing premises and taking out the finished products for sales and distribution, and as such we call that inbound and outbound logistics. Transportation has significant cost due to rise in fuel prices and energy cost. Appropriate strategies need to be developed to contain the cost of transportation and logistics. These issues have been discussed in greater detail in the chapter on transportation (Chapter 6).

Businesses are required to deliver incremental value on a sustainable basis to ensure survival and growth and, therefore, unlocking the hidden value in the entire supply chain is of primary focus. Also, because of the very dynamic nature of the business, demand fluctuates and SCM has to gear up to meet the fluctuating demand. Manufacturing operations need to be flexible and agile. That has influenced the development of a flexible and agile supply chain to reduce the response time. To manage today's supply chain thus requires an integrated view supported by competitive operational strategies. Sustainability is another key area that requires attention and focus including environmental concerns which will require judicious selection of technology and processes ensuring green logistics and so on, which are the key concerns of the global supply chain and logistics operators. These issues have been adequately covered in the book. This book has been designed to get the integrated view of the supply chain for providing a holistic approach for SCM.

KEY CHALLENGES

With increased awareness and concerns about the protection of environment, a supply chain has added complexity and challenges. The regulations regarding environment protection are forcing businesses to view the whole task of organizing supply of products and making that available what customers want. The recent challenges of government asking FMCG companies such as Hindustan Unilever Limited (HUL) and Procter & Gamble (P&G) to be responsible to take care of their own waste coming from the use of packaging material, particularly non-biodegradable packaging material used for production of items that the companies sell, are a pointer in that direction. Environment-friendly countries such as Ireland have decided to do away with the inner box that is normally used for packing toothpaste tubes. In Ireland, now toothpaste tubes are sold without the box. Food regulatory authorities have now banned the use of recycled plastic for packing food products. The virgin polyester (PET) is non-biodegradable and also a costly packing material for food products such as sauces, ketchups, beverages and mineral water. PET is a product from petroleum refinery. Processes have now been developed to completely decompose the used and recycled PET by pyrolysis and then reconstruct the virgin PET material again from the components to recycle the used food grade polyesters. New technologies are developed to overcome and address these challenges.

There are also new security concerns with respect to the movement of stocks in global trade. Terrorism, cross-border tension, trade rivalry, political conflict, piracy and so on are becoming and posing increased threat for the movement of cargo in global trade. The increased security concerns and related regulatory issues pose additional challenges for logistics and SCM in terms of securing the cargo and conforming to the country-specific regulations. In addition to all these, there are issues related to piracy, theft and pilferage and tempering of cargo as challenges to global logistics operators.

As transportation is an integral part of logistics operation, with rising fuel cost, transportation cost is also increasing, which is the key challenge to logistics operators. Sulphur content of the bunker fuel and new regulations for that are coming as a big challenge. With rising cost of transportation, global logistics players are trying many alternative strategies to contain those to be competitive. As a result, many acquisitions and strategic alliances are now being seen to be happening. Sustainable transportation is another challenge to logistics operators.

Handling of a hazardous and inflammable cargo requires additional safety measures, and there are regulations with respect to those to be complied with. SCM covers wide areas and functions in a business. Large parts of capital investment are also made in these areas to be effective. A supply chain represents key components of costs in business; managing a supply chain effectively and efficiently is therefore the key imperative to derive a competitive advantage in business. Businesses are seen to be experimenting with new ideas and strategies to create a competitive advantage in the business. This book has discussed many such practical cases to drive the point. Managing a supply chain better also improves the success rate of new business, new products and start-ups.

The book is an attempt to see SCM and logistics management as an integrated discipline in terms of managing the new challenges in a supply chain, which is very vital for succeeding in the marketplace.

CHAPTER SUMMARY

This chapter discusses the new concepts of SCM as we know today, covering a wide range of business functions which were earlier managed in silos and are now being managed as integrated holistic functions. The chapter also addresses the importance of SCM in terms of delivering improved business performance and to remain competitive to ensure survival and growth. The increased complexity and management challenges of a supply chain are elaborately discussed, highlighting the interrelationship of various functions now included and considered as part of the supply chain. The new regulatory, safety as well as packaging and environmental issues are also discussed, which are posing new challenges to be effectively managed. Lastly, the chapter addresses the new-found importance of logistics management in a supply chain and key issues that make a very valid case of managing the supply chain and logistics as an integrated function.

DISCUSSION QUESTIONS

1. What are the key functions that SCM encompasses in the current context?
2. Why is SCM so important in business in terms of delivering a competitive advantage?
3. How has logistics management emerged as a key discipline and is part of supply chain now?
4. What are the key considerations to manage SCM as an integrated discipline?
5. Discuss the key complexities and challenges of SCM function

REFERENCES

Chen, I. J., and A. Paulraj. 2004. 'Understanding Supply Chain Management: Critical Research & Theoretical Framework'. *International Journal of Production Research* 42 (1): 131–163. Published online in February 2007.

Deloitte. 2018. *Global Manufacturing Competitiveness Index* (report). New York: Deloitte.

BIBLIOGRAPHY

Fisher, Marshall L. 1997. 'What Is the Right Supply Chain for Your Product?' *Harvard Business Review* (March–April): 83–93.

Kopczak, Laura R., and M. Eric Johnson. 2003. 'The Supply-Chain Management Effect'. *Sloan Management Review* (Spring): 27–34.

Robensen, James F., and William C. Copacino, eds. 1994. *The Logistics Handbook*. New York: The Free Press.

Slone, Reuben E. 2004. 'Leading a Supply Chain Turnaround'. *Harvard Business Review* (October): 114–121.

2

Evolution of Integrated Supply Chain and Logistics Management

LEARNING OBJECTIVES

- Understand how SCM has evolved over the years as a discipline
- Get exposure to scope and key components of a supply chain and their implications
- Get insights into the historical perspective of an integrated supply chain and logistics management
- Know the role and functions of an integrated supply chain and its key deliverables

INTRODUCTION

SCM in the current context covers a very wide area of business functions. What had started in the early 1980s as a new concept initiated and introduced by consultants in the USA to improve business performance is now a full-grown integrated end-to-end supply chain from procurement to production to distribution and customer order processing and customer service. Even some of the erstwhile sales and distribution functions including debtors management and channel partners management are now covered under integrated SCM. SCM as we understand now covers a very wide range of activities, including procurement, warehousing, transport and logistics, inventory management, production, demand management, distribution and customer services. It, thus, assumes great importance in managing the business in terms of cross-functional expertise, efficiency and effectiveness. We can say that organizations are very large cost centres and everything we do inside the organization is only cost which has to be transacted with the prospective customers with a margin of profit. In an ever-increasing competitive environment, margins are getting squeezed, and to retain the desirable level of margin, businesses have to drastically improve the efficiency of SCM, including logistics. And as end-to-end SCM represents the major part of the cost in the business, an efficient and effective integrated SCM largely determines the overall business performance and profitability in the current context and new business environment.

SCOPE OF SCM

By the way we understand SCM now, we can define it as the integration of key business processes across the end-to-end supply chain for the purpose of creating value for customers and other stakeholders. SCM revolves around efficient integration of suppliers, manufacturers, warehouses, stores, wholesalers, retailers and customers. It also optimizes the organizational resources to ensure the ideal level of servicing the customer demand or requirement at all times.

This would mean that SCM is the management of a network of interconnected businesses involved in the ultimate provision of product and service packages required by end customers (Harland 1996). To compete in the global market and networked economy, an interorganizational supply network can be acknowledged as a new form of organization itself. An ideal level of SCM performance needs synchronization of various other direct and indirect business functions, starting from demand forecasting, procurement, production, warehousing, distribution, logistics and so on. SCM now covers a wide variety of functions, and therefore, we look at these interconnected functions in business and try to manage as integrated activities because of their functional interdependencies. And as such, inefficiency in one function will impact the performance in other associated and interlinked functions. In the context of current global business environment and complexity, SCM, therefore, has to be viewed as a unified integrated function. This function is so important that businesses have to derive their competitive advantage through significant innovation in the entire SCM functions. What had started initially in the early 1980s as global procurement challenges has now evolved as an integrated as well as very critical discipline in business.

The three main streams of integrated SCM are as follows:

1. Sourcing, procurement and supply management
2. Materials management and demand management
3. Logistics and distribution management

A customer will be buying the product from the end selling point and that could be a retail store in the neighbourhood. But to make the product available in time for the customer to buy, there are numerous interconnected activities and associates, vendors and suppliers are involved in a networked environment, all working in harmony to make that happen in an integrated and effective chain of activities as has been shown in Figure 2.1.

The supply chain is thus dynamic and essentially involves the constant flow of information, product and funds among various interconnected partners. In e-commerce, a customer will place an order online on say Amazon or Flipkart's website and transfer the money to buy a particular product after going through the information available on the website about the product, price and availability. An e-retailer like Amazon may decide to supply it from their warehouse or even from their registered suppliers' network stock points, involving either courier services or delivery service vendors, to ensure that the product is delivered within the agreed delivery terms of the order of the customer which needs to be processed immediately. Upon receiving the product, if the customer finds it defective or not as per the expectation, he/she can either return the product or get it replaced within a prescribed time, giving reasons thereof. The e-retailer then has to take back the product and credit the customer and debit the supplier or vendor and also adjust the inventory

FIGURE 2.1 Scope of Supply Chain Management

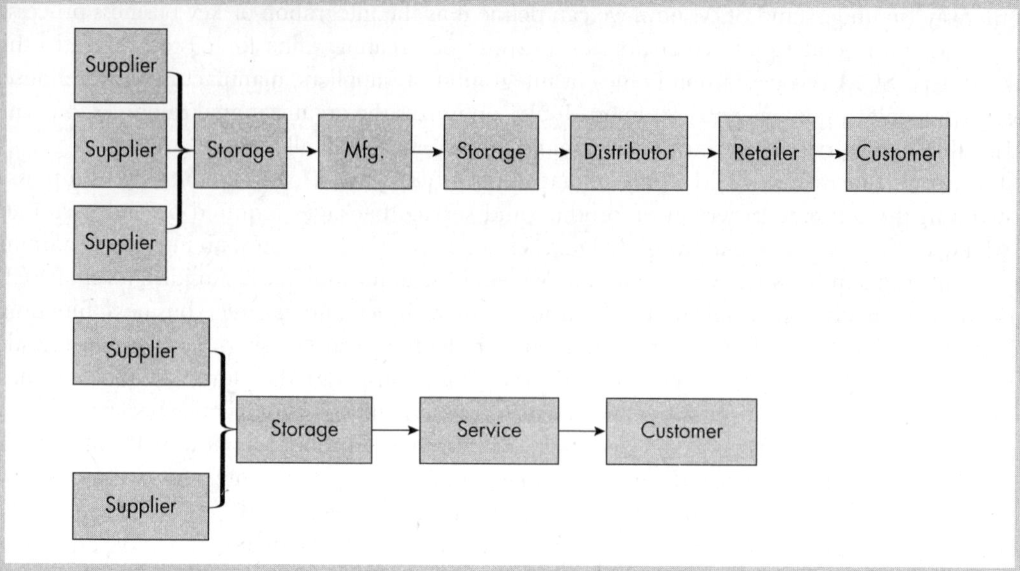

record immediately, which is in fact a reverse logistics task to be managed. The operation as described, in fact, comes under the SCM and as can be seen, it is highly complex.

Sourcing and procurement are important areas of SCM. Earlier, procurement was considered a very mundane function, but soon businesses realized its importance in terms of cost reduction possibilities, which has drawn the attention of top management. The **materials management** function, in fact, includes multiple functions such as forecasting, inventory management, stores management, warehousing and stock keeping as well as scheduling. **Logistics and distribution** were initially derived from military parlance dealt with movement and maintenance of armies, but when its application came to be recognized in business, it was intended to cover physical movement of goods and services across a supply chain till it reaches the end consumer for better service and satisfaction.

EVOLUTION OF SCM: THE HISTORICAL PERSPECTIVE

The integrated SCM has evolved over the years as a result of several business development challenges in a global supply chain.

There are five major movements or major industry-led initiatives that we can observe as the evolution of the SCM as we understand now. These are as follows (Magretta 1998):

1. **Creation era:** SCM was first coined by a US industry consultant in the early 1980s. At that stage, SCM included the need for large-scale changes, re-engineering and downsizing, driven

by cost-reduction programmes to remain competitive in the marketplace in global business environment. Cost was always considered as a major competitive advantage for business. Offering same or more benefits at a lower cost is always a winning strategy and in the creation era, SCM was focused on many cost reduction programmes. We have seen since then that there are initiatives on business process re-engineering (BPR), total quality management (TQM), continuous improvement, kaizen and so on. The primary objective of all these initiatives was to eliminate the non–value-adding activities in the business to make the business more cost competitive, proactive, flexible and responsive to the ever-changing and competitive business environment. The competitive forces of businesses during those years have made these changes a logical imperative.

2. **Integration era:** After the initial phase came the integration era to cash on the various initiatives the businesses have been seen to be undertaking in order to absorb the benefits of those initiatives in the business as a whole or the organization itself. This was triggered by the development of electronic data interchange (EDI) systems in the 1960s and developed through the 1990s by the introduction of enterprise resource planning (ERP) systems. In this phase, industry was concentrating on productivity improvement as well as on resource optimization, and ERP was making inroads into business. Organizations were seen to be implementing ERP at a huge cost in the 1990s, which is now available at 10% of the original cost of the package in those days. Even relatively smaller businesses have also now implemented a customized ERP package in their business for optimizing the resource allocation and uses that is linked with the sales order processing. It was always debated by the businesses whether huge investment in implementing ERP packages such as SAP, BAAN and BPCS has really delivered the commensurate result or benefits to the business. But large industries thought that their existence would be threatened if they do not go ahead with such large investment programmes in ERP. In the 1990s, all large global businesses implemented SAP or other costly ERP packages at a huge cost and time, and those large investments coupled with the engagement of trained IT professionals to help running the system and churning out various kinds of management reporting systems to understand the efficiency and effectiveness of the management functions. ERP did not help reduce manpower in the organization which was originally thought of but definitely brought in a new view of the business performance and helped businesses to take an integrated view of many interconnected functions which were earlier viewed and managed in silos.
3. **Globalization era:** During the third phase, which was in the 1990s, globalization, regionalization and so on had started impacting businesses. There were global realignments of businesses. Large acquisitions and mergers happened during that time. Manufacturing was shifting to the countries where it was most economical to produce. The third phase of the movement of SCM development was triggered by the globalization era and can be characterized by the attention given to global systems of supplier relationships and the expansion of supply chains over national boundaries and into other continents. During this phase, we have seen that manufacturing locations were moving to places where it was costing the least to produce and global sourcing as well as outsourcing in a major way increasing the complexity in business. In this era, raw materials and input materials were sourced from the countries where best quality and reliability were ensured at least cost, and final production was carried out in yet another country where cost of production was the least to be shipped

to the world market as per customer requirements. During this phase, China had emerged as a global manufacturing hub for most of the global brands and as such it was able to attract global investors to set up global factories to satisfy their customer requirements around the world. This complexity of movement of raw materials and finished products has thrown many challenges in terms of logistics as well as regulatory to be effectively managed to run a global factory.

4. **Specialization era I—Outsourced manufacturing and distribution:** The specialization era was experienced in two phases during which SCM was realized to be a service function like many other functions in business such as finance and marketing, and that has enlarged its scope to include customer services and distribution as well. During this era, everything in business was seen as a way to provide better service to the customer, and organizations were seen to be totally focused on customer retention by providing better service and satisfaction in relation to its own competition. Service quality, customer retention, flexibility and mass customization gained importance, and these were the additional challenges for an SCM team in any business to be addressed as an added complexity. Many changes were noticed during the two phases of the specialization era of SCM.

   In the 1990s, industries began to focus on 'core competencies' and adopted a specialization model. Companies abandoned vertical integration, sold off non-core operations and outsourced those functions to other companies which could perform these better at a lower cost. Most of the organizations are now focusing on their core competence which they can do better than others, and the rest of the activities and business functions are outsourced. In the early 1990s, outsourcing of manufacturing and production operations was seen to be the beginning of this era, but today most of the large and global enterprises have divested their own production and manufacturing facilities and started sourcing from the third parties whom they have developed over the years, and that has also increased the complexity in the management of business processes. Domestic companies have also been seen shifting manufacturing operations to areas where tax holidays and other investment-related incentives were available. They were flexible to shift manufacturing locations only to reduce the cost of production, taking into account the tax incentives that were made available to attract investors in areas which were less industrialized.

5. **Specialization era II—SCM as a means of providing service:** During this phase, the logistics function gained tremendous importance, as it was realized that logistics is the next largest cost after procurement that businesses are incurring, and the performance of logistics greatly influences the SCM performance. During this phase, third-party logistics (TPL) and so on were greatly studied and investigated. Logistics which was earlier synonymous with the transportation was now being addressed as a holistic function and a fully-grown discipline.

Specialization within the supply chain began in the 1980s with the inception of transportation brokerages, warehouse management and non-asset-based carriers, and has matured beyond transportation and logistics into aspects of supply planning, collaboration, execution and performance management. During this phase, which is clearly visible in the current business context, we were witnessing the importance of logistics as a key function with a lot of opportunities for improvements and cost reduction and also a focus on integrated end-to-end SCM. Logistics has now evolved as one of the key drivers of providing competitive advantage to the business, and it also has to be seen as the integral part of the extended SCM.

As logistics is an integral function of end-to-end SCM, we will be discussing SCM and logistics functions together as an integrated function.

KEY OBJECTIVES AND CHALLENGES OF SUPPLY CHAIN INTEGRATION

For integrated SCM, a great degree of internal as well as external factors of the business need to be aligned to improve the overall performance of SCM. This also results in networking as well as technology selection and implementation. For efficient SCM integration, one has to consider the various components and put together appropriate structure and framework in place in order to produce the desired results. For efficient management of an integrated SCM, businesses need to have an elaborate planning and control mechanism and work process structure, management methods and practices as well as organization structure to ensure smooth flow of materials and facilities supported by appropriate information flow and system. This is possible with competent and capable leadership with a well-defined organization structure and design and favourable organization culture and attitude with adequate risk mitigation strategies wherever required including a reward structure. This aspect will be clearer when we will be taking up case studies in this chapter itself.

The primary objective of all supply chains has to be to maximize the overall value generated in the chain which would also mean to generate supply chain surplus which can be defined as follows:

$$\text{Supply Chain Value} = \text{Customer Value} - \text{Supply Chain Cost}$$

The customer value is in fact the price a potential customer is willing to pay for the product offering, which depends not only on the product type, quality and benefits that it offers to the target customers but also on how the product has been positioned in the customers' minds and how it is promoted and marketed. The customer value, therefore, has got to do with the effectiveness of the marketing function in the business. However, marketers need support and cooperation to succeed in the marketplace in a competitive environment. The distribution which was earlier a sales function is now integrated into the supply chain function. A supply chain, thus, now plays a more integrated role. Without the cooperation, involvement and effectiveness of the supply chain, it would be difficult for the marketers to create a steady and growing demand for the product. A supply chain, therefore, plays a complimentary role for the marketing function, and if the supply chain fails, marketing will also fail.

OBJECTIVES AND CHALLENGES OF SCM

The key objectives that reflect the performance of SCM in a business world would ultimately depend on achieving the cost reduction objective and to achieve that we have many challenges. We need to coordinate activities across the SCM to improve performance by:

1. Reducing total cost
2. Increasing customer service level

3. Reducing the impact of bullwhip effect
4. Utilizing the organizational resources in a better way
5. Effectively and proactively responding to changes in the marketplace

To achieve the above-listed objectives, businesses have to have well-defined and actionable strategies to manage the SCM functions across the entire value chain. As the entire supply chain has to be managed with the sole objective to meet the customers' real-time demand, estimating the demand accurately will hold the key to managing the supply chain effectively. The performance of a supply chain is also led by a few critical or key drivers, including inventory control and management, transportation, facilities planning and information flow and accuracy. Unless these key strategic drivers are managed well, the integration benefits will not emerge. These strategic drivers illustrate the opportunities and challenges associated with SCM integration, which will include the following:

1. Supply chain strategies: Push, pull and push–pull systems
2. Demand-driven strategies
3. Effective distribution strategies

Pull strategies are always better in the sense that in a pull strategy, the demand is managed from the point of view of the real-term demand of the customers and it is the task of the marketers to create the customer demand by effectively executing demand pull marketing strategies and promotion including advertisement, whereas a push strategy, which is manufacturers and marketers driven, often leads to artificial demand, raising the level of the trade stock which in turn can cause other problems such as increase in expiry stock and stock return and high debtors. The aim of the efficient supply chain is to optimize the two apparently opposing objectives so that the real-term demand is satisfied and we do not lose out on sales and at the same time we also do not overstock the trade by overtrading, raising the working capital locked up in the system leading to underperformance.

ROLE OF SCM

SCM really works by bringing positive impact by servicing the customers better, thereby helping business to grow faster in terms of increased sales, growth and profits. The primary role of SCM is to optimize the organizational resources to maximize the sales and profit by servicing the real-term customer demand. In this task, SCM primarily performs the following activities:

- Communicating the customer's demand from the point of sale (POS) to the supplier
- Physical flow process that engineers the movement of goods
- Optimizing the organizational resource to satisfy the customer's demand

The key benefits that can accrue from the efficient SCM are, therefore, many and include the following:

- Reduction of product losses in transportation and storage by making the processes and functions more efficient and effective

- Providing a competitive advantage to the business by unlocking a lot of hidden value in the entire supply chain
- Increase of sales resulting from better customer service, ensuring customer satisfaction
- Dissemination of technology, advanced techniques, capital and knowledge among the chain partners, thereby helping the channel partners to be more competitive and efficient in their own businesses

It is a common practice of large businesses to help the contract manufacturers and contract packers to become more cost-effective by infusion of technology and knowledge and even sometimes investment in vendor's facilities and then share the added value so created for the benefit of both. This is a win-win situation for both principal and vendors. Sometimes it is much easier to either experiment or practise in vendor's premises, rather than in the facilities and premises of large global players because of rigidity and inflexible policies and practices which require time to change. We will discuss a P&G case to bring in more clarity in this regard. P&G is generally recognized as more proactive and innovative in relation to its own competitive sets, and it is constantly experimenting to find better solutions to the newer challenges of the global market. The case will, therefore, reveal some of their key strategic drivers to find innovative solutions which can significantly improve business performance and reduce risk of failures.

Supply Chain in Competitive World: A Case of Li & Fung

Victor Fung of Li & Fung gave an interview which was published in *Harvard Business Review* (Magretta 1998). He said:

> Say we get an order from an European retailer to produce 10,000 garments. For this customer we might decide to buy yarn from a Korean producer but have it woven and dyed in Taiwan. So we pick the yarn and ship it to Taiwan. The Japanese have the best zippers ... so we go to YKK, a big Japanese zipper manufacturer, and we order the right zippers from their Chinese plants.... The best place to make the garments is Thailand. So we ship everything there.... The customer needs quick delivery, we may divide the order across five factories in Thailand. Effectively, we are customizing the value chain to best meet the customer's needs.

The complexity as explained in this case of Li & Fung is explained diagrammatically in Figure 2.2, which shows the complexity of the whole process of executing the European order of garments by Li & Fung in order to deliver the best value to the ultimate customer to ensure the sustainability of the whole business process which is hinging on the ultimate customer satisfaction with quality, time and price. Li & Fung is Hong Kong's largest export trading company. It has also been innovative in SCM. In the interview example, it can be seen that Li & Fung has created a supply chain for the purpose of meeting a customer's needs. In general, this case is more an exception than a rule but serves to illustrate some of the pieces of a global supply chain which is not only complex but also requires management knowledge and expertise.

FIGURE 2.2 Complexity in Supply Chain in Li & Fung Business Model

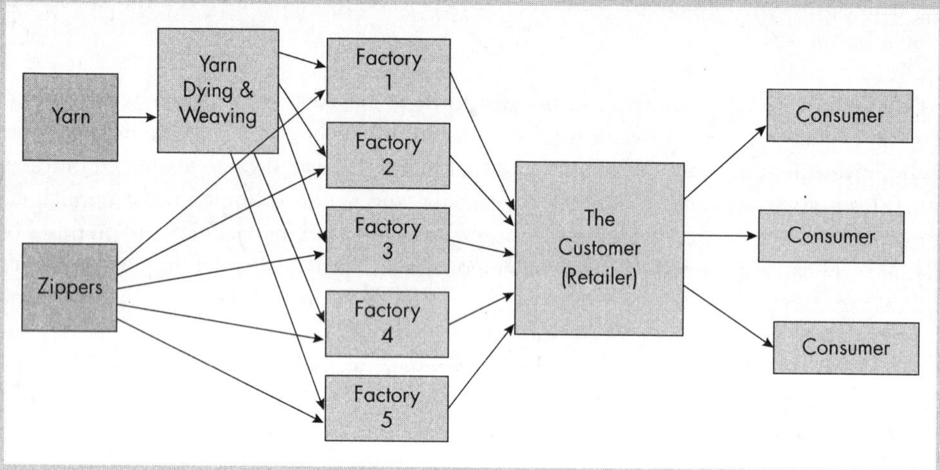

A value chain is another name for a supply chain. The concept of value chain was introduced by Michael Porter (1985), and what we understand today by a value chain is in fact another name of an extended end-to-end supply chain. A supply chain is a sequence of organizations—their facilities, functions and activities—that are involved in producing and delivering a product or service.

In a supply chain, the members linked in the chain serve as both customers and suppliers as they receive input materials from someone else and convert that to the finished product to sell to their own customer, and as such, each partner performs both the roles. In the case of Li & Fung, as discussed above, the Korean yarn producer and Japanese zipper producer are probably suppliers and also the customer's customer. SCM, therefore, links the organizations within the supply chain for meeting the demand across the entire chain efficiently. In a typical non-brokered supply chain, one or more of the organizations in the chain can also provide the management function.

WHY IS SCM SO IMPORTANT?

In today's business, sourcing is done from places and factories where it costs the least and is most efficient in terms of quality and delivery. As mentioned by Fung of Li & Fung, worldwide there are various products now being produced in China or in East European countries by sourcing components and raw materials from various parts of the world and that makes SCM so vital and important for the performance of the business by impacting numerous criteria of performance such as cost, quality, time, customer service, reduction of wastage, environment-friendly processes, productivity, skill level of people, innovation and sustainability. Efficient management of SCM is thus essential and critical to the performance of business, and that is why it is so important. SCM is managed to provide multiple benefits to the business, which include the following:

- Improving efficiencies from procurement, distribution and logistics
- Making outsourcing activities more efficient
- Reducing cost of transportations of inventories
- Managing the inventories required across the supply chain
- Making businesses more cost-effective and globally competitive
- Managing the complexities of the supply chain
- Managing the new challenges from e-commerce
- Absorbing competitive pressures from shorter development cycle time, more new products and demand for more customization
- Meeting the challenges of globalization and longer supply chains

However, managing a supply chain to achieve the desired outcome is not an easy task simply because different organizations in the supply chain may have different conflicting objectives and other internal constraints, including resource constraints and business objectives. For example, partners in the supply chain can have typically conflicting interests and objectives as mentioned below and those need to be optimized for overall performance:

- **Manufacturers:** long-run production, high quality, high productivity, low production cost
- **Distributors:** low inventory, reduced transportation costs, quick replenishment capability
- **Customers:** shorter order lead time, high in-stock inventory, large variety of products, low prices
- **Consumers:** availability, affordable cost, value for money, after-sales service, product performance

Supply chains are, in fact, dynamic in nature in any organization, and they evolve over time and also change with the change in the business environment. A supply chain thus needs to be managed as a vertically integrated function. For any organization, vertical integration will involve taking either one or more suppliers backward or one or more of the distribution activities forward. For example, a backward vertical for say a peanut butter manufacturer would be deciding to start growing peanuts instead of buying peanuts from the supplier for processing, and forward vertical integration for the same manufacturer would entail that the peanut butter manufacturer decides to market their peanut butter directly to the grocery stores and retailers instead of going through the existing channel partners. In a supply chain, some functions related to suppliers as well as distribution might be performed by the manufacturers directly if that provides cost competitiveness to the business. Such decisions are normally taken when businesses realize that some of those functions can be better managed by themselves instead of getting these done by third parties on whom manufacturer-marketers have no control and such decisions are taken when those functions are better managed with lesser costs by manufacturers themselves.

LOGISTICS: A NEGLECTED AREA—NOW AN INTEGRAL PART OF SCM

Peter Drucker (1962) has said, 'Logistics is the economy's dark continent. It is the most neglected but very promising business area.' Global sourcing has posed serious challenges and also opportunities for the logistics companies. Businesses are still learning how to use logistics effectively, and logistics has thus become a key source of a competitive advantage.

Efficient logistics function management is the key driver to deliver a competitive advantage to business. Businesses, therefore, need to develop a strategic plan for the effective logistics function to unlock the value in logistics management chain, and logistics has thus emerged as one of the key functions in business.

Logistics is the integral part of SCM encompassing the planning and management of all activities involved in sourcing and procurement, conversion and all logistics management activities. In addition, it also includes coordination and collaboration with channel partners, which can be suppliers, intermediaries, third-party service providers and customers. In essence, SCM integrates supply and demand management within and across companies. And logistics is the integral part of all interfaces. Logistics, in fact, takes care of the way a company acquires materials such as raw materials, packaging materials or parts, spares and components and intermediates, how a company handles them once they arrive at the company's manufacturing premises and how they are shipped out. Logistics, therefore, is the intervening facilitator from the time material input is sourced and brought inside the company's manufacturing locations till it reaches the end customer as the final product to be consumed. On the basis of this, very broadly logistics can be divided into inbound logistics and outbound logistics. While inbound logistics deals with the input material, outbound logistics deals with physical distribution and marketing logistics.

Physical distribution means the way a company delivers its product to the market, which could be the intermediaries, customers or retailers and end users, and marketing logistics are basically the physical distribution of goods. Marketing logistics involves planning, delivering and controlling the flow of physical goods to a market as well as the material and information necessary to meet customers' demands. Marketing logistics even covers market returns which need to be either disposed of or reprocessed, as required, and that is a part of reverse logistics. The demands of the customer must be met at a profit that increases revenue for the organization.

WHY IS LOGISTICS IMPORTANT?

Logistics can help improve value delivery to customers, and therefore, it can also improve customer satisfaction and help businesses to become more competitive in the marketplace. And that is the key to success. In order to succeed in the marketplace, businesses have to consistently deliver superior value to their target customers and consumers in relation to their own competitive set. All businesses have their identified competitors with whom they compete, and it is essential that you deliver superior value in comparison to your identified competitors to succeed. In this regard, it should also be mentioned that all players in the same business are not necessarily competitors and that same strategy will not address the challenges of all competitors, and therefore, it is essential that businesses identify their competitors judiciously. And in that task, effective and efficient logistics management holds the key.

Things began changing with the advancement in transportation systems. Population began moving from rural to urban areas and to business centres. No longer did people live near production centres, nor did production take place near residential centres, where goods and services are mostly consumed. The geographical distance between the production point and the consumption point thus increased. And logistics also thus gained importance.

Logistics is one of the most important functions in business today. No marketing, manufacturing or project execution can succeed without logistics support. For companies, 10–35% of gross sales are logistics cost, depending on types of business, geography and weight/value ratio of the product.

Other factors have also come into play recently. Since the early 1990s, the business scene has changed. Globalization, free market and competition have required that the customer gets the right material, at the right time, at the right point, in the right condition and at the lowest cost, which has its implication in the global competitive environment where players try to outsmart their competitive counterpart in order to thrive in the business.

> Businesses spend a huge sum on managing logistics activities within the supply chain. For example, in the USA, 25–35% of a product's sale value is attributed to the logistics cost for international logistics and 8–10% for domestic logistics. In 1993, the USA had spent 10.7% of GDP to cover the cost of logistics, twice of that spent on national defence. In 2000, the USA spent 10% of the price of all goods which was attributed to the cost of logistics. Costs of logistics in any organization and in businesses depend on three major factors, namely level of economic activity, efficiency and the transition of managing SCM from the perspective of goods to orientation towards providing better services to customers.

CORE CONCEPT, DEFINITION AND SCOPE OF LOGISTICS

Logistics is the function that enables the flow of materials from suppliers into an organization through operations within the organization out to the customers. It is derived from the Greek word *logistikos*, which means 'to reason logically'. It basically consists of all operations required for goods (both tangible and intangible) to be made available in markets or at specific destinations.

According to CLA (USA), 'Logistics is the process of planning, implementing and controlling the efficient, effective flow and storage of goods, services and related information from the point of origin to the point of consumption for the purpose of conforming to the customer requirements.'

The Council of Supply Chain Management Professionals (CSCMP), the largest professional organization on logistics, has provided the most useful definition of logistics, and according to that,

> Logistics management is that part of the supply chain management that plans, implements, and controls the efficient, effective forward and reverse flows and storage of goods, services and other related information between the point of origin and the point of consumption in order to meet the customers' requirements.
>
> Logistics management activities typically include inbound and outbound transportation management, fleet management, warehousing, materials handling, order fulfilment, logistics network design, inventory management, supply/demand planning, and management of TPL service providers.

> To varying degrees, the logistics function also includes sourcing and procurement, production planning and scheduling, packaging and assembly, and customer service. It is involved in all levels of planning and execution—strategic, operational and tactical.

Based on this, it can be said that logistics management is an integral function which coordinates and optimizes all logistics activities with the other functions in the business, including sales and marketing, productions, operations and manufacturing, finance, and information technology (IT; Council of Supply Chain Management Professionals [CSCMP] 2013, https://cscmp.org/CSCMP/Educate/SCM_Definitions_and_Glossary_of_Terms/CSCMP/Educate/SCM_Definitions_and_Glossary_of_Terms.aspx?hkey=60879588-f65f-4ab5-8c4b-6878815ef921 [accessed on 3 September 2019]).

The early years of the 21st century were characterized by a slow evolution from logistics to SCM in both academic and business circles.

The small and medium-sized companies have been seen to be slower in terms of accepting the emerging concept of SCM. However, large professional organizations continued to be active in assisting academicians and practitioners in the logistics and supply chain discipline.

The logistics side is well represented by CSCMP. It defines SCM as follows: 'Supply chain management encompasses the planning and management of all activities involved in sourcing and procurement, conversion, and all logistics management activities' (CSCMP 2013). The handbook *Transportation and Logistics Basics* states: 'The supply chain includes all partners in the logistics process. The idea is to have integrated information sharing among all trading partners (vendors, manufacturers, and customers)' (Southern 1997, 248).

In business terms, logistics means the physical movement of goods from the supplier point to the receiver point. The basic functional activities under logistics including transportation, packaging and storage, loading and unloading, handling, distribution, information system management, etc., are organically integrated based on the practical needs of the businesses.

BASIC ELEMENTS OF LOGISTICS

Whereas the term logistics covers a very wide area of activities and functions as discussed above, the basic elements of logistics include the following functions:

1. Transportation
2. Warehousing
3. Inventory management
4. Packaging and utilization
5. Information and communication

LOGISTICS AS A DISCIPLINE

Logistics, over the years, has evolved as a discipline or management science and covers strategic planning, forecasting, material-handling, warehousing, transportation, distribution and operation research. Logistics is now a multidisciplinary function. The scope of study of logistics as a discipline depends also on the types of logistics including logistics costs and financing and TPL.

TYPES OF LOGISTICS

We can see that logistics is involved in every human endeavour and activity. Some of the activities where logistics is the key to meet the objectives such as war logistics and disaster logistics have become an independent area or discipline for study now. There are activities and services where logistics will determine the performance and success which include tourism logistics and medical logistics. Broadly, we can have the following types of logistics, which are only indicative but not exhaustive:

- Business logistics: moving cargo
- General logistics: moving cargo and moving people

The activities involved in managing the logistics function for moving cargo which we consider as business logistics will be different from when it has to be for moving people. Although transportation is a common function in both, their objectives and criteria of performance would be different.

We normally refer to moving cargo or business logistics in this book. Although airlines or travel services are part of the logistics functions, we will refer to only business logistics in the sense that it relates to moving cargo or goods. Other types of logistics will include the following:

- Inbound logistics or procurement logistics
- Production logistics or internal logistics
- Outbound logistics or distribution logistics or marketing logistics
- Reverse logistics
- Green logistics
- Defence logistics
- Medical logistics
- Disaster logistics
- War logistics
- Agricultural logistics
- Tourism logistics

As the names indicate, the types of logistics will have their own performance criteria and objectives as well as their own challenges to be managed, and each type of logistics now needs to be discussed in specialized training and academic programmes. A great deal of research activities are undertaken to make these logistics more cost effective and efficient.

LOGISTICS ACTIVITIES AND GOALS

Logistics is about getting things to where they need to be and is much broader than transportation of goods from one location to another. The overall goal of logistics, thus, would be to achieve a targeted level of customer service at the lowest possible cost. Logistics activities cover a wide range of tasks including the following:

- Network design
- Information processing
- Transportation
- Inventory management
- Warehousing, material-handling and packaging

The operational objectives of a logistics system can have several objectives including the following:

- Rapid response
- Minimum variance
- Minimum inventory
- Movement consolidation
- Quality
- Life cycle support

Logistics, thus, is a support function to operations. Also, integrated logistics emphasizes the need to coordinate with suppliers and customers.

EVOLUTION OF LOGISTICS: THE HISTORICAL PERSPECTIVE

In the initial years, logistics was synonymous with transportation, but today transportation is only one of the sub-functions, but a very important one, of logistics. Logistics as a discipline has developed into a very important function and part of the end-to-end SCM. Today, logistics covers a wide range of activities and serves as a key integrator of SCM. It has developed during last five decades, although in the beginning it was relevant to military operations and focus was on transportation.

However, during the last few decades, it has developed from the narrowly defined distribution management to the integrated management and linked to the global supply chains. The mission of logistics management is to plan and coordinate all activities to achieve desired levels of delivered service and quality at the lowest possible cost. In order to succeed in today's global marketplace, companies must be ever cognizant of these trends and develop a logistics management strategy that capitalizes on the best-of-breed technology solution available today, so that they can meet the demands of their customers today and be well prepared for the future. The logistics function has evolved through five distinct phases as narrated below from transportation to business logistics.

THE 1950s' TRANSPORTATION ERA

During the 1950s, the emphasis was on transportation and at that time several university programmes were offered in transportation as major which did not include topics such as logistics, physical distribution, physical supply and SCM. Computers or even calculators were not available to calculate or quantify the data, nor was there much discussion on the systems or total cost approach as we take today. Also, the idea of the collaboration with the vendors and suppliers or customers was not the priority or concern of the businesses in those days, and the term logistics was used in military or defence context only, whose primary focus and key imperative were to get the right supplies to the right place at the right time during wartime conditions.

James A. Houston (1996) surveyed the significance of logistics in the military and said, 'This work is a general historical survey of logistics in the American Military experience.'

Although initial work on logistics was focused on military logistics, today logistics covers a vast range of subjects.

THE 1960s' PHYSICAL DISTRIBUTION ERA

During the 1960s, all studies related to transportation were related to physical distribution and to a lesser degree on logistics. The National Council of Physical Distribution Management (NCPDM), USA, representing professional physical distribution managers, was formed in 1963, which changed into CLM in 1985 and again changed its name to CSCMP in 2004. Today, CSCMP has more than 14,000 members. Physical distribution (outbound logistics) and physical supply (inbound logistics) were considered as two distinct functions.

During this decade, physical distribution received a lot of attention in the literature. And one of the first textbooks titled *Physical Distribution Management Logistics Problems of the Firm*, written by Smykay, Bowersox and Mossman (1961), that focused on physical distribution and logistics was published during this decade). And this subject got a great deal of attention of the researchers during the 1960s. The first issue of the *Transportation Journal* was published in 1961 by the American Society of Traffic and Transportation, and in 1966, US President Lyndon B. Johnson signed 'Public Law 89-670' establishing the Department of Transportation, and Alan S. Boyd was selected as the National Secretary of Transportation.

During this decade, a great deal of emphasis was laid on the importance of logistics in economy and business and as a consequence, a lot of academic activities were seen to have initiated.

THE 1970s' PHYSICAL SUPPLY AND PHYSICAL DISTRIBUTION

During the early 1970s, physical supply or materials management, which is basically inbound logistics, received considerable attention and later in the decade there was a move to combine physical distribution with physical supply to emphasize on the much broader concept of logistics management. Also, during that time, when there was an advancement of basic concepts of logistics, we found that universities and academic journals and textbooks as well as professional organizations contributed to make that a productive decade for the development of logistics as a discipline that we know today.

Rails and roads are the most important modes of transport of goods within many countries as well as in international logistics operation, and their cost, performance criteria, service quality, effectiveness and efficiency and so on received attention.

THE 1980s' TRANSPORTATION DEREGULATION AND PHYSICAL DISTRIBUTION

By the 1980s, the term physical distribution was phased out and the term logistics was emphasized. To cite an example, the authors James C. Johnson and Donald F. Wood had even changed the title of their textbook from *Contemporary Physical Distribution* to *Contemporary Physical Distribution and Logistics* in 1982.

THE 1990s' BUSINESS LOGISTICS

During the 1990s, business logistics continued to be an important discipline, and most of the cost-focused businesses became aware of the opportunities for savings in cost through better negotiations with their freight carriers and implementation of the system approach and total cost concept to management.

During that time, many transport companies also picked up the concept of the logistics function and tried to promote the idea that they were not simply a transport company or truck operators and also tried to position themselves in the market as providers of total logistics solutions. During the same time, the major factors affecting logistics were developments in electronics and communication technology such as Internet and EDI. Also, there was growth with regard to TPL organizations as well as strategic alliances and partnerships, and businesses started to view the logistics function as an integral component of their overall business strategy.

The logistics management as a discipline got importance that a leading *Journal of Supply Chain Management* published a lead article titled 'Thirty-Five Years of *The Journal of Supply Chain Management*: Where Have We Been and Where Are We Going?' (Carter and Ellram 2003). This article provided a much greater understanding of the evolution of purchasing and supply research during the journal's existence from 1965 to 1999. The authors concluded that the legal and regulatory issues were the major focus during the earlier years between the 1960s and 1970s. The procurement function was considered important during the later 1970s. The areas of importance during the 1990s included procurement strategy, strategic impact on business through purchasing as well as role of procurement in new product development, involvement of purchasing function in supplier or vendor development and strategic supplier alliances. And it was only after 1994 that the emphasis was on the broader areas of supply chain issues.

PROCUREMENT AND OUTSOURCING KEY FOCUS FOR COST COMPETITIVENESS IN LAST DECADE

We now understand that logistics is part of total SCM. In the era of globalization, businesses were facing stiff competition from players around the world and in order to compete in that global environment, businesses were constantly struggling to improve on competitiveness. One of the key criterion of competitiveness was delivering goods and services at a lower cost than competition. In the last decade, businesses have focused on procurement functions to reduce the procurement cost and significant result was achieved. In the last decade itself, we have seen a shift of manufacturing operations where it is costing least, and we know that China has emerged as the choice destination for global manufacturing. Businesses have also resorted to outsourcing the manufacturing or production function. Most of large multinational corporations (MNCs) have now stopped manufacturing themselves and are sourcing from cheaper and smaller contract packers to reduce the cost of goods and services. And contract packers are identified close to the customers' cluster to further reduce the distribution, redistribution and customer servicing costs. Material procurement functions have also now been done through e-auctions to get most competitive rates. There are numerous developments that have taken place using technology to reduce the product cost, and this area seems to be totally exploited. In procurement functions, bill discounting as well as competitive discounting is now being practised to make the entire process of procurement more cost-effective and competitive.

INCREMENTAL VALUE DELIVERY THROUGH EFFECTIVE LOGISTICS MANAGEMENT

Currently, the entire focus of the business community is on logistics which acts as a critical chain in the entire end-to-end SCM. We will gradually understand the role of international logistics in terms of its capability to deliver superior value.

And, therefore, let us clarify the core concept of value. It is defined as benefits divided by cost. The benefits include both tangible and intangible benefits. Intangible benefits are associated with brand. And cost would mean the cost of acquiring the product. We can, therefore, see that value can be improved by either increasing the benefits or decreasing the cost or even both. And effective and efficient logistics management can impact both numerator and denominator positively and can thereby improve the value delivery very significantly.

While effective and efficient logistics management can create incremental value in the business, only creating value is not enough; it is also essential that you capture the value so created and deliver that for the customers' benefit. Only then business results will be forthcoming. In this connection, Kenichi's strategic 3C's model (Kenichi 1982) makes abundant sense that the corporation and competitor are both trying to deliver value to the customers but they themselves only differentiate by costs (Figure 2.3).

FIGURE 2.3 Corporation and Competition Differentiate Only on Cost

Strategic Triangle of 3C's (Kenichi Ohmae 1982)

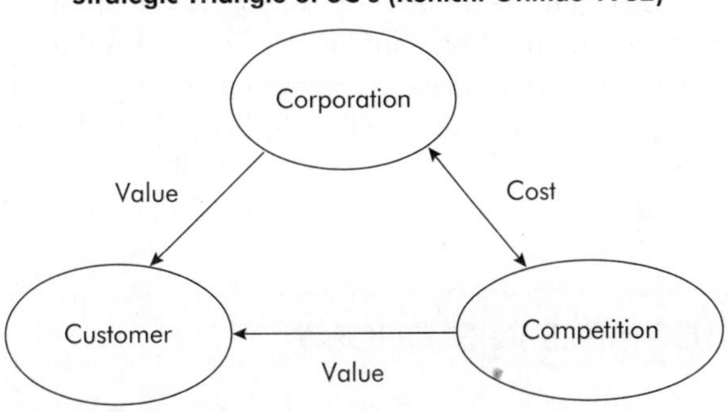

STRATEGIC TRIANGLE OF 3C's (KENICHI OHMAE 1982)

The practical significance of Strategic Triangle 3C's is that your 'corporation' has to perform against your 'competition' by delivering better and higher value to the 'customer' based on the differential cost between your product against that of your competitor.

Peter Drucker (1962) long ago said that logistics is the most neglected area till now. Businesses are trying to learn to improve that function. A lot of work has been done in the recent past in this area and today we understand logistics in a much broader sense of the term.

THEORETICAL FOUNDATIONS OF INTERNATIONAL LOGISTICS

Let us now discuss how international logistics has evolved over the years and also theoretical foundations of international logistics, which means as to how several factors lead to internationalization of logistics management.

Four key management functions of logistics management within a company like any other business are as follows: operational, financial, marketing and informational. When such systems of interlinked companies are located all over the world and when one such function is shared, it is called international logistics.

Operational cooperation at international scale often has similar objectives like lean management or agile management. Using shared services often provides services like IT services or HR services at a much lower cost and shared risks with consequential benefits. In such an environment, businesses often apply a similar concept of inventory management such as co-managed inventory (CMI), vendor-managed inventory (VMI), and collaborative planning, forecasting and replenishment (CPFR). The environmental concern and regulatory issues in many countries encourage the concept of green logistics and reverse logistics.

The other triggering factors for international logistics are use of similar methods of goods flow management such as JIT and Kanban, implementation of latest transportation technologies and tracking system, implementation of latest warehouse management systems (WMSs) and technologies, automated control and monitoring system, use of robots and artificial intelligence and so on. Other factors responsible may include uniform measures and standardization of methods and processes and construction of vast computer networks, implementation of modern communication system, video conferencing, internet and so on, with an overall objective to improve the functional efficiency of the entire interlinked organization itself.

The global forces have also compelled businesses to collectively improve things and operations such as joint cost reduction programme and joint financial control and management including cost control. Collaborative marketing such as making common face and image and making joint bid for a business to make it more competitive using collective strength using integrated IT system that supports and facilitates in pricing and policy areas as well as through use of Global Data Synchronization Network (GDSN) and exchange information via Electronic Data Interchange (EDI).

IMPORTANCE OF LOGISTICS IN ECONOMY

Why is logistics so important for the economy of a country? Globally, logistics is about 10% of the GDP. In the USA it is about 8%, in India it is 15%, in China it is about 12%, in Slovenia it is reported as 11% and in Germany it is 9%. What is important is that logistics cost has a relationship with the economic health of a nation. The logistics cost also has a direct relationship with the status of the infrastructure in a country. Because of poor infrastructure and complex tax structure, cost of logistics in India is still quite high when compared with other developed countries of the world.

> It has been established that Logistics Performance Index (LPI) is correlated with the country's international trade performance. Countries with stronger logistics performance generally tend to see a higher percentage of their overall services export, although it flattens after achieving a peak level performance. In India, logistics infrastructure is now developing and is still poor, resulting in high logistics cost in the business. Because of poor logistics infrastructure, many large public projects get delayed, resulting in time and cost overrun. In fact, most of our large projects, as per a Planning Commission's report, incurred huge overrun up to three times of the original budgeted cost of the project and the main reason could be logistics failure. Many hydropower projects got delayed just because it was found that the road leading to the project site was not suitable to take the load of a large turbine to be carried to the site for generation of power which was not originally visualized when the project was planned, and constructing yet another road could come under the purview of many agencies including state governments and other local bodies, which is time consuming to overcome due to complexity and other associated issues and problems including legal issues that need to be resolved. The result is delay and huge cost overrun.

There are many firm-level data which prove the point. For example, Shepherd (2011) has reported that poorer trade facilitation data as measured by longer lead times of export and import are always associated with higher level of trade-related corruption, as poor performance always acts as an incentive to flout the rules by paying money.

WORLD COMPETITIVENESS

Competitiveness has a direct relationship with the level and state of logistics infrastructure.

It has also been reported that the variety of trade business environment constraints affects trade performance and logistics costs as well as competitiveness measurement in the international market. Similarly, Li and Wilson (2009) also demonstrated that the time to export is an important determinant of firm-level trade behaviour and competitiveness.

Competitiveness is normally measured at three levels—country level, industry category level and firm level. Country-level competitiveness impacts all players similarly, whereas industry category-level competiveness impacts all players in the same category (e.g., steel or cement) similarly. But companies compete with each other at firm level and, therefore, managing firm-level competiveness effectively demands that logistics parameters are managed better than others.

Logistics cost has a direct bearing on a country's competitiveness and an organization's profitability. For a country, an improved infrastructure results in efficient logistics sector, which encourages investment from domestic as well as international investors, fuelling production and consumption and, therefore, the economic growth.

FIGURE 2.4 Dependence of World Competitiveness on Logistics

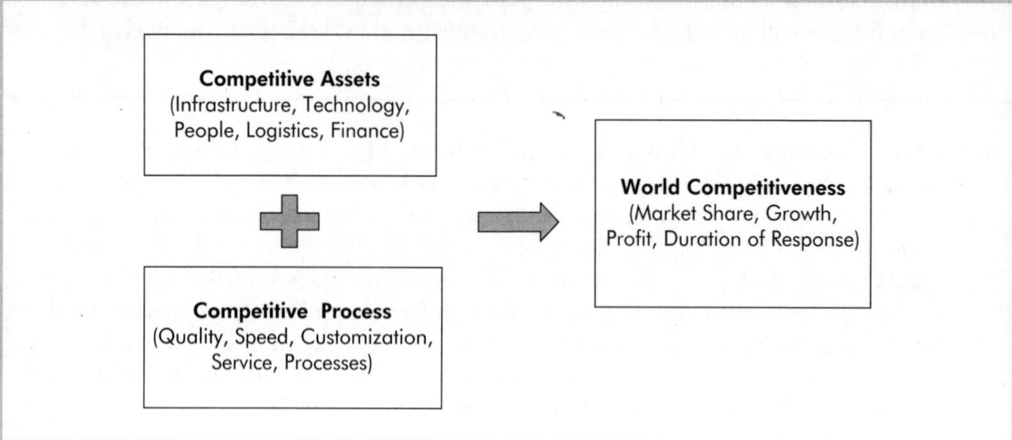

For an organization, efficient logistics management reduces the cost of delivering products, increases trade, opens a new market, and improves sales, revenue and profit margins.

Global Competitiveness report defines competitiveness as the ability to increase market share, profit and growth in value-added products and services and to stay competitive for a longer duration. Reducing logistics costs and ensuring faster delivery to customer premises, therefore, can increase enterprise competitiveness. Logistics, therefore, has a distinct role in enterprise competitiveness (Figure 2.4).

Competitive assets and competitive processes can only help you to get benefits of world competitiveness. Competitive assets can include infrastructure, technology, people, logistics and finance; competitive process can include quality, speed, customization, service and process; and world competitiveness would ensure market share, growth, profit and duration of response. This has been demonstrated in Figure 2.4.

PHYSICAL INFRASTRUCTURE AND SCM PERFORMANCE

In some areas, the performance of a supply chain largely depends on the physical infrastructure in place. A supply chain becomes inefficient if the infrastructure is not up to the mark or is deficient. For example, for an agricultural or horticultural supply chain, cold chain storage facilities and infrastructure are the key determinants of the performance of the agricultural supply chain. Industries which use agricultural or horticultural products as raw material incur higher cost resulting from poor infrastructure for managing the inventories from the stage of post harvesting of the crops. These infrastructures are normally developed either by the publicly funded organizations or by the government or even by private companies, and the efficiency as well as effectiveness of these infrastructures determine the cost of the input and also the performance of the agro-based

FIGURE 2.5 Cost Build-up and Trade Margins for Agro Commodities in India

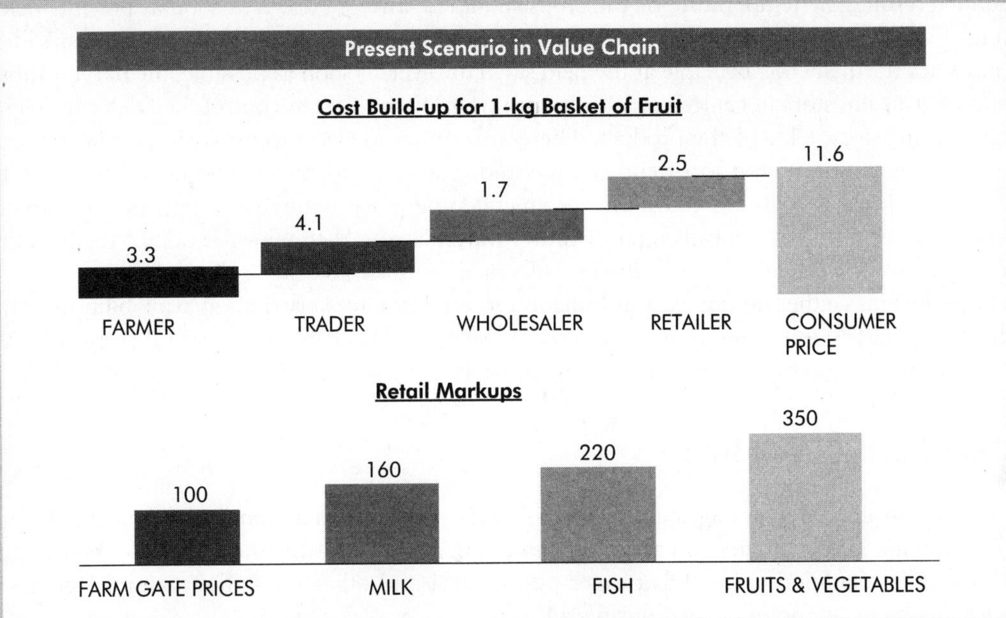

industries, including food-processing industries. In India, an agricultural supply chain is still in its infancy, resulting in very high farm-level wastages. We have a scenario where farm gate price, as well as cost of farm labour, is one of the lowest in the world, but the market price or price at which these agricultural items are delivered to customers is almost 3.5–4 times the farm gate price (Baisya 2012) as shown in Figure 2.5.

The agricultural supply chain needs the support of the necessary infrastructure for reducing the wastage. The poor infrastructure results into high logistics cost pushing the price of agricultural commodities and making them globally uncompetitive. The agricultural logistics effectiveness is thus a key for growth of agro-based industries in India. These are as discussed further.

COLD CHAIN FACILITIES

For managing an integrated supply chain in the agriculture sector, cold chain facilities are essential to control quality, shelf-life and wastage of the primary agricultural produce. For this purpose, we need the following:

- Industrial cold stores in the production zones
- Refrigerated vehicles for long-distance transport
- Refrigerated rooms in wholesale markets

FIELD HEAT REMOVAL FACILITIES

Upon harvesting, the temperature of the crops should be brought down as soon as possible before storage in cold chain facilities, which normally helps in extending the shelf-life of the crop. These facilities are normally not available at the field site. However, as soon as possible, the harvest should be brought to the storage centres or warehouses where temperature control facilities can help in extending the storage life of the product. There are various low-cost technologies available for the storage of agricultural crop to extend the life and quality of the crop. The key concern of the storage of grains is to bring down the product temperature upon harvesting by immediately transferring the crop to a controlled temperature warehouse, as the major fraction of the heat load needs to be removed that influences the rate of reactions during storage.

These facilities either do not exist in India as required or have very limited availability, resulting in high post-harvest losses and also higher cost of the agricultural and horticultural crops, which in turn make the agro-based industry non-competitive in the global market.

WAREHOUSING FACILITIES

To store the grains and other agricultural crops, we also need adequate warehousing facilities which should provide ideal storage conditions to maintain the quality of the grain and also temperature and humidity conditions as well as proper pest control and other infestation control facilities to ensure that crops are not damaged during storage.

Criticality of Supply Chain Efficiency in Agriculture Sector: A Case of Food Corporation of India (TOI Report)

In the period 2010–2012, the Food Corporation of India (FCI) has allowed 46,658 tonnes of food grains to rot in 1,889 warehouses across the country. Again, 143.74 tonnes were reported stolen. The *Times of India* reported (https://times of india.indiatimes.com/India/India-waste-21-million-tonnes-of-wheat-every-year-Report/articleshow/17969340.cms) that this much of food grains could have fed 800,000 people from priority families under the National Food Security Act for an entire year. It could have fed 10% of Bengaluru's population or 6% of Mumbai's citizens, if each person received 5 kg of food grains per month.

Such problems have been plaguing FCI for over decades, and it is trying to reduce the buffer storage. A study by the London-based Institution of Mechanical Engineers (IME) on global food wastage found that about 21 million metric tonnes (MMT) of wheat goes waste in India. The Indian government buys food grains from the farmers but does not have the space to store it. FCI has insufficient number of grain silos (modern storage facilities), and grains are stored in outdoor depots across the country. This makes grains prone to rodents, moisture, birds and pests. Unexpected rainstorms and bad weather make matters even worse.

FCI had an excess of 15.65 MMT of food grains of the prescribed buffer norms as of 1 April 2016. But according to the norms which were reviewed in January 2015, FCI should have stocked only 21.04 MMT of food grains as on 1 April but had 36.65 MMT. This suggested that the problem of storing additional grains would plague FCI next year (2017) also.

One of the reasons for the wastage of food is that grains are not moved out of the warehouses in time and distributed. Due to this inefficiency in transporting grains out of the warehouses and to the ration shops, massive quantities of grains pertaining to years 2008–2009 were found in the FCI warehouses even in March 2012.

In June 2012, the grain stock with the state agencies had crossed 75 MMT for the first time in the country's history, whereas the covered storage area available was only for 50 MMT, which means that 25 MMT of food grain had to be kept in open storage with either *kachcha* or *pucca* plinths, and thus was exposed to large-scale damage and pilferage. How much would get damaged and lost is anyone's guess. The quality of the covered storage in many places was also questionable. While the record production would give satisfaction to many, when they will see that a sizeable chunk of this stock was likely to get wasted as they would get soaked and damaged in rain, it will definitely be a disappointment for everyone. However, if some measures were taken on war footing, some quantity of that surplus could possibly be saved. This quantity is estimated to be about 9–10 MMT out of the surplus of 25 MMT. Still the wastage to the extent of about 15 MMT is a distinct possibility and that itself is a huge loss. The initiatives that the government could take were to provide incentive to state governments to lift and transport the stock to various public distribution system (PDS) stock points so that those could be sold to the public through PDS.

A question that normally arises is how we got into this situation. Good monsoon in the earlier four years had resulted in an increase in crop production from 231 MMT in 2007–2008 to 252 MMT in 2011–2012. But consumption of cereals had not been going up. The demand of cereals, in fact, had not gone up and on the contrary people were consuming more of protein and fruits and vegetables and less of cereals. The dietary habits had changed significantly over the years, thanks to the sustained campaign of food marketers. The export of wheat was banned in February 2007, and it was opened again only in September 2011 coupled with good harvest which had led to accumulation of stocks, whereas the storage capacity had not increased commensurately. Some state governments, notably Madhya Pradesh, had given a bonus of ₹100 per quintal in wheat, which had thrown private operators out of the market, and government procurement had increased significantly from less than 2 MMT in 2009–2010 to more than 6 MMT in 2012. Rajasthan had also followed the same example in 2012, and its procurement had increased by almost 194% in 2012–2013 compared to 2010–2011. Also, states such as Punjab and Haryana had put much higher statutory levies on wheat and rice at 14.5% in Punjab and 12.5% in Haryana, which had again pushed private traders out from the market and significantly pushed the state procurement upwards. It was like the state takeover of grain trade in these states which had created an unprecedented problem and scarcity of storage space.

Rice could have been exported if we had encouraged export; possibly excess rice stock could have been taken care of. In 2011–2012, India was expected to export about 6.5–7 MMT of rice, and the same could have been repeated in 2012–2013, making India the second-largest rice exporter in the world. But wheat export was not possible as Russian and Ukrainian wheat really pulled down the price of wheat in global trade. As such, the real challenge was to store the wheat stock. The cost of carrying the stock which includes storage and interest costs would be about 20%, and this amount could possibly be given as incentives to state governments to lift the stock and send that to PDS. The payment of bonus by certain states as well as the demand of statutory levies by certain states has added to the problem by keeping private players out of the grain trade. FCI, therefore, is a source of loss of precious food grains for not having adequate storage facilities for storing grains. The scenario is same even for fruits and vegetables, and as a result, India, as a country, loses huge amount for not having logistics infrastructure which is so vital to the economy.

Inadequate storage facilities can result in huge losses to the exchequers. In a country where there are people who still do not have two square meals a day, losing such magnitude of grain due to shortage of storage space and resulting wastage is criminal. Such a thing can only happen for not having the right procurement policies and also not having the required supply chain infrastructure. This is the state of affairs with respect to grain storage, which can be stored at ambient storage conditions. The situation is still worse with respect to perishables where refrigerated storage conditions or cool chambers are required to store the surplus. This situation of food grains rotting in FCI's warehouses which are ill equipped for proper storage is not something new. A few years ago, it was reported that the government had approached the Delhi School of Economics (DSE) to suggest them what to do with the bumper crop for which FCI did not even have facilities to store, and large-scale wastage and damage were inevitable. Economists from DSE suggested that surplus grains might be distributed free to the poor. Obviously, the government did not act on their advice, though giving food free to people who were starving would have been a good thing, instead of allowing the food grains to rot due to lack of storage facilities.

The government is granting many incentives for setting up storage facilities including cold chains. I know couple of entrepreneurs who have set up cold storage in northeastern regions. But they are not very happy with the utilization of space as those cold storages are running less than 50% of their capacities. I asked them why they had gone for such projects without making any detailed study of the surplus stock to be stocked in the region. The answer given by them was very simple. They said that the government is giving 50% subsidy on the cost of the project. Giving a blanket subsidy for locating the storage warehouse at any place has led to a very peculiar situation. On the one hand we have inadequate infrastructure, and on the other, we have unutilized space. This can happen only when the facilities created are not well planned, following an appropriate strategy.

What we need is a comprehensive plan and actions. Sporadic decisions are not going to be yielding the expected result. The whole infrastructure will have a consequential impact on the price of the commodities as well as of fruits and vegetables, which in turn will influence the product prices in the market. And price is a key influencer on demand and thus the growth of the entire industry. A holistic view is thus necessary to be taken to build the supply chain infrastructure for the food industry. Only talking about the need for the supply chain infrastructure is not enough. It needs to be comprehensively planned and implemented. The criticality of the infrastructure needs to be understood in view of what the industry needs and how it can be provided. An efficient supply chain is actually the backbone of the industry. The industry clearly understands the fact that over about 70% of the cost of product is contributed by the material cost and, therefore, efficient SCM is the key to providing the competitive edge. And a large part of the infrastructure has to be provided, by design, by the government, and that is the country's role to make the industry category competitive in global trade.

Source: https://timesofindia.indiatimes.com/india/Grains-rotting-with-FCI-could-have-fed-8L-for-a-year/articleshow/52068428.cms (accessed on 24 March 2019).

INNOVATIONS IN SUPPLY CHAIN

To make a supply chain efficient and competitive, there have to be constant innovations in every facets and interface of SCM, starting from product development, procurement, production and distribution in order to have a sustainable growth in revenue and profits. These innovation approaches need a company-wide programme and not isolated affairs of sporadic development taking a quick-fix approach. Not many companies have been able to achieve that objective, although businesses are pursuing their own innovation agenda. In this connection, P&G seems to be ahead of others in competition, which has helped it to triple the innovation success rate in a highly competitive market. Let us examine the model that P&G has been following to have key learning from its experiment and success stories.

How P&G Tripled Its Innovation Success Rate

P&G has very elaborate innovation management and new product development practices, and the company takes direct feedback from its over three million customers with whom it interfaces to understand the customer expectations, which it takes into consideration in its development and innovation efforts.

Tide is the biggest brand in the company's fabric and household care category. The laundry detergent is almost a 60-year-old detergent brand and still dominates its core markets, but of late it is not growing fast enough as expected. P&G pursued its systematic innovation-led strategic growth which resulted in almost doubling its revenue from US$12 billion to US$24 billion. How could this be achieved through P&G's creativity, speed and reliability? Their leaders devised a 'new growth factory', which is still ramping up. It has already helped the company strengthen its core businesses and also its ability to capture new growth opportunities. P&G spends almost US$2 billion on R&D, which is almost double of what its nearest competitors spend. In spite of big investment in R&D, in the early 2000s only 15% of its innovations were meeting its revenue and profit targets, and to address this, the company set about building organizational structures to systematize innovation to drive new growth target. In 2004, Gilbert Cloyd, then chief technology officer (CTO), and A. G. Lafley, then chief executive officer (CEO), tasked two P&G veterans John Leikhim and David Goulait with designing a new growth factory, whose intellectual underpinning would derive from the Harvard Business School Professor Clayton Christensen's disruptive innovation theory. They formed groups of new growth business guides to help teams working on disruptive projects. For example, these small groups augmented an existing entity to create new brands and new business models, and dedicated teams within the groups conducted market research, developed technology, created business plans and tested project-specific assumptions to produce a process manual containing step-by-step guidelines for creating new growth business. This manual describes opportunities and identifies requirements for success, as well as monitors progress and makes go/no-go decisions for running demonstration projects for showcasing the merging factories' work. One of these is a line of pocket-size products called Swash, which can quickly refresh clothes. For example, if someone is in a hurry, he/she can give a not-quite-clean shirt a spray rather than putting it through the normal wash.

P&G's four types of innovations are sustaining, commercial, transformational sustaining and disruptive. Sustaining innovations bring only incremental improvements in existing products and processes. Commercial innovations use creating marketing and promotional approaches to grow existing offering. Transformational sustaining innovations reframe existing categories. They normally bring some fundamental changes to a business that can lead to some breakthrough in the market. In 2009, P&G introduced a wrinkle-reduction cream Olay Pro X launching at US$40 a bottle, which was possibly a questionable strategy, but P&G went ahead as it was a clinically tested product and the first-year revenue was US$250 million from food retailers and drug stores alone. The disruptive innovations represent new-to-the-world business opportunities. A company enters entirely new businesses with radically new offerings as P&G did with Swiffer and Febreze.

By 2008, P&G had a working prototype factory, which was able to dramatically increase the innovation output by focusing on fewer but bigger initiatives and in that direction, McDonald's and Brown's team drove three critical improvements. First, it increased emphasis on transformational sustaining innovations, which deliver major new benefits in existing business categories. Second, P&G strengthened organizational supports for the formation of transformational sustaining and disruptive businesses. It established several new business-creation groups, larger in size and scope than any previous growth factory team, whose resources and management are kept carefully separate from the core business. These groups' dedicated teams led by a general manager develop ideas that cut across multiple businesses and also pursue entirely new business opportunities. Third, P&G revamped its strategy development and review process. Innovation and strategy assessments had historically been handled separately. Now CEO, CTO and chief financial officer (CFO) explicitly link company, business and innovation strategies. This integration, coupled with new analyses of such issues as competitive factors that could threaten a given business, has surfaced more opportunities for innovation. The process has also prompted examinations of each unit's 'production schedule', or pipeline of growth opportunities, to ensure that it is robust enough to deliver against growth goals for the next 7–10 years.

P&G has also customized formulations for emerging markets. Ethnographic research showed that about 80% of consumers in India washed their clothes by hands. They had to choose between detergents that were relatively gentle on the skin but not that good at cleaning clothes and more potent but harsher agents. With the problem clearly identified, in 2009 a team came up with Tide Naturals, which cleaned well without causing skin irritation. Mindful of the need in emerging markets to provide greater benefits at lower cost—more or less—P&G priced Tide Naturals 30% below comparatively effective but harsher products, and that made Tide brand accessible to 70% of Indian consumers and helped to significantly increase Tide's market share in India. Now Tide Dry Cleaners represent an entirely new business model. It started when a team began exploring ways to disrupt the dry cleaning markets, using proprietary technologies and a unique store design grounded in insights about consumers' frustration with the existing options. Many cleaning establishments are dingy, unfriendly places. Customers have to park, walk and wait, and often the cleaners' hours are inconvenient. P&G's alternative: bright, boldly coloured cleaners featuring specialized treatments, drive-through windows and 24-hour storage lockers to facilitate after-hours drop-off and pick-up. Tide's innovation efforts have been closely coordinated through regular dialogues among several leaders—CEO McDonald, CTO Brown, the vice chair of the household business unit and the president of the fabric care division (Brown and Anthony 2011).

Lessons for Leaders

Efforts to build a new growth factory in any company will fail unless senior managers create right organizational structures, provide proper resources, allow sufficient time for experimentation and learning, and personally engage themselves. That journey for P&G suggests six lessons for leaders looking to create new growth factories:

1. **Closely coordinate the factory and the core business:** Leaders sometimes see efforts to foster new growth as completely distinct from efforts to bolster the core. A healthy core produces a cash flow that can be invested in new growth. A core business is rich with capabilities that can support new growth efforts. P&G has excellent relationships with major retailers. Those relationships are a powerful, hard-to-replicate asset that helps the factory expedite new growth opportunities. Some of the tools for managing core efforts, particularly those that track a project's progress, are also useful for managing new growth efforts, and finally the factory's rapid learning approach often yields insights that can strengthen existing product lines. Critical discovery: Babies who wore disposable diapers fell asleep 30% faster and slept 30 minutes longer than babies wearing cloth diapers—an obvious benefit for infants and their parents. This campaign helped make Pampers the number one brand in several emerging markets.
2. **Promote a portfolio mindset:** P&G communicates to both internal and external stakeholders that it is building a varied portfolio of innovation approaches ranging from sustaining to disruptive ones. It uses a set of master-planning tools to match the pace of innovation to the overall needs of the business. It also deploys portfolio-optimization tools that help managers identify and kill the least promising programmes and nurture the best bets. The portfolio approach helps to set up the expectation that different projects will be managed, resourced and measured in different ways just as an investor would use different criteria to evaluate an investment opportunity.
3. **Start small and grow carefully:** Remember how the new growth factory began—with a simple two-day workshop which then followed to small-scale pilots in several business units before becoming a company-wide initiative. It also provides targeted experimentation. A staged approach also helps in avoiding any quick-fix solutions which will not be lasting solutions.
4. **Create new tools for gauging new businesses:** Anticipated and nascent markets are notoriously hard to analyse. P&G now conducts 'transaction learning experiments' or TLEs, in which a team 'makes a little and sells a little', thus letting consumers vote with their wallets. New sales organizations or new selling methods and processes can be experimented before these are implemented company wide.
5. **Make sure you have the right people doing the right work:** Building the factory forced P&G to change the way it staffed certain teams. At any given time, the company has hundreds of teams working on various innovation efforts. In the past, most teams consisted mainly of part-time members—employees who had other responsibilities pulling at them. But the disruptive and transformational sustaining efforts require undivided attention, as the old saying goes that nine women cannot make one baby in a month. There need to be people who wake up each day and go to

sleep each night obsessed about the new business and new business models of growth, but the team has to be small.

6. **Encourage intersections:** Successful innovation requires rich cross-pollination both inside and outside the organization. P&G's Connect+Develop (C+D) programme is part of a larger effort to intersect with other disciplines and gain new perspectives. P&G has shared people with non-competing companies. In 2008, P&G and Google swapped two dozen employees for a few weeks. P&G wanted greater exposure to online models of business, and Google was interested in learning how to build power brands.

P&G has engaged even more outside innovators. In 2010, it refreshed its C+D goals. It has expanded the programme to forge additional connections with government labs, universities, small and medium-sized entrepreneurs, consortia and venture capital firms. It has also brought in outside talents. It traditionally promoted from within but recognized that total reliance on this approach could stunt its ability to create new growth business. So it began bringing in high-level people to address needs beyond its core capabilities, as when it hired an outsider to run Agile Pursuits Franchising to acquire expertise in franchise-based business models which would have otherwise taken years to build organically.

P&G's efforts appear to be working well. Today, 50% of its innovation efforts are meeting the profit and revenue targets as against only 15% earlier. Its experience tells us that although individual creativity can be unpredictable and uncontrollable, collective creativity can be managed. This innovation process can create sustainable source of revenue growth, no matter how big a company becomes.

Dell's Direct Business Model of Virtual Integration

Dell is a US multinational computer technology company that develops, sells, repairs and provides support for computer and related products. Founded in 1984 by Michael S. Dell who also is the company's CEO. The revenue increased to US$90.62 billion in 2019 with a net income of US$2.31 billion, a growth of 9% over the previous year. Dell is an innovative company and practises a very cost-effective supply chain management model which distinguishes itself from other players in personal computers. This has helped them to keep leadership position in highly competitive PC market. Dell displayed and delivered consistent growth and profitability in personal computer market because of their distinctive SCM policy to produce and assemble computers against firm order and creating a very realistic budgeted forecast aligned with customer orders taking a bottom-up approach for optimum resource allocation and management which has been discussed in this case.

Dell has a very successful and well-performing global supply chain model of virtual integration. Advantages of a tightly coordinated supply chain traditionally facilitated by vertical integration combined with focus and specialization. Dell has also leveraged the investments others have made and focused on delivering solutions and systems to customers. It has been able to greatly take partners' support to its advantage, which has led it fewer things to manage, which means that only few things can go wrong. Suppliers' engineers are part of Dell's design team and Dell also has few partners who are selected to work in association with Dell to co-create significant value.

Dell is an example that enjoyed tremendous success based on its supply chain design, planning and operation by adapting its supply chain in response to shift in technology and customer expectations.

With channel partners, Dell shares information in real-time basis and stitches together a business with partners that are treated as if they are inside the company. The focus changes from how much inventory there is to how fast it is moving, which is in fact a model of asset collecting risks around it one way or the other. Their product also requires limited or no testing for using Sony monitors.

Dell has only three manufacturing centres in Austin, Ireland and Malaysia. The information flow is at real-time and inventory levels, and replenishment needs sometimes are conveyed to vendors on hourly basis. Also information related to inventory can be sub-categorised as 'inventory and ship' only when company has real demand from real-end customers. Clever segmentation and focus on institutional markets helped them to achieve better performance. For example, 70% deliveries going to very large number of customers with annual purchases exceed US$1 million. During 1993–2006, Dell experienced unprecedented growth in both revenue and profits by structuring a supply chain that provided customers with customized personal computers (PCs) very quickly and at a very reasonable cost.

Dell had exited from retail business after making a wrong entry in 1989. Customer segmentation by remaining close to customers and have access to valuable information helps in better customer service delivery and performance. Demand forecasting is done with the involvement of partners, and Dell developed a critical tool in demand forecasting. It helped global customers manage their total purchase of PCs by selling them a standard product globally. And Dell server loaded the software on customers' computers and met customers' needs faster and more efficiently than any other model. This innovative virtual integration model worked well for them. By 2006, Dell had a net income of more than US$3.5 billion on revenues of just over US$56 billion. This success was based on two key supply chain features that supported rapid and low-cost customization. First, Dell decided to sell directly to the end customer bypassing distributors and retailers, making it more cost effective and responsive to customer's demand. Second, the centralization of manufacturing and inventories in a few locations where final assembly was done was postponed till receiving the confirmed order from the customer. Dell was also able to supply a large variety of PC configurations as required by the customers while keeping very low levels of component inventories.

Dell also responded to changing market environment when it was seen that customers were going for very low level of customization and buying standard products and were seen to be satisfied with few standard models when they adjusted to the changing market structure by adjusting their supply chain with regard to both direct selling and building to order when they also started selling their PCs through retail chain like Walmart in the USA and GOME in China.

CHAPTER SUMMARY

This chapter discusses the evolution of SCM and logistics management through last few decades from their early stage of development as a discipline to what we understand today, and also the core concept of integrated SCM in terms of its definition, scope, objectives and challenges. Key components of SCM are discussed in detail with examples and short cases. The chapter also discusses why supply chain and logistics functions are so important for sustaining a business in the current context of global competitive environment and how effectively managing these functions can help provide a competitive advantage to the business. It also discusses why and how logistics management performance contributes to the country's economic growth. Key components and basic elements of SCM and logistics function are explained as well as various types of logistics are discussed. The complexity of integrated SCM are demonstrated taking the case of Li & Fung. The chapter covers in detail the evolution of logistics now as a full-grown discipline and also outlines the importance of international logistics and its implication in business. Logistics which started initially as transportation gradually emerged as product distribution, and finally as business logistics covering the scientific research and development work including the technology development and interface of various information technologies and ERP in the current context in terms of running the modern businesses now. How robots and artificial intelligence are now being used for managing the logistics and warehouse functions as well as material-handling functions in modern factories is discussed briefly. Two case studies are discussed—one of FCI to discuss how poor logistics infrastructure resulted in huge losses and wastage of food grain in FCI warehouses and the other a case of P&G to discuss how innovations in SCM and related areas helped it to gain a competitive advantage following disruptive innovation for radical improvement in business performance. Also, a case on Dell is discussed showing how Dell decided to change its supply chain network to improve both cost and response time to significantly improve the performance of the business.

DISCUSSION QUESTIONS

1. Discuss the core concept of SCM as it is known today and its scope and coverage.
2. How did the SCM functions evolve over the years? What are the basic elements of logistics and how is it now an integral part of SCM?
3. How can efficient SCM practices provide the key competitive advantage to the business? Discuss taking a case.
4. How important is the logistics function in business as well as the overall economy? What are the different types of logistics?
5. Discuss the key role of SCM in delivering the business performance. Discuss the criticality of the supply chain efficiency in India's agriculture sector.
6. Discuss the key success criteria which have helped P&G to triple its innovation success rate. What are the key lessons learnt from their innovation management and new product development practices?

REFERENCES

Baisya, R. K. 2012, June. Criticality of Supply Chain Efficiency in Agriculture. *Processed Food Industry*, 15 (9): 18–20.

Brown, Bruce, and Scott D. Anthony. 2011. 'How P&G Tripled Its Innovation Success Rate'. *Harvard Business Review* (June): 65–72.

Carter, C., and L. Ellram. 2003. 'Thirty-Five Years of the *Journal of Supply Chain Management*: Where Have We Been and Where Are We Going?' *Journal of Supply Chain Management* 39 (1): 27–39.

Council of Supply Chain Management Professionals (CSCMP). 2013. http://cscmp.org/about-us/supply-chain-management-deficition (accessed on 19 August 2019).

Drucker, Peter F. 1962. 'The Economy's Dark Continent'. *Fortune* (April): 103, 265, 268 and 270.

Harland, C. M. 1996. 'Supply Chain Management: Relationships, Chains and Networks'. *British Journal of Management* 7 (S1): S63–S80.

Houston, James A. 1996. *The Sinews of War: Army Logistics, 1775–1953*. Washington, DC: Government Printing Office.

Kenichi, Ohmae. 1982. *The Mind of Strategist: The Art of Japanese Business*. New York: McGraw-Hill.

Li, Y., and J. Wilson. 2009. 'Time as a Determinant of Comparative Advantage'. Policy Research Working Paper 5218. Washington, DC: World Bank.

Magretta, Joan. 1998. 'Fast Global and Entrepreneurial: Supply Chain Management, Hong Kong Style'. *Harvard Business Review* (September–October): 102–114.

Movahedi, B., K. Lavassani, and V. Kumar. 2009. 'Transition to B2B e-Marketplace Enabled Supply Chain: Readiness Assessment and Success Factors'. *The International Journal of Technology, Knowledge and Society* 5 (3): 75–88.

Porter, Michel E. 1985. 'The Structural Analysis of Industries'. *Competitive Advantage: Creating and Sustaining Superior Performance*, 11–15. New York, NY: The Free Press.

Shepherd, Ben. 2011. 'Logistics Costs and Competitiveness: Measurement and Trade Policy Applications'. MPRA Paper 38254. Munich: University Library of Munich.

Smykay, Edward W., Donald J. Bowersox, and Frank H. Mossman. 1961. *Physical Distribution Management: Logistics Problems of the Firm*. New York, NY: Macmillan Publishers.

Southern, R. Neil. 1997. *Transportation and Logistics Basic*. Continental Traffic Publishing Company.

BIBLIOGRAPHY

Cavinato, Joseph L. 2002. 'What's Your Supply Chain Type?' *Supply Chain Management Review* (May–June): 60–66.

Fuller, Joseph B., James O'Conner, and Richard Rawlinson. 1993. 'Tailored Logistics: The Next Advantage'. *Harvard Business Review* (May–June): 87–98.

Lambert, Douglas M. 2004. 'The Eight Essential Supply Chain Management Processes'. *Supply Chain Management Review* 8 (6, September): 18–26.

Lee, Hau L. 2002. 'Aligning Supply Chain Strategies with Product Uncertainties'. *California Management Review* 44 (3, Spring): 105–119.

Marien, Edward J. 2000. 'The Four Supply Chain Enablers.' *Supply Chain Management Review* 2 (3, March–April): 60–68.

Robeson, James F., and William C. Copacino, eds. 1994. *The Logistics Handbook*. New York, NY: The Free Press.

Slone, Reuben E. 2004. 'Leading Supply Chain Turnaround'. *Harvard Business Review* (October): 114–121.

3

Demand Estimation in a Supply Chain

LEARNING OBJECTIVES

- Understand the role and importance of forecasting in managing a business as well as a supply chain
- Identify the characteristics of forecasts and factors influencing forecasts
- Identify the types and levels of forecasts
- Get acquainted with various qualitative and quantitative methods of forecasting
- Analyse demand forecasts and estimate forecasting errors

INTRODUCTION: ESTIMATING CUSTOMER DEMAND

Businesses are created for serving and satisfying customer demands, and only through satisfying the customer demands and expectations organizations generate revenue from sales and make profit for the shareholders, and that is the sole purpose of the existence of a corporation. SCM functions and processes are designed to effectively service the demand. However, the task of creation of demand rests with the sales and marketing teams of the business, whereas meeting and satisfying the projected demand is the job of the SCM team. Marketers are relentlessly trying and working hard to increase the demand and delivering the projected growth of the business, and they are always under pressure to deliver growth often more than realistically possible and they often try to push stocks in the market. The SCM team has to meet that ever-changing demand in a dynamic market and ensure customer satisfaction. Management gives a higher target to the sales and marketing teams of the business. However, growth can come only from increased customer demand, and as same customer is unlikely to consume more, new customers need to be created. New customers can come either from deeper penetration in the existing market of the business or through the geographical expansion. The sales team will try to exploit both avenues. Either way, the task of SCM changes in terms of complexity of demand management. These two very important functions of the business, therefore, have to work in harmony and in tandem with each other and support each other, which makes a valid case for discussing the integrated SCM.

The market is highly dynamic as well as competitive; satisfying a customer, therefore, in this complex and challenging environment, is all the more difficult. But satisfying the customer requirement is always a sacrosanct task of the business. A customer has many choices; businesses are dependent on the customers. The pressure on the SCM team in that environment is therefore immense. We will separately discuss in this chapter how a corporation's sales team can make SCM teams' life all the more difficult. To deliver business performance to be effective is more important, but to be effective one also needs to be efficient. The efficiency and effectiveness of the SCM function is therefore of paramount importance to ensure the delivery of budgeted cost and profit of the business. Although customer demand has been created by the marketers, the demand has to be managed effectively by managing the inventory optimally. Large part of the profit of the business is linked with the efficiency of the supply chain, which is again a function of developing a realistic demand forecast in its totality, considering the seasonal fluctuation in demand, if any, as well as due to dynamic nature of the business environment beyond the control of the business and also considering the fact that a stock-out situation has to be avoided for the reason that in a fiercely competitive marketplace, a customer has many choices and alternatives to choose from. Losing a loyal customer will have negative impact on business. As inventory has to be optimized to effectively manage the demand, two very important aspects of the business are also being discussed together in this chapter.

UNREALISTIC DEMAND CAN MAKE SCM INEFFICIENT

The business planning exercise in any organization starts with the sales numbers projected in a given year by the company, involving its sales, marketing and planning teams, following the view, goal and objective of the top management. The top management expresses the desire to achieve a certain goal and market share, and the sales management team has to deliver that. Involving these three teams to prepare the corporation's annual budget is therefore a very vital and important task of the business every year. Once sales numbers are finalized and approved, the planning function works with the SCM team to ensure that the production planning is robust enough to produce and deliver those quantities as per the sales requirement. SCM, in fact, has to be dependent on the accuracy of the demand forecast emanated from the sales department and approved by the top management, who in turn approves other resources, including financial and manpower, for the business. Achieving the sales target including in terms of its periodicity at stock-keeping unit (SKU) level is a key imperative to the business. But it is not an easy task to project demand to that level of accuracy, and there will always be a mismatch between the actual demand of the market and the budgeted sales forecast. Thus, a constant adjustment in terms of production planning and procurement planning would be necessary to align the supply chain with the change in demand resulting from changed business environment. This often results in a conflict between the sales and SCM teams. The sales team is also responsible for achieving top-line value performance month wise, and in order to do that, they often demand more quantity of items to be sold for which the company may not have the capacity to produce to pass the blame to the SCM team for lack of supply for their underperformance. The sales team sometimes even do it deliberately, knowing well that the SCM team cannot deliver the incremental demand over and above the budgeted numbers. We have, therefore, observed that in a business, there is a constant rift between the sales and SCM teams. This conflict is mostly unavoidable, but the more accurate the demand forecast will be, the less the conflict and friction will be between the two departments which are very vital for organizational performance. Sales is the most difficult function in the business, but everything else and all other functions in business depend on the sales. Everything else becomes meaningless if the sales function does not perform. The sales team is therefore always under pressure to perform, and often demand is to outperform. Sometimes the top management even pushes the sales team to deliver something unrealistic, creating additional pressure in the system which can even escalate the conflict.

It makes good sense that SCM is geared to deliver realistic customer demand and not pseudo demand, and to achieve that, a demand forecast must consider that opportunities for growth are fully captured so that there is no loss of sales for non-supply, and at the same time the demand should not be over-projected resulting in stock built-up, blocking working capital and high debtors. A demand forecast is therefore a very important task and an annual exercise reviewed periodically for any correction for the business to be undertaken with all seriousness and rigours to ensure minimal forecasting error. A great deal of past experience in the business helps in this task.

FORECASTING IN SUPPLY CHAIN

For effective SCM, businesses need a reasonably reliable forecast to start with, as a demand forecast is the basis of all supply chain planning exercises. The businesses which have product lines with a regular pattern of established demand are much easier to manage in terms of designing, planning and implementing their end-to-end supply chain. For such businesses, there is a pull of brands and product lines already exist. But when products need to be pushed in the market to achieve targeted sales volume, forecasts may not be that much accurate. The pull process is triggered from the customer demand, whereas the push process is triggered by the managers of the company based on what they want to achieve, which may not have any real-term relationship with customer demand or requirement. Businesses which have multiple locations have to generate forecasts from each location and then collate the same for company-wide forecasts. Also, businesses which operate franchise models need to generate collaborative forecasts based on an established process.

For large MNCs, forecasts have to be globally aggregated, collecting local country-specific forecasts. The accuracy of the forecasts is a key concern for the both SCM performance and overall business performance. Even resource allocation has a bearing on the quality and accuracy of the forecasts. Forecasting, therefore, is a very important function of the business done annually, although in reality, many or even large numbers of businesses do it just as a ritual. Such businesses just keep a growth factor in mind every year and build on the actual sales performance of the previous year. In general and broadly, two approaches are followed for demand forecasting, which can be classified as bottom-up approach and top-down approach. In bottom-up approach, a corporation attempts to generate the sales forecast, taking the projections from the front-line salespersons who really know what can be realistically delivered given a certain support and competitive scenario. To help the front-line salespersons to generate the primary numbers of forecast for the coming financial year, corporations normally prepare and share a document where business portfolio analysis, competition analysis, business environment analysis as well as company's focus on certain categories of products including any plan for new products to be introduced during the year, as well as marketing and promotional support are available so that businesses can deliver the expected level of performance. This document normally outlines the expectation of the shareholders of the company. The bottom-up approach generates some sales numbers which will invariably fall short of meeting management's expectation. A process then starts which is in fact an iterative process of discussion to find out ways and means to come closer to the management's expectations, and finally democratically agreed figures are canned as the year's sales budget, product group wise, broken down to individual brands as well as SKUs. Then calendarization is done taking into account any seasonal fluctuations and then progressed to get sales projection even salesman wise in details.

> Reckitt Benckiser, an Anglo-Dutch MNC in FMCG sector, starts the annual budgetary exercise from late August for the next financial year. There will be a global business review document covering the company's own business performance review and futuristic perspective and forecasts, including competitive analysis globally as well as for regions. This document becomes the basis of country-specific initiatives for generating the sales projection in each country, which creates yet another document discussing similar parameters for the country itself and gives indications of future growth avenues where the company intends to focus, which include the existing business and brands giving reasons why. This document is discussed in the country's management committee and approved for sharing with the sales and marketing teams and then percolated down to front-line salesmen. The bottom-up figures are generated and collated from all regions and then checked if those figures are matching or coming closer to the top management's perspective to translate shareholders' expectation both locally and if it also integrates and delivers the expectation of the global headquarters in London. Once approved, this becomes the finally canned budget which is a sacrosanct document for the business unit to deliver. This entire process is spearheaded by the corporate planning and business development department at both at headquarters and local country levels. The final budget document gets the approval of the topmost authority like the board of directors in their meeting. This entire process normally takes about three months to complete. And this approved document finally becomes the starting or basis of SCM planning and implementation. Large companies will invariably have their ERP software like SAP which supports the monthly production and procurement and dispatch planning. It is needless to say that in spite of following such an elaborate and rigorous system of budgeting with milestone and involvement of everyone in the organization, occasional trouble related to short supply, out of stock or even excess stock and overtrading leading to higher debtors could not be avoided. It can therefore be understood that SCM is a very complex and dynamic document requiring frequent review and course correction. And the reasons are many, which we will discuss in this chapter. Some of the MNCs even prepare what they call 'Goal Book', which contains the budget document for five years; the first year is firm and next four years are tentative, and this is in fact a rolling forecast which is reviewed, revised and updated every year. No business accepts the growth rate lower than the industry category growth rate because if the growth rate of a product category is projected or forecasted lower than that, it would mean that the business is losing market share in that product category itself, which consciously no business can accept as it will trigger the downward journey for that brand and product category. The growth forecast is thus normally higher than the category growth rate but how much is determined by all the factors influencing the performance of the product in the marketplace, including competitive actions. While doing the budgetary exercise, businesses also give more emphasis on volume forecast and not value forecast, and value is normally derived and also impacted by any inflationary factor resulting in price increase. The real measure of growth is thus volume growth.

CHARACTERISTICS OF FORECASTS

In spite of best intention, forecasts can be in general inaccurate and only degree of inaccuracy might differ from company to company or even product to product in a company. For an established product, a forecast will be more accurate but a new product forecast will be inaccurate and to manage that supply chain, constant adjustments and flexibility will be required. Forecasts can also be inaccurate for unrealistic growth ambition of the business. For this reason, any forecast must have both expected value of demand and a measure of the forecast error or demand uncertainty. Businesses do not normally keep any record for discrepancies of real-term demand against the projected or forecasted demand, nor do they normally try to analyse the reasons for such errors simply for the fact that reasons of error in different times would be different and also the focus for the business is always to deliver budgeted profit and that focus many a time forces businesses to either overtrade on certain brands and SKUs or create artificial demand on item(s) to get to the desired profit figures. These actions from the sales and marketing sides of the business are always supported by the management obviously at the cost of disorientation of all plans of the SCM team. But this is the reality of the uncertain and dynamic nature of the business environment and competitive actions which make all forecasts very difficult to implement by the SCM team. In spite of all the efforts to make the sales and SCM teams to work in tandem and harmony, the problems and conflicts still surface. Take the case of two businesses in a similar product category, both expecting a healthy growth rate and delivering similar numbers in terms of sales volume, but a forecast error can make the SCM plans different for these two companies. The lesser the forecast error, the better it is to manage.

Demand forecasts are normally made for short term, medium term as well as long term. A short-term forecast, say for a month, will be more realistic and deliverable than a medium-term one, say for a quarter, or a long-term one, say for a year. As such, long-term forecasts are less reliable and hence have greater errors than the short-term forecasts. Long-term forecasts have larger standard deviation of error in relation to mean than short-term forecasts.

P&G, a couple of years ago, implemented a project called 'Project Golden Eye', applying the Pareto principle that 20% distributors generate 80% of the sales volume. They decided to focus on and deal with these 20% distributors, and remaining 80% distributors were put under the 20% which had reduced the complexity of the business hugely. P&G was able to get rid of large numbers of sales force and create a lean organization which was more efficient. By reducing the numbers of the direct distributors to be serviced, a lot of cost saving was made possible. And by implementing an ERP software package such as SAP, P&G was able to directly link the small numbers of distributors and replenish the stock sold in the earlier period. The frequency of servicing the distributors and stockists also improved, resulting in lower stockholding in the trade, and hence lower working capital and higher profit. Customer service levels also increased significantly.

However, aggregate forecasts are normally more accurate than disaggregate forecasts for the reason that they have smaller standard deviation of error in relation to the mean. It is not difficult to forecast the GDP of a country with less than 2–3% error. But it is really difficult to forecast the sales revenue of a company in the same country with that much of accuracy. It is in fact even more difficult to forecast the sales volume of a product with the same level of accuracy which arises due to the degree of aggregation. The greater the aggregation, the greater will be the level of accuracy of the forecasts.

FACTORS INFLUENCING FORECAST

The forecast for a company's product lines depends on many internal as well as external factors. Internal factors largely include the company's advertisement and promotional plan, product's past demand in the same market, whether any new product variant in different price segment is being introduced or not, competitive action in the same market, economic growth, product category growth rate and so on. If the product has long performance history and has a dominant position in the marketplace, having strong brand, projection or forecasting becomes easier and that is more reliable also. The problem starts when the forecast has to be made for other products including new products. Depending on the amount of valid information and data available in a given situation, forecast methodology is decided. When heavy promotion is resorted to for an established and strong brand to raise short-term demand, then customers might even decide to stock the product when such promotional or price discounting is announced and then buy less in subsequent months when the price is brought back to normal. It happens when there is a steady demand for the product and artificial demand is created by price discount and/or the promotion has resulted in excess stocking but not consumption by the customers. But for a lesser known brand or a product, such schemes are directed to generate trials and create new sets of customers. A forecast in such a scenario will impact the supply chain plan as well as performance.

WHY FORECAST?

The entire ERP commences when the sales forecasting exercise is completed and approved. The forecast of the annual budgetary revenue is therefore very important for all businesses, irrespective of their types, nature and character. The bigger the company, more complex the forecast processes would be. Many decisions including recruitment or staffing, organization structure and design are linked with the business forecast as well brand marketing plan to achieve the forecasted volume.

Inaccurate demand predictions can have disastrous consequences on business performance and profitability.

> For example, Hewlett Packard was unable to predict the proper product mix for its customers for two quarters in a row many years ago (Hograth 1975). The demand for low-end printers and workstations was high, while the demand for commercial printers was low. As a result, earnings were 14% less than the prediction or forecast given by the analysts. The stock market also reacted sharply by knocking the company's stock price down by 5% in one day. This demonstrates the importance of being able to measure the size of the market opportunities as well as kind of opportunities following a reliable forecasting method that suits better for a company's product category in a given market.

MARKET POTENTIAL

Market potential is actually the maximum demand over a given period of time based on the number of potential users and their purchase rate. In fact, actual industry sales are normally less than the market potential. Some potential always remains unexploited for various reasons. However, a business must know about the total potential to identify as well as understand the gap in the market. A company's sales projection can only be a part or portion of the total industry demand for the particular product category. It is the maximum the company can sell at a given period of time which again will depend on many other factors including the state of the product life cycle the product currently is in and also on the competitive actions and company's own sales marketing plans and promotions.

TYPES OF FORECASTS

The entire end-to-end supply chain planning actually stems from the sales forecast, and the main purpose of planning is to allocate company resources in such a manner that it achieves the targeted and budgeted sales figures. A company can forecast the sales by forecasting market sales which we can call as market forecasting and then making a prudent assumption of the percentage of that market which the company can expect to get in a given environment, and that share of the total market can become the company's sales forecast. However, this estimate will be at an aggregated level when business planners will be interested in forecasts at product level and even product SKU level. There are numerous techniques that can be used for preparing sales forecasts which will be discussed in this chapter. Let us look at the three basic levels of short-, medium- and long-term forecasts and their practical utility.

1. **Short-term forecasts:** These short-term forecasts are usually for periods up to three months. The general sales trend is not important here, and these forecasts are normally used for tactical purposes such as production planning to take into consideration any fluctuation in sale.
2. **Medium-term forecasts:** Medium-term forecasts are usually for a period of one year. This is thus the annual budget of the business and has significance for the planners. This is, in fact, the starting POS forecast, and if sales forecast is incorrect, the entire budget is incorrect. If the forecast is overoptimistic, then the company will have unsold stock in inventory which has to be funded from working capital. Or it will be lying as unsold stock at the channel partners' warehouses, resulting in higher debtors or even expiry of the stock resulting in write-offs, reprocessing, and so on, impacting the bottom-line performance of the company. If the forecast is pessimistic and is lower than the market opportunity for the company, there will be loss of opportunity, resulting in underperformance and loss of market share to competition which will have longer-term implication to the business. Establishing the required process and rigours within the business to develop annual sales budget realistically is the key to deliver the business for realizing its potential.
3. **Long-term forecasts:** These are usually for periods of three years and more but not more than five years as beyond five years it is not realistically possibly to forecast considering the expected changes in business environment including technology and so on. In industries, three years is generally considered as long term, but in steel industry or even energy sector, 10 years' horizon is generally considered as long term. Long-term forecasts are worked out from macroeconomic and environmental factors such as government policy and economic trends. These are normally referred to and discussed by corporate finance and board of directors for long-term capital investment or for allocation of other resources, as such

decisions might even involve the construction of new factories or new technology and/or upgradation of existing facilities.

In addition, other functions in a business can be directly and indirectly affected in their planning considerations as a result of the sales forecast, and such functions include the following:

- The production and operations department needs to know the sales forecasts so that they can arrange production planning. There needs to be close coordination and liaison between production and sales to determine customer priorities in the short term. Production also needs to know long-term forecasts so that capital plant investment decisions can be made in order to meet anticipated sales in future.
- The purchase department normally gets its cues to purchase from production via purchase requisitions or bill of materials. For long-delivery items or for strategic sourcing of key inputs, it is useful that the purchase department gets some advance intimation or even warning for such a situation might be arising so that they can better plan their purchases in terms of pricing and delivery schedule requirement.
- The human resource department is also interested to know the sales forecast from the manpower planning point of view.
- The finance and costing department needs to know the medium-term sales forecast for their budgeting purpose. Longer-term forecasts are required by financial accountants and top management for critical decisions related to capacity building and resource planning.
- The R&D department also needs to know the forecasts, although their requirement is more for technological point of view. They are particularly interested to know the expected life of the existing products and how technology is impacting their costs, performance and so on in relation to competition to plan and direct their R&D activities. They also use the market research reports to design and develop the future products for the company suited to the changing marketplace. Such a view reflects a marketing-oriented approach to customer requirements.
- All sales promotion and marketing activities are aligned with the sales forecast to ensure that the budgeted numbers are achieved and therefore the sales forecast forms the critical input for the business to align all activities to happen in an integrated manner.

LEVELS OF FORECASTING

Forecasts can be prepared at different levels of aggregation, starting from global level to national and ultimately to SKUs, month wise as well as weekly, salesperson territory wise, taking into account the seasonal impact on sales performance and consumer demand which can really help the corporation in designing and planning the supply chain to satisfy the projected demand of the customers. For example, an organized retail store buyer can take an easy approach to ask the store manager of each store to give a forecast for his/her store and then the buyer can add up the individual store-level forecasts to get the total ordering quantity for the company. It is based on the local market intelligence that the store has, but store managers are forecasting well ahead of the actual demands, and therefore might even go wrong and forecasts might be inaccurate. In this case, it is better to forecast the demand at the aggregate level for ordering with the supplier, particularly for long-delivery or long-lead time items, and then ask the store managers to forecast when they want the stock to be delivered to their stores nearing the season when local market intelligence of the store management team will be more closer to the reality and hence more accurate.

SEASONAL VARIATIONS

In large companies, a forecast is always an annual exercise when the annual sales budget is approved and canned for planning purpose from which monthly budgets are also derived and the supply chain function is planned to meet and service those targets. As the environment is dynamic, a constant or at least periodic review is generally done. The seasonal impact is normally taken into consideration when monthly budgetary figures are drawn up for production planning and control taking more realistic views of numerous issues including seasonality. If seasonality is not considered, a good forecast may ultimately turn out to be poor because of the failure to consider seasonal factors. When historical sales figures are taken to forecast, the accuracy of the forecast improves if suitable adjustments are done to eliminate the seasonal effects (Table 3.1). It should be noted that seasonal adjustments are widely used in business, and they reduce forecasting errors.

TABLE 3.1 Determining a Seasonal Index from Historical Sales Data

Quarter	Year 1	Year 2	Year 3	Year 4	Four-Year Quarterly Average	Seasonal Index
1	45	52	53	71	55.25	0.72[a]
2	72	92	85	95	86.00	1.13
3	86	85	90	96	89.25	1.17
4	77	58	87	76	74.50	0.98
Four-Year Sales = 1250/16 = 76.25 (average quarterly sales)						

Note: [a] Seasonal index = Average sales for four quarter/Average quarterly sales = 55.25/76.25 = 0.72.

Some of the businesses are highly seasonal. For example, carbonated soft beverages such as Pepsi and Coke are dependent on the impact and duration of summer season, and in India more particularly the sales in northern territories, sales can be highly skewed in summer months to the extent that about 45–50% of the year's sales can happen in a few summer months. The impact of the summer season is there in every region, but it may not be that much skewed as in North India. For Mumbai or western India, the impact could be around 30–35%, and in eastern India, it could be about 35–40%. Similarly, for a product like ice cream, sales in winter months in northern regions come down drastically. Seasonal factors, therefore, have to be invariably considered for certain categories of products for determining the sales forecast. Besides, in a country like India, the festival season of October–November, and in Western countries, the Christmas and holiday season, when all brands and businesses offer heavy discounts to clear the inventory, automatically put pressure on the SCM function to meet the unrealistic demand. For many businesses, last three months of sales could be as high as 35–40% of the sales of the year. During these festival periods, there will be overtrading for artificial demand when consumers get their annual bonus which will invariably make the beginning of the new year to start with a low volume of business. All these types of fluctuations have to be managed optimally by effective SCM practices.

DEMAND FORECASTING

Broadly, we can divide the methods of forecasting into the following:

- Qualitative or subjective or judgemental
- Extrapolation
- Quantitative

Table 3.2 summarizes the possible methods that can be applied under each broad classification of forecasting methods. We will be discussing some of these methods with case studies and examples in this chapter for better clarity. The industry uses these methods to various degrees. The sales force composite, which is in fact a bottom-up approach, is quite commonly used by the industry and more particularly by the FMCG industry for their reliability and confidence.

A major component of demand management is forecasting the amount of product that will be purchased by consumers or end users. In an integrated supply chain, all other demand will be derived from the primary demand. The key objective is to anticipate and respond to the primary demand as it occurs in the marketplace. Primary, secondary and tertiary sales (consumer offtake) need to be balanced with excess stock at each level linked to the service frequency of the business to avoid disharmony of having excess stock resulting in overtrading. As integrated supply chain decisions are normally derived from primary sales numbers, primary sales projection must have some good correlation with real-term consumer offtake for which marketers must have a sense of reading the pulse of the ultimate consumers.

TABLE 3.2 Different Methods for Forecasting

Type of Methods	Actual Methods
Qualitative/Subjective/Judgemental	• Sales force composite • Jury of executive opinion • Intention to buy survey • Industry survey
Extrapolation	• Moving average • Per cent rate of change • Leading indicators • Unit rate of change • Exponential smoothening • Line extension
Quantitative	• Simple regression • Multiple regression • Econometric models

In a typical channel distribution of FMCG, the actual consumer demand needs to be managed by managing channel partners. The manufacturers need to satisfy the demand reflected by consumer offtake by ensuring adequate stock level at wholesalers', distributors' as well as retailers' end, which calls for managing adequate inventory levels at all points. Businesses normally subscribe to the retail survey (audit) data that are routinely done by market research organizations like AC Nielsen. Referring to these database will provide insight into trade stocks as well as consumer offtake in different customer segments as well as geographical territories to understand the reality of product movement in each customer segment even at the SKU level. Subscribing to these database helps in forecasting and planning and also taking corrective action wherever required, and therefore serves as a useful tool in terms of managing the demand and inventory in the system.

There are three basic types of forecasting models, namely (a) judgemental, (b) time series analysis and (c) cause and effect relationship. Qualitative forecasting is also sometimes referred to as judgemental forecasting which involves using judgement and intuition and is preferred in situations where there are limited or no historical data available such as with a new product introduction. Judgemental forecasting techniques include surveys and analogue techniques, among others. Judgemental techniques are subjective as they are dependent more on opinion and less on mathematics in their formulation, and as such they are often used in conjunction with other quantitative techniques.

Consumer–User Survey Method

The method essentially involves asking customers about their likely purchase intention during the forecasting period. For an industrial product where numbers of customers are not too many, such research are often carried out by involving the salespersons responsible for servicing those customers. But if there is competition in the product category that your business represents, then it may not be easy to ascertain what percentage of that incremental demand of that customer will really be sourced or purchased from you. Yet another problem is that the salespersons as well as the customers tend to become optimistic when forecasting the future requirement, and that might lead to a higher degree of inaccuracy in the resulting forecast. Clearly, this way only a small sample size can be covered, and therefore, it has limited utility for forecasting for FMCG where customers are wide and large in numbers and spread all over.

Panel of Expert Opinion

This is also sometimes referred to as the jury method where specialists or experts on the product categories who have knowledge of the product and industry are asked to forecast. Most often, these experts come from outside the company and can also include management consultants who operate within the particular industry. Sometimes external experts may also include the customers who are in a position to advise from a point of view of the buying company and as such the panel of experts may finally consist of both internal and external experts. These experts come with a prepared forecast and defend their projection in the committee in presence of other members on which the discussion follows. The individual projections may subsequently be altered based on the opinion and discussion that follow in the committee and in the end, if disagreement still follows, a mathematical aggregation may even be necessary to arrive at a compromised forecast. This is in fact a 'top-down' exercise for an industry category from which a company can derive its own share from the overall growth of the industry in that category. This method also has its limitation in the sense that even if the company is in a position to estimate a demand from the total projected industry demand volume, getting into an individual product and its variants level in different sales territory is still not easy and involves some elements of guess from the past experience. This method is thus again subjective and inaccurate (Kahn 1988).

Sales Force Composite

This method involves salespersons making a product-by-product forecast for their particular sales territory. The sum total of all salespersons' forecasts covering the entire sales territory would normally be equal to the company's sales forecast taking a bottom-up approach and sometimes it is also considered as a 'grass-roots' approach. This approach can sometimes be realistic as salespersons involved in generating or forecasting the numbers in their own territory are eventually responsible for delivering these forecasted numbers and hence company can rely on this forecast. However, there is an inherent problem or shortcoming in this approach, that is, as salespersons' own remuneration and incentive depend on realizing the forecasted numbers they themselves project, there is a natural tendency to underreport the projected forecast volume. Hence, a better approach could be the fusion of both bottom-up and top-down figures.

Delphi Method

This method bears the resemblance of the 'expert opinion' method and a forecasting team is chosen using a similar criterion. The main difference is that they do not meet in a committee. The project administers a structured questionnaire to each member of the team. The questionnaire can be administered in different stages to ultimately bring out a forecast for the company covering the product categories that the company sells. The questions addressed normally are of behavioural nature. For example: Do you envisage that new technology products would replace some of our product lines in next three–five years? If so, by what percentage of market share? This question can then proceed to ask more pointed questions about a specific individual company with the ultimate objective to translate opinion into some form of forecast. After each round of questionnaires, the aggregate response from each is circulated to the members of the panel before they complete the questionnaire for the next round so that the members of the panel are not completing their questionnaire in a void but can moderate their response in the light of the aggregate results.

As the members do not meet in a committee, their responses are not influenced by majority opinion and, therefore, a more objective forecast may result from the Delphi method. However, it has a greater value in terms of generating industry trends and as a technological forecasting tool in addition to providing useful information regarding new products and processes to direct company efforts in the development of new products. For developing a forecast sales territory-wise and product line-wise, its usefulness is still limited.

Bayesian Decision Theory

This theory has been placed under qualitative techniques of forecasting, although it is in reality a mix of both subjective and objective techniques. The technique is similar to the critical path analysis in that it uses a network diagram, and probabilities must be estimated for each event over the network. Bayesian decision theory is a relatively new and somewhat controversial method for dealing with future uncertainties. The technique, however, incorporates the firm's own parameters as data inputs into the calculation of a sales forecast.

Let us assume that the management feels that the country's economy can go either of the following ways in the next 12 months: continue to be buoyant (Event A), a moderate downturn (Event B) and a serious recession (Event C). Each of these can be considered as an external event on which the management has no control. If, however, the management wishes to take a decision to maximize the profit, they can assign subjective prior probabilities to each of the possible events. These are expected external events which impact the sales performance of the company but are actually not within the control of the company. The management takes three possible scenarios on expected profit, which are shown in Table 3.3.

TABLE 3.3 Expected Profit in Three Scenarios

Events (E)	Export Now (£)	Delay 1 Year (£)	Delay 2 Years (£)
Economic condition remains good	800,000	600,000	500,000
Moderate downturn in economy	500,000	390,000	250,000
Economic recession	–350,000	60,000	100,000

Management wishes to make the decision that can maximize the firm's expected profit after assigning the probability factor on each expected event happening. The impact of that is shown in Table 3.4.

TABLE 3.4 Impact of Probability Factors on Expected Profit

Event	Profit for Optimal Act	Probability	Expected Value (£)
A	800,000	0.5	400,000
B	500,000	0.4	200,000
C	100,000	0.3	30,000
			630,000

These prior probabilities are now incorporated into a decision tree which is made up of series of nodes and branches as shown in Figure 3.1.

FIGURE 3.1 **Decision Tree for Three Expected Events**

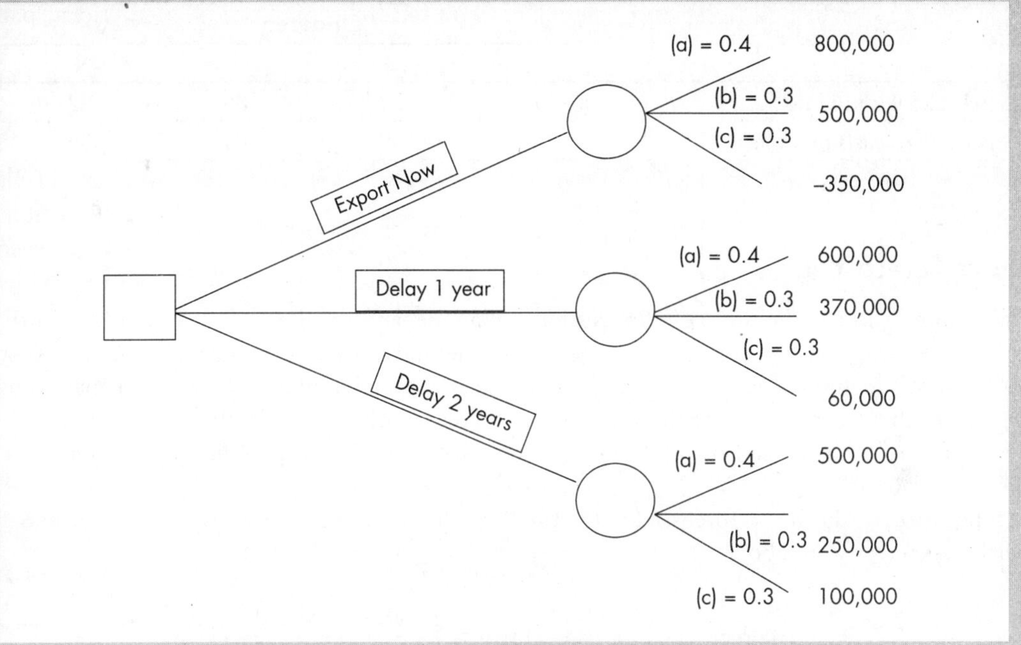

If more information is available based on the survey conducted by the company to further improve upon the forecast, then those survey indicators should influence the probability factors to be considered which in turn can change the decision tree.

Quantitative Forecasting Techniques

This is also sometimes referred to as objective or mathematical techniques. Quantitative techniques are based on the manipulations of historical data.

An underlying assumption of time series forecasting is that the future demand is solely dependent on the past demand. For example, this year's demand is 10% more than the last year's actual sales. Time series analysis takes into account the historical sales over a longer period of years to arrive at a realistic level of the projected sales. Cause and effect forecasting (also referred to as associative forecasting) assumes that one or more factors are related to the demand and that the relationship between cause and effect can be used to estimate the future demand. This uses simple as well as multiple regression techniques. In simple regression, the demand depends on only variable, whereas in multiple regression, the demand depends on two or more variables. For example, the financing option can increase the demand or a high interest rate can decrease the demand of a particular commodity or product.

TABLE 3.5 Naive Forecasts from the Earlier Period Actual Sales

	Quarter			
	1	**2**	**3**	**4**
Actual Sales in Units	59	65	85	92
Naive Forecasts in Units		59	65	85

Naive Forecasting

Naive forecasting is the simplest forecasting technique and is often used as the standard of comparison with the forecasts derived from other methods. A large number of companies (over 30%) use this method of forecasting on a regular basis. This method actually assumes that nothing is going to change and therefore the next quarter's forecast will actually be the current level of sales performance. Table 3.5 can be used to predict the sales for the next quarter, taking actual sales of the earlier quarter.

The error in the naive forecast for quarter 2 is the difference between 59 and 65, and the percentage error would be:

$$\text{Percentage forecasting error} = \frac{\text{Forecast} - \text{Actual}}{\text{Actual}}$$
$$= (59 - 65) / 65 = 58\%$$

If the data are adjusted for seasonality, the forecasting error for quarter 2 will come down to a much lower value (7.6%), which is an acceptable figure.

MAPE Method

When you like to compare the forecasting accuracy over several time periods, the mean absolute percentage error (MAPE) method is the method used by most of the businesses (Lancaster and Wright 1983)). The MAPE can be calculated using the following formula:

$$\text{MAPE} = \frac{(\text{Forecast} - \text{Actual}) / \text{Actual}}{N} \times 100\%$$

$$\text{MAPE} = \frac{\sum_{i=1}^{n} (\text{Forecast} - \text{Actual}) / \text{Actual}}{N} \times 100\%$$

where N is the number of forecasts to be made. The main advantage of the MAPE method is that it allows easy comparison of forecasting errors across product categories and companies.

Businesses normally prepare their annual budget, containing projected sales numbers, which is also calendarized month-wise for production planning. The budget numbers are very broad, and the same undergo many iterations during the budget year as several things change including unforeseen activities in the market changing the demand which SCM has to consider in a continuous manner. The budget document includes the market analysis in detail and competition analysis reports to decide on at what rate possibly a business can grow under the given market and competitive environment and in a given resource availability scenario for delivering business growth. The broad figures for sales contained in the budget can be generated following several methods, and the easiest of those is applying the projected growth factor over last year's actual sales achievement. The projected growth factor has to be at least equal to or more than the industry category growth rate to retain the market share by the business. A higher growth rate can be taken if any special activity or resource allocation is planned by the business to gain incremental market share. Usually, projecting the next year's sales forecast from the last year's actual sales applying the growth factor is normally practised by the industry. This, however, is the simplest approach or method for estimating or forecasting the demand. A more elaborate sales forecast can, however, be generated by the Delphi technique involving experts, time series analysis and so on. Whatever may be the method, generating a demand forecast with about 10% accuracy is a reasonable figure to plan production, procurement and inventory. By resorting to the correction factor in every production and inventory cycle based on actual achievement is likely to lead to an effective SCM plan for implementation.

Moving Average Method

The moving average method actually predicts the future sales on the average sales performance for the same product categories in the recent past. As such, average sales revenue actually achieved for several periods in the recent past is used to predict or forecast the sales for the next period, using the following formula:

$$F_{t+1} = \frac{S_t + S_{t-1} + S_{t-2} + \cdots + S_{t-n+1}}{N}$$

where
F_{t+1} = forecast for the next period
S_t = sales in the current period
N = number of periods in the moving average

The moving average method assumes that the future will be the average of the past achievement. Therefore, when there is a strong trend in a time series, a moving average forecast without the trend adjustments lags behind. However, this lag can even be an advantage when there is sudden increase and decrease in sales volume because in that case, the moving average forecast will be more accurate. It should be pointed out here that the limitation of moving average is that it does not consider the dynamic nature of the business environment where each period can behave differently. However, it must be remembered that moving average really does move. For example, sales data from Table 3.1 can be used to make two periods' moving average as follows:

	Quarter			
	1	2	3	4
Actual Sales	45	72	86	77
Two Periods' Moving Average			58.5	79

Exponential Smoothing

An important feature of exponential smoothing is its ability to emphasize the recent information and data and systematically discount old information. A simple exponentially smoothed forecast can be derived from the following equation:

$$\bar{S}_t = \alpha S_t + (1 - \alpha)\bar{S}_{t-1}$$

where
S_t = smoothed sales for period $t + 1$
α = smoothing constant
$\bar{S}_t$ = actual sales in period t
$\bar{S}_{t-1}$ = Smoothed forecast for the period $t - 1$

The above equation in fact combines a portion (α) of current sales with the discounted value of the smoothed average calculated for the previous period to give a forecast for the next period.

Using the data given in Table 3.5, we can work out taking smoothing constant of 0.4 as follows:

	Quarter			
	1	2	3	4
Actual Sales	45	72	86	77
Smoothed Forecast			57.8	77.6

The forecast for quarter 3 can be obtained by multiplying the smoothing constant 0.4 with the current sales for quarter 2 plus 0.6 times of current sales of quarter 1 which will work out to 57.8; similarly, for quarter 4, the smoothed forecast will be 77.6. The critical decision with respect to exponential smoothing is selecting an appropriate value for the smoothing constant (a) which actually ranges from 0 to 1, with low value indicative of stability and high value allowing a rapid response to sales changes. And as such, if we use the smoothing constant as 1.0, it will give the smoothing forecast same as that is obtained by the naive method. Forecasts produced with a low smoothing constant, for example, 0.2, lag behind and forecasts generated with high values of smoothing constant such as 0.8 will likely overestimate sales at turning points. If a business has the historical data, it must try to find out an optimum smoothing constant by trying out different values of 'a' to see which one fits the best. Regression techniques have advantages in situations in which managers wish to incorporate other variables which can influence the sales volume in their forecasting programme.

Linear Regression

In a simple linear regression equation, the relationship between sales (X) and some variable (Y) can be assumed as linear, and therefore it can be represented by a straight line. The equation then would be: $X = a + bY$, where a is the intercept and b is the impact of the independent variable. The main step for deriving a linear regression equation is to find the values for coefficients a and b that gives the line that best fits the data and that can be obtained by employing a least-squares procedure as illustrated in Figure 3.2, where sales (X) have been plotted against time (Y). The equation is: $X = 63.9 + 3.5Y$. Two variable regression equations can thus be easily calculated. However, a limitation in this is the assumption that sales follow a linear pattern which is not correct. And there are cyclical sales patterns as well for many parameters impacting the sales which a linear equation cannot capture. In that case, the sales analyst can base the forecasting equation on the logarithm of the time series data to generate an improved version of forecasting equations. Another problem is to decide how much of the past data should be included in the calculation to forecast. Although all past data points can provide greater stability, sometimes shorter period regression can do a better job of tracking changes.

The simple regression equations that have been described use time as an independent variable, which is very common in sales forecasting, and with time as an independent variable, a regression

FIGURE 3.2 **Fitment of Trend Regression to Seasonality-adjusted Sales Data**

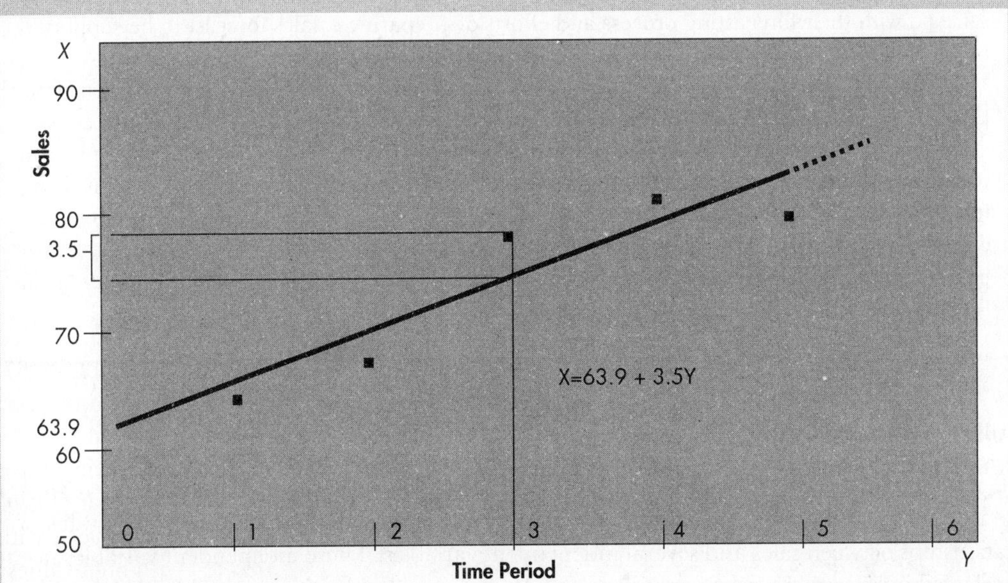

approach also becomes a trend forecast. However, other variables which are closely related to sales forecast such as income growth of the targeted consumers and frequency of use can also be used. But when sales seem to be associated with the several independent variables, a multiple regression procedure can be used to build the forecasting model.

How P&G Forecasted Its Detergent Sales in Italy

P&G is a global leader in detergent. It is considered as the most innovative company in the FMCG sector, and to keep its supremacy, P&G invariably brings in some new features on tangible and, if not, at least on intangible platforms to differentiate its products from others and most importantly to differentiate from its immediate competitor Unilever. P&G's Italian subsidiary produces both liquid and powder detergents, and the Italian company had a staff strength of 400. Their annual sales volume used to be about US$385 million per year. They regularly prepare sales forecasts for two variants of powder detergents and one variant of liquid detergent for use in washing machines. In addition, P&G Italy also prepares sales forecasts for one more brand of powder and liquid detergents which are used in hand as well as bucket clothes wash. For established brands like Ariel, P&G Italy uses their historical sales data and adjusts those for incremental advertisement and promotional plan for the brands during the year and then uses a computer program to prepare sales forecasts. Under normal circumstances, they use previous three years' sales data to prepare the forecast for the current year. Forecasts of sales volume for P&G Italy are prepared for medium term to long term, and their most detailed forecasts are for three years. For new products, the forecasts are normally prepared from the targeted market share to be built up to the targeted level over a given period of time. As the liquid detergents are a new category, there is no historical sales figure available to go by. As the forecasting error in P&G is normally a few percentage points only, they are fully satisfied with their forecasting process and efforts of preparing a sales forecast to be supported by an elaborate supply chain planning to meet the projected demand.

It can be pointed out here that sales forecasting in most of the FMCG companies is done through projection from historical data of say three years to see the trend, taking into consideration the impact of marketing and advertisement plan for the year. This plan is in addition to taking a bottom-up approach for generating a product category-wise sales forecast involving front-line sales staff. It is also important to note that a sales forecast is generated product category wise and brand wise, taking into account the brand marketing plan to achieve the projected numbers and in that respect the entire plan is integrated as a common objective and goal for the year.

Multiple Regression

When the projected sales volume depends on multiple variables, we need to use multiple regression, and if there are a number of variables, a computer is used to build forecasting based on historical relationships between sales and several independent variables. These independent variables need to be selected judiciously based on past trends and experience to identify those which have significant impact on sales. The multiple regression equation must capture some of the best indicators of sales performance. The suggestive factors can be economic growth rate, marketing and promotional budget for the category, industry category growth rate, interest rates, growth in target population and so on. However, these factors need to be predicted for future time periods before loading them into the forecasting equation. There are other variables which would be product specific such as growth of infrastructure and real estate in a given geographical area; new investment in certain projects can also impact the sales volume, and those impacts on sales will not be very difficult to predict. The decision whether to use a simple or multiple regression forecasting model often depends on the values of three statistics that are calculated by the computer forecasting program. For example, if the R^2 value is 0.70, your equation explains 70% of the variation observed in your data. Forecasting equations with a high R^2 value are generally preferable to equations that explain only 5–10% of the variation. The standard error of the estimate tells you the range within which you can expect to find the true value of the variable that you are predicting. Also, errors in the coefficients for the variables in your equation should be smaller than the coefficients. If, however, the errors are larger than the coefficients, there is a good reason to drop that variable from the forecasting equation. With regression forecasting, you need five observations for every independent variable in your equation. Thus, an equation with 1 predictor variable would need 5 observations, and an equation with 3 variables would need 15 observations. If your data set does not meet these requirements, then another forecasting method should be selected. Despite complexities of multiple regression forecasting, this technique is most popular of all the quantitative methods mentioned in Table 3.2 and has been reported to be used regularly in almost 13–15% of the firms. A real data set that you can use to build a multiple regression forecasting equation is discussed under the section 'Demand Management' in Chapter 5 for better clarity and understanding.

Trend- and Seasonality-Corrected Holt–Winters' Exponential Smoothing

The trend-corrected exponential smoothing as per Holt's model is appropriate when the demand is assumed to have a level and a trend in the systematic component but no seasonality, which would mean that

$$\text{Systematic Component of Demand} = \text{Level} + \text{Trend}$$

Both trend- and seasonality-corrected exponential smoothing as per Winters' model are appropriate when the systematic component of the demand has a level, a trend and also a seasonality factor, which thus would mean that

$$\text{Systematic Component of Demand} = (\text{Level} + \text{Trend}) \times \text{Seasonal Factor}$$

Once data have been captured for the time series to be forecasted, the analyst's next step is to select a model for forecasting. Various statistical and graphic techniques may be useful to the analyst in the selection process. The best place to start with any time series forecasting analysis is to graph sequence plots of the time series to be forecasted. A sequence plot is a graph of the data series values, usually on the vertical axis, against time usually on the horizontal axis. The purpose of a sequence plot is to give the analyst a visual impression of the nature of the time series. The presence/absence of such components can help the analyst in selecting the model with the potential

TABLE 3.6 Applicability of the Methods

Forecasting Methods	Where Applicable
Moving average method	No trend or seasonality
Simple exponential Smoothing	No trend or seasonality
Holt's model	Trend but no seasonality
Winters' model	Trend and seasonality

to produce the best forecasts. After selecting a model, the next step is its specification. The process of specifying a forecasting model involves selecting the variables to be included, selecting the form of the equation of relationship and estimating the values of the parameters in that equation. The model can be selected based on the trend analysis and historical data and data quality available.

The forecasting methods we have discussed in this chapter can be used in different situations as given in Table 3.6.

We normally obtain an initial estimate of the level and trend by running a linear simple regression between demand D_t and time period t of the form:

$$D_t = at + b$$

Running a linear regression between demand and time periods is appropriate because in Holt's model, assumption is that the demand has a trend but no seasonality, and therefore their relationship is linear. The constant b measures the estimate of the demand at period $t = 0$ which can be taken as the initial estimate L_0. The slope a measures the rate of change in demand per period and the initial estimate of the trend T_0. In period t, from the given estimates level L_t and trend T_t, the forecast for the future period will be as follows:

$$F_{t+1} = L_t + T_t \text{ and } F_{t+n} = L_t + nT_t. \tag{3.1}$$

And, on observing the demand for the period t, the estimates of level L_t and trend T_t, the forecast for future periods are expressed as

$$L_{t+1} = \alpha D_{t+1} + (1 - \alpha)(L_t + T_t), \tag{3.2}$$

$$T_{t+1} = \beta (L_{t+1} - L_t) + (1 - \beta) T_t, \tag{3.3}$$

where α is the smoothing constant for the level and β is the smoothing constant for the trend, having value between 0 and 1. You should observe that for two updates of level and trend and a weighted average of the observed value and the old estimates.

For Winters' model, assume the periodicity of the demand to be p. We need the initial estimates of the level L_0, trend T_0 and seasonal factors $S_1 - S_p$. In period t, the estimates level L_t, trend T_t and seasonal factors $S_t, \ldots, S_{t+p-1}$, the forecast for the future period can be obtained from the following:

$$F_{t+1} = (L_t + T_t) S_{t+1} \text{ and } F_{t+l} = (L_t + lT_t) S_{t+1}. \tag{3.4}$$

After observing the demand for the period $t + 1$, we can revise the estimates for level, trend and also seasonality factors as follows:

$$L_{t+1} = \alpha\,(D_{t+1}/S_{t+1}) + (1-\alpha)\,(L_t + T_t), \tag{3.5}$$

$$T_{t+1} = \beta\,(L_{t+1} - L_t) + (1-\beta)\,T_t, \tag{3.6}$$

$$S_{t+p+1} = \gamma\,(D_{t+1}/L_{t+1}) + (1-\gamma)\,S_{t+1}, \tag{3.7}$$

where α is the smoothing constant for the level, β is the smoothing constant for the trend and γ is the smoothing constant for the seasonal factor being between 0 and 1. We can observe each of these impacts, and the revised estimate is a weighted average of the observed value and the old estimate.

WHEN TO USE QUANTITATIVE FORECASTING METHODS

Quantitative forecasting techniques are best employed in situations where we have access to historical data, and these are also helpful if the time series we are trying to forecast are stable and do not often change the direction. Quantitative methods have a distinctive advantage in situations where frequent forecasts are to be made for very large numbers of products and product categories which may also need the use of computers and forecasting software because of large numbers of calculations. Forecasters also need to be conversant and familiar with various statistical tools and procedures used by these techniques. Additionally, quantitative techniques are most useful in situations where the management understands and also endorses their application to sales forecasting problems. However, it should be remembered that simple procedures such as naive, moving averages and exponential smoothing often have lower forecasting errors than other complex methods (Dalrymple et al. 2003).

CHANGING BUSINESS ENVIRONMENT

The numerical methods for forecasting sales normally attempt to make projections from historical data and often do not take into consideration the impact of any significant development in the business environment on sales numbers. Percentage rate of change, unit rate of change and two variable regression are in fact poor predictors of series under a significant turning point in business. Naive, moving average and exponential smoothing are somewhat better because they tend to lag and then adapt to new realities. If the identification of such a turning point is important for business, the use of qualitative procedures is often a better approach. These methods can pick up environmental cues that signal the turning points which are missed quite frequently by numerical methods. Leading indicators can be included in multiple regression equations to help predict those unexpected turning points.

FORECASTING IN PRACTICE

For deriving realistic forecasts, a close coordination between sales and SCM teams and also the channel partners including the IT team of the company is very much desirable. Share only those data which are valuable for the specific business function. The value of the data depends on where one is located in the entire chain. For example, a retailer finds point-of-sales data very valuable in terms of measuring the performance of the store. However, a manufacturer selling to a distributor or wholesaler who in turn sells to the retailer does not find point-of-sales data that useful and instead manufacturers find the aggregate demand data to be very useful. Historical sales data should not be confused with the historical demand because there can be occasions of loss of sales due to stock shortages and also there can be occasions when businesses resort to overtrading creating artificial stock pressure in the system which results in high debtors but the volume so traded appears in their official sales figures. Those situations of overtrading and undertrading need to be corrected to get to the exact demand forecast.

WHAT INDUSTRY PRACTICES

Industry tends to use simplistic methods to forecast sales as has been explained earlier. The only concern is the degree of errors in their method. If the degree of error is very low and/or does not put the SCM tasks in difficulty in terms of handling a possibly stock-out situation resulting in loss of sales or a sudden spurt in demand offering short-term opportunities to capture and grow, then the methods that are being employed are for all practical purposes working well for the company.

But quantitative methods are also used under certain circumstances and situations. For example, quantitative forecasting techniques are best employed in situations where you have access to historical numerical data and also when time series that you intend to forecast are stable and do not often change the direction. Quantitative methods have distinct advantages where forecasts need to be generated frequently and that too for hundreds or thousands of products. Because large numbers of calculations are required by quantitative forecasting methods, it often requires the use of computers and forecasting software, and in addition one has to be well versed in statistical procedures used by these techniques. Most importantly, quantitative techniques are most useful where the management understands and endorses their application to sales forecasting problems.

DEMAND MANAGEMENT

Demand management is one of the key areas which impact the supply chain performance. The ideal performance of a supply chain will, however, be when the end-to-end chain and link in the entire value chain is led by the real-term customers' demand. If a business can achieve that status of seamlessly meeting the customer demand by coordinating and managing the production operations as well as inventory without any excess stock at any stage, that would be the ideal situation. Demand management thus is a very critical area of influence that determines the performance of the business.

Demand management can be defined as focused integrated efforts to realistically estimate and manage the customer demand with an intention of using these information to shape the operating decision related to production and operations strategies and plan of the business. The essence of demand management is to continuously improve the ability of the firm's SCM practices on flow of product, services, information and capital through a collaborative approach involving customers, or in other words, the demand has to be managed as customer demand led by SCM. The desired end result should be to create a greater value for the end user or consumer, for whom all supply chain activities should be undertaken. Estimating the demand as accurately as possible will result in the better supply chain decisions and will likely result in benefits flowing through the supply chain. The demand can be generated through either push or pull methods. Demand pull creates better and ideal SCM practices, whereas creating demand by push strategy can often lead to unnecessary stock hold-up in the trade channel if such a demand is not corroborated by the real-term customer demand, and that can negatively impact supply chain performance and also corporation's business performance.

Demand management is a complex subject in the sense that accurate forecasting in terms of what items we need, where we need and when we need is not easily determined. Besides, in a dynamic business environment, it always changes and fluctuates. Oversupply will add to build-up of trade stock, resulting in higher working capital. Overstocking the trade can also lead to wastage and write-off and bad debts, resulting in significant negative impact on the business. On the other hand, restricted supply may lead to loss of sales, and in some cases and for some categories of products such as perishables and food products, it may be a permanent loss of sales which also has the risk of customers shifting to competitors' products and that would mean a possibility of losing the customer permanently as well and not simply short-term loss of sales. Demand management has to be seen from these perspectives. The effective demand management will help to unify channel members with the common goal of satisfying customers and solving customer problems. However, for effective demand management, accuracy of demand estimate is an essential prerequisite. The accuracy of demand depends on many factors which can include the following:

- Customer data relating to the demographics, consumption pattern and their buying habits
- Seasonality of demands, if any
- Break-up of demands by customer segments including institutional customers and bulk customers
- Information regarding how, when and where the expected demand has to be met; also, information regarding channel intermediaries
- Common trade practices and trade terms
- Developing and executing the best practices for logistics, transportation and distribution methods to deliver products and services to consumers in the desired format

Gathering these information and analysing knowledge about customers, their problems and their unmet needs would help. It is necessary to design the supply and distribution chain and identify partners to perform the functions needed in the demand chain. And also, it needs to help the channel members/partners to perform effectively and efficiently. Sharing the knowledge about consumers and customers, available technology, and logistics challenges and opportunities with all members of the channel are essential to improve channel effectiveness.

Efficient Demand Management

Efficient demand management would mean servicing the customer requirement on real-time basis at least cost or at affordable cost which would entail delivering the customer order wherever required and whenever required at minimal cost of servicing. Some companies have developed systems and processes to deliver customer orders most efficiently. Their service level and frequency are much higher than their competitors. For example, Kao Corporation of Japan competes with MNCs such as Unilever, Colgate-Palmolive and P&G and can service its 200,000 retailers in Japan within 24 hours of receiving orders irrespective of the location of the customer. Efficient demand management requires efficient communication management. Sales order processing is the primary information for implementation of ERP which most of the companies now have to bring in cost economy and service efficiency in the business.

Communication between various departments within the business results in little or no coordinated response to demand information. Sometimes too much emphasis is placed on forecasts of demand with little attention paid to collaborative efforts and strategic and operational plans that need to be developed from the forecasts. Demand information is often used more for tactical and operations purposes than for strategic purposes. Primary emphasis should be on using demand information to create likely scenarios of the future as they relate to product supply alternatives. Resulting business successes will be an outcome of the better match of demand to product availability.

As end-user demand begins to decline, the situation clearly shifts to one of oversupply. This is largely due to the industry's planning processes and systems, which are primarily designed to use previous period demand as a gauge. The net result of these behaviours in aligning supply and demand is that a large majority of product is sold during the declining period of profit opportunity, thereby diminishing substantial value-creation opportunities for industry participants.

Estimating the Total Market Demand

An industry always tries to follow the method that suits it best and that will be industry category specific as well as individual business itself. For this purpose, businesses must get a good fix on the overall market demand for an industry category in order to forecast the demand of the product(s) for the individual business itself which again will be a factor of the company's existing and past real-term demand and market share data as well as the projected market share which will have a direct bearing on category growth rate, past growth rate, and marketing and promotional plan for the current year. To arrive at a reasonably reliable estimate of the total demand, following steps will be useful (Barnett 1988).

Define the Market

While defining the market, it is necessary to consider the potential and existing substitute of your product. There are several ways that you can make sure that you include all important current and potential substitute products. Market research can lead to insights about consumer products, and speaking with experts in the relevant technologies can help you identify potential developments that could threaten your industry. The demand curves will have their relationship between price and volume. With an appropriate definition, the total industry demand curves will often be steeper than the demand curves for individual products in the industry. For example, consumers are more likely to switch from Nescafé to Brooke Bond's coffee if Nescafé's prices increase. But if prices of both brands increase, there could be a fall in the demand of coffee as a category itself.

Divide the Industry Demand into Its Principal or Main Components

The second step in forecasting is to divide the total demand into its main components or segments for a separate analysis. There are two criteria to keep in mind when choosing segments: (a) make each category small and homogeneous enough so that the drivers of demand will apply consistently across its various elements and (b) make each category large enough so that the analysis will be worth the effort. In thinking about market divisions, managers need to decide whether to use existing data on segment sizes or to commission research to get an independent estimate.

Forecast the Key Drivers of Demand in Each Segment and Project How They Are Likely to Change

The third step is to understand and forecast the drivers of demand in each category. Here, you can make good use of regressions and other statistical techniques to find some causes for changes in historical demand. But this is only a start. The tougher challenge is to look beyond the data on which regressions can easily be based to other factors where data are much harder to find. Then you need to develop a point of view on how those other factors may themselves change in the future.

Conduct Sensitivity Analyses to Understand the Most Critical Assumptions and to Gauge Risks to Base Line Forecast

Managers who rely on single-point demand forecasts run dangerous risks. Some of the macroeconomic variables behind the forecasts could be wrong. It is necessary to identify potential risks and discontinuities like what things could cause this forecast to change dramatically or developments in competing technologies, in customer industry competitiveness and in supplier cost structures. So once a baseline forecast is complete, the challenge is to determine how far it could be off target. At one level, such a sensitivity analysis can be done by simply varying assumptions and quantifying their impact on the demand. But a more targeted approach usually provides better insight.

Even when the work is sound, uncertainties remain; discontinuities are still difficult to predict, especially if they are rooted in momentous political, macroeconomic or technological changes. But managers who push their thinking through the steps in this framework have a better chance of finding these discontinuities than those who do not. And those who base their business strategies on a solid knowledge of demand stand a much greater chance of making wise investments and competing effectively.

We would like to discuss a case of demand estimation in the pharmaceutical distribution industry. Pharmaceutical, like FMCG, is a category where competition is intense and distribution system and structure are highly complex. Added to this, India is a huge country with huge population living in rural settings which makes the task of FMCG marketers all the more difficult.

CASE STUDY: APOLLO PHARMACY

The pharmaceutical industry is a highly regulated market. Most of the pharmaceutical products are sold as prescription drugs. There are some products that are sold as over-the-counter (OTC) drugs. Regulations restrict most of the prescription drugs marketing strategies directed to generate prescriptions following canvassing and convincing medical doctors like general practitioners to prescribe the company's prescription drug. Whether a particular doctor is prescribing or not can be understood from the sales performance of the chemists and pharmacies around the area. The prescription sales impact inventory management policy. Trade channel partners and distributors mostly decide on stock ordering and inventory levels based on their past experience.

While non-availability of prescription items in one pharmacy is not usually life-threatening for any patient, the inconvenience caused due to delay may result in loss of customer loyalty. Hence, a product should be available at retail outlets when customer demands. Apollo Pharmacy retail chain does not follow any established demand forecasting technique. However, such forecasting can help the distributor to better manage the inventory of critical drugs as well as fast-moving drugs including OTC drugs.

Forecasting aims at reducing uncertainty that confounds future decisions. However, difficulties arise while fulfilling the assumptions of the economic order quantity (EOQ) model, which includes a continuous, constant and known rate of demand (Hill 1988). Prescription items can be substituted for one another (generic substitution and me-too drugs with similar active molecules), which obviates EOQ assumptions.

For products where demand history is available, the future demand can be predicted better using quantitative models from sales in the previous cycle (Tersine 1994). Time series analysis predicts future attributes from the historical past and prior experience. This method uses time as the independent variable to predict the demand. The causal relationship is applicable under the assumption that there exists a cause and effect relationship between an input variable and its corresponding output (Wheelwright and Makridakis 1985).

The sales data of Apollo Pharmacy belonging to Alwal region of Hyderabad, Telangana, are given in Table 3.7, specifically adopted for the study. Apollo Pharmacy belongs to a large umbrella group organization that follows consistent marketing/sales policies across all its retail outlets.

The case study attempts to identify a suitable forecasting model for use by Apollo Retail group from the various methods discussed in order to recommend one based on the best fit from the values of mean absolute deviation (MAD), mean squared error (MSE) and MAPE.

Forecasting Methods

The simple moving average technique is chosen for its simplicity of use. It is easy to understand and implement. The simple exponential smoothing technique takes into account the weighting factor/smoothing factor and thus helps in adjusting better to recent changes in demand. The Winters' exponential smoothing (WES) uses a seasonal component in addition to the trend component, making it the most appropriate technique for the forecast of the study. The chosen forecasting models were recorded in Microsoft Excel spreadsheets and simple Excel functions were used following equations given in the literature. These simple models formed the basis of the study with an objective to delineate/identify the most suitable forecast model for the chosen product, by comparing the actual sales value and predicted sales value.

The forecasting techniques are evaluated based on their accuracy in forecasting actual demand data. Thus, MAD, MSE and MAPE are used to measure the error of forecast obtained by using various techniques. Because MAPE is a percentage, it is a relative measure, and is thus sometimes preferred to the MAD. The MSE, which is a squared measure, is selected as it helps in penalizing errors more heavily.

Results

The actual demand data obtained from Apollo Pharmacy retail are recorded in Table 3.7 of the supporting data. Table 3.8 depicts the measurement errors, obtained by using each of the three forecasting techniques for the two prescription drugs. The following observations were made from Table 3.8.

For Okacet (Seasonal Demand)

WES captures the seasonality in sales of Okacet. Seasonality is evident in the sales volume of Okacet, which peaks in early December compared to reduced sales in the month of April (774 units vs 118 units). WES provides sales forecast most accurately compared to the other three models (MAD = 92.28, MAPE = 27.50, MSE = 14,635.74).

For Stamlo Beta (Non-seasonal Demand)

Six-month moving average best predicts the demand for Stamlo Beta, which has a relatively stable demand during an entire year or the time period in question. It accurately provides sales forecast (MAD = 47.19, MSE = 394,719.07, MAPE = 45.62) compared to the other models, although Winters' model forecasts the demand equally well.

In summary, comparative values indicate that WES is a superior forecast model to predict sales of pharmaceuticals whose demand fluctuates and/or varies seasonally. And six-month moving average is a better forecast model to predict the sales of pharmaceuticals whose demand remains fairly constant. Average works reliably for non-seasonal pharmaceuticals for the chosen Apollo Pharmacy retail.

TABLE 3.7 Comparison of Measurement Errors Obtained for Okacet and Stamlo Beta Using Time Series Forecast Models

	Okacet			Stamlo Beta		
Technique Error	**6-Month Moving Average**	**Simple Exponential Smoothing**	**Winters' Exponential Smoothing**	**6-Month Moving Average**	**Simple Exponential Smoothing**	**Winters' Exponential Smoothing**
MAD	117.35	420.01	92.28	47.19	615.74	83.21
MSE	21,048.03	198,950.33	14,635.74	3,158.69	394,719.07	10,305.11
MAPE	42.43	157.39	27.50	45.62	550.30	61.86

Sales Data

Daily sales data for the two products mentioned were collected for the period starting from December 2010 and ending in November 2013. Data were obtained by contacting the selected retail outlet manager. As observed, Apollo Pharmacy maintains electronic data of its daily product sales using an ERP solution. Data such as number of units sold, product code and number of items remaining in inventory were of particular importance for this study.

TABLE 3.8 Sales Data of Apollo Pharmacy

Period	Month and Year	No. of Okacet Issued	No. of Stamlo Beta Issued
1	Dec 2010	413	233
2	Jan 2011	399	171
3	Feb 2011	307	258
4	Mar 2011	350	96
5	Apr 2011	277	169
6	May 2011	341	82
7	Jun 2011	536	133
8	Jul 2011	383	142
9	Aug 2011	486	167
10	Sep 2011	503	97
11	Oct 2011	485	86
12	Nov 2011	482	167
13	Dec 2011	744	66
14	Jan 2012	371	174
15	Feb 2012	376	81
16	Mar 2012	216	168
17	Apr 2012	118	32
18	May 2012	208	84
19	Jun 2012	202	135
20	Jul 2012	288	165
21	Aug 2012	415	180
22	Sep 2012	434	145
23	Oct 2012	301	236
24	Nov 2012	269	91

Period	Month and Year	No. of Okacet Issued	No. of Stamlo Beta Issued
25	Dec 2012	359	174
26	Jan 2013	267	156
27	Feb 2013	281	190
28	Mar 2013	193	141
29	Apr 2013	216	171
30	May 2013	143	120
31	Jun 2013	255	293
32	Jul 2013	228	122
33	Aug 2013	419	118
34	Sep 2013	405	96
35	Oct 2013	286	63
36	Nov 2013	480	145

Source: Anusha et al. (2014).

Case Questions

1. Which of the forecasting models, among simple moving average, exponential smoothing and WES, yields least error? The quantitative indicators to be used to assess the forecast error are MAD, MSE and MAPE.
2. Which of the forecasting models, among simple moving average, exponential smoothing and WES, most accurately predicts the demand for a seasonal pharmaceutical item, Okacet 10 mg tablet?
3. Which of the forecasting models, among simple moving average, exponential smoothing and WES, most accurately predicts the demand for a random pharmaceutical item, Stamlo Beta tablet?

Source: The case is based on the data reported by Anusha, Alok and Shaik (2014).

CHAPTER SUMMARY

The chapter starts with explaining the critical role of forecasting in a supply chain. A realistic demand forecast actually forms the basis of all supply chain planning, management and control. The basic approach to demand forecasting is explained, and various types of forecasts and their implications in terms of efficient SCM are then discussed. Various methods of forecasting including time series analysis, moving average method, exponential smoothing and so on are elaborately discussed with examples to explain where these methods can be used and will be useful. How historical data regarding the actual performance of companies help in generating forecasts in the business and the forecasting methods used in real-life business with case studies are also discussed in this chapter. Lastly, the role of IT in demand forecasting as well as forecasting practices is discussed. A sales forecast many a time is higher than the real-term demand from the customer, and it is important to manage the supply chain to cater to the realistic demand which necessitates that companies learn to distinguish between sales target and real-term demand. Chasing an unrealistic sales target can create distortion in trade and also business in terms of their performance in real term which is not desirable, whereas meeting the real-term customer demand really serves the purpose of managing the supply chain effectively. The demand management in supply chain is discussed taking examples of unusual demand due to the introduction of new product or even fluctuating demand during season for seasonal products.

DISCUSSION QUESTIONS

1. What are the various approaches to demand estimation, and what are the types of forecasts businesses make and for what purpose?
2. Why do we need a forecast, and what internal and external factors influence the forecast and how?
3. Which criteria decide the level of forecasting? Discuss how seasonality influences the forecast taking examples.
4. Discuss different methods of demand forecasting. Discuss the advantages and disadvantages of sales force composite and industry survey methods.
5. When should you use the quantitative methods of forecasting? Discuss the multiple regression technique with an example.
6. Why is the MAPE method useful? Discuss the moving average and exponential smoothing methods of forecasting.
7. How does P&G forecast its detergent sales in Italy, and why are they satisfied with their method and approach?
8. What is the normal industry practice for forecasting the demand while doing their annual budgetary exercise?
9. Discuss the criteria which influence the accuracy of demand. What do you understand by efficient demand management?

REFERENCES

Anusha, S. Lakshmi, Swati Alok, and Ashiff Shaik. 2014. 'Demand Forecasting for the Indian Pharmaceutical Retail: A Case Study'. *Journal of Supply Chain Management Systems* 3 (2): 1–8.

Barnett, William P. 1988. 'Fore Steps to Forecast Total Market Demand'. *Harvard Business Review* (July): 1–9.

Dalrymple, Douglas J., L. Cron William, and Thomas E. Decarlo. 2003. *Sales Management: Concepts and Cases*, 228–246. 7th ed. Singapore: John Wiley & Sons (Asia).

Hill, W. J. 1988. 'Alternative Inventory Control Methods for Use in Managing Medical Supply Inventory'. MS thesis, AFIT/GLM/LSM/88S–35. School of Systems and Logistics, Air Force Institute of Technology, Air University, Wright-Patterson AFB, OH.

Hograth, R. 1975. 'Cognitive Processes and the Assessment of Subjective Probability Distributions'. *Journal of American Statistical Association* 70 (350): 271–289.

Kahn, Kenneth B. 1998. 'Revisiting Top-Down versus Bottom-Up Forecasting'. *Journal of Business Forecasting Methods & Systems* 17 (2, Summer): 20.

———. 1999. 'Benchmarking Sales Forecasting Performance Measures'. *The Journal of Business Forecasting Methods & Systems* 17 (4, Winter): 20.

Lancaster, G. A., and G. Wright. 1983. 'Forecasting the Future of Video Using a Diffusion Model'. *European Journal of Marketing* 17 (2): 2.

Tersine, R. J. 1994. *Principles of Inventory and Materials Management.* 4th ed. Englewood Cliffs, NJ: Prentice Hall.

Wheelwright, S. C., and S. Makridakis. 1985. *Forecasting Methods for Management.* 4th ed. New York, NY: John Wiley & Sons.

Zachary, G. Pascal. 1989. 'Hewlett to Post about Flat Net for 3rd Period'. *The Wall Street Journal*, 15 August, 10.

BIBLIOGRAPHY

Brown, Robert G. 1959. *Statistical Forecasting for Inventory Control.* New York, NY: McGraw-Hill.

Georgoff, David M., and G. Murdick Robert. 1986. 'Manager's Guide to Forecasting'. *Harvard Business Review* (January–February): 2–9.

Gilliland, Michael. 2002. 'Is Forecasting a Waste of Time?' *Supply Chain Management Review* (July–August): 16–23.

Gilloth, V. R., Ohi, Jack F. Jr and Wells, Willaim A. 1979. 'An Evaluation of Seasonality in the United States Air Force Medical Material Management System'. MS thesis, LSSR 13–79B. School of Systems and Logistics, Air Force Institute of Technology, Air University, Wright-Patterson AFB, OH.

Hanke, J. E., and A. G. Reitsch. 1992. *Business Forecasting.* 4th ed. Boston, MA: Allyn & Bacon.

Jobber, David, and Geoff Lancaster. 2005. *Selling and Sales Management,* 411–442. 6th ed. Pearson Education (Singapore).

Makridakis, Spyros, and Steven Wheelwright. 1989. *Forecasting Methods for Management.* New York, NY: Wiley.

Pilinkienė, V. 2008. 'Selection of Market Demand Forecast Methods: Criteria and Application'. *Engineering Economics* 3 (58): 19–25.

Rachmania, I. N. 2013. 'Pharmaceutical Inventory Management Issues in Hospital Supply Chains'. *Management* 3 (1): 1–5.

Saffo, Paul. 2007. 'Six Rules of Effective Forecasting'. *Harvard Business Review* (July–August): 122–131.

Sarang, D. N., and M. Laxmidhar. 2006. 'Exploratory Investigation of Sales Forecasting Process and Sales Forecasting System'. Master's thesis. Jönköping International Business School, Sweden.

Sarker, S. 2010. 'Increasing Forecasting Accuracy of Trend Demand by Non-linear Optimization of the Smoothing Constant'. *Journal of Mechanical Engineering* 41 (1): 58–64.

4

Warehousing and Distribution Management: Complexity and Challenges

LEARNING OBJECTIVES

- Understand the purpose, scope, functions and types of a warehouse
- Design criteria and layout of a warehouse for efficient warehousing activities
- Calculate the warehousing cost and identify the criteria impacting warehousing performance
- Understand warehousing management system and performance metrics
- Understand distribution management: objectives, tasks, methods, channels, strategies, policies and challenges
- Recognize key performance indicators of distribution and design a distribution network
- Create a distribution organization and channel structure for specific product categories

INTRODUCTION

Finished goods' warehouses are located in strategic locations from where ultimate customers as well as trade channel partners are serviced. The objective of locating a warehouse is to respond to the customer demands in the quickest possible time and at least cost. Companies do a lot of surveys as well as mathematical modelling to decide the location for finding out an optimum solution for transportation and distribution of products, which is a subject matter of operations research. Dynamic programming and simulations such as Monte Carlo simulation are carried out to take appropriate and logical decisions for such crucial activities in a business.

Warehousing has a significant cost in terms of total logistics cost (TLC). Besides, effective and efficient warehousing is critical to distribution efficiency. Location and type of warehousing and its management are thus critical decisions to a business. Complexity of warehouse operation depends on the number of SKUs to be handled and the number of orders received and filled. Order-filling rate and stock-filling rate have to meet customer requirements as per the order conditions in addition to meeting the delivery time and schedule to ensure high level of customer satisfaction. The most performed activity in a warehouse is material-handling, which improves the warehouse operational efficiency and helps reduce wastages and damage. But material-handling also adds a significant cost in terms of both capital and operational costs, and as such, a warehouse has to be designed to minimize the need of material-handling. Distribution efficiency is also linked with the warehouse management efficiency in addition to the location of the warehouse. A specific warehouse can only service that many customers around its location. The management perspective is to consider managing both warehouse and distribution functions as an integrated function. And as such, in this chapter, two interrelated subjects warehousing and distribution are discussed together.

WAREHOUSING PURPOSE AND SCOPE

Warehousing is actually a large intermediate storage space for holding stocks of finished goods till the time these stocks are sold to be delivered to the customer as per the customer ordering quantity and input materials such as raw and packaging materials, spares and components to be transferred to production and manufacturing departments as and when required. Depending on types of inventory kept in a warehouse, the customer could be internal or external. For example, raw material and packaging material kept in a warehouse will be used internally by the production department, whereas finished goods kept in a warehouse will be used for the external customers or buyers. For distribution, warehouses are located in strategic locations identified in relation to customer concentration. A distribution warehouse, therefore, normally holds finished goods for sales, whereas a warehouse located in the vicinity of the manufacturing or production location contains both finished goods and input materials, and for finished goods it normally serves as a feeder warehouse to distribution warehouses. Businesses incur storage cost in a warehouse as well as the handling cost. A warehouse needs to be designed to improve the movement of stock for dispatch unhindered with minimal or nil handling to reduce the cost. Efficient warehouse management will help the business to improve profitability. From this point of view, a warehouse can be defined as part of a logistics management system that stores the products for subsequent distribution to meet the customer demands. Warehousing provides time and space utility for raw and packaging materials and other inputs including spares and consumables, industrial goods and finished products to help customers as a dynamic value-adding tool, which can ultimately provide a competitive advantage to the business. Warehouses, if located in a strategic location, can significantly increase the value to the customers by reducing the delivery time and cost as well as helping the customers in lowering their inventory level, which helps customers to improve their profitability and in that sense warehousing can play a strategic role in a business.

PRIMARY FUNCTIONS OF WAREHOUSE

A warehouse, in fact, has multiple functions, and those include the following:

- **Consolidation for transportation:** Depending on the customer's order, the lot size is consolidated collecting stocks in various SKUs as per the order from various storage locations within the warehouse before transportation.
- **Mixing of products:** Products are grouped under various product mix configurations which can facilitate their identification and also consolidation to execute customer's orders expeditiously.
- **Docking:** Products of various groups as identified are kept and stored at designated docking stations for loading and dispatch immediately on demand without holding the stock. In docking stations, products come and are unloaded and reloaded to another destination.
- **Customer service:** Meeting the customer requirements in terms of both ordering quantity, product mix configuration as well as SKUs and service frequency for both internal and external customers is the responsibility of the designated warehouse itself.
- **Buffer against contingencies:** It helps in meeting the fluctuating customer demand including seasonal demand and other variable demand situations during unusual situations in the marketplace.

EFFICIENT WAREHOUSE MANAGEMENT

The designated warehouse performs its primary function to achieve the objective as listed above, but the functional efficiency of the warehouse is determined by many performance criteria which are the primary objectives of efficient functioning of the warehouse. These performance criteria are as follows:

- **Providing timely service to the customer:** Customer orders have to be executed as fast as possible to ensure that the customer never goes out of stock and also for customer satisfaction. These days, customers demand more frequent deliveries in small quantity rather than large deliveries to reduce the cost of stockholding that needs higher service frequency which can add to the cost to marketers. In a competitive environment, cost has to be contained by bringing in savings in production and operations.
- **Keeping track of items to find them readily and correctly when needed:** This helps in faster execution of customer orders and also in terms of managing the warehouse better. This is essential for computerization of warehouse management and is part of the design and implementation of an efficient WMS.
- **Minimize the physical effort and material-handling to save cost:** The design of the warehouse and stock storage plan should be such that movements inside the warehouse are managed most efficiently at least cost. The layout design should be such that material-handling is minimal which is a non-value-adding activity and is kept at the minimal level to save cost incurred on moving goods into and out of the warehouse. Material-handling can

be minimized by properly designing the layout following the industrial engineering principles and ensuring linear movement of stocks and using material-handling equipment to improve efficiency by reducing cost and wastages.

- **Providing communication links with customers:** A warehouse has to be an important link for sales system of the company and the customers, and for that purpose warehouse records have to be accurate and up to date. Real-time information often needs to be provided to sales force as well as to customers so that they can also plan their activities more efficiently.

TYPES OF WAREHOUSE

As warehousing is a significant cost in business, several alternative methods and models are experimented and followed in real-life practices. Businesses are constantly exploring possibilities of reducing the cost of warehousing, and we can see various types of warehouses that are in use including the following:

Public warehousing: Public properties are available for businesses to be used as warehouses on rent or lease. For example, Port Trust Authority, which owns the warehouse space in the port areas, is normally given on long- or short-term lease to private businesses through a public tendering process. These warehouses are operated by the warehouse operators and are given on fixed or variable commercial terms to manufacturers and marketers for use. Businesses having international operations prefer stockholding facilities in the port areas from the considerations of cost and convenience.

Private warehousing: Privately built or constructed warehouses are available on rent or lease at convenient locations to service the customers. For example, before entering a large city like Mumbai, most of the companies have their warehouses located in Bhiwandi at a lower cost instead of bringing the stock to Mumbai city where the cost of a warehouse is many times higher. The same is true for other large and smaller cities around the country. Locating a warehouse in the outskirts of large costly cities also saves the tax to be paid for entering and other constraints like longer waiting time incurring cost before transport vehicles are allowed to enter the city limits and hence works out to be more economical.

Third-party warehousing or contract warehousing: In this type of warehousing, the goods are given to a third party on contract basis under some agreed commercial terms to be stored on behalf of the company. The traditional carrying and forwarding (C&F) agents also serve the similar purpose. Post implementation of Goods and Services Tax (GST), the role of C&F has become irrelevant in the traditional sense, but they also serve the purpose of warehousing for their principal as well as for redistribution of stocks as C&F agents actually function as an extended arm of the marketers from where a company can bill to distributors, wholesalers as well as other categories of customers, including institutional customers and large retailers such as organized retailers and e-retailers in e-commerce.

Multi-client warehousing: Here, one warehouse is used by many clients, and this helps in terms of sharing the space as per requirement of the individual companies and also sharing the common area including utilities and security services and cost thereof. This often becomes economical. In this model, warehousing can even be directly linked dynamically with the space utilized for keeping the stock instead of paying for a fixed storage space to make it 'as used payment basis'—meaning that you pay for the space you use dynamically and that will be very economical.

WAREHOUSE LAYOUT DESIGN CRITERIA

The internal layout of the warehouse has to be designed keeping the following design criteria in mind with the object of efficient operations at least cost. The warehouse should be located in a single-storey building having maximum height and least numbers of columns inside to ensure large space availability. A square building is preferred as space utilization is maximum in a square building and wastage of space is minimum. This helps in making an effective storage plan. The layout design must ensure maximum utilization of the height and available space of the storage area. Maximizing aisle space for efficient movement of material-handling equipment like fork lifts should also be ensured. The material-handling equipment that is used in warehousing must be efficient, the movement of the goods should always be in a straight line and the entire layout design must follow the principles of industrial engineering. Any forward or backward movement should be avoided or eliminated. A typical layout design of a warehouse and activities performed in different sections is shown in Figure 4.1.

WAREHOUSING COST

There are two broad elements of warehousing cost, namely capital cost and operating cost. Capital costs include the costs of space and material-handling equipment and also WMS software which, of course, are incurred by those who have implemented a computerized WMS. A large part of the cost of warehouse is the material-handling systems and equipment. The operating costs, however, include the cost of direct labour, utilities as well administrative cost and communication and documentation costs.

WAREHOUSE ACTIVITIES

To perform the objectives and functions as mentioned above, there are numerous activities that a typical warehouse has to perform which are as follows:

Receive goods: This entails accepting goods from suppliers and vendors as well as outside transporters and other factories, checking the quantities received against orders and the bill of lading, inspecting goods as per order specifications and reporting discrepancy, if any, and also checking for damages and report as necessary for replacement or adjustment in record. Goods are normally received at receiving docks for inspection and issuing a goods receipt note (GRN) for tracking the goods against each order subsequently, which is also required for making suppliers' payment. Goods are also returned for damage or otherwise unsellable stock from the customers and market.

FIGURE 4.1 Warehouse Layout Design and Activities Performed

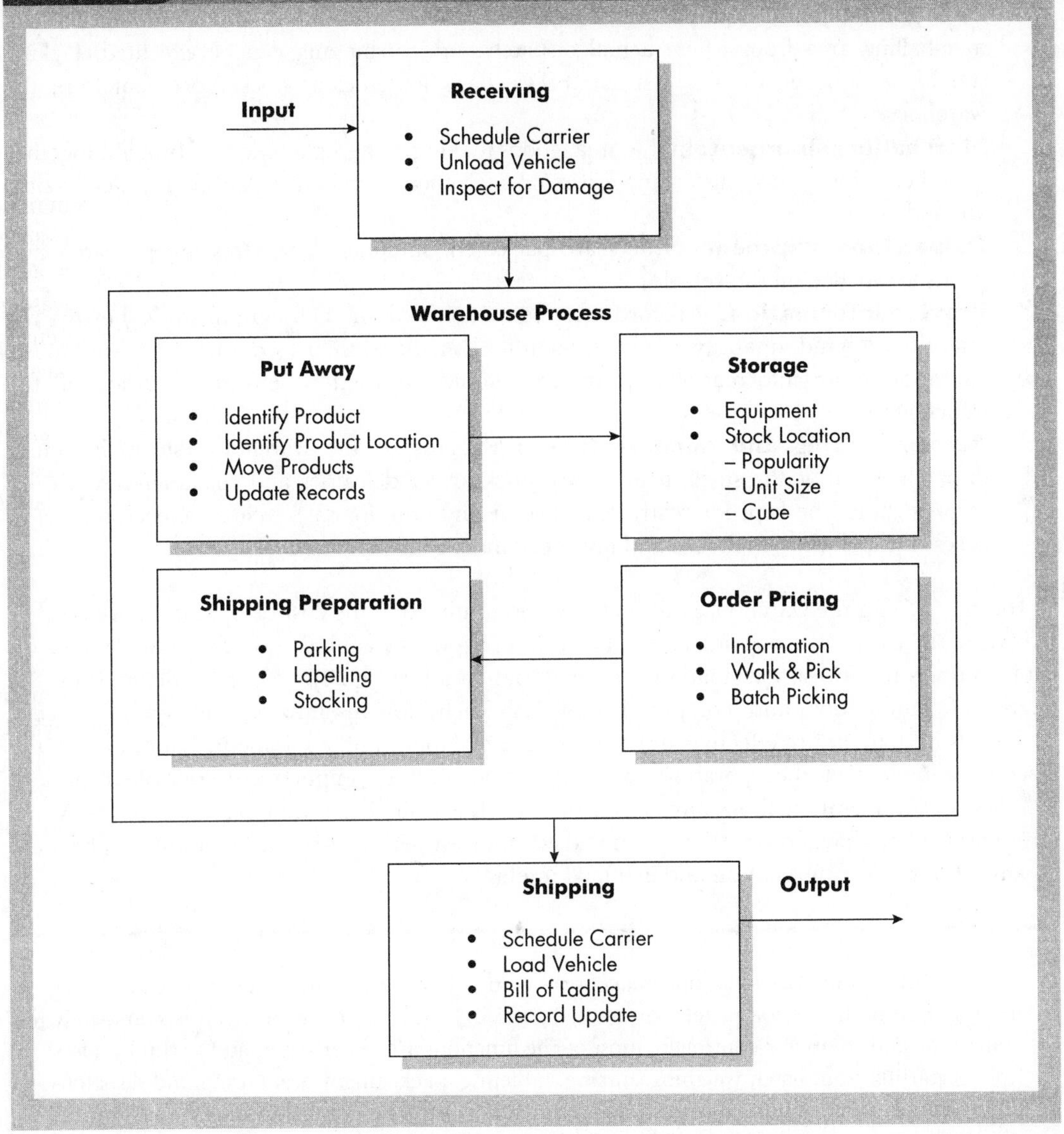

Identify goods: Items are identified with the appropriate SKU number and/or part number as the case may be and the quantity received has to be recorded.

Transfer goods to storage area: Goods are sorted and put away at their designated storage locations so that as and when required it is easy to trace and retrieve to ensure that there is no loss of time while we need to retrieve for using and/or further dispatching.

Hold goods: Goods are kept in storage in their designated storage locations well protected to avoid any damage and to facilitate subsequent utilization when needed.

Pick goods: Items required from stock must be selected from storage and brought to a marshalling area from where actual dispatch and/or shipping can be executed. Picking should be done on first-in, first-out (FIFO) basis for efficient stock movement from the warehouse.

Marshalling shipment: In this area, goods making up a single order are brought together and checked for omissions or any errors or any other discrepancy. And then order records are updated.

Dispatching shipment: Orders are packaged, shipping documents are prepared and goods are loaded on the vehicle.

Provide information: A record must be maintained for each item in stock showing the quantity on hand, quantity received, quantity issued and their location in the warehouse. An appropriate information system (IS) should be used to ensure accuracy of the information.

Record-keeping and documentation: Records of the warehouse stock, locations, dispatches, age of the stock, near expiry stock, order deliveries and customer-wise service records should be kept for ready reference at any time for sales system and customers to access through the warehouse and inventory management system.

For maximizing the warehouse productivity and minimizing the cost of operation, we need to maximize the use of space which forms the largest part of the capital cost. The other significant capital cost is the investment made in the material-handling equipment which depends on the degree of automation and computerization. As such, for minimizing the operating cost, businesses have to ensure effective and efficient use of labour and equipment. Labour being the largest component of the operating cost, automation and a computerized controlled modern warehouse can operate without any labour or with drastically lesser numbers of workers. Many large corporations have completely automated warehouse operations running without involvement of any labour using automation and artificial intelligence.

For example, an international pharmaceutical company KRKA's (pronounced as Karka) factory in Europe has a completely automated WMS. Their factory in Slovenia is completely automatic and computer-controlled; most of the functions are either automatic or run by a few robots starting from batch weighing, mixing, tableting, packaging, warehousing and dispatching. There is no manpower involved in certain functions. The entire warehouse function for finished goods, raw materials and packaging materials is being managed through a pre-programmed computer-controlled trolley and fork lifts moving on guided rails. The goods are automatically picked from the designated storage areas and being loaded in transport vehicles for dispatch against a particular order of a client or sales invoice which is entered in the system and rest is automatic. Another auto seat manufacturer TVP, producer of automobile seats for all brands of cars and supplies worldwide, is completely managed by robots and controlled through artificial intelligence.

FACTORS INFLUENCING EFFECTIVENESS OF WAREHOUSE

There are many factors impacting effectiveness of a warehouse such as cube utilization and accessibility, stock location, order picking and assembly, and physical control and security of stocks.

Cube utilization and accessibility: Goods are stored not just on the floor but also in the cubic space of the warehouse; warehouse capacity depends on how high goods can be stored. The available height of the warehouse and volume of space should therefore be fully utilized. For fork lift operation, a minimum of 18–20 ft high warehouse is selected. Those who use telescopic fork lifts in automatic operation even go for still more height. Utilizing the complete volumetric space reduces the cost significantly. Accessibility means being able to get at the goods wanted with a minimum amount of work. The warehouse design and storage patterns and identification and location codes should facilitate by taking minimum time to access the items stored whenever required. Utilizing both horizontal and vertical spaces to the extent possible determines the cost of holding the stock (Figure 4.2).

FIGURE 4.2 Cube Space Utilization and Accessibility

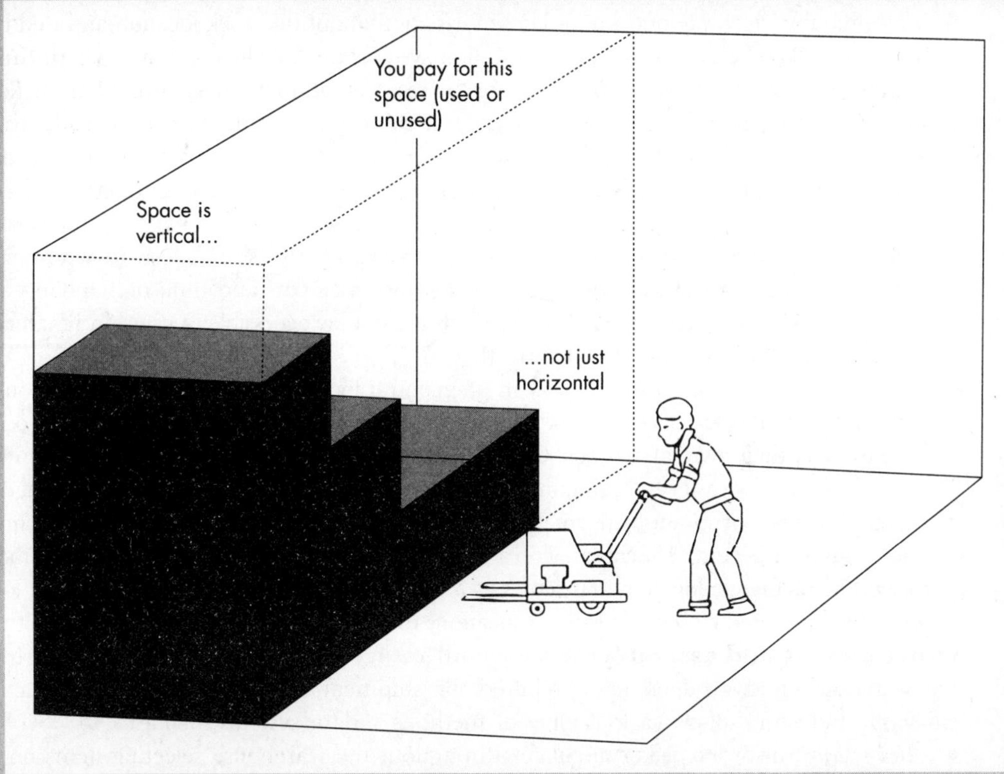

Stock location: Objectives of designating a specific stock location are to provide the required customer service and also to keep track of where items are stored to minimize effort to receive, put away and retrieve items.

Locating various kinds of stocks within the warehouse to facilitate identification and shipment when needed can follow different types of stock locating systems as follows:

- *Basic stock locating systems:* Classify the goods stored in the warehouse in some order based on their functions or use to facilitate easy identification in a large warehouse. Several such systems with respect to grouping of stocks are in use such as:
  - Functionally related items together
  - Fast-moving items together
  - Physically similar items together
  - Working stock and reserve stock separately
- *Fixed location:* In this system, an SKU is assigned a permanent location, and no other item is stored there. But fixed location systems usually have poor and less efficient cube utilization and, therefore, are usually used in small warehouses where throughput is small, and there are few SKUs to be handled and managed. A fixed location, however, helps in terms of easy identification and audit of the stock. When stocks are scattered, conducting an audit becomes difficult.
- *Floating or random location:* Goods are stored wherever there is an appropriate or suitable space available, and the advantage of this system is that cube utilization is significantly improved. It also requires accurate and up-to-date information about the stock location and quantity SKU wise. Warehouses using floating location systems are usually computer based. In the industry, this practice is widely prevalent for the reason that no businesses would like to keep space unutilized as space is money. Whenever a delivery van comes to deliver stocks, there is an urgency to unload the stock to make space for the next van to arrive and park. Under that kind of a situation, goods are kept after unloading wherever space is available.
- *Point-of-use storage:* Inventory is stored close to where it will be needed and normally used in repetitive manufacturing and JIT systems. Keeping the stock close to where it is required for use has several advantages, including lesser cost and time of handling and movement. The key advantage is that materials are readily accessible to users and material-handling is reduced or eliminated altogether.
- *Central storage:* It contains all inventory in one central location which helps in reduction of cost, and materials are accessible all the time. Safety stock level is reduced as users do not need to carry their own safety stock. Central storage is much easier to control, and inventory record accuracy is easier to maintain. Central storage also facilitates specialized storage, if required. Large corporations normally follow this practice for better control and accurate information in a central location. For a large business, a central warehouse is normally located in a strategic location and serves as a feeder warehouse to feed stock to other local warehouses located closer to customer locations to facilitate better service and flexibility.

Order picking and assembly: When an order is received, items must be obtained from the warehouse and grouped and prepared for shipment, and to manage that function efficiently, industries follow various types of methods and/or systems such as:

- *Area system:* An order picker circulates throughout the warehouse selecting items on an order, and an order is ready to ship when the order picker is finished picking the stocks as per the order requirement. This requires a little longer time to assemble one order for delivery. This is practical for a small warehouse dealing in limited numbers of products and SKUs.

- *Zone system:* A warehouse is divided into several zones, and each picker works only in an assigned zone. The order is normally divided by zone, and the items from each zone are sent to the marshalling area for executing the order. When product groups are large and each one is managed as a separate profit centre and/or strategic business unit (SBU), zone system is better. For example, a company deals with FMCG, industrial products as well as pharma products. Zone system also avoids intermixing of stocks and ensures better control.
- *Multi-order system:* It is same as the zone system, except that each picker collects items for a number of orders at the same time. In reality, this multi-order system is practised. In large retail stores, orders are picked up throughout the day and in the evening all orders are executed to facilitate deliveries indicated in the order.

Physical control and security elements: The goods stored inside the warehouse have to be secured and safe at all times and should be in control of the warehouse management team. Some standard practices must be followed to ensure security and safety of the stock. These are as follows:

- Goods parts numbering system should be simple but unique to facilitate easy identification. It should also have a simple and well-documented transaction system involving identifying the item, verifying the quantity, recording the transaction and physically executing the transaction.
- Inventory must be kept in a safe and secured (locked) place with limited general access or access through identity checks by those who are authorized. It should be accessible only to the authorized people. A well-trained workforce should be engaged to manage the warehouse to eliminate damages and wastages and pilferages as well as thefts. An adequate surveillance system such as CCTV monitoring will help. But in spite of all these precautions, pilferage still happens and businesses have to absorb that cost. Needless to say that all those costs have to be ultimately borne by the end customer. To be competitive, businesses have to control all such possible pilferage.
- Modern warehouses are fully automated and computerized, and customer orders are processed by picking up stock from the designated locations and managed through central data processing and inventory control stations. Most of the large ports these days have warehouses including bonded warehouses where stocks are kept and taken as per need paying the custom duties. This type of operation has brought in significant improvement in operational efficiency in the business. Some of these warehouses are used by many clients on a space-sharing basis, providing space utilization efficiency.

WAREHOUSE MANAGEMENT SYSTEM

WMS AS AN ENABLER

A WMS is a proven, advanced software solution for manufacturing, distribution and retail enterprises and TPL providers that can be used by enterprising organizations of all sizes. It helps companies maximize product placement strategies, prioritize tasks, implement fair productivity standards and increase logistics efficiency.

The evolution of WMSs is very similar to that of many other software solutions such as ERP and material requirements planning (MRP). There is an overlap in functionality among planning, transportation management systems, supply chain planning, advanced planning and scheduling, and manufacturing execution systems will only increase the level of confusion among companies looking for software solutions for their operations. Businesses have to decide on an appropriate software system out of many such options available and that task is not easy. Only those businesses which are very clear about their requirement can find an ideal solution for them. An efficient ERP like SAP can serve as a useful tool and control software system for managing the warehouse for a business. But still many businesses opt for WMS software. The effectiveness of a WMS depends on how efficiently information processing and organization and handling of stock and type of automated environment as well as material-handling equipment are installed and managed. A WMS, therefore, also involves significant investment in capital expenditure to derive commensurate benefits.

WHY AND WHEN IT IS NECESSARY

WMS is not always useful and has to be implemented when it is necessary and there are valid reasons for taking such decisions.

- Not every warehouse needs a WMS. Certainly any warehouse can benefit from some of the functionality, but businesses need to assess the benefits that can be derived to justify the initial and ongoing costs associated with a WMS. WMSs are big, complex, data-intensive applications. Large automated operations can definitely benefit.
- You need to manage your WMS efficiently to derive the full advantage. Otherwise, a WMS can end up as an additional complexity and cost in your business. Many a time, large operations end up creating a new IS or IT department with the sole responsibility of managing the WMS. And that cost and complexity can offset the benefits of the WMS. This is therefore a tricky decision that businesses need to take with utmost care. Otherwise, a WMS can only add to complexity and cost with no commensurate benefit forthcoming.

ADVANTAGES OF IMPLEMENTING WMS

A WMS, if implemented properly and supported by the necessary inventory data, can lead to several benefits such as:

- Reduction in inventory
- Reduction in labour costs
- Increase in storage capacity
- Better customer service
- Increase in inventory accuracy
- Better management of complex warehouse structure
- Optimized warehouse activity

- Increase in trace and track ability of materials in warehouse
- Facilitate mobile data entry
- Increase in efficiency
- Reduction in customer complaints

The implementation of a WMS along with automated data collection is likely to give a business better inventory data accuracy, reduction in labour costs and a greater ability to service the customer by reducing cycle times. The predominant factors that control inventory levels are lot sizing, lead times and demand variability. However, a WMS is unlikely to impact these factors. Beyond labour efficiencies, the determining factors in deciding to implement a WMS tend to be more often associated with the need to do something to service the customers that the current system does not support (or does not support well) such as FIFO, cross-docking, automated pick replenishment, wave picking, lot tracking, yard management, automated data collection and automated material-handling equipment.

IMPLEMENTING AND SETTING UP WMS

There are various requirements for implementing and setting up WMS, which are listed below.

- The set-up requirements of a WMS can be extensive and also expensive. The characteristics of each item and location must be maintained either at the detail level or by grouping similar items and locations into categories, as discussed earlier. And these details include exact dimensions and weight of each item in each unit of measure the item is stocked (such as inches, cases and pallets) as well as information such as whether it can be mixed with other items in a location, whether it is rack-able, maximum stack height, maximum quantity per location, hazard classifications, finished goods or raw material and fast- vs slow-moving items.
- Although some operations need to set up each item this way, most operations benefit by creating groups of similar products. In reality, most operations have a much more diverse product mix and require much more system set-up. Setting up the physical characteristics of the product and locations is only part of the picture. The real-term requirement is very extensive in terms of organizing the layout, data regarding inventory type and group and logic of taking decisions based on which a WMS will operate.

WHEN WMS CAN BE ADVANTAGEOUS

A WMS can lead to many other operational benefits in addition to those listed above as functional benefits that can accrue to the business if it is implemented properly. It should be pointed out here that only very large and complex business organizations with very diversified product portfolio and very large and well-dispersed customer base to service can really benefit from the implementation of a WMS. Some of those other benefits are as follows:

- **Wave picking/batch picking/zone picking:** Support for various picking methods varies from one system to another. In high-volume fulfilment operations, picking a logic can be a critical factor in WMS selection. An appropriate picking logic is therefore a key criterion for efficient WMS operations.

- **Task interleaving:** Task interleaving describes functionality that mixes dissimilar tasks such as picking and putting away to obtain maximum productivity. Used primarily in full-pallet-load operations, task interleaving directs a lift truck operator to put away a pallet on his/her way to the next pick. This requires a very standard operating system to be implemented in warehouse operations.
- **Integration with automated material-handling equipment:** If you are planning on using automated material-handling equipment such as merry-go-round, automated storage and retrieval system (ASRS) units, automated guided vehicles (AGVs), pick-to-light systems and sortation systems, you will want to consider this during the software selection process. Since these types of automation are very expensive and are usually a core component of your warehouse, you may find that the equipment will drive the selection of the WMS. If the WMS is integrated with an automatic material-handling system, efficiency improves significantly.
- **Advanced shipment notifications (ASNs):** If your vendors are capable of sending ASNs (preferably electronically) and attaching compliance labels to the shipments, you will want to make sure that the WMS can use this to automate your receiving process.
- **Cycle counting:** Most WMSs will have some cycle counting functionality. Modifications to cycle counting systems, as required, are common to meet specific operational needs. A WMS needs to support the prevailing cycle counting practices.
- **Cross-docking:** In its purest form, cross-docking is the action of unloading materials from an incoming trailer or rail car and immediately loading these materials in outbound trailers or rail cars, thus eliminating the need for warehousing (storage) altogether. This requires synchronized operations and planning as well as coordination.
- **Pick-to-carton:** For parcel shippers, the pick-to-carton logic uses item dimensions/weights to select the shipping carton prior to the order-picking process. Items are then picked directly into the shipping carton. Shipping cartons are normally standardized to ensure ideal usage, and items to be shipped are normally picked directly into the shipping cartons.
- **Slotting:** Slotting describes the activities associated with optimizing product placement in pick locations in a warehouse. There are software packages designed just for slotting, and many WMS packages also have slotting functionality and need to be selected to match the requirement.
- **Yard management:** Yard management describes the function of managing the inventory of trailers parked outside the warehouse, or the empty trailers themselves.

  It is generally associated with cross-docking operations and may include the management of both inbound and outbound trailers. For efficient yard management, goods truck parking queuing needs to be programmed based on a logic.
- **Activity-based costing (ABC)/billing:** This functionality is primarily designed for TPL operators. It allows them to calculate billable fees based upon specific activities. It also helps in terms of improving in cost criteria by eliminating non-value-adding cost from the process. Billing is linked with the activities required to be performed and is therefore more logical and efficient.

TABLE 4.1 Warehouse Performance Metrics

Category	Measure	Definition
Order fulfillment performance	On-time delivery	Orders delivered on time as per customer requirement
	Order fill rate	Orders filled completely on first shipment (delivery)
	Order accuracy (pack fill rate)	Orders picked, packed and shipped perfectly according to customer order
	Line (product category) accuracy	Lines picked, packed and shipped perfectly
	Order cycle time	Time from order placement to shipment
	Perfect order completion	Orders delivered without changes, damages or invoice errors
Inventory management measure	Inventory accuracy	Actual inventory quantity to system-reported quality
	Damaged inventory	Damage measured as a percentage of the value of the inventory
	Storage utilization	Occupied space (square foot) as a percentage of the total storage capacity
	Dock to stock time	Average time from carrier arrival until product is available for picking
	Inventory visibility	Time from physical receipt of goods to customer service notice of availability
Warehouse productivity	Orders per hour	Average number of orders picked and packed per person hour
	Lines per hour	Average number of order lines picked and packed per person hour
	Items per hour	Average number of order items picked and packed per person hour
	Cost per order	Total warehousing costs: fixed space, utilities and depreciation including operational cost Variable: labour/supplies and administration overheads
	Cost as a percentage of sales	Total warehousing cost as a percentage of total company sales revenue

DEVELOPING A RESPONSIVE WMS

If a large corporation implements a responsive and well-functional WMS, there are various other benefits and supports that will be available for improving the business performance. A WMS (Table 4.1) can also thus lead to other advantages including the following:

- Support goods returns processing and reverse logistics
- Use task interleaving to minimize deadheading
- Improve order consolidation, wave planning, inventory allocation and pick sequencing
- Identify consolidation opportunities to free space and reduce outside storage requirements
- Support bill of material, work order and value-added processing
- Update inventory records as events occur
- Provide accuracy that allows replacement of full physical with scheduled cycle counts
- Time stamp each transaction and identify the operator who performed it
- Provide feedback to the workforce and support performance measurement
- Measure supplier and carrier performance

NEW TRENDS IN WMS

The recent trends in WMSs are resulting in further consolidation of the industry as well as in terms of alliances with ERP and other enterprise system providers. A WMS now facilitates ABC, which in turn helps in cost reduction. Latest WMS-embedded profiling tools are used for space use analysis to facilitate relay out and inventory slotting. Also, introduction of object-oriented toolkits for requirements of modelling and WMS development has helped in the warehouse management performance

PRODUCTIVITY IMPROVEMENT TOOLS OF WMS

Barcode

A barcode is magnetic stripe against a light background normally used to identify a stock. It is usually instantaneously identified by a barcode reading system. A barcode is read through the reflectance and absorption of light. A light of a given wavelength is beamed and moved across the barcode at a consistent speed and the reflected light is measured with a photo receptor. The pattern of the barcode creates an electrical wave which is sent to a computer chip called 'decoder'. Barcode technology is a widely used method of automatic identification. Automatic identification encompasses automatic reading of information most commonly through printing and reading of information encoded in the barcode and thus eliminates any human error.

Barcode System Requirement

Bar coding system has to perform some typical tasks as described below:

- **Barcode label and printer:** Barcode labels are printed using barcode label printers. These printers are normally faster printers than the normal laser printers. These labels are then attached to an asset class or product for easy identification.
- **Scanning equipment for data collection:** The scanner accurately identifies, reads and deciphers the information contained in each barcode label.
- **Capturing the data to an external database:** To be able to effectively use the codes, a database is required to relay the information.

- **Put to light and pick to light:** In a 'pick to light' system, lights will guide the operators to a specific SKU location where they will pick or select the orders from. And in a 'put to light' system, light modules will guide the operators to the correct location to sort or to 'put' the item into where it belongs.

If the products are barcoded, a 'put to light' system helps in faster sorting of products based on their SKUs and product category. In large manufacturing organizations with large numbers of products and variants, this system will really help the business. As mentioned earlier, to make a WMS very effective, the inventories and IS need to be organized to make the warehouse performance efficient and effective.

With a 'put to light' system, the operator simply grabs an item and scans the label with a radio frequency (RF) unit. Lights illuminate at locations where the particular item resides as well the quantities required to fill a customer order. The process is thus repeated till the customer order is fulfilled. This is extremely fast, accurate and error-free. 'Pick to light' and 'put to light' systems can be remarkably fast and accurate, helping a significant increase in warehouse productivity. It is also the most cost-effective means of providing dramatic improvement in warehouse cost reduction and in increased productivity. Pick to light is a paperless solution that increases the **pick rate productivity**, accuracy and cost efficiency of this otherwise labour-intensive operation by reducing the walk time, eliminating reading errors and also simplifying the task throughout the process.

DISTRIBUTION MANAGEMENT

Distribution is an essential part of the sales function, but now it has come under the broad umbrella of integrated SCM. The key task of distribution is to make goods and services available from where consumers would like to buy it. Efficient distribution is, therefore, key to ensure consumer offtake, and the success of any product is largely influenced by the effective and efficient distribution management.

DISTRIBUTION TASK

It depends on the product(s) to be distributed, target consumers to be reached and serviced, geographical areas to be covered, width and depth of distribution to be achieved, and service levels and frequency of service desired. The distribution objective is normally influenced by the customer expectations and also the company's sales and distribution policy. It defines the extent of time, place and possession utilities which the customer can expect out of the channel network.

DEFINITION AND SCOPE

The scope of distribution covers many activities to ensure timely availability of goods and services wherever required. The scope thus includes:

- It is the management of the efficient transfer of goods from the place of manufacture to the POS or consumption.

- Distribution management encompasses activities such as warehousing, material-handling, packing, stock control, order processing and transportation.
- According to Mossman and Norton (1965), 'Distribution is the operation which creates time, place and form utility through the movement of goods and persons from one place to another.'

DISTRIBUTION CHANNELS

Distribution channels are sets of interdependent organizations involved in the process of making a product or service available for use or consumption? Seven R's of distribution are the right product in the right quantity in the right condition at the right time and at the right place for the right customer at the right cost.

Channel partners are intermediaries or middlemen. They help in the management of the distribution process. They also perform various roles and facilitate distribution and redistribution of stocks. The other benefits that are accrued from distribution include the following:

- They exist because producers cannot reach all their consumers directly and therefore need partners or channel associates to reach ultimate consumers.
- They multiply, reach and provide efficiency to the marketing process as channel partners can help accelerate the distribution process and improve efficiency.
- They can facilitate smooth flow of goods and services and create time, place and possession utilities.
- They are selected based on their core competence, infrastructure and facilities as well as reach.
- They provide contact, experience, specialization and scales of operation.

An example: A consumer wants to buy a tube of toothpaste (a product) from a retail outlet located close to her residence (the place) to be made available at 8 PM on a Tuesday evening when she wants it (time) from where she can pay for the toothpaste and take it away (possession).

The company's distribution function has made all this possible in the most cost-effective manner. The situation would be similar if a customer wants to buy a soap, a refrigerator or medicine or even an electric motor.

DISTRIBUTION METHODS

Distribution methods normally are determined based on several issues and criteria as well as on the company's policy to decide the best method of achieving the distribution objective to effectively service the target customers.

The distribution methods to be adopted generally depend on the following:

- Product types
- Buying behaviour
- Consumption pattern
- Buying frequency
- Buyer types and demographics
- Market characteristics

- Infrastructure, complexity and reach
- Competitive practice on distribution
- Geographical area to be covered
- Service frequency and service levels desired

Basically, the management has the choice of one of the following different types of distribution systems and practices prevailing in the industry:

1. **Direct:** The manufacturer does not use a middleman and sells and delivers direct to the end customer. The channel length is short but effective. In a business-to-business (B2B) model, this is a preferred mode of distribution.
2. **Selective:** The manufacturer sells through a limited number of middlemen who are chosen because of their special abilities or having facilities to enable the product to be distributed better. The company can even choose to have its own distribution outlets instead of having a channel partner.
3. **Intensive:** Maximum exposure at the POS is needed and the manufacturer sells through as many outlets as possible. Servicing and after-sales service are less important, for example, FMCG products such as food, cigarette and detergent. The channel length is longer in this case. For intensive distribution, multiple channel intermediaries are involved for reaching and servicing the clients covering very wide range of socio-economic strata.
4. **Exclusive:** The manufacturer sells through a restricted number of dealers normally used for high-value durable items like cars where the distributor must provide a level of desired stockholding, after sales-service and so on. Investment from distributors in this case is also high. Exclusive distribution is also practised for very high-end products and services like fashion stores or beauty parlours which can also be owned by the manufacturer-marketers. Exclusive stores provide special ambience and decor as well as specialized customer service by well-trained customer service executives who are capable of answering all questions of a prospective customer and influence the decision of such customer visiting such distributor's premises and as such it also acts as a sales promotion centre.
5. **Multi-level marketing (MLM):** Is a product distribution and marketing strategy in which the sales force is compensated not only for sales they generate but also for the sales of the other salespeople that they recruit? This recruited sales force are referred to as the participant's 'down-line' and can provide multiple levels of compensation. MNCs such as Amway and Oriflame created successful global brands through MLM production, distribution and marketing strategies. In this system, sales force are really working as independent agents and not as company's employees. Agents engaged in MLM are self-motivated individuals who work as commission agents taking product from the company's warehouses located in strategic locations and selling directly to the customers and developing their own line of sub-agents to drive the process at multiple levels of the operations, and as the chain expands, they gain collectively. MLM has been discussed in detail later in this chapter.
6. **Online marketing:** In e-commerce, businesses receive orders online on their portal and deliver the stock directly to the end customers. The typical channel partners are non-relevant for online retailers such as Amazon and Flipkart. However, many manufacturer-marketers are also taking advantage of online trade to significantly improve their performance and growth as that helps in getting faster penetration in the market at a lower cost. Some global established brands are also now distributing online. The online sales have helped Dell to

significantly improve its performance for customized servers in terms of both responsiveness and cost. For standardized laptops, however, the online channel is significantly less attractive because its main strength which is reduction of inventory through aggregation is not as valuable for standardized configurations. Simultaneously, the weaknesses of online channel which are poorer responsiveness and higher transportation costs become more significant for standardized configurations.

DISTRIBUTION CHANNEL STRATEGY

It is derived from the corporate strategy and the marketing strategy. Primarily, distribution objectives as mentioned below have to be defined first for designing a distribution strategy:

- Defining customer service levels
- Distribution objectives and goals
- Sales target
- Set of activities
- Distribution organization
- Geographical area to be covered
- Key performance indicators (KPIs)
- Critical success factors (CSFs)
- Distribution policy

Once there is clarity regarding the customers to be targeted, penetration to be achieved, and service level and frequency of service to be achieved, a distribution strategy is developed with regard to what would be the best distribution methods and strategy to achieve the desired goal. The channel strategy has to be implemented through an efficient distribution organization.

Customer Service Level

As a policy, company has to decide a competitive service level for its customers for implementation in the business based on the following criteria:

- It is defined by the nature of the industry, products, competition and market shares.
- Affordability also decides the service level.
- It should at least match the competition.

Customer expectations have no limit—the more you do, the more they expect. However, a distribution strategy has to satisfy the customer expectation. A desired level of customer service is a key decision of the management.

Distribution Objectives

The distribution objective depends largely on the type of product and the level and extent of reach a corporation intends to achieve over a period of time in a given geographical area. It also depends on the company's resources, competitive environment and available distribution infrastructure.

The primary objective is to service the target segments effectively at least cost and without facing any stock-out situation so that there is no loss of sales and at the same time maintaining a healthy level of stock without unnecessary stock build-up of trade stock reflecting on the age of the stock as well as high debtors.

Distribution Organization

The type and structure of the distribution organization depend on the distribution methods adopted which again depend on the type of products. Distribution is normally achieved through a third party who participates as a channel partner. The organization normally maintains a lean structure to deal with the external channel partners following the company's policy and guidelines. As the channel partners are external to the organization, they are selected on the basis of the partners knowledge, infrastructure, experience and financial status. The company's own distribution organization is very lean and mostly stocks controllers responsible for a defined geographical area. Stock controllers and distribution managers coordinate with the sales department and channel partners for servicing customer orders.

Activities in Distribution

These depend on the manner in which the company and its marketing channels go about achieving the customer service levels. Some of these steps could be as follows: sales forecasts, dispatch plans, market coverage beat plans, journey plans for service engineers and sales staff, collection of sales proceeds and carrying out promotional activities. The company also decides as to who is to perform which task. Distributors are the key link with the other channel partners such as wholesalers and retailers to reach the ultimate customers, and as such they need to service the market as per the defined and agreed service frequency. These days FMCG companies' and more particularly multinationals like HUL's frequency of service has increased to twice or thrice a week, and for achieving such level of services distributors must have required infrastructure and system in place.

Distribution Policy

All businesses have their well-defined distribution policies and implementation guidelines described in their operating manuals, and these can vary depending on companies as well as on the product category and distribution methods.

Broadly, the policy guidelines include the following:

- A code of conduct for channel members
- Stock management including ordering and inventory levels
- A pricing and credit policy
- Pricing and stocking policies including stock level to be maintained
- Promotional scheme operational processes
- Margins, billing and customer service levels
- A system for redressing customer complaints
- Any additional subsidies or margins
- Handling institutional business policy

- Utilization of promotional and point-of-purchase promotional materials
- Record-keeping and documentation
- A rural market and van operation policy
- A stock return and quality control policy
- An out of warranty and expiry of stock handling and management policy

Key Performance Indicators

For the measurement of effectiveness of distribution, some of the indicators are as follows:

- Consistent achievement of targets by product groups, periods and territories
- Achievement of market shares
- Achievement of profitability
- Zero complaints from customers
- No stock returns
- Ability to handle emergencies and sudden spurts in demand
- Balanced sales achievement during a period—no period-end skews in sales
- Market coverage with ready stocks against taking order to be delivered later—advantages vs disadvantages
- Excellent management of accounts receivables
- Minimized losses on account of stock-outs
- Minimized damages to products
- Very low incidence of complaints and settlement of complaints

Critical Success Factors

A distribution strategy also needs the support and encouragement of the top management to succeed. Some of the CSFs are as follows:

- A clear, transparent and unambiguous policy and procedure
- Settling the claims and grievances of the channel partners expeditiously
- Serious commitment of the channel partners
- Fairness in dealings
- A clearly defined customer service policy
- High level of integrity
- Equitable distribution at times of shortage
- Timely compensation of channel partners
- Transparent and fair distribution and compensation policy
- Competitive practices as per industry standards

Sales Target

Achieving sales target is the key objective of the business, and hence also of the distribution channel strategy. The channel types and number of intermediaries will change with the sales target to be achieved.

Geographical Area to Be Covered

For business growth strategy businesses often need to extend the geographical boundaries, and thus distribution channels need to consider that in terms of formulating distribution strategy as some area(s) are covered sometime with different channel partners depending on the potential of the area.

TYPICAL CHANNEL PARTNERS

C&F Agents and Carrying and Selling (C&S) Agents

Both C&F and C&S agents are on contract with the company, and both are transporters who work between the company and its distributors, collect products from the company, store in a central location, break bulk and dispatch to distributors against indents. Goods belong to the company till the time they have not changed hands through transactions.

C&F agents also act as an extended arm of the manufacturer-marketers and represent them in the market. Sometimes companies use C&F agents' locations and addresses to bill the company's product to avoid interstate sales taxes. Before the implementation of GST, we had both central and state taxes such as CST and ST, and in that environment, C&F played a very useful role to save taxes.

Distributors, Dealers, Stockists, Value-Added Re-sellers

They are the channel partners in the business performing the role of stocking the company's product(s) and then redistributing and or reselling to retailers and customers. Stockists will keep the company's stock from where customers and retailers can buy, whereas value-added re-sellers sometimes carry out some additional functions on behalf of the company and as directed by the company. Their role is thus very important in terms of delivering company's distribution objective and performance.

- Their name denotes the extent of redistribution done by them.
- Distributors invest in the products—buy products from the company.
- They are on commission, margins or mark-up.
- They may or may not get credit—but extend credit to the market.
- Distributors cover the markets as per a beat plan. All others merely finance the business.
- Distributors could be exclusive for a company.
- Sometimes same distributors are working for multiple marketers.
- Agents bring the buyer and the seller together.

Super Stockists

They perform multiple functions of the channel intermediaries, which are as follows:.

- They perform the roles of both C&F agents and distributors.
- Small companies as well as new entrants prefer to appoint them for distribution.
- New businesses as well as new products prefer this method of appointing super stockists to make it simple and for better control.

Agents and Brokers

They represent the company.

- Agents and brokers canvas for a company's products and solicit business.
- They have their own distribution network.
- They are often independent and work for many clients.

Franchisees

Following are the features of franchises:

- They are given the right to represent a company's product as given to them.
- Franchisees work under given agreed terms independently.
- Their performance is periodically audited.

Electronic Channels

Following are the features of electronic channels:

- These are used by online players and in e-commerce.
- These are accessible only where internet access is there.

Wholesalers

They are required for redistribution of products for the markets which a company cannot cover directly. They are an important part of the product distribution. Their functions include the following:

- They operate out of the main markets.
- They deal with a number of company products of their choice.
- They are not on contract with any company.
- They sell to other wholesalers, retailers and institutions and even to end consumers.
- They negotiate about 15 days credit from company distributors—also provide credit to their customers. However, all companies do not extend credit. Also some wholesalers don't extend credit and work only on cash basis with very low margin.
- They operate on high volumes and low margins.
- They cover rural distribution and areas where a company's own dealer–distributors network cannot reach.
- They are the redistributors and help taking stocks to places covering the tertiary market.

Retailers

Retailers have the following features:

- They are the ultimate link with the customers.
- They are the final contact with consumers.

- They operate out of their shops and sell a large assortment and variety of goods.
- They sell multiple and competing brands and products.
- They are located closest to consumers.
- They buy from companies, distributors or wholesalers.
- They have highest margins in the network.
- They provide personalized services to their customers.
- They can influence customers' buying decision if higher margins are available to them. Smaller companies depend on them to push sales by influencing them with higher margins.

DISTRIBUTION COST

Distribution costs typically include the following:

- Transportation
- Travel cost of sales force and distribution staff
- Channel sales force wages and distribution organization
- Channel partners margin
- Handling and storage costs
- Damages, wastage and out-of-warranty costs
- Insurance and taxes
- Warehousing and inventory and stockholding costs
- Insurance and administrative costs
- Infrastructure and documentation costs

Normally, additional sales force are kept on distributors' payroll and are also included in the cost of distribution. These salespersons recruited under distributors or channel partners are also known as pilot salesmen who are normally used to canvas and collect orders from the market to be handed over to the distributors to execute.

EFFICIENCY OF DISTRIBUTION

Criteria of effectiveness and efficiency include the following:

- Cost of distribution
- Level of service
- Incidence of consumer/customer complaints
- Stock turnover ratio
- Damages and stock return
- Outstanding and payment discipline
- Inventory age and level

Although the efficiency of distribution is determined by various criteria as mentioned above, their relative weightage on overall performance and efficiency will be different. The most important criteria, however, is the cost of distribution which has to be within budgeted limits and level of service accomplished reflected by customer complaints. The level of service has to match at least competition and industry practice.

FACTORS IMPACTING DISTRIBUTION NETWORK DESIGN

The distribution effectiveness is of primary concern of any business. More so, if the product is a mass consumption product, then the effectiveness of the distribution channel is the key, and therefore, it receives attention at the highest level. Top management's perspective on the performance of a distribution network of a company would essentially consider two broad factors:

1. Value provided to the customer
2. Cost of satisfying customer needs

When businesses evaluate various distribution network options, they must assess the impact on customer service and cost. The revenue is generated by satisfying identified customer needs by delivering the product through the distribution network. The distribution cost, thus, determines the profitability of the delivery network. Although customer value delivery depends on various factors, businesses need to focus on measures that are influenced by the structure of the distribution network which are not only measurable but also controllable and that include the following:

- **Response time:** the amount of time it takes for a customer to receive an order
- **Product type:** the number of different products or variants that are offered through the distribution network
- **Product availability:** the probability of having a product in stock when customer order arrives
- **Customer experience:** the ease with which a customer can place and receive orders and the extent to which this experience is customized including how customer experience is positively impacted by sales staff dealings and other interfaces with the customers
- **Time to market:** the time it takes to bring a new product to the market
- **Order visibility:** the ability of the customers to track their orders from ordering to receiving the orders
- **Returnability:** if the customer is not happy with the product or if it does not meet the specification, how easy it is to return the merchandise and the ability of the network to handle such stock returns
- Product movement in the market in the sense whether fast moving or slow moving
- Product category and distribution methods

It is not necessary that a customer always wants a high level of performance in all these stated dimensions. The customer can even trade off with some dimension for any other tangible benefit. For example, a little longer delivery period may be acceptable to the customer against a lot of varieties or even better quality and competitive price available in a store like Amazon. To give a unique experience to the customers, businesses have to design the network for which they might be incurring a significantly higher cost. For single-day delivery commitment, a traditional store will be required to have many stores in a defined geographical area or market which may even run into hundreds as against relatively much lesser number of stores at say Amazon.

Changing the distribution network design can, therefore, impact various supply chain cost drivers such as inventories, transportation, facilities and handling as well as information, in addition to sourcing and pricing drivers.

DISTRIBUTION MANAGEMENT: KEY CHALLENGES

Through effective distribution, consumer demand is serviced. Consumers would like to buy products from the nearest available sales outlet and that could be a retailer, distributor or showroom as the case may be. Adequate stock level needs to be maintained as required to avoid any eventual stock-out situation resulting in loss of sales and in some cases even permanent loss of sales. The distribution function is therefore extremely important. Effective distribution is essential to succeed in the marketplace.

Logistics management offers significant complexity for businesses in India to service the end customers particularly for the reasons of very long distribution channels involving multiple partners. Distribution cost also, therefore, is relatively higher in relation to overall product cost. Bringing down distribution and logistics costs thus can provide a competitive advantage to the business. Large businesses, particularly in business-to-consumer (B2C) models in the FMCG segment such as Unilever, Nestlé and ITC, as well as online retailers such as Amazon and Flipkart, are trying innovative methods to deliver to their end customers in most cost-effective ways, which is a big challenge to the businesses in a highly complex and large market like India. This chapter attempts to trace the complexity of logistics management issues for the B2C segment with particular reference to organized retailing and e-retailing. Producing in multiple locations either directly or through a contract manufacturing route is common for liquid, bulky and light-weight goods of daily use. Using a local channel partner and a wholesale route for redistribution of goods to reduce the cost of handling and storage is very common triggered by the complex tax structure in India. Businesses here in India are trying to be smart in managing the complexity. In India, it is not smart logistics but very smarter ways to manage the challenges of logistics issues.

Distribution is one of the essential elements for the success of any product or brand. And having distribution strength is what new multinational entrants into a new market like India are lacking in comparison to their Indian or local counterparts. If a brand has to be big, it has to achieve a high level of penetration among the target consumers by extending both depth and width of distribution. New MNCs in India, therefore, have options of gradually developing their own distribution infrastructure or acquiring a local company that is engaged in a similar business. It is the latter route that is preferable because it takes long time and high cost to develop effective distribution strength. MNCs are not even aware of and have experience of complexity of distribution in Indian business environment. Marketers generally believe that if distribution is achieved for a product up to a desired level, half of the battle is already won. Getting required distribution of the product is also indicative of the fact that trade channel has accepted and agreed to stock the product, and if desired level of stocking as per norms which is directly related to the type of the outlet and type of products is achieved, then it is all the more desirable and encouraging. Also, simply having the distribution infrastructure may not be enough. It should also be geared to reach the right place for the target consumers. Distribution infrastructure must be developed in line with product types and target market. For example, an industry having good rural distribution will not be suitable for a product which is designed predominantly for urban higher-income group upper-class consumers and vice versa. Optimization of distribution cost vis-à-vis the desired reach is therefore what all marketers look for. Worldwide, several experiments for this optimization have been tried and attempted. In India, we seem to have got stuck with our traditional mode of distribution, although, of late, other alternative models are being tried and also tested. Traditionally, in India we have distribution through a wholesale route which is a preferred option for new entrants and small companies in the SME sector. The other option is through appointed distributors and stockists serviced from either the company warehouse or through stock points and clearing and forwarding agents. The latter is also a necessity because of our federal tax structure and system of multiple tax points of state and central tax and interstate tax including entry tax. This scenario has now changed after GST is implemented. In the current system, the distribution cost will come down as the tax structure is rationalized through the implementation of a unified tax regime, GST.

In the current system, the cost of distribution can range between 25% and 35% of the product cost because of the involvement of multiple agencies depending on whether it is for an established brand or a new brand. Additionally, a high level of trade inventory gets locked up which has its own cost.

Ultimately, a consumer has to pay for all these hidden costs, also for system inefficiencies. But if goods and merchandise can be directly taken from the company warehouse to the consumer, much of these costs can be avoided. In today's context of increasing global competition, organizations explore ways and means to optimize the distribution cost to reach the end consumer in quickest possible time at least cost.

Towards this, the lead is taken again by multinationals.

Oriflame, a Swiss cosmetic manufacturing company, entered the Indian market in the early 1990s with a range of high-priced cosmetic products. Obviously, the products are targeted for upper-income group segment, and the company had opted for direct home-to-home selling through appointed agents who only work on commission. The commission offered to the agents is about 25%, which is much lower than the traditional cost of distribution appointing stockists, distributors, wholesalers and finally retailers to reach the end customers. As the products are directly reaching the ultimate consumers, trade stocks are thus avoided. This mode of direct marketing has not only proved to be little cheaper, but it also helps the company to remain in direct contact with the target consumers, which itself is a great advantage to brand marketers. The negative side of this mode of direct distribution is that the process is slow but sure. This negative aspect of the whole system of direct to home distribution has also been resolved by Amway—a 10 billion-dollar American multinational and largest home-to-home consumer goods company. Amway manufactures daily-use, high-quality household products. In India, they entered by importing the products in the first phase but later on got their products also manufactured through the contract route. They appoint individuals as distributors who work and sell the product directly to end consumers. Direct appointed distributors do not have to invest in the business but earn high commission. These first-layer distributors again appoint others known to them as agents who also get supplies directly from the company and sell the products to homes. These second level of distributors again appoint sub-distributors, who again can extend the chain further through their own known circles and thus the link extends, and as a result the whole multi-level distribution system as we call them spreads like wildfire as long as the link continues to grow. As long as the chain continues to grow, each link in the whole chain benefits from each other's performance and, therefore, making an effective and enterprising individual as distributor can positively impact the growth further and can make it more effective and efficient. A company will have stock points at convenient and strategic locations to service the target market. In MLM, there are advantages as well in the sense that there is no damaged stock, stock return, write-offs, outstanding, trade debtors, doubtful debts and consumer complaints to deal with as opposed to the indirect traditional system of distribution. With absolutely no hassle, companies provide 100% money-back guarantee for dissatisfied customers to ensure reliability and consumer confidence by giving quality assurance and guaranteed satisfaction. Amway has, in fact, written a new chapter by establishing multi-level distribution in India for FMCG products, and others have learnt from their experience and experiments.

COMPLEXITY IN LOGISTICS MANAGEMENT IN INDIA: A CASE OF FMCG INDUSTRY

In the last decade, there were couple of end-to-end TPL providers offering solutions to businesses, but their offering was limited to the B2B model. Even multinational logistics companies such as DHL and FedEx, and local competition such as Gati and Safexpress, are also active in India offering end-to-end solutions to the businesses, of course, at a cost (Baisya 2015a).

In India, we have about 13 million small retail outlets which cater to the consumers. These retailers are serviced by the distributors and wholesalers who are in turn serviced by the manufacturers from their strategically located stock points or warehouses, and depending on the market penetration, businesses can have even over 200 such stock points. TPL companies deliver company stock to those stock points from company manufacturing locations. The competition has forced manufacturers to decentralize the manufacturing operations and go for contract manufacturing routes. Earlier, MNCs were having their own manufacturing facilities, but many of them including Unilever, Reckitt Benckiser, P&G and so on have been increasingly outsourcing their manufacturing operations primarily because it also reduces the logistics cost as contract manufacturing locations can be established close to the distribution point. Companies like P&G are sourcing from their Thailand manufacturing plant for their Indian market requirement to optimize on the global logistics cost.

The bigger the enterprise is, the more complex their logistics issues are. Earlier logistics used to mean transportation (freight) and warehousing, but now we mean it in a more holistic sense. Logistics operators now are required to provide an integrated solution covering raw materials and packaging materials shipment to production plants to warehousing and distribution of finished goods to end consumers. In a dynamic market, demand fluctuates which results in interlocation transfers and retransfers of goods adding to the complexity.

A typical large FMCG company will have about 3–4 company-owned manufacturing locations, about 10–12 contract manufacturers (co-packers), about 8–10 warehouses, over 1,000–1,200 distributors and wholesalers, and 13 million retail universe. Normally, through direct distribution about 1–1.5 million retail outlets are covered, and rest are covered through a redistribution route. For companies like Unilever, direct reach can be little higher. The vendors supplying input to the manufacturing locations will be numerous and that will include even imported raw materials and packaging materials. This will explain the complexity of the logistics management task in a country like India with population of over 1.20 billion.

Depending on the size of the operation and their geographical spread, the distribution will be intensive, selective or exclusive. For example, an organic food brand can have selective distribution designed to cover its target segment, but an FMCG company, manufacturing daily-use products like tea and biscuit, will have to have an intensive distribution network and in the Indian context, the task is very complex.

India as a Country Adds to Complexity

India is a huge country with land mass of 3,287,240 sq. km (largest is Rajasthan with land mass of 342,239 sq. km and smallest is Goa with land mass of 3,702 sq. km) and 29 states. While Rajasthan is the largest in size, population is largest in Uttar Pradesh (200 million). The population of India is 1.25 billion (2.4% of world's land area, but 17.5% of world's population), and over 50% of the population falls in the age group of less than 25 years (a high spending segment in many markets), about 31% in the age group of less than 14 years and about 25% in the age group of 20–35 years. India is thus a young country contrary to developed countries such as Europe, which has an aging population.

The market is so diverse in the sense that demographic and psychographic profiles of the consumers in various regions vary widely. The country is so huge that in one part there could be flood when the other part is facing serious drought conditions. In addition, it also offers sociocultural complexity.

Seventy-two per cent of the population lives in rural areas in 638,000 villages. The rural market is, therefore, very large and still untapped. MNCs and large FMCG companies derive 20–40% revenue from the rural market.

Life expectancy is 69 years; literacy rate is 64%. We are a trillion-dollar (US$2.24 trillion in 2017) economy and GDP growth rate is 6.7%. In India, we have 100 million internet users. You cannot, therefore, ignore India if you want to do business on a global scale.

Entry of Organized Retailers and E-Retailers

Leading global retailers such as Walmart and Tesco have already entered the Indian market through joint ventures or on their own in a big way. Walmart has recently acquired majority stake in Flipkart, the largest e-commerce player in India, to have their entry into e-retailing to fight Amazon outside the USA. Besides, there are host of domestic retailers such as Big Bazaar, Reliance and Aditya Birla Group competing with global retailers. Of late, online retailers like Amazon have also entered the fray competing with local online retailers such as Flipkart and

Snapdeal. These companies have been investing heavily in their business, hoping to make good sense of their investment in the long run. In wholesale trade in cash and carry mode, we have global players like Booker and Metro (Makro) competing with our traditional distributors and wholesalers. Walmart also has 25 Best Price large format wholesale cash and carry stores in India. The success of these ventures into retail and wholesale operations will depend on how effectively they will be able to manage the logistics cost in terms of the following parameters:

- Time to deliver the goods to the customers
- Reducing the inventory in the system without losing out on delivery commitment
- Cost of logistics

These parameters will essentially provide them a competitive advantage as only other parameter that they have to control and manage is procurement efficiency, and major suppliers are large global players and organized retailers or even cash and carry operators do not have any incremental buying power with them (Baisya 2015b).

Distribution Challenge for the Base of the Pyramid Population

According to National Sample Survey Organisation's (NSSO) definition, persons spending less than US$75 per month on consumables fall under the bottom of the pyramid (BOP) of population and according to that definition about 114 million households or 76% of the rural population actually come under BOP. Delivering goods and services to this section of population is really a challenge for the marketers in India. There are three major factors that explain the complexity of distribution for BOP. These can be depicted as shown in Figure 4.3 (Hammond et al. 2008, Huhmann 2004).

FIGURE 4.3 **Distribution Challenges of BOP Market**

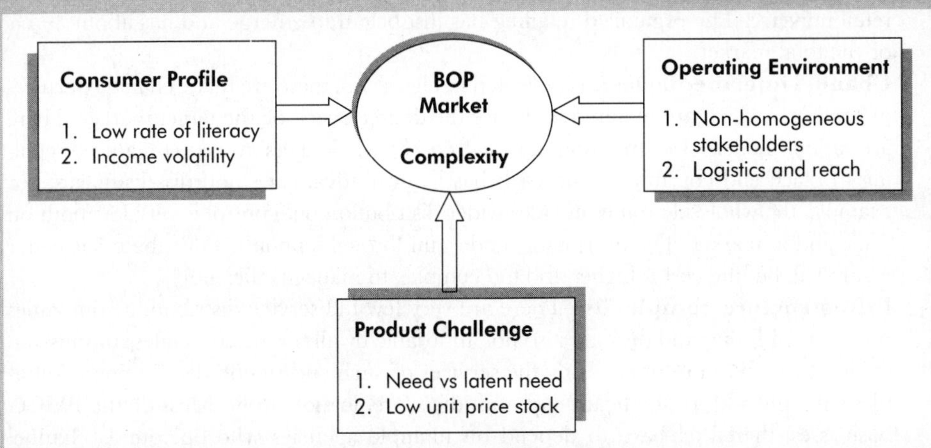

Source: Shukla et al. (2011).

In the rural market which constitutes the BOP segment, the only way to reach is through the redistribution route involving wholesalers who have small rural redistributors to cover rural retail outlets. Very slow-moving vehicles including bullock carts, cycle-rickshaws, auto-rickshaws and even boats running through waterways (as in Kerala) are used to manage the logistics issue. Salesmen using bicycle or even delivering door-to-door customers or village retailers and tobacco shops on foot are also common sights in rural and sometimes even in urban distribution system for FMCG like food or even tobacco products. A unique system is being followed to cover every opportunity to deliver growth in a complex market like India, particularly to face challenges of BOP opportunity. For the BOP segment of the market, marketers need special product pack and pricing keeping in mind the consumer profile in that segment and also for overcoming the distribution challenges offered by the typical environment as well as incremental cost involved in the distribution reach. To penetrate this market, smart logistics is not enough but what is needed to act street smart (Shukla and Bairiganjan 2011).

Drivers of Distribution Complexity

The overall retail market is estimated to be about US$300 billion growing at an average of about 6%. India has been a host of many consumer products of multinationals including giants like Unilever, ITC and Nestlé operating in India for several decades. Still for many, India is relatively a new territory with a number of interrelated factors which make the task of distribution very challenging. These factors are as follows:

Dispersed population: There are 30 cities in India which have over 1 million population, but this constitutes only 15% of the total population. The rural market still constitutes 30–50% of the market. The market again is not homogeneous with many income groups and demographic and psychographic variations.

Retail density: With about 13 million retail outlets, India has one of the highest retailing densities in the world. Mom and pop stores account for about 95% of the total retail universe. The organized retailing has just began to emerge and has about 4–5% of the total market.

Channel intermediaries: As indicated in Figure 4.3, there are many channel partners or associates which are required to ensure the desired reach of the target market. There are various models of distribution starting from the wholesalers' route to organized retailing to reach end consumers, and each has its own advantages and disadvantages. For example, the wholesale route provides wider distribution but control is very low both on trade and in market. The distributor model run through appointed distributors is better controlled, but the cost is higher and too complex to manage efficiently.

Infrastructure complexity: There are very few full-service distribution companies operating in India, and they are also not affordable by all businesses. Unless brands can fetch a very premium price, using the services of such end-to-end distribution companies will only add to significant cost and, therefore, loss of profit. Most of the FMCG businesses, therefore, have to depend on multiple agencies who operate as channel partners in this complex logistics management task.

Consider a case of a typical FMCG like a biscuit manufactured in the northern state of Himachal Pradesh, in Baddi—a tax-free zone where manufacturers prefer to make new investment in production facilities to get excise and sales tax holidays. When this biscuit has to be sold in a place in a state like Tamil Nadu in down south, first the stock is handed over to a local transporter who keeps the stock in his warehouse in Baddi and then this trucker takes almost 15 days to reach the manufacturer's distributor in the state headquarters in Chennai in Tamil Nadu passing through eight states and multiple checkpoints. From the company's distributor in state headquarters, the stock is moved to the district town distributor in a smaller truck or even in a three-wheeler. This district town distributor also gives stock to local wholesalers from whom rural retailers buy, and these wholesalers sell stock to rural distributors and the stock in smaller quantity move either in state transport buses or even in bullock carts. The whole process can take over a month. Only very large companies have been able to reach through their distribution network to markets with say about 50,000 in population. A smaller market uses local transport to reach the rural market, and their efficiency depends on the pull of the product. A company's stock moving from say state headquarters to smaller district-level distributors and rural distributors in state-owned buses, three-wheelers or bullock carts are very popular sights in India. In addition, small orders are also executed by companies through the government-owned postal system in value payable parcels (VPPs) and railways which have much greater reach but are time consuming, having no control over their operations, and therefore no commitment can be given about the time to reach customers. Still goods for PDS such as wheat, rice and salt largely move in rail transport just because state-controlled railways have to get business and not for cost or efficiency reasons.

Unorganized markets: For most of consumer products, the market will be unorganized. Large businesses will work with about 1,000–1,200 appointed distributors. Companies like P&G have made a two-tier distribution system following 80:20 principle, as 20% of the distributors deliver 80% of the sales. They, thus, a decade ago implemented a project called 'Project Golden Eye' and directly sold the goods to company-appointed large distributors (20%) who have under them smaller distributors (80%). With this change and consolidation, P&G has reduced the strength of the sales force drastically and also simplified the complexity in the system. Manufacturers have varying degree of distribution structure designed to meet their objectives.

Choosing the right mix: Organizing an efficient channel of distribution is thus an enormous task for businesses. One has to, therefore, strike a right balance between various models. The evolution of distribution is shown in Figure 4.4, which indicates the degree of sophistication.

In India, we have a mix of all in a typical manufacturing–marketing company of FMCG products.

The more sophisticated the market, the higher the control of the marketers in the distribution system but lower the reach as depicted in Figure 4.4 (Bhalla, Bhattacharya, Singhi and Verma 2007).

FIGURE 4.4 Degree of Sophistication in Distribution

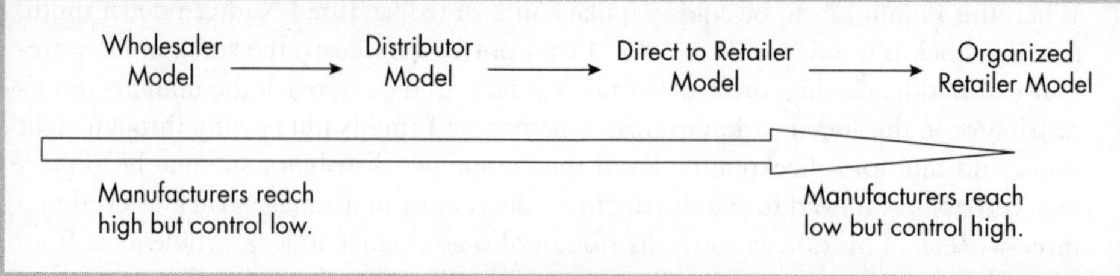

Source: Adapted from a BCG analysis (Mossman and Norton 1965).

Current Scenario: A Mixed System

In order to reduce the transit inventory of goods, constant en-route and live monitoring of vehicles are being used by incorporating devices like RFID or a similar GPS-based monitoring technology. With connectivity being available, this online and real-time monitoring is now being done by select and large TPL providers. However, technology solutions are not offered by all TPL providers, and majority of freight and transport service providers in India are only geared to provide point-to-point transport service. As market is highly fragmented, the requirement of goods in certain areas is low, resulting in not having full load of goods and that adds to the problem, and it goes through multiple handling causing delays in delivery, and as a result, consumers also get relatively older stock compared to high consumption market in metro and mini metros where relatively fresh stock is available. For low-shelf-life goods and for the goods which require refrigerated storage and transport system, cost of distribution is significantly high and efficiency low. Small towns and villages get stock through the redistribution route which is not serviced directly by the manufacturers. The complexity is mounted by a multiple tax regime when goods and services move from one state to another which includes central sales tax (CST), state sales tax (VAT), entry tax and so on, and complexity is more if the goods are excisable such as liquor which has to move in a bonded warehouse while even on the move in a transport vehicle. Typically, FMCG companies have flow of goods as shown in Figure 4.5. With the introduction of GST, tax structure has broadly been rationalized but it is still not uniform and leaves aside some products like liquor which has been kept out of GST purview. While the introduction of GST made the movement of transport vehicles carrying goods faster resulting in reduction in transportation time to some extent, the complexity of the distribution function has still remained because of the huge retail universe spread over in such a diverse country with varying degree of logistics infrastructure that businesses need to service.

Figure 4.5 explains the complexity of the goods distribution system in a long chain intensive distribution category of products like FMCG such as processed foods and daily consumables.

The distribution complexity and cost forces businesses to go for the contract manufacturing route to set up small third-party manufacturing units to cater to the smaller market in a highly dispersed and scattered market like India. And if the product is bulky and light weight or heavy or liquid, the logistics cost would even be much higher in relation to other products. As per the labelling requirement, the name and address of manufacturing locations are to be mentioned

FIGURE 4.5 Logistics Complexity of FMCG Category

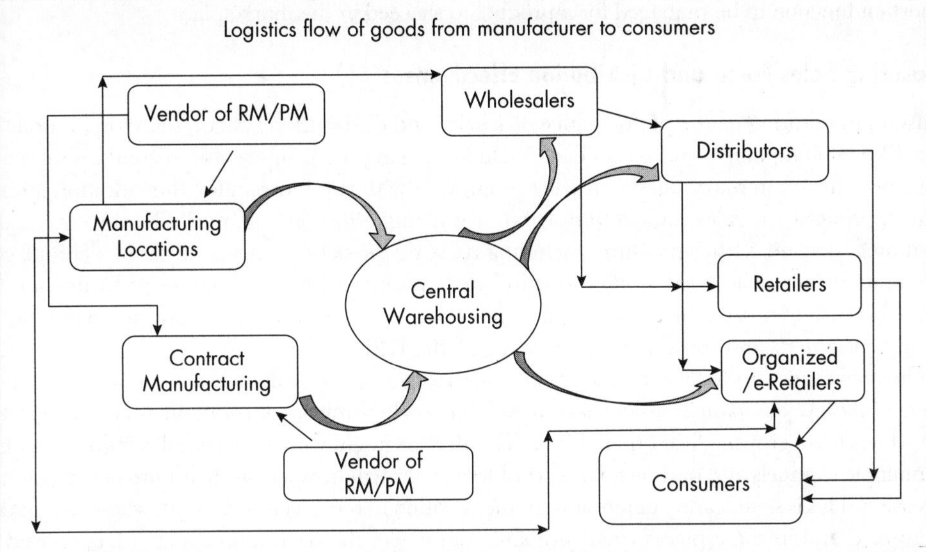

statutorily in the product label. And if one takes a look at the label of a national brand of tea, he/she can see the manufacturing locations which can run up to even 10–15 locations. Liquid products like bottled water or beverages are also manufactured in multiple locations to save on the distribution and logistics costs.

Developing Efficient Sales and Distribution Structure

It takes years for businesses to develop an efficient sales and distribution infrastructure. Successful companies give as much attention in keeping right distributors with appropriate infrastructure and goodwill in the trade to work for them for long as they give in appointing senior employees. Companies that provide training programmes, coaching and sales support to their distributors to perform better in the marketplace when compared to their competitors are expected to perform better. Sales force effectiveness is thus important for companies to derive competitive advantages.

Having an efficient and well-entrenched distribution system in India holds the key to success. Many MNCs have failed on that ground and many were seen to acquire local companies simply to get the control over the distribution system. For example, Coca-Cola acquired local beverages company Parle Beverages only to get the control over and entry into the local beverage distribution system which takes years to build, and Coca-Cola acquired it paying a huge price. Coca-Cola left India in 1977 and at that time, it had 26 franchised bottlers and they were controlling over 80% of the soft beverage market in India. Second to Coke was Parle Beverages and its subsidiary Bisleri which owned the rest 20%. When Coke decided to come back again post liberalization, the market structure reversed by then and Parle was controlling close to 75% market in the same product category and Coke found the acquisition of Parle brands and business the best route to get access to local distribution when their arch-rival PepsiCo was already there well entrenched. Even PepsiCo also acquired Dukes from Pandoles to get entry into soda water distribution. Distribution is the most important function to be managed for a product to succeed in the marketplace.

Measuring Sales Force and Distribution Effectiveness

Constant monitoring of the performance of a sales and distribution system, therefore, is done by most FMCG companies, and parameters include tracking the primary and secondary sales and consumer offtakes (tertiary sales) market segment wise with rural–urban focus in addition to sales volume, profit of the sales route and distributor ranking, order fill rate, pack fill rate, cost of distribution and so on. Other measures including tracking the debtors, age analysis of debtors, cost of operations per unit of sales, sales growth rate, customer-wise sales volume and value, profitability by customer segment or even customer wise, new customer creation and retention of existing customers, and sustainability are some of the KPIs.

The magnitude of the task to manage the logistics in FMCG companies as can be seen is enormous. Only few companies which have a well-entrenched mixed distribution system to get the desired reach are growing faster than others. The BOP segment which is a complex segment requiring multiple channels and partners offers considerable growth prospect as their purchasing power is increasing. This is significantly different from the situation in the developed world, where the market is saturated and in some places even shrinking and where the distribution system has evolved to reach every prospect. But doing business in India requires different skills and knowledge. Learning that or acquiring that is essential for success. Only having a smart logistics solution is not enough. In India, you need to act smarter. Otherwise, you will only scrape through the surface of the total market opportunity and can never be a partner to take advantage of all-inclusive growth.

The sociopolitical conditions including climatic conditions in various markets in India including the consumer buying behaviour are so different that each market requires separate attention. The market is heterogeneous—there is thus no one uniform solution that will work in all markets. Each market needs separate attention for finding a solution, as it will offer different degrees of complexity to the business depending on their products profile, characteristics and target market's requirement.

Source: Baisya (2015a).

CHAPTER SUMMARY

Warehousing is a very critical function to be managed effectively which determines the productivity and cost-efficiency of the entire supply chain. A warehouse is required to be located in a strategic location from the consideration of providing ideal level of customer service at least cost which is a prerequisite for survival in a dynamic market environment. Warehousing, therefore, plays a key role in distribution management, and the efficiency of distribution management determines the success of the business itself. Distribution management is an area that demands the attention of the top senior-level management team, and key decisions are taken at the highest level of the corporation. The decisions related to the distribution strategy and performance criteria are taken by the senior management team in the business. The chapter deals with the functions and activities undertaken in a warehouse as well as types of warehouses and which type suits for what kind and size of business. Warehouse design and construction for efficient warehouse management, warehouse cost, activities and warehouse location decision criteria are discussed with examples. Strategies and planning of taking warehousing decisions as well as WMSs and warehouse operation are also discussed. WMS implementation strategies and advantages as well as challenges are discussed in detail. Warehouse performance metrics and factors influencing the performance of a warehouse are also discussed in detail. Criticality of warehouse management and their implication on distribution performance are discussed. Distribution challenges and complexity are discussed particularly in the context of the Indian market environment. Finally, a case of FMCG products' distribution is discussed to explain the typical complexity and challenges and how those are tackled by the marketers of FMCG products. Also, distribution management task, scope, organization, channel management and channel partners role, distribution cost, performance criteria and what it takes for efficient distribution management are discussed in this chapter.

DISCUSSION QUESTIONS

1. Discuss the various functions of warehousing. What are the key indicators of efficient warehousing management?
2. What are the different types of warehousing that the industry uses and for which conditions those are preferred?
3. Discus the key design criteria for the layout of a warehouse for efficient operation. What constitutes warehousing cost?
4. What are the key activities being performed in a warehouse and what are the factors that influence the effectiveness of warehouse performance?
5. Discuss the advantages of implementing WMS and when can WMS be advantageous?
6. Discuss the key performance matrix of a typical warehouse and the productivity improvement tools.
7. Define distribution objective and scope. What are the various distribution channels available for FMCG products? How are channel partners selected?
8. Discuss the channel distribution strategy for a new product to be introduced under consumer durable category. Also design a distribution organization for this product.
9. Discuss the distribution policy and KPIs of the effectiveness of a distribution system. What are the CSFs?
10. How is distribution cost calculated? What factors impact the distribution network design?

REFERENCES

Baisya, R. K. 2015a. 'Challenges in Logistics Management—I: Complexity of Covering BOP Market'. *Processed Food Industry* 18 (3, January): 9–11.

———. 2015b. 'Challenges in Logistics Management—II: Choosing the Right Distribution Mix and Building Efficient Distribution System'. *Processed Food Industry* 18 (4, February): 10–12.

Bhalla, Vikram, Arindam Bhattacharya, Abheek Singhi, and Sharad Verma. 2007. *Creating a Distribution Advantage in India*. India: Boston Consulting Group Publications.

Hammond, Allen L., William J. Kramer, Robert S. Katz, Julia T. Tran, and Courtland Walker. 2008. *The Next 4 Billion: Market Size and Business Strategy at the Base of the Pyramid*. Washington, DC: World Resource Institute and International Finance Corporation.

Huhmann, S. 2004. 'Tapping India's Rural Market'. *Journal of Student Research:* 92–99. http://www.uwstout.edu/rs/2004/article1.pdf (accessed on 20 August 2019).

Mossman F., and N. Norton. 1965. *Logistics of Distribution System*, 3. Boston, MA: Allyn & Bacon.

Shukla, Sachin, and Sreyamsa Bairiganjan. 2011. *The Base of Pyramid Distribution Challenge*. IFMR Research. Centre for Development Finance.

BIBLIOGRAPHY

Eisenhart, Tom. 1990. 'Drawing a Map to Better Sales'. *Business Marketing* (January): 59–61.

Maher, P. 1984. 'National Account Marketing: An Essential Strategy, or Prima Donna Selling?' *Business Marketing* (December): 34–45

McDonald, M., and B. Rogers. 1995. *Key Account Management*. London: Butterworth-Heinemann.

Millman, T. 1996. 'Global Key Account Management and System Selling'. *International Business Review* 5 (6): 631–645.

Millman, T., and K. Wilson. 1995. From Key Account Selling to Key Account Management'. *Journal of Marketing Practice* 1 (1): 9–21.

———. 2001. 'Structuring and Positioning Global Account Management Programmes: A Typology'. *Journal of Selling and Major Account Management* 4 (1): 11–38.

Moss, C. D. 1979. 'Industrial Salesman as a Source of Marketing Intelligence'. *European Journal of Marketing* 13 (3): 94–102.

Tally, W. J. 1961, January. 'How to Design Sales Territories'. *Journal of Marketing* 25 (3): 7–13.

5

Managing Inventory for Satisfying Customer Demand

LEARNING OBJECTIVES

Section I: Managing Inventory to Satisfy Customer Demand

- Understand why businesses need inventory and how it impacts business performance
- Identify types and classification of inventories and inventory cycle
- Explain inventory cost, control and management
- Understand the replenishment of inventory, EOQ, business responses to excess stock as well as to stock-out situations
- Recognize the impact of trade discount and trade promotions on cycle inventory

Section II: Dealing with Demand Uncertainty in Supply Chain

- Describe different measures of product availability and key concerns to manage them
- Appreciate the role of safety stock in terms of managing the supply chain performance
- Identify the various factors that influence the required level of safety inventory
- Detect the ways and means of reducing the levels of safety stock without compromising product availability
- Understand the impacts of uncertainties in a supply chain and estimating safety stock

SECTION I
MANAGING INVENTORY TO SATISFY CUSTOMER DEMAND

INTRODUCTION

The inventory management policy of any organization has to be designed to hold minimum inventory at all stock points including stocks of input materials and finished stocks in manufacturing locations, intermediate stock points and warehouses as well as trade stock of distributors and retailers to ensure servicing customer demands on real-time basis, which would mean that there is no stock-out situation so that sales is not lost as well as there is no extra stock increasing the working capital requirement in the business. Inventory has to, therefore, be linked with sales order processing, and sales order processing has to be linked with the production planning and procurement. The problem starts when the sales order does not match the real-term consumer offtake as determined by the sales happening from the front-end retailers in any business. Retailers are selling directly to the end customers, and that is exactly the measure of the real term sales. Corporations many a time lose out on that focus for not knowing the exact sales to the end consumers. The longer the channel length is, the higher the trade inventory or even total inventory in the system will be. The trade channel, therefore, has to be efficient and short to make the task of inventory management more controllable.

All organizations have an inventory policy determined on the basis of several criteria which include service frequency, consumer demand, the cost the product(s), replenishment time, industry and trade practices, commercial terms to be implanted and enforced, consumer offtake data as revealed from the company's own sales report as well as retail audit data which companies subscribe from AC Nielsen, seasonality of demand, company's own marketing and promotional policy including activities during a particular period which can spur the demand, production and procurement lead time, manufacturing plant capacity and so on. In spite of the best intention, inventory level is always seen to be a matter of great concern for all companies.

The production plant has to run as per its optimal capacity, otherwise manpower and other overheads will not be fully utilized. The manufacturing plant capacity also has to be aligned with the demand forecast. If the capacity utilization of the plant becomes an issue, the cost of the production will go up because underutilization of the capacity will lead to underabsorption of the overhead expenditure, which will impact both SCM performance and productivity. Managing inventory, therefore, is very critical to the management of the SCM performance as it has to optimize several factors, both controllable and uncontrollable. Efficient and effective inventory management requires not only the reliable and historical data of the business but also the experience of the operations manager who is entrusted for delivering the key objectives and goals of SCM performance. Inventory management also requires close coordination between departments in the business, including production, distribution, warehousing and sales departments, within the business, and customers who need to be serviced effectively, outside the business. It is therefore a very challenging task.

INVENTORY MANAGEMENT

Inventory constitutes the stock levels of raw, packaging material and other input material such as standard spares and also the finished goods, as well as work in progress (WIP) carried in the business to service the demand in the market. More often than not, the inventory in a business is disproportionately higher than the required or optimal level, resulting in very high working capital locked up in business impacting the performance of the organization itself. Managing inventory effectively to avoid high level of stock of input material and finished goods is therefore the key to improve business profitability. Most of the time, management is not well informed about the inventory it is carrying, which leads to high level of stock tied up in the system costing a huge sum of money. In such a situation, company also often faces write off, wastage and obsolescence and expiry or even redundant stock, particularly when a model and or design of a product is changed or when a product formulation is changed and earlier product is substituted by a new product.

The inventory, therefore, is the material that a firm obtains in advance of need, holds until it is needed and then used, consumes, incorporates into a product, sells or otherwise disposes of. A business inventory is temporary in nature. In that respect, inventories are stock of any kind such as fuel and lubricants, spare parts and semi-processed materials to be stored for future use mainly in the process of production, or these can be known as the ideal resource of any kind with some economic value.

In a supply chain, one of the key variables which have to be managed is inventory. The inventory includes a vast spectrum of materials that are being transferred, stored, consumed, produced, packaged or sold in one way or the other during a firm's normal course of business. The planning, storing, moving and accounting for inventory are the bases for all logistics. Inventory has a financial value, which for accounting purposes is considered a floating asset. However, it may be very difficult to convert physical inventory into liquid assets; hence, the inventory is a very risky investment. The problem of liquidating excess inventory normally results from the very basic reasons of overestimating the current demand. The demand can be wrongly estimated, but sometimes businesses deliberately target a higher level of market share to be achieved and plan the production and sales to achieve the higher level of performance but in reality they might even fail to achieve the target resulting in stock pile-up and loss of profitability. It has been seen that sometimes it becomes an unmanageable proportion.

All businesses want to improve the performance of their operations over the previous year. As such, it can be noticed that at year-end, sales figures are abnormally high. In order to show the year-end closing performance of the business better, businesses often overtrade and invoice more stock than the requirement of the market in the last quarter of the financial year and more so in the last month of the year closing. For example, businesses are seen to invoice large stocks to their distributors before the close of the year on credit basis. As this is not aligned to the customer requirement, the distributor does not pay for the stock and agrees only to take a book entry with a clear understanding that the company will take that excess stock back after the close of the year. The last day of the year is always seen for all companies to sell a very large stock to clear the inventory as the company's account will show better result with lower stock. For this purpose, companies even resort to extra promotional drives to liquidate the stock by giving a discount. The excess stock that was sold stock but which distributors could not sell is then often brought back to the company's warehouse or stock point. This is what we can call pseudo-sales and helps only dressing the books of accounts. Such practice can only create distortion in the level of inventory. While year-end inventory will be lower than actual, soon it will show a higher value because of stock return.

If sales can be achieved with minimal or no inventory, that would be the ideal. Most of the businesses do not have any idea how much inventory the business is carrying at any given point of time and as such, the management sometimes wakes up with a shock when they come to know about huge stock that they are carrying in inventory in the factory, warehouse and also trade channel. The retail industry normally takes physical inventory at regular intervals to manage the stock better just because the entire profit of the operation normally depends on the efficient management of store inventory. In spite of using ERP packages for managing the store operations, the stock discrepancy still happens because of pilferage that are happening within the retail stores which often go undetected in spite of having a CCTV monitoring system in place. The book inventory and physical inventory often do not match. The organized retailers take about 1–1.5%

of the stock which can disappear from the system as acceptable due to pilferage, and there is a constant surveillance and monitoring of stock movement to control the pilferage. Anything in terms of reduction of losses due to pilferage can be considered as an incremental profit straight sitting at the bottom line of the profit and loss statement. From all these considerations and issues, managing inventory assumes additional importance.

INVENTORY MANAGEMENT GOAL

Inventories represent the largest single investment in assets as current assets for many manufacturers, wholesalers and retailers. Inventory investment represents over 20% of the total assets of manufacturers and more than 50% of the total assets of wholesalers and retailers. Thus, one goal in operations is to keep the level of inventory in the supply chain as low as possible and to free up funds for other productive purposes.

Holding the inventories is connected with significant costs. Despite all the efforts and technological innovations, inventories are often still the asset with lowest return in the company. Arguably, majority of companies hold 25–40% more inventories than actually needed. Unreasonably high inventory levels lower the company's profit and return on assets. The stated goal or objective, therefore, is to reduce or minimize the level of the inventory without any loss of sales. For some products such as seasonal products and food products, loss of sales would mean permanent loss and that cannot be retrieved. Moreover, in such situations, your customers will also shift to your competition, resulting in losing a customer for non-performance and non-delivery, which itself is a big loss to the company. It takes a long time and effort to create a customer and, therefore, losing a customer will always be considered as a big loss for the business. It takes six times more effort to create a new customer, and by switching to your competition if your customer is satisfied, bringing him/her back will be all the more difficult. The goal of inventory management, thus, is to manage inventory without facing a stock-out situation but also not to overstock.

WHY DO WE NEED INVENTORY?

Ideally, inventories should be as low as possible or if we can manage JIT inventory, it is excellent as in that case we can eliminate the inventory altogether. Although that will be an ideal situation, it cannot be possible to manage it in all situations and, therefore, in business we invariably need to have inventories of all kinds. There are several reasons of having inventories and these include the following:

- **Improves customer service:** Ready in stock can make faster delivery for any customer orders. Delivering immediately on receipt of customer order or reducing the lead time of customer servicing helps in improvement in customer service, and hence also satisfaction. In FMCG, retailing is normally done with ready stock so that orders from the retailers are executed immediately and this also eliminates the possibility of the retailers changing their mind later on and cancel orders.
- **Provides immediacy in product availability:** Having inventory means a product is always or even immediately available.

- **Encourages production, purchase and transportation economies:** Inventory policy and holding also trigger other associated activities such as transportation, procurement and production.
- **Allows for long production runs:** Higher inventory would mean larger production capacity utilization.
- **Takes advantage of price-quantity discounts:** Buying larger quantity of input materials can help getting quantity discounts.
- **Allows for transport economies from larger shipment sizes:** A larger volume shipment can be more cost effective in terms of transportation cost.
- **Acts as a hedge against price changes:** A higher level of inventory would also mean a hedge against any fluctuation or increase in price of the input and thus saves on any eventual input cost increase.
- **Allows purchasing to take place under most favourable price terms:** If the inventory of finished goods is adequate, businesses can buy the input material at most attractive price and can also avoid purchasing under pressure arising out of reaching zero inventory situation.
- **Protects against uncertainties in demand and lead times:** With an adequate inventory level, businesses are protected from any uncertainties in demand and lead time of delivery.
- **Provides a measure of safety to keep operations running when demand levels and lead times cannot be known for sure:** Inventory also provides adequate safety stock in uncertain situations in the market.
- **Acts as a hedge against contingencies and buffers against unusual events such as strikes, fires and other disruptions in the supply line:** Inventory also acts as buffer stock in terms of calamity, disaster as well as other types of disruptions in production and operations such as riots, fires, strikes or even any other sociopolitical upheaval and uncertainties.
- **Buffers against such events disruptions in supply:** If the critical material suppliers are either facing a difficult situation or acting tough because of a monopoly supplier, a comfortable level of inventory can provide sufficient breathing time to face such situations and still can continue the supply line.

INVENTORY IMPACTS BUSINESS PERFORMANCE

Inventory blocks capital in the form of working asset. It is therefore a cost to the business and hence impacts performance of the business. The best way to run a business is without having any inventory and, if possible, on 'made to order' basis or as JIT inventory to be delivered which is produced against a confirmed customer order. In some business categories in B2B model, this may be possible. However, it is almost impossible to operate with zero inventory unless businesses are willing to forego the sales and lose customers under certain situations. Businesses can decide to trade off the cost of holding buffer stock to address certain situations and not servicing or accepting customer order beyond a cut-off date, keeping the bottom-line performance of the business as sole criterion for decision. It is also possible to manage with very low–almost zero level inventory for short supply items. Normally, short-supply items are overstocked by customers and, therefore, possibility of losing a customer for non-delivery is very low. Such items are also normally monopoly products; thus, in those situations one can take a policy decision of either 'made to order' or 'JIT' inventory.

But it may be impossible to manage in the FMCG category without having any inventory. The level and quantum of stock in inventory depends on the type of distribution channel chosen for distribution as well as redistribution of products and also width and depth of distribution. And that will block a large resource in working capital. Efficient management of working capital, thus, holds the key to reduce the negative impact of inventory holding cost on business. Inventory utilizes capital resources that might be possible to put into better use in the business. It also diverts management's attention away from careful planning and control of supply and distribution channel.

In many European countries which are small having only a couple of million population and as such customers' base is small and are serviced through the organized large format retail outlets and also Cash & Carry wholesale format. These stores can be directly connected to the company's distribution system, and a daily production programme can be linked with daily sales from these stores which can be replenished on the next working day. In this situation, a procurement programme is also linked with the production plans of the day, and vendors are contracted to make the input material to be made available well in time for the day's production to start. This JIT line can be managed in an environment where the information of the customer requirement is made available on real-time basis to be synchronized with daily production, procurement and customer services and associated logistics issues. But in a complex, diverse market like India or in other Asian countries, having JIT production lines is almost impossible to practise. We have discussed this complexity in Chapter 4.

TYPES OF INVENTORY

There are many types of inventories. The form of inventory depends upon the type of concern or business. All types of inventories do not require same treatment, and therefore, policies with regard to each may also differ. Inventory can be classified based on business requirement for better control and management for least cost of holding the inventory and better supply chain performance. Broadly, one approach of classifying types of inventories could be based on the type of use of the item(s) to be stored or stocked. Based on the type of use, the classification can be as follows:

- **Raw material inventories:** These are raw materials and other supplies, parts and components, which enter into the product during the production process and generally form part of the product.
- **Packaging material inventories:** These can include all types of packing material required to be used in the manufacture or production of an item such as primary packaging, secondary packaging, tertiary packaging and shipping cartons.
- **WIP inventories:** These are semi-finished, WIP and partly finished products formed at various stages of production.

- **Spare part inventories:** Maintenance, repairs and operating supplies which are consumed during the production process and generally do not form part of the product itself are referred to as spare part inventories.
- **Finished goods' inventories:** These are complete finished products ready for sale. In a manufacturing unit, they are the final output of the production process. Finished goods are intended as ready for sale. These itself can be further classified as follows:
  - *Movement inventories:* These include inventory for items that are held due to a process delay while some inventory is moved from one location to another.
  - *Lot size inventories:* From considerations like quantity price discounts, shipping costs, setup costs, etc., make it more economical to offer inventory in one economic lot.
  - *Anticipation inventories:* These are stock or inventories built in excess anticipating sudden levels of demand and are kept on hand to deal with uncertainty in customer demand. Fluctuations in buying activity or seasonal demand or even demand arising out of unusual activities in the market can lead to complexity in inventory management and to be managed under demand uncertainties.
  - *Fluctuation inventories:* It is an inventory system in which the balance in the inventory account is adjusted for the units sold each time a sale is made.
  - *Physical inventories:* It is a manual count of the on-hand inventory. Physical inventory thus would mean the actual count on a given date or at the end of a period.
  - *Transit inventories:* These are inventories of items between two stock points or points of use.

ALTERNATIVE APPROACH FOR CLASSIFICATION OF INVENTORIES

Inventory classification can have several approaches, and these approaches depend on the company's primary accounting and recording approach so that data can be captured accordingly from the corresponding location where physical inventories are lying, and in what form and for what period that will facilitate the accounting and recording process and system software that are being used by the company. Corporations can even have their own approaches to facilitate accounting and make stock management easier for them. There are many such approaches but broadly, we can have the following approaches for classification also:

By the position in company's production/operation process: This facilitates in locating the inventory in relation to production and operation processes of the company and can include the raw materials, packaging materials, WIP and finished goods as well as goods purchased for resale and advance payments to suppliers (suppliers holding inventory on business owner's cost). This approach has been discussed in the preceding section.

By the financial accounting rules: This approach deals with and facilitates accurate accounting of the inventories under a specific class. This facilitates the management to take an action on those classes where the inventory level is higher than projected or anticipated.

- **Cycle stock:** These are inventories for satisfying usual (predicted) demand between replenishments (receiving new ordered quantities).

- **In-transit inventories/pipeline stock:** These are items that are en route from one location to another. They may be considered part of cycle stock even when they are not available for sale or shipment until after they arrive at the destination.
- **Safety or buffer stock:** It is held in excess of cycle stock because of uncertainty in demand or lead time. The amount depends on the extent of demand fluctuation, replenishment lead time and planned availability level for customers. It makes the majority of inventory in the typical logistic system.
- **Speculative stock:** It is held for some reasons other than satisfying the current demand such as getting quantity discounts, forecasted purchase price increase or materials shortage and protecting against strikes/natural disasters. Production economies may also lead to the manufacture of products at times other than when they are in demand.
- **Seasonal stock:** It is a form of speculative stock that involves accumulation of inventory before a seasonal period begins like festival season or say harvesting period in agriculture.
- **Near-expiry stock:** It is the stock that is nearing expiry and therefore needs to be sold on priority basis through special promotion or even price reduction and, if necessary, directly to the end consumers bypassing the channel partners. Near-expiry stock can be sold by heavily discounting the price or can even be donated for a cause. Pharmaceutical and food manufacturers are often seen donating the near expiry stock to NGOs who in turn redistribute that to the needy and poor for immediate consumption and use which helps them to create a goodwill as well as a positive image for the company.
- **Expired stock:** The expired stock sometimes is possible to be reprocessed to make it good for sale again. Sometimes and for some categories of products, a small quantity of the expired stock is added to the fresh batch of production without compromising the quality of the final products. Every organization has its unique method and policy that it follows to deal with such inventory permitted under law instead of just throwing it out as useless stock. However, under normal circumstances, expired stock needs to be written off impacting the financial performance of the company. Sometimes, the out-of-warranty or expired stock requires special treatment for disposal as waste which is an additional cost for the business. This is true for stock which is hazardous in nature and therefore cannot be directly disposed of without special treatment of processing.
- **Dead stock:** These are the items for which no demand has been registered for some specified period of time (obsolete products, demand season ended, fashion changed rendering existing stock out of fashion and so on). Dead stock needs a special disposal plan and depending on the products is sometimes sold as scrap or waste. When the design of a model of a product changes in the marketplace, the inventory related to that older model is normally a dead stock. Such things happen in business, although companies make a transition plan from one model to a newer model to minimize such dead stock. But even a best plan for such transition will also leave behind some dead stock to be dealt with in the best possible manner. If nothing else, dead stock can be sold as scrap material.

It can be mentioned here that all companies have their own methods of dealing with dead stock and out-of-warranty stock as well as for scrap or waste disposal which are approved and accepted as standard norms of accounting practices.

Inventory has a significant impact on the material flow time, meaning the time that elapses between the point at which material enters a supply chain as input material and the point from where it exits at the time of delivery to the customers in the supply chain. In a supply chain, sales throughput normally dictates the inventory level. For example, sales throughput S, material flow time T and inventory I can be correlated by Little's law as follows:

$$I = ST \tag{5.1}$$

If an organized retail outlet like Flipkart or Walmart holds 150,000 units in inventory and sells 1,500 units everyday, Little's law tells us that the average unit will spend 150,000/1,500 = 100 days in inventory. If, however, the flow time is reduced, the inventory holding will also reduce. For example, if flow time is reduced to say 50 days from 100 days while sales throughput is still constant, the inventory holding will reduce to 75,000 units. This is valid only when inventory and sales throughput have consistent units.

An example: Reckitt Benckiser has very fast-moving products in its portfolio such as Dettol antiseptic liquid, Harpic toilet cleaners and Mortein household insecticide. It also has slow-moving products such as Brasso and Silvo metal polishers. Dettol and Harpic require fast response time and the sales happen more or less in predicted lines as per budgeted sales forecast. For fast-moving, regular selling, high-volume products, inventory is maintained at all stock points and in company-operated and -managed warehouses, whereas for slow moving products which sell in select locations such as Brasso and Silvo, the inventory level is low. Sometimes these products are produced once or twice in a year to be sold throughout the year, which is possible if the product has a very long shelf life like the one mentioned in this example. However, for low shelf-life, low-demand products, a better policy is to produce only against confirmed customer order.

Amazon sells a wide variety of books. Almost all authors and publishers prefer to keep their books stocked in Amazon. Some books are in high demand whereas others are not and therefore are slow moving. Bestselling books are kept in all regional stock points and warehouses so that they are closer to the customer locations and the response time to service the order is low. But for slow-moving books, the inventory is not kept and books are procured from the publisher and distributors to execute the order on receipt of the customer order.

These days, some of the best-known publishers like Taylor & Francis take very small print run. And even if the books are marketed or launched globally, they are printed on demand and sold.

From these examples, you can understand that both inventory levels and locations have a direct relationship with the product demand and material flow time.

COMPONENTS OF INVENTORY DECISIONS

For creating the most efficient and responsive supply chain, operations managers must take decisions related to major inventory types.

CYCLE INVENTORY

Cycle inventory is in fact the average inventory used to satisfy the demand between receipts of supplier shipments. As such, the size of the cycle inventory is a result of the production, transportation or purchase of material in large lots. Businesses normally produce or purchase in large lots to benefit from the economies of scale in the production, procurement and also transportation processes. But with increase in lot size, holding cost also increases. Supply chain managers have to, therefore, balance or optimize these two apparently opposing impacts from a careful cost–benefit analysis. The basic trade-off a manager will face is the cost of holding larger lots of inventory when the cycle inventory is high against the cost of ordering more frequently when the cycle inventory is low.

SAFETY INVENTORY

Safety inventory is held to cater to the excess demand than what has been anticipated. It helps if the demand is more than expectation and thus acts as buffer against any uncertain situation. A prediction is often not correct and if a reasonably reliable futuristic prediction is possible, we do not need to have safety stock. In that environment, cycle inventory would be enough. Companies normally keep safety stock only to satisfy an unexpectedly high demand. But it is not easy to determine that how much safety stock is enough to be considered as safe. If there are past records of unusual seasonal demand, then one can go by the past experience to avoid losing sales when all of a sudden the demand spurts or increases which would otherwise mean that determining the safety inventory involves making a trade-off between the cost of having too much inventory and the cost of losing sales for not having enough inventory.

SEASONAL INVENTORY

Some products are highly seasonal such as soft drinks and ice cream. For these products in a tropical country like India, the demand significantly increases during summer months. Also, during the festival season like Diwali in India and Christmas in Western countries or even during Eid in Muslim countries, there is a sudden increase in demand. There are two ways companies can manage this situation of significant higher demand during a season. One is to produce a higher amount in the lean season and sell the inventory during the peak season. The other is to create capacity of the production plant to take care of the incremental demand during the season. In the first option, there will be some incremental cost of holding stock piled up during the lean season. And in the second option, there will be incremental capital cost to be incurred for setting up larger production plants. Another option could be to source from third parties during the peak season. If the stock is build up during the lean season, it is likely to get aged when it is offered for sale during the peak season and for some products like food products, consumers do not like to buy old stock. However, for a consumer durable category, building stock for sale during the lean season is an acceptable practice. Still there are products for which input material is available only during a certain period of the year to be sold throughout the year. For example, marine products—a particular type of fish is caught during the season but is sold throughout the year, all over the world. The fish is processed and frozen during the season for meeting the demand during the whole year till the time next catching season arrives. Such practices are true for many other product categories as well.

LEVEL OF PRODUCT AVAILABILITY

A high level of product availability ensures a high level of responsiveness, but it also increases the cost of holding a higher level of inventory. The level of product availability is actually the fraction of the demand that can be served from the inventory of the product. Although the low level of product availability lowers inventory holding costs, it increases the fraction of customers who are not serviced on time. The trade-off for determining the level of product availability, therefore, is the cost of inventory to increase the product availability and the loss from not serving the customers on time.

INVENTORY COST MANAGEMENT

Inventory is the single largest cost that businesses incur in terms of working asset. Inventory, therefore, needs to turn around as fast as possible, and we thus consider sales to working asset ratio as an important parameter to be monitored. We also need to ensure that the inventory which has entered the system first has to also exit first following the FIFO principle. Most of the companies do not have any idea about how much money is locked up in various kinds of inventories at various locations. It gets revealed only when physical stock audit is done. To manage the inventory more effectively, corporations have to know the location-wise inventory and also the type of inventory which constitutes the inventory holding cost.

Inventory costs are traditionally categorized into four basic cost groups:

1. **Purchase cost:** For items that are purchased from outside the firms, this is usually the unit price that the firm pays to its vendor. As an item moves through the logistics system of the firms, its purchase cost in the inventory analysis should reflect its fully landed cost, which would mean the cost to acquire and to move the item to that point in the system from where it will be used.
2. **Ordering cost:** In addition to the per unit purchase cost, there is usually an additional cost which is incurred whenever we order, record and/or replenish the inventory. If we produce items internally, then there will be an organization set-up cost. This happens because we have to shut down the manufacturing line, and change over and reconfigure the line to make a specific item. This is the cost involved with the processing of the order, involving paying the bill, auditing and so forth.
3. **Holding cost:** It is the cost that accrues due to the actual holding of the inventory over a period of time. Many different kinds of costs can be considered as holding cost. The key characteristics of holding cost vary with the amount of inventory being held and the time that the inventory is held.

   The holding cost can also be classified as follows: Storage cost or cost of space, damaged spoiled goods cost and handling labour and insurance cost.
4. **Storage cost:** When a demand arises which cannot be satisfied from available inventory, an inventory shortage occurs.

Purchase, ordering and holding costs can be thought of as the costs of having inventories, while shortage cost results for not having inventory, or for not having enough inventory at the right place and at the right time.

INVENTORY CONTROL

Inventory control is the process of managing materials inventory of right quality and quantity to be made available as and when required at least cost without facing any stock-out situation resulting in loss of either production or sales. The desired level of inventory can be neither high nor low because a high level of inventory will lead to an increase in carrying cost, while a low level of inventory will lead to an increase in ordering cost.

The main criterion for managing inventory is deciding on an inventory policy regarding the level of inventory to be maintained based on the classification and types of inventory, the buffer stock as well as reorder points (ROPs) and lead time and EOQ. Periodically, an inventory control policy is reviewed to see how the policy is working in terms of cost and availability in real life.

The primary objective of inventory control is to ensure smooth flow of stock in terms of supplying the required quantity and quality of materials at minimal cost and investment locked up in inventory. The control processes must also take care of the fluctuating demand and production, providing adequate flexibility and minimizing the associated risk and uncertainty as well as obsolescence.

EFFECTIVE INVENTORY MANAGEMENT

Inventory management means the methods that are used for organizing, holding and replenishing stock. The main purpose of inventory management is minimizing differences between customers' demand and availability of items. These differences are caused by three factors: customers' demand fluctuations, suppliers' delivery time fluctuations and inventory control accuracy.

The main goal is to keep the inventories on an optimal level, without stock-outs and excesses. For this, two controversial but simultaneously mutually dependent tasks, such as the loss of sales due to stock-out situation and cost of holding additional inventory to meet sudden demand of customers, should be solved. It is necessary to have enough inventories to fulfil orders of external and internal clients to satisfy their requirements.

ORDER FILL RATE AND PACK FILL RATE

Usually, customer service level is measured as availability or by order fill rate. Businesses normally keep track of order fill rate and pack fill rate by having a budgetary objective to achieve a target order and pack fill rate and every year trying to improve upon that target. Many have achieved above 99% of order and pack fill rate targets and have well-controlled inventory and demand management systems in place.

By order fill rate we mean that the customer order in terms of value and volume has been satisfied. When the inventory of a particular item is not there, the order value can still be managed by replacing one type of stock by another if that is acceptable to the customers. Sometimes customers are persuaded to take another product in place of the product that they ordered, and they normally accept such requests for maintaining the relationship with the business and even sometimes when the product offered in place of the product that customer ordered is a fast-moving product and is in demand.

But marketers' and business objective is not only to fill the order but also the pack. By pack fill rate we normally mean that the customer order is fulfilled not only in terms of product types and categories as well as the value of the order but also in terms of SKUs that the customer ordered. And as said earlier, businesses target to achieve above 90% or even 99% pack fill rate, and to achieve that kind of perfection both demand forecast and production planning and control need to be managed well, and there has to be enough flexibility built into the process to achieve that targeted pack fill rate. Businesses who do not achieve such high order fill and pack fill rates try to improve upon these criteria and budget that target to be achieved every year as an improvement target.

To minimize inventory carrying costs, a trade-off between the cost of capital tied up and business profitability has to be achieved following EOQs and timing. This would mean having an accurate, complete and timely inventory transactions record and avoiding differences between accounting and real inventory levels. Two tools commonly employed to ensure inventory accuracy and control are ABC analysis and cycle counting. Inventory management includes all activities of planning, forecasting and replenishment.

For effective inventory management, other techniques and tools that can be employed are as follows:

> **Cross-docking:** This involves unloading goods arriving from a supplier and immediately loading these goods onto outbound trucks bound for various retailer locations. This eliminates storage at the retailer's inbound warehouse and cuts the lead time. It has been used very successfully by Walmart and Xerox, among others.
>
> **Delayed differentiation:** This involves adding differentiating features to standard products late in the process. For example, Benetton decided to make all of their wool sweaters in undyed yarn and then dye the sweaters when they have more accurate demand data which arrives nearing the season. Another term for delayed differentiation is postponement.
>
> **Direct shipping:** This allows a firm to ship directly to customers rather than through retailers. This approach eliminates steps in the supply chain and reduces lead time as well as pipeline inventory. Reducing one or more steps in the supply chain is known as disintermediation. Companies such as Dell use this approach.

INVENTORY TRANSACTION

Inventories normally move positions and/or locations for being used for various purposes. The transactions of inventories can therefore happen for various reasons. When transactions of inventories take place, there is legal transfer of ownership of the inventories in case of sales. But transactions of inventories can also take place internally from one section to another, and thereby control mechanism as well as authority, and responsibility can also shift. Some of the routine transactions of inventories that take place within as well as outside the business may include the following:

- Normal stock receipt: from previously issued purchase orders and transfers
- Unexpected stock receipts: the stuff that just shows up on receiving stock
- Requisitions: a request for material to be consumed within a company
- Emergency requisitions
- Sales

Transactions of various types can arise out of numerous reasons such as a sales orders to be delivered to the client, orders to be picked up, cash sales from stock point and warehouse, direct shipment to end customers, transfer to other warehouses or facilities when required, stock return, returning the material to suppliers for say non-conformance to standards, scrapping and writing-off stocks.

STOCK-KEEPING UNIT

The inventory control is made by an SKU. An SKU is an individual product that differs from other products in some way, and inventories are kept SKU-wise. The difference could be in size, colour, brand, model, package, function or some other relevant characteristic such as flavour and fragrance, or a combination of these. Each SKU has its own unique identification code (product code) in the inventory accounting system, and it is counted and stored separately from other items.

Much of inventory control is directed at controlling each SKU in the inventory. Although daily operations of inventories may require SKU-level control, strategic planning of inventory levels can be accomplished by substantially aggregating products into broad groups by some characteristic—product groups. A basic approach is when managing the inventory investment of all SKUs collectively is the issue.

As the number of SKUs increases in a business, the complexity of inventory management also increases and as such businesses need to rationalize the SKUs based on their performance in terms of sales volume in the customer segment it served and the importance of that segment in business as well as profit contribution it makes. Sometimes, small-volume SKUs are also carried in business inventory in order to be a player in all sub-segments of the business category for other strategic reasons. The strategic reasons could be the need to be present in all sub-categories and sub-segments of the business to keep the leadership position in the category. For example, Reckitt Benckiser is a leader in shoe care category and its brand is Cherry Blossom. There are many sub-categories in this shoe care range and that include wax, liquid, cream, cleaners, shoe shampoo, chalk for canvas shoes, handy shine and so on. Some of these sub-categories have very small volume of business contributing small amount in sales and profit but to keep their leadership position in the market, Reckitt has to keep inventory of all these products adding complexity to the system. But the fact remains that SKUs add to complexity in inventory management. If a corporation has the leadership position in certain types of products or product categories and is growing at a healthy rate, the competition is normally seen to be making attempts to break that monopoly and to do that, the competition will constantly explore the possibility of finding a suitable entry point to carve out a niche for them from the leader. This niche will be some segment of the customers who would be looking for some differentiation or they even might be left uncovered and not serviced. To eliminate those possibilities of entry points, new SKUs are often introduced by the marketer just to cover all segments even if some segments are either small or not profitable. SKUs thus increase and so does the complexity in inventory management in particular and SCM in general.

BULLWHIP EFFECT

Manufacturers like to produce in large lot sizes because it is more cost-effective. The problem, however, is that producing in large lots does not allow for flexibility in terms of product mix. It also adds to the inventory which a business may not require immediately. The downside is that ordering/ producing large lots can result in large inventories of products that are currently not in demand while being out of stock for items that are in demand.

Retailers find benefits in ordering large lots for benefits such as quantity discounts and advantages of many trade schemes and promotions. And it also provides enough safety stock. Distributors and wholesalers like to stock more of products which are fast-moving and for which schemes and other promotions are being announced to meet the demand coming from the retailers they serve.

Ordering and producing in large lots can also increase the safety stock of suppliers and its corresponding carrying cost. It can also create what is called the bullwhip effect. Everyone linked in the supply chain has a natural tendency to keep enough margin of safety stock when they place their demand. This makes a multiplier effect in the whole chain, impacting the performance. This effect is what we call the bullwhip effect.

The bullwhip effect is the phenomenon of orders and inventories getting progressively larger (more variable) moving backwards through the supply chain. This is illustrated graphically in Figures 5.1–5.3.

FIGURE 5.1 Wholesalers/Distributors' Orders to the Manufacturers

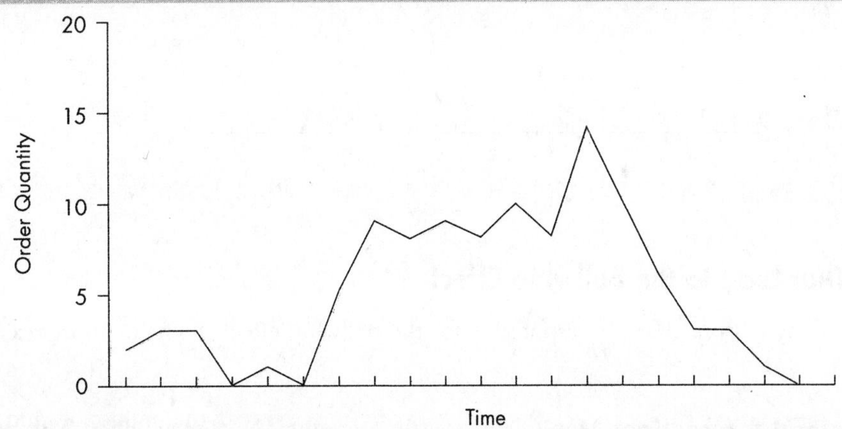

FIGURE 5.2 Consumer Offtake at Retail Sales Point

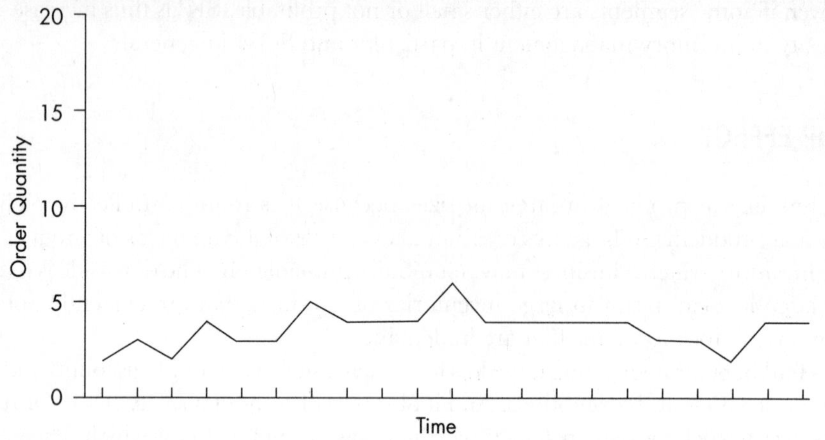

FIGURE 5.3 Manufacturers' Orders to the Suppliers/Vendors

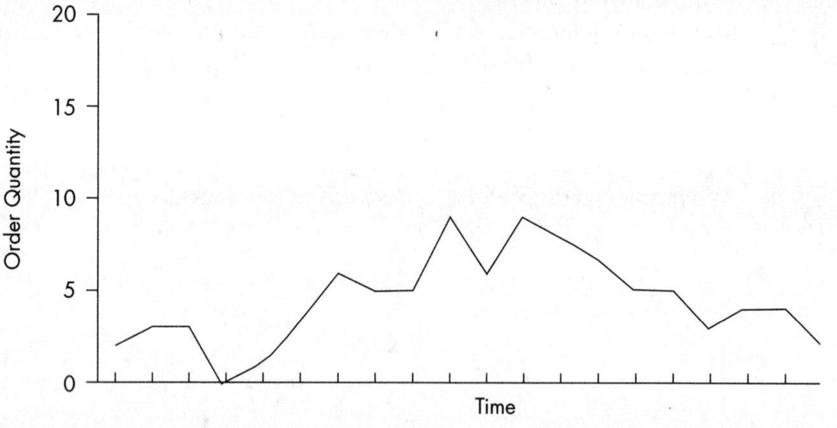

Causes That Lead to the Bullwhip Effect

There are many reasons that are responsible for the bullwhip effect. Some of those reasons are as follows:

Demand forecasting: Many firms use the min–max inventory policy. This means that when the inventory level falls to the ROP (min), an order is placed to bring the level back to the max, or the order-up-to-level. As more data are observed, estimates of the mean and standard deviation of customer demand are updated. This leads to changes in the safety stock and order-up-to-level and, hence, the order quantity. This also leads to variability.

Lead time: As lead time increases, safety stocks and order quantities are also increased. This also leads to more variability.

Batch ordering: Many firms use batch ordering such as with a min-max inventory policy. Their suppliers then see a large order followed by periods of no orders followed by another large order. This pattern is repeated such that suppliers see a highly variable pattern of orders.

Price fluctuation: If prices to retailers fluctuate, then they may try to stock up when prices are lower, again leading to variability.

Inflated orders: When retailers predict that a product will be in short supply, they tend to inflate orders to ensure that they will have ample supply to meet the customer demand when stocks are unlikely to be made available when needed. When the shortage period comes to an end, the retailer goes back to the smaller orders, thus causing more variability.

The Effect on Supply Chain Performance

To contain the impact of the bullwhip effect, there is a great deal of coordination required within the business among various departments. The lack of such coordination may impact the performance of the business negatively. The consumer offtake or retail sales normally follow an established pattern. However, most of the time, wholesalers' and distributors' orders that come to manufacturers do not reflect the real-term demand of the customers and there are various reasons for that including retailers deciding to stock a higher quantity when some offer or quantity discount is announced by the company or during festival season or even on hearing the news of possibility of short supply. Besides, for fast-moving items retailers always like to stock a higher quantity (Crowther 1964).

Wholesalers on the other hand trade on heavy discounts to liquidate the stock and for that reason they order a higher quantity from the manufacturers. Wholesalers have a tendency to rotate the stock faster even if it is necessary to sell at a low margin because by increasing the stock turnover ratio, the total profit will be higher. But this approach can lead to overstocking the market as consumer offtake in most of the cases follows a more or less uniform pattern. The result is the bullwhip effect. Wholesalers also perform the role of the redistributors where traditional channel partners cannot directly reach. They also have the tendency to trade in other's territories whenever an opportunity arises, creating distortion of the sales figure. Manufacturers, therefore, order for the input materials from their vendors and suppliers which varies widely, and vendors are not in a position to estimate the manufacturers' requirements and plan their production schedules to meet their clients' requirements. These variabilities have been shown in Figures 5.1–5.3.

This distortion due to the impact of the bullwhip effect results in the rise in various costs like manufacturing costs, as the company and its suppliers have to cater to the orders which are at variance with the customer demand. This also increases the inventory costs because the company as well as the trade channel partners has to keep a much higher level of the inventory in comparison to the real-term customer demand. Because of the bullwhip effect, transportation requirements fluctuate significantly over time because a higher quantity needs to be transported during a high demand period, raising the transportation costs. The bullwhip effect also increases the cost of handling for receiving the goods as well as for shipping the goods out. This can also result in occasional stock-out situations, particularly with the retailers who do not order more and others corner the stocks by buying more than required which in turn results in loss of sales. It should be noted that a company's real-term sales will be the quantity sold by the retailer to the ultimate consumer or consumer offtake. The fluctuation and all the distortion of sales take place because of the bullwhip effect, not only impacting the performance and profitability of the business but also creating confusion and misunderstanding in the whole supply chain.

Reducing Impact of Bullwhip Effect

Centralizing demand information occurs when customer demand information is available to all members of the supply chain. This information can be used to better predict what products and volumes are needed and when they are needed so that manufacturers can better plan for production. However, even though centralizing demand information can reduce the bullwhip effect by reducing the uncertainty, it will not eliminate it totally. Therefore, other methods that are needed to cope with the bullwhip effect include the following:

Reducing variability: This can be accomplished by using a technique made popular by Walmart and then Home Depot called everyday low pricing (EDLP). It eliminates promotions as well as the shifts in demand that accompany them. Large retail stores and wholesale stores run the EDLP programme regularly on select stock to reduce the impact of the bullwhip effect.

Reducing lead time: Order times can be reduced by using EDI with the partners in the supply chain. Access to the database by the concerned people reduces the lead time of ordering.

Strategic partnerships: The use of strategic partnerships can change how information is shared and how inventory is managed within the supply chain. These will be discussed later in greater detail.

BUSINESS RESPONSE TO STOCK-OUT

In spite of the best plan and best forecast, businesses can still face a stock-out situation for various reasons including disruption of regular production schedules and a sudden spurt in unusual demand as well as disruptions due to strikes, riots and other natural disasters. In that environment, there are standard responses that businesses can display. Some of these are as follows:

Back-ordering: The quantity requested by the customer is placed on a separate order called a back order and the special order is filled as soon as the product is available from the internal or external source. In some cases, the back order is shipped directly from its original source to the customer to ensure that the customer order is fulfilled in shortest possible time.

Substitution: It occurs when a product acceptable for the customer is substituted for the product that is not available. Sometimes customers are persuaded to accept alternative products or SKUs in place of what they have ordered by offering a special discount to attract them so that they still remain loyal to the product and company. If the substitution is done with a product or SKU which is in regular demand, customers normally accept that.

Lost sales: It occurs when an unsatisfied client annuls the order. This is common in retail situations as retailers very willingly offer customers with an alternative but equivalent product from the competition, and in that environment it is permanent loss of sales for the corporation. If a product not much in demand is substituted by another product, the loss of sales of that product is a permanent loss. Also, if a customer switches over to the competition when there is a stock-out situation, there is permanent loss of sales.

REPLENISHMENT OF INVENTORY

The aim of inventory replenishment is to ensure that the level of each SKU is kept at a level, optimal for an established customer service level (availability). Inventory replenishment is done after determining the demand and current availability for satisfying that demand and information regarding pending orders yet to be received. Based on these inputs, you can work out what stock will need to be ordered and when will the orders need to be released (ROP).

There are various approaches followed to determine what needs to be ordered, how much to be ordered and when. These are as follows:

Periodic or fixed interval review system: The periodic review system is very widely practised in the industry by taking the inventory details once in a fixed predetermined time interval to decide the ordering quantity. This time interval for review is determined based on the company's past practice as well as experience and lead time for ordering of long delivery items.

ROP system: The point triggers when reordering has to be done taking the information related to stock level as well as other input regarding any delay in receiving stock than the normal lead time as well as if there is any excess consumption arising out of unusual demand. At this point, procurement is initiated. The ROP is actually average daily consumption multiplied by the lead time of procurement plus the safety stock (Figure 5.4).

Time-phased order point (TPOP) system: TPOP is a computerized management tool that plans inventory needs in a priority-sequenced, time-phased manner to meet customer and forecast demand as it occurs. This technique is at the heart of MRP and distribution resource planning (DRP) systems used for the control of manufacturing and distribution channel inventories. The main advantage is that inventory actions are triggered by matching the supply with the anticipated demand as it occurs in time. At the point where the demand exceeds the supply, the system will alert the inventory planner to order the item according to the predetermined lot size and to have it available at the anticipated date on which stock-out will occur. In addition, each time a TPOP is generated, the system will resequence demand and supply relationships and suggest a new set of required order actions for the order planner.

FIGURE 5.4 **ROP for Inventory**

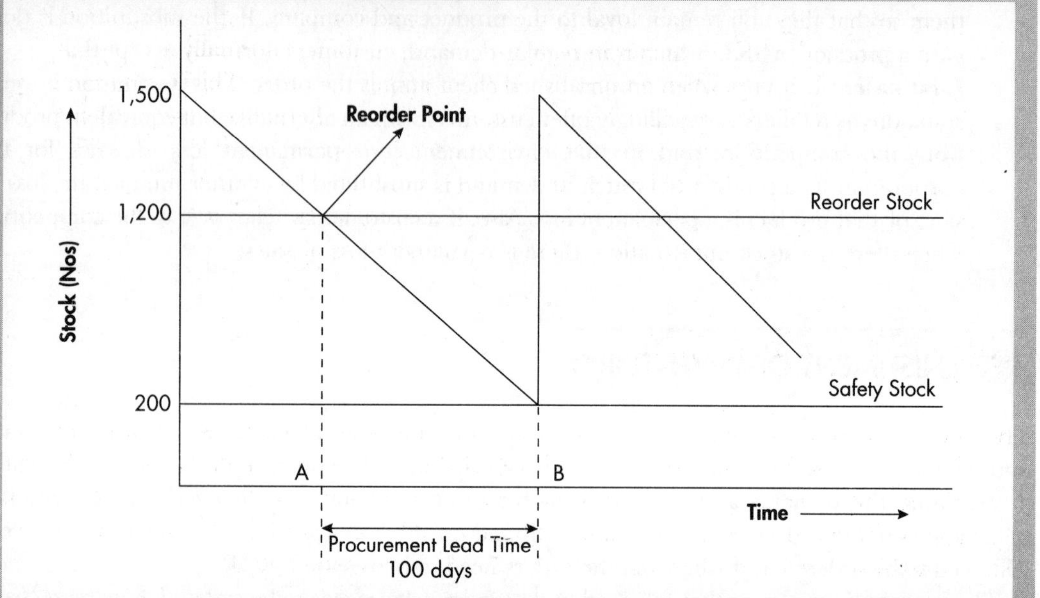

Notes: A—ROP triggered and procurement initiated.
B—material received.

The information or inventory management system must generate data regarding order level, average inventory level, lead time of ordering, demand during lead time and safety stock. The average inventory level is max level + min level/2 or ½ of the replenishment order. As SKU stock is a sum of cycle and safety stocks, the average inventory is: ½ replenishment order + safety stock. The normal practice in the industry is, however, a periodic or fixed interval review system. Order cycle time is actually the ratio of estimated total annual demand to average ordering quantity.

INVENTORY POSITION

The replenishment decision is made when an inventory position of item reaches the ROP. The replenishment decision model includes the following components:

- **On-hand inventory:** The quantity that the inventory system shows as being physically in stock. This value should never be negative. This is the starting point for the replenishment calculation.
- **Available inventory:** It is found by subtracting all order demand quantities, whether allocated or unallocated, from the on-hand inventory. The balance remaining is the quantity

available to immediately satisfy new customer demands. This value can be negative, if open customer orders exceed the on-hand inventory.

- **On-order inventory:** It is the replenishment stock that has been ordered but has not yet been received. Although the inventory position calculation considers the on-order inventory as if it were on hand, this stock should not be allocated to open customer orders or existing back orders within the replenishment lead time.
- **Inventory position:** It is the value that is determined for a given item by subtracting the inventory requirements generated by open customer and inter-branch transfer orders allocated (committed) and back orders from the total on-hand stock and expected on-order inventory.

AVERAGE INVENTORY

It is the average quantity or value of whole stock or quantity. If an SKU is in a warehouse at max level valued at US$5,000 and at min level valued at US$2,000, the difference between these two levels (5,000–2000) or US$3,000 is the order quantity resulting in the cycle inventory of US$1,500. At the beginning of the cycle, the stock level is at max. Customers deplete the inventory when it reaches its min level. Average inventory is therefore max level + min level/2 or ½ of the replenishment order. As SKU stock is a sum of cycle and safety stocks, the average inventory is: ½ replenishment order + safety stock.

ORDER CYCLE TIME

Interval between Orders

Order cycle time is the time period between placing one order and the next order or the time period between two successive orders.

$$T = Q/D$$

where T = order cycle time, Q = quantity and D = assumed annual demand.

For example, if assumed annual demand is 5,000 units and order quantity is 60 units, then order cycle time T = 60/5,000 = 0.012 year or 0.012 × 52 weeks or 0.012 × 365 days = 4 days.

IMPLICATIONS OF EOQ

Following are the implications of EOQ:

- A formula is used for calculating optimal production batches as a 'lot size' formula, and S is the set-up cost and V is the manufacturing cost.
- While EOQ may not apply to every inventory situation, most organizations find it beneficial in at least some aspect of their operation. At any time if having repetitive purchasing or planning of an item, EOQ should be considered.

FIGURE 5.5 **Economic Ordering Quantity**

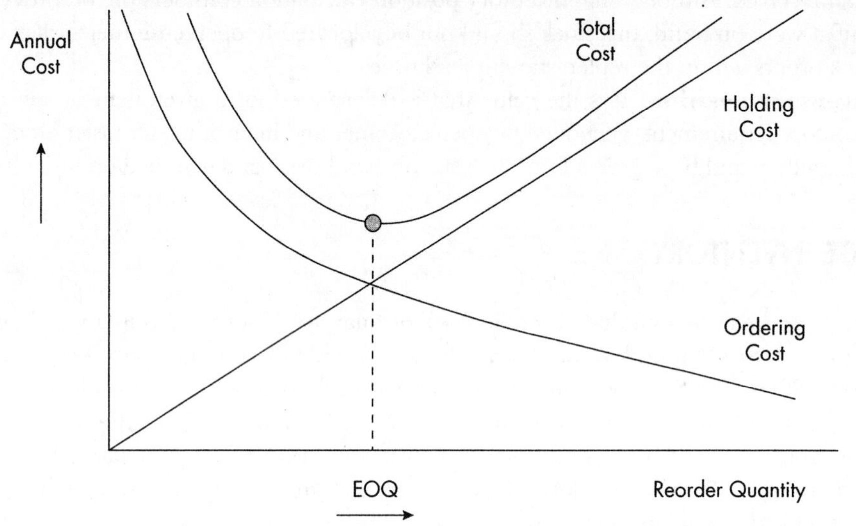

- Obvious applications for EOQ are purchase-to-stock distributors and make-to-stock manufacturers; however, make-to-order manufacturers should also consider EOQ when they have multiple orders or release dates for the same items and when planning components and sub-assemblies.
- Repetitive buy maintenance, repair and operating (MRO) inventory is also a good application for EOQ.
- Although EOQ is generally recommended in operations where demand is relatively steady, items with demand variability like seasonality can still use the model by going to shorter time periods for the EOQ calculation.

In the EOQ model, it is assumed that there is no time lag between ordering and procurement of materials. Therefore, the ROP for replenishing the stocks occurs at that level when the inventory level drops to zero, and because of instant delivery by the suppliers, the stock level bounces back to the desired level (Figure 5.5).

In reality, however, there is always a lead time of ordering, and the stock required during that period needs to be there in the inventory. In a real-life situation, one never encounters a zero lead time. There is always a time lag from the date of placing an order for materials and the date on which materials are received and as a result, the ROP is always higher than zero. If a firm places an order when the inventory reaches the ROP, the new deliveries will arrive before the firm runs out of goods to sell. In a JIT line which is not easy to practise, receiving the stock when needed is possible. It will always be the endeavour of the procurement manager to reduce the lead time of ordering in an attempt to reduce the stockholding in the system and the associated reduction of working capital and save the interest on the same for the business.

MATERIAL REQUIREMENTS' PLANNING

The objective of MRP is to prepare procurement plan to meet the production target derived from the company's sales order processing. This, therefore, helps the business to optimize production, procurement and inventory for better performance.

- **Principle:** The MRP starts with sales order processing. The sales orders are generated by the company's sales system, and each order generated by the salesman is required to be serviced by a defined time limit which we normally call order delivery schedule. The purpose of MRP then is to work backwards to generate the bill of material to deliver that order as per the schedule, check the existing inventories to determine what needs to be ordered and when based on their lead time of delivery and finally release the orders as per the material requirements plan. This is a complex task and most often managed by having ERP software. If it is known what final product should be produced, it is also known how much materials and components are needed for manufacturing that product. Theoretically, there is no need for safety stock of materials. If the quantity of finished products and production schedule are known, then received inputs will be immediately used. But the reality is different from what could be theoretically possible simply because there are uncertainties and failures on the part of vendors to meet the commitment. These uncertainties can also occur if there is a fluctuating demand in a dynamic and highly competitive business environment. Safety stock, thus, needs to be provided for considering these issues, but the quantity of safety stock is determined by businesses based on their own past experience. And as such, one can find that some businesses work with very low level of safety stock and some have a relatively higher level of safety stock.
- The timing of incoming material flows according to the production schedule and is the basis of MRP. MRP links procurement operations with manufacturing or material management functions.

WHAT MRP INDICATES

The MRP indicates the following:

- The types of materials and the quantity that has to be purchased from outside, taking into account current inventory levels
- The types of materials that need to be manufactured internally and in what quantity, taking into account current inventory levels
- At what time to place these orders, either by purchasing from outside or for manufacturing inside

COMPONENTS OF MRP II

MRP II stands for manufacturing resource planning. Manufacturing Resource Planning (MRP II) is an integrated information system which subsequently came in business to be known as enterprise resource planning (ERP). Many ERP packages since then have been launched and all businesses are using this to optimally manage various business functions.

Master Production Schedule

It is the list of the products and services to be supplied within a specific period of time. This period must be sufficiently long to allow for the ordering and delivery of required sub-assemblies and parts, as well as allow sufficient time for manufacturing the product in question. It may be made up of the forecast demand and actual known demand. It also lists the required outputs for the system and when the goods and services are required through the use of due date.

Bill of Materials

It is a diagram, engineering drawing or list of all materials at various levels. The product structure is often presented in a hierarchical form, where the end product is at the highest level (level 0 or 1) and then components that go into making this product are at a lower level.

Inventory Status File

It is a complete record of the quantity of each material held in the inventory. A detailed file shows transactions, receipts, disbursements, scrapped materials, planned orders, order releases, projections of delivery dates, quantities of each material to order and when to place orders. It also shows the lead times, or the time required to produce a production lot in-house or receive a lot purchased from a supplier. To take into account the lead time, a requirement in a one-time period necessitates the release of the order in some earlier period according to the established delay or lead time.

OUTPUT OF MRP

It is a list of purchase requirements, which includes what needs to be purchased and when including the following:

- A manufacturing schedule, which lists what will be made and when it will be made
- The closing stock of parts, components and sub-assemblies after the master schedule has been completed
- The closing capacity available after the master schedule has been completed
- A list of anticipated shortfalls in production—these may be due to shortages of parts of capacity

The differences between order point system and MRP system are summarized in Table 5.1.

TABLE 5.1 Order Point System vs MRP System

Criteria	Order Point System	MRP System
Demand	Independent	Dependent
Ordering philosophy	Replenishment	Need based
Control principle	ABC grouping	All items are equally important
Forecasting	Based on demand	Based on a master production schedule
Purpose	Satisfying customer needs	Satisfying production needs
Order size determination	EOQ	Firm request for concrete items
Design Pattern	Unvaried	Changing but predictable
Inventory types	Finished product, spare parts	WIP, raw material

Source: https://www.vkok.ee/logontrain/wp-content/uploads/2014/03/Riga-3-july-2014.pdf (accessed on 20 August 2019).

MIN–MAX REPLENISHMENT SYSTEM

It is the most popular replenishment method and is normally practised by the industry as it is easy to operate. It is a variant of the ROP model with two differences:

1. If the SKU inventory level reaches the ROP or below it, the variable size order is made to raise the inventory level on to a predetermined maximum level (which is EOQ + ROP).
2. If the inventory level of some SKU drops to the ROP or below it, the inventory levels purchased from the same supplier are reviewed, despite these being above their ROPs. Besides ROP, each SKU has a predetermined minimal order quantity. Replenishment orders for SKUs which need replenishing in quantities above the minimal size (but have not reached ROP) are added to the order submitted to the given supplier. So this approach enables joint ordering, therefore decreasing the number of submitted orders and increasing order sizes.

An example: Let us take an example to explain how this popular method works in the industry by taking the data presented for two items in Table 5.2. A company manufacturing two products say edible oil requires two items (Item 1 and Item 2) to manufacture. If the stock and data related to ROP and EOQ are as given in Table 5.2, we can work out the order size.

From the above example as presented in Table 5.2, we can see that the stock level of Item 1 has dropped to a ROP. Also, the level of Item 2, ordered from the same supplier as Item 1, is reviewed. The difference between the max and current levels of Item 2 is (1,800–1,000) = 800 units. As the difference of 800 units exceeds the predetermined min order size for Item 2, the order for this item is also placed in addition to the order for Item 1.

TABLE 5.2 Principle of Min–Max Replenishment System

	Item 1 Mustard Oil (Units)	Item 2 Corn Oil (Units)
ROP	200	400
EOQ	1,000	1,400
Maximum stock level (ROP + EOQ)	1,200	1,800
Minimum order size (½ of EOQ)	500	700
Stock at the moment	200	1,000

Source: https://www.vkok.ee/logontrain/wp-content/uploads/2014/03/Riga-3-july-2014.pdf (accessed on 20 August 2019).

HOW MUCH SHOULD BE ORDERED?

Majority of inventory replenishment methods are the variations of following three theoretical basic models:

- Periodic review system or fixed interval system
- ROP system
- TPOP system

TOTAL COST OF INVENTORY

The objective of most companies is to buy every item at the lowest total cost per unit. The total cost is the sum of three elements:

1. **Material cost (landed cost):** It is the purchase price of product plus freight and any other charges that are related to specific shipment including taxes, transportation and so on, or manufacturing cost in production.
2. **Ordering cost:** It is the cost of issuing, receiving and paying a vendor. It is associated with ordering frequency, not with the quantity ordered.
3. **Inventory carrying or holding cost:** It is the cost of maintaining the inventory in a warehouse before it is sold, transferred or otherwise used. It is associated with the quantity ordered, not with ordering frequency.

OUT-OF-STOCK COSTS

It is an additional cost element related to inventories—cost incurred when an order is placed but cannot be filled from the inventory from which the order is normally assigned. Finding these costs is quite complicated and inaccurate.

There are two kinds of out-of-stock costs:

1. **Lost sales cost:** When a customer faces an out-of-stock situation, he/she chooses to withdraw the request for the product. This relates to cost of lost sales which is equal to unearned profit from the sales which is lost plus possible negative impact on future sales as customer might even switch to competition or divide orders between suppliers.
2. **Back-order cost:** When customer is willing for out-of-stock goods resulting into delay in the execution of the order. The sale is not lost, only delayed, but it incurs back-order processing costs and additional transportation and handling costs (if the back order is processed and delivered as a separate shipment).

INVENTORY-CARRYING COST

Inventory is part of the working capital in the business and consists of raw material, packaging material and other input material including spares and components, work-in-progress, as well as finished inventory. Following are its features:

- It is the cost associated with having inventory in hand.
- The term 'inventory carrying cost' may be used in two different contexts:
  - Determining the firm's TLC.
  - Calculating EOQ for SKU.

Inventory is a significant part of the working capital of the company. Keeping excess inventory leads to loss in terms of interest cost the capital blocked in the inventory. As such, total cost as well as location-wise and/or under account head-wise inventory should be periodically reviewed to ensure that there is no unnecessary stockholding at any point. Excess inventory can also become a deterrent for the company to consider introducing a new model or a new design and/or new formulation, as the case may be. The inventory can also become obsolete and waste. Some inventory of raw and packaging materials and more particularly finished goods can become waste after their prescribed expiry period. Organized retailers take inventory audit almost every month to see that the records in the books are correct and also if anything is becoming dead inventory soon. If they identify near-expiry stock or even dead stock, a special disposal and salvation plan is worked out to recover as possible from such a situation. Inventory needs a very close scrutiny and valid periodical audit to ensure that inventory management practices are as planned in the budget document.

TOTAL COST APPROACH

Capital cost is a major cost component of inventory-holding. It is the opportunity cost of money tied in a firm's inventory which may represent over 90% of total inventory-carrying cost in certain cases, although the cost can be subjective depending on the interest rates used for calculating the opportunity cost. The interest rate can be based on:

- WACC (weighted average capital cost)—considered most objective for a realistic cost overview
- Hurdle rate—minimal acceptable return on investment (ROI) accepted by the company
- The lowest bank loan interest rate (currently around 10–12% in India), which can be different in other countries
- Inventory service costs—include, typically, insurance and taxes on inventory
- Storage costs—part of warehousing costs depending on inventory level
- Inventory risk costs—obsolescence, damage, pilferage and relocation costs

STRUCTURE OF INVENTORY-CARRYING COST

The structure of inventory-carrying cost is as follows:

Capital cost: 82%
Inventory service cost: 0.75% (insurance 0.25% and taxes 0.5%)
Storage cost: 3.25%
Inventory risk cost: 14.0%
Total: 100%

If the total inventory-carrying cost is found, it can be divided by the average inventory investment or average stock value and can be expressed as a percentage of the average. This helps in determining how much it costs to maintain a unit worth of inventory in a business which typically ranges from 18% to 28%. The inventory risk cost should be included while calculating EOQ.

If a company uses a private or rented warehouse, mistakes in calculating the storage cost are common in EOQ implementations. Generally, companies include all costs associated with the warehouse. This tends to include costs that are not directly affected by the inventory levels and do not compensate for storage characteristics. Carrying costs for the purpose of the EOQ calculation should only include costs that are variable based upon inventory levels. For a storage area, the proportionate share of depreciation and rent and communication cost need to be included, whereas shipping, receiving and other working areas are not included (https://www.vkok.ee/logontrain/wp-content/uploads/2014/03/Riga-3-july-2014.pdf).

DEMAND ESTIMATION

Reorder Point

ROP is the level of inventory which triggers an action to replenish the particular stock of inventory item, and it is normally calculated from the demand forecast during the replenishment lead time plus safety stock. As such, ROP is a method to determine when to order for a particular material, but it does not address the issues related to how much to order.

$$\text{ROP (R)} = \text{Normal consumption during lead time} + \text{Safety stock.}$$

As such, two factors that determine the appropriate order point are (a) the delivery time stock which is the inventory needed during the lead time which is the difference between the order date and the receipt of the inventory ordered and (b) the safety stock which is the minimum level of inventory that is required to be held as a protection against shortages due to fluctuation in demand.

Exercise 1: When Demand and Lead Time Are Constant or Fixed

Problem: An online paint store is open 311 days per year. If the annual demand is 10,000 gallons of iron coat paint and the lead time to receive an order is 10 days, determine the ROP for paint.

Solution: In this problem, both demand and lead time are constant, and hence as per the basic EOQ model, with constant demand and constant lead time to receive an order, the ROP is equal to the amount demanded during the lead time.

ROP = Normal consumption during lead time.

$$R = D \times LT, \tag{5.2}$$

where
D = demand rate per period (day or week)
LT = lead time in days or weeks
Demand (D), 10,000 gallons/year
Store opens 311 days/year
Daily demand = 10,000/311 = 32.154 gallons/day
LT = 10 days
R = D × LT = 32.154 × 10 = 321.54 gallons

CASE STUDY: VMI AT TATA STEEL

VMI is one of the outcomes of integrated SCM approaches designed to improve the supply chain performance. This is one of the methods applied to reduce the impact of the bullwhip effect and to help to achieve a better inventory accuracy. VMI is a means of optimizing supply chain performance in which the manufacturer is responsible for maintaining the distributor's inventory levels. Manufacturers thus will have access to the distributors' inventory data and accordingly will raise the purchase orders. The objective and goal of VMI is to streamline and optimize the supply chain operations for both the suppliers and the manufacturers. This means that vendors monitor the buyer's inventory level and replenish the stock as required, which would be equal to the sales performance of the distributors, or it will be optimized keeping the manufacturer–marketer's sales objective and the real-life inventory data into consideration. In this system, although the manufacturer manages the distributor's inventory, that does not mean that the manufacturer will have the liberty to overstock the distributors because in that case the whole purpose of optimization will be lost. As such, a lean manufacturer will be able to make use of this concept to significantly improve their performance. The data related to physical inventory of the distributors actually help the manufacturer to control the trade inventory without loss of sales or facing any stock-out situation. The success in SCM is drawn from the clearer understanding of the relationship between inventory cost and customer service levels. VMI in that perspective helps to reduce cost by reducing the inventory level without any negative impact on the performance of the business. On the contrary, VMI in reality helps increasing the customer services frequency by delivering smaller quantities as required by the consumer demand.

The distributors who are the first-level customers benefit by the lower cycle stocks and not just low end-of-the-month stock.

To achieve this objective, the focus should be on reducing or minimizing the total supply chain cost which helps to achieve cost saving benefits for all the parties linked in the supply chain. Before implementing VMI on a full scale, one should first do it on a pilot scale which might involve select distributors for select SKUs, a clear understanding on the relationships and responsibilities covering the EDI protocol standard to transmit information at the end of each working hour every day and a common understanding of the performance measures of the distributor's performance. The success of VMI depends on EDI which provides vendors with essentially the same POS and inventory information retained by the consumer which enables improved forecasting because the vendors can observe demand for their product(s) over a wider range of customers and can incorporate the effects of sales promotion activities, competing products and also seasonal variations in demand, if any. Many global businesses including Walmart and P&G have implemented VMI in their business and derived significant advantages and demonstrated improved performance. P&G implemented a project called 'Project Golden Eye' to reduce the distributors' stock significantly to improve profit. We have discussed this earlier in this chapter.

Strategic Consulting Group at Tata Steel uses analytical skills and cross-functional expertise from within Tata Steel and its suppliers involving their dedicated group of analysts from different streams. Each of those commodity analysts is attached to the asset class of specific commodities, and they identify, evaluate and negotiate with suppliers, manage overall pricing issues along with the segment leader and commodity analyst, are responsible for meeting the objectives, and are constantly looking for ways to reduce cost and formulate the sourcing strategy for the assigned commodities by working with cross-functional teams called 'commodity competence teams' (CCTs).

These analysts provide tools, resources and knowledge through techniques such as benchmarking, quality improvement programmes (QIPs) and VMI, e-procurement, and knowledge management. These tools contribute to optimize the overall costs, material flow and response time with respect to suppliers as well as customers. Tata Steel has steering committees, strategic sourcing teams, CCTs as well as strategic sourcing groups working together to reduce the number of discrete one-time purchase orders and include more products and suppliers in its annual rate contract.

Tata Steel's B2B procurement platform is one of the first among similar initiatives taken by other large competing companies. The site offers web-based multi-directional flow of transaction and business information among transaction participants. All cross-organizational elements of the inbound supply chain including enquiry and/or request for quotation (RFQ) details, order placements, delivery compliance monitoring, order amendments, material receipts and payment tracking are covered. Value-added services such as a negotiation chat room with bid revision tracking or reverse auction, transactional correspondence and e-mail notifications and acknowledgements are also offered, and the site is constantly upgraded and revised with new releases.

Tata Steel is self-sufficient in iron ore, the key raw material for steel production, through its captive mines, which is a distinct advantage. It is 60% self-sufficient for coking coal and the rest is procured mostly through imports. However, for Corus (Tata Steel Europe Ltd) operations, the company needs to source raw materials through contracts with mining companies in UK and the Netherlands and is striving towards raw material security through joint ventures in Thailand, Australia, Mozambique, Ivory Coast in West Africa and also Oman. In addition, it has signed an agreement with Steel Authority of India to establish a 50:50 joint venture coal mining company in India and acquired 19.9% stake in New Millennium Capital Corporation, Canada, for iron ore mining, exploration of opportunities for titanium dioxide in Tamil Nadu, commissioning of a ferro-chrome plant in South Africa and setting up of a deep seaport in coastal Odisha to meet the company's long-term growth objective. All these initiatives intended to have greater control over raw material resources and achieve its security across global operations.The procurement division of Tata Steel plays a critical role for business to make it a successful, profitable global organization which is working under the overall guidelines for conformance to the company's policies, its governance model and Tata Code of Conduct.

The SCM department of Tata Steel is one of the core departments interfacing between the suppliers and the operations, and therefore is a huge cost centre responsible for indenting of stock items that are ordered by all departments of Tata Steel. They strictly follow the quality objectives and parameters following procedures as laid down for material procurement for both consumption-based material and also materials based on direct supplies. The first materials management system in Tata Steel was that of Burroughs, then came IBM in 1993 which took six years to mature and meet the company's SCM requirement and then came Enterprise Solutions to integrate all the business functions comprising SCM, logistics, human resource management (HRM), marketing and finance. In 2001, the management implemented SAP in record nine months' time with the help of PricewaterhouseCoopers.

Tata Steel was finding it difficult to manage the inventory which was rising impacting the bottom line. To reduce the inventory level, Tata Steel eventually came up with the idea of implementing VMI which was successfully implemented in retail as well as the automotive sector. VMI, if not implemented properly, can have a negative impact in the whole system as well. This requires well-thought-out preparation in advance. The modification that Tata Steel did was segregating the materials into A, B, C and D classes of items for easy reference and close monitoring of the level of inventory. This classification was made on the basis of two identified criteria, namely consumption quantity and last year consumption (LYC) value.

ABC Classification

ABC classes of items are actually regular-moving items. And D class items are slow-moving items. ABC is again further subdivided on the basis of LYC value on the basis of the following:

Top 80% of LYC value = A class (high consumption value)
Next 15% of LYC value = B class (medium consumption value)
Next 5% of LYC value = C class (low consumption value)

High-cost and slow-moving items are classified as D class items which are not stocked in large quantities. Based on this classification, the inventory levels at Tata Steel were found to be as given in Table 5.3.

TABLE 5.3 Class of Inventory at Tata Steel

Class Type	Total Value in ₹	Total No. of Items	% Shares in Value
A	76,792,478.7	180	0.3206
B	3,317,455.93	24	0.0138
C	317,833.81	15	0.0013
D	159,126,366.22	3,821	0.6643
Grand total	**239,554,134.66**	**4,016**	**1.0000**

As can be seen, the total inventory cost of these items at Tata Steel was valued at ₹2,390 million (₹2.39 billion), which was of course alarming with a high amount blocked in D class items representing about 67% of the total inventory. This prompted Tata Steel for implementing VMI way back in the year 2002–2003, and Vesuvius being one of the prominent vendors along with Tata Refractories was associated in implementing VMI. These two vendors represent about 50% of the total inventory in the system and were involved in the implementation of VMI. Some of the vendors and their production data are given in Table 5.4.

TABLE 5.4 Refractories' Purchase Records of Tata Steel

Vendor	Vendor's Name	Quantity in kg	Value in INR (₹)	% of Total Purchase Value
TC81	Tata Refractories Ltd	6,965,719.230	258,236,182.910	37.12
V216	Vesuvius Ltd	2,256,805.400	88,127,436.030	12.67
TF2F	TRL China Ltd	2,495,144.800	70,810,110.500	10.18
A751	Ace Refractories Ltd	1,226,606.800	57,550,881.210	8.27
O009	OCL India Lts	734,681.000	36,688,701.220	5.27
R50F	RHI Refractories Asia Ltd	483,335.300	31,478,567.880	4.53
O083	Orient Abrasives Ltd	859,268.200	20,354,446.830	2.93
S489	Singhbhum Refractory	1,162,032.970	16,875,752.760	2.43
M165	Maithan Ceramic Ltd	1,265,720.000	16,824,363.430	2.42
R48F	RHI Refractories	218,351.700	16,652,000.200	2.39
C92F	Calderys	168,110.400	14,714,737.180	2.12
GA21	Foseco India Ltd	152,195.000	12,971,292.830	1.86
M340	Murugappa Morgan Thermal	72,294.590	9,498,421.970	1.37
A02H	Aegis Business Ltd	194,688.000	7,669,605.320	1.1
N53F	Sojitz Chemical Corporation	58,549.000	6,421,295.240	0.92

VMI was implemented in Tata Steel before implementing an ERP system like SAP. Post implementation of SAP in the year 2005, the whole system of inventory management was further integrated. The values of VMI items as compared to the total consumption value were monitored and measured by SAP. It was also possible to compare plant-wise and storage location-wise inventories, and it also enabled Tata Steel a detail analysis using various other measuring criteria. By implementing VMI in Tata Steel, the level of inventory holding at the warehouse and inventory holding cost had come down from ₹2,390 million to as low as ₹280 million.

Large MNCs like HUL or even large companies like Reliance Industries derive great advantage from their strength of buying power, and vendors are extending credit to them when companies' own sales are all on cash. HUL, for example, manufactures almost all of their requirement through the contract manufacturing route buying inputs from the suppliers and approved vendors extending credit. Companies like HUL and Reliance can afford to get long supply line credit and because their own sales are in cash, these companies have a distinct advantage over the others in terms of inventory holding and inventory carrying cost.

Case Questions

1. On what will the success of the implementation of VMI depend?
2. How did Tata Steel go about implementing VMI in the company?
3. Discuss the approach of Tata Steel towards inventory analysis.
4. What was the outcome of the implementation of VMI at Tata Steel?

Source: The case is based on the data reported by Chakraborty and Swain (2011).

SECTION II
DEALING WITH DEMAND UNCERTAINTY IN SUPPLY CHAIN

MANAGING UNCERTAINTY IN SUPPLY CHAIN

Due to dynamic nature of businesses and changing environment, demand fluctuates. A higher level of inventory increases the cost of holding and other associated problems related to a company's performance, but the company also cannot afford to lose sales on account of non-availability of stock. Safety inventory, therefore, is carried in the system to satisfy the demand that exceeds the demand forecast. The two factors that determine the appropriate order point are the **delivery time stock,** which is the inventory needed during the lead time, that is, the difference between the order date and the receipt of the inventory ordered, and the **safety stock,** which is the minimum level of inventory that is held as a protection against shortages due to fluctuation in demand.

$$\text{ROP (R)} = \text{Normal consumption during lead time} + \text{Safety stock.}$$

In the context of today's business environment, customers can go around and search across stores for a stock of an item that they are looking for. If Amazon is out of stock of a book title, a customer can easily check if the same title is available on Flipkart or even other stores like Barnes & Noble. Searching online is easy and that makes a more valid case to ensure that the stock is available. For any supply chain, following questions are required to be considered when the business is planning for safety stock: What is the appropriate or desired level of product availability? How much safety stock is required for the desired level of product availability? What actions can be taken to reduce safety stock without compromising product availability level?

MEASURING PRODUCT AVAILABILITY

There are several ways to measure the product availability. One of those measures is product fill rate, which means the fraction of the product demand that is satisfied from the product available in the inventory. It is the corporation's decision about the fill rate but in an intensely fought competitive environment, companies aim at a very high fill rate nearing 99%.

$$\text{Product fill rate} = \text{Product demand/Product available in inventory} = 99/100 = 99\% \quad (5.3)$$

The other measure of product availability is order fill rate, which again means a fraction of the order received that is filled by the inventory of the product itself and that also measures the specific numbers of the orders. Besides, product fill rate and order fill rate companies also measure pack fill rate to ensure a higher degree of customer satisfaction. In addition to these measures, product availability can also be determined by cycle service level (CSL) which is the fraction of the replenishment cycles that end with all the customers' demands being met. The replenishment cycle is the interval between two successive replenishment deliveries, and therefore CSL is the probability of not having a stock-out in a replacement cycle and is measured over a specific number of replenishment cycles.

ESTIMATING SAFETY STOCK

Safety stock is the average stock on hand when a replenishment order arrives. Therefore, for example, when the lead time of the order is LT weeks for a product, say mobile phone, and mean weekly demand of the product is D,

$$\text{Expected demand during the lead time} = \text{LT} \times \text{D}. \quad (5.4)$$

Given that the distributor places the replenishment order when the ROP of the product (mobile phones) is on hand,

$$\text{Safety stock (SS)} = \text{ROP} - (\text{LT} \times \text{D}). \quad (5.5)$$

This we will work out taking some examples.

Example 1. Estimating Safety Stock from Replenishment Policy

Let us assume a distributor of mobile phones having weekly demand with a mean of 3,000 and standard deviation of 500. Let us also assume that the manufacturer takes about two weeks to fill the order (lead time of order). The distributor currently orders 12,000 mobile sets when the inventory on hands drops to 7,000.

As per the replenishment policy of the distributor,

- Average demand per week = D = 3,000
- Standard deviation of weekly demand = αD = 500
- Average lead time for replenishment = LT = 2 weeks
- ROP = 7,000
- Average lot size (ordering quantity) = 12,000
- Safety stock = SS = ROP – (LT × D) = 7,000 – (2 × 3,000) = 7,000 – 6000 = 1,000.

The distributor thus will carry 1,000 safety stock as a safeguard against uncertainty in demand.

- Cycle inventory = 12,000/2 = 6000
- Average inventory = cycle inventory + safety stock = 6,000 + 1,000 = 7,000

The distributor thus carries on an average 7,000 mobile sets in stock.

Average flow time = Average inventory/Average demand = 7,000/3,000 = 2.33 weeks, which means that each mobile set thus remains in the distributor's stock for 2.33 weeks.

Example 2. Estimating Safety Stock from Desired CSL

CSL is the probability of not getting into a stock-out situation in a replenishment cycle. Thus, CSL = The probability of demand during lead time should be less than or equal to ROP. And to evaluate this probability, we need to determine the distribution of demand during the lead time which again follows a normal distribution with a mean of DT and a standard deviation of αT.

Taking the earlier case of mobile phone in a store with an average sales per week of 3,000 and standard deviation of 500, the lead time of ordering is 2 weeks. If the store reviews the replenishment policy continuously, then let us estimate the safety stock that the store should carry to achieve a CSL of 90%.

Here we have

- Demand per week = D = 3,000
- Mean standard deviation = αT = 500
- CSL = 0.9
- Lead time = T =2 weeks.

Because demand across time is independent, we can have

- DT = 2 × 3,000 = 6,000
- αT = √T αT = √2 × 500 = 707

Thus, safety stock will work out as NORMSINV(0.90) × 707 = 906.

(Note: NORMSINV(P) returns the standardized normal deviate Z corresponding with one-tailed probability P, where P must be a value between 0 and 1. NORMSINV is the inverse function of the NORMSDIST function. NORMSINV(0.9) = 1.28155.)

Therefore, to achieve the cycle inventory service level of 90%, the safety stock is 906 mobile sets.

Businesses need to have a measure of product availability from the business performance criteria like service level or order fill or pack fill rate, and using those criteria of measures, companies will work out the safety stock in the business but most importantly it is critical to business to use available managerial levers to lower the safety stock without hurting product availability or losing out on sales and impacting customer service levels as per the objective of the business.

REORDER POINT

Example 1: When there is variable demand and constant lead time, the inventory level might be depleted at a faster rate during the lead time (Figure 5.6).

FIGURE 5.6 ROP with Variable Demand

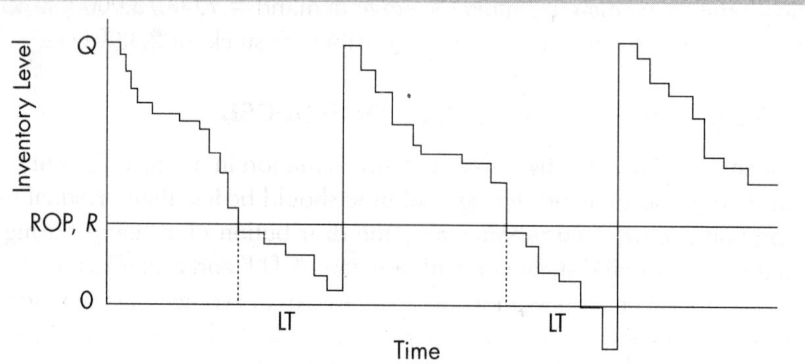

FIGURE 5.7 ROP with Safety Stock

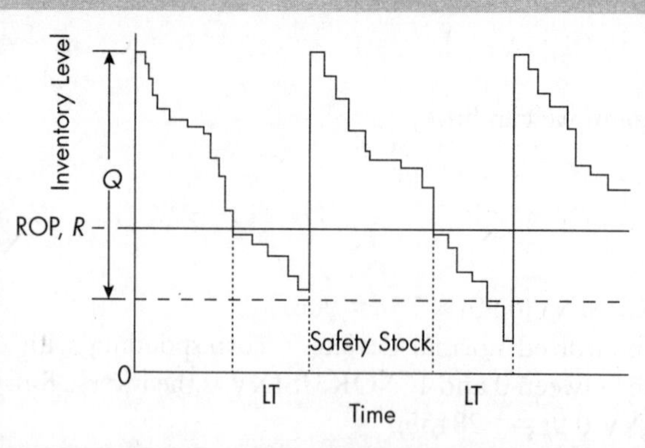

When the demand is uncertain, a safety stock of inventory is frequently added to the expected demand during the lead time (Figure 5.7).

SERVICE LEVEL

Service level to be achieved provides an assurance to the customers regarding what will be the lead time to meet the demand of a customer from the time of receiving the supply order to what level of accuracy. Following are its features:

FIGURE 5.8 Service Level Determines the Safety Stock

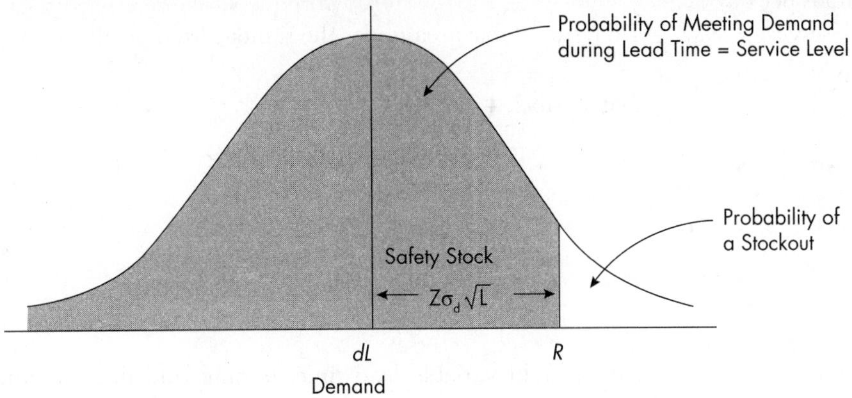

- The probability that the inventory available during the lead time will meet demand.
- Stock-out means an inventory shortage.
- A service level of 90% means that there is 0.90 probability that the demand will be met during the lead time and the probability that a stock-out will occur is 10% (Figure 5.8).

When there is variable demand and constant lead time,

$$R=\bar{d}\text{LT}+z\sigma_d\sqrt{\text{LT}} \tag{5.6}$$

where
$\bar{d}$ = Average daily demand
LT = Lead time
σ_d = Standard deviation of daily demand
Z = number of standard deviations corresponding to the service level probability
$z\sigma_d\sqrt{\text{LT}}$ = safety stock

The term $\sigma_d\sqrt{\text{LT}}$, in this formula for the ROP is the square root of the sum of the daily variances during the lead time.

$$\text{Variance} = (\text{Daily variance}) \times (\text{Number of days of lead time}) = \sigma_{d^2}\text{LT}$$

$$\text{Standard deviation} = \sqrt{\sigma_{d^2}\text{LT}} = \sigma_d\sqrt{\text{LT}},$$

Example 2: For the same e-Paint internet store, let us assume that the daily demand for iron coat paint is normally distributed with an average daily demand of 30 gallons and a standard deviation of 5 gallons of paint per day. The lead time for receiving a new order of paint is 10 days. Determine the ROP and safety stock if the store wants a service level of 95% with the probability of a stock-out equal to 5%.

Solution:
$\bar{d}$ = 30 gallons per day
LT = 10 days
σ_d = 5 gallons per day
For a 95% service level, Z = 1.65 (from table area under the standardized normal curve)

$$\text{Safety stock} = z\sigma_d\sqrt{\text{LT}},$$
$$= (1.65)\,(5)\,(\sqrt{10})$$
$$= 26.1 \text{ gallons}$$
$$R = \bar{d}\text{LT} + z\sigma_d\sqrt{\text{LT}}$$
$$= 30(10) + 26.1$$
$$= 326.1 \text{ gallons}$$

When there is constant demand and variable lead time, if only lead time is variable, then $\sigma_{d\text{LT}} = d\sigma_{\text{LT}}$

$$R = d\overline{\text{LT}} + zd\sigma_{\text{LT}}, \tag{5.7}$$

where
d = Demand rate
$\overline{\text{LT}}$ = Average lead time
σ_{LT} = Standard deviation of lead time
Z = Number of standard deviations corresponding to the service level probability

Example 3: A motel uses approximately 600 bars of soap each day, and this tends to be fairly constant. The lead time for soap delivery is normally distributed with a mean of six days and a standard deviation of two days. A service level of 90% is desired.

1. Find the ROP.
2. How many days of supply are on hand at the ROP?

Solution:
d = 600 bars per day
SL = 90%, so z = 1.28 (from table area under the standardized normal curve)
$\overline{\text{LT}}$ = 6 days
σ_{LT} = 2 days

$$R = d\overline{\text{LT}} + zd\sigma_{\text{LT}}$$
$$= 600 \times (6) + 1.28 \times (600) \times (2)$$
$$= 5{,}136 \text{ bars of soap}$$
$$\text{No. of days} = R/d = 5{,}136/600 = 8.56 \text{ days}$$

ROP: Variable demand and variable lead time Expression

If both demand and lead time are variable, then

$$\sigma_{dLT} = \sqrt{\overline{LT}\sigma^2_d + \bar{d}^2\sigma^2_{LT}}\ .$$

$$R = \bar{d} \times \overline{LT} + z\sqrt{\overline{LT}\sigma^2_d + \bar{d}^2\sigma^2_{LT}},$$

where
$\bar{d}$ = Average demand rate
$\overline{\text{LT}}$ = Average lead time
σ_{LT} = Standard deviation of lead time
σ_d = Standard deviation of demand rate
z = Number of standard deviations corresponding to the service level probability

Example 4: The motel replaces broken glasses at a rate of 25 per day. In the past, this quantity has tended to vary normally and have a standard deviation of three glasses per day. Glasses are ordered from a Cleveland supplier. The lead time is normally distributed with an average of 10 days and a standard deviation of 2 days. What ROP should be used to achieve a service level of 95%?

Solution:
$\bar{d}$ = 25 glasses per day
SL = 95%, so z = 1.65 (from table area under the standardized normal curve)
$\overline{\text{LT}}$ = 10 days
σ_{LT} = 2 days
σ_d = 3 glasses per day

$$R = \bar{d} \times \overline{LT} + z\sqrt{\overline{LT}\sigma^2_d + \bar{d}^2\sigma^2_{LT}}$$

$$= 25(10) = 1.6\sqrt{10(3)^2 + (25^2)(2^2)}$$

$$= 334 \text{ glasses}$$

SINGLE PERIOD MODEL

Sometimes referred to as the newsboy problem, it is used to handle ordering of perishables (fresh fruits, vegetables, seafood, cut flowers) and items that have a limited useful life (newspapers, magazines, spare parts for specialized equipment). It focuses on two costs: shortage cost and excess cost.

As the product is perishable and has a very limited shelf life or useful life, if there is excess stock then businesses lose as the unsold stock is lost. Also, if there is shortage of stock, then the loss will be arising out of loss of sales, dissatisfied customer and customer moving to the competition.

Shortage costs may include a charge for loss of customer goodwill as well as the opportunity cost of lost sales. Generally, shortage costs are simply unrealized profit per unit.

$$\text{C shortage } (C_s) = \text{Revenue per unit} - \text{Cost per unit.}$$

Excess cost pertains to the items left over at the end of the period. In effect, excess cost is the difference between the purchase cost and salvage value.

$$\text{C excess } (C_e) = \text{Original cost per unit} - \text{Salvage value per unit}$$

CONTINUOUS STOCKING LEVELS

Demand from customers should not ideally exceed the stocking level of the inventory. As per the demand of the customers, inventory is constantly adjusted and replenished with fresh stocks to keep the stocking level at optimum. Following are the features:

- The stocking level equalizes the cost weights.
- The service level is the probability that the demand will not exceed the stocking level, and computation of the service level is the key to determining the optimal stocking level (S_o). Service level has to be determined from the experience to avoid excess stock and not losing the customer for shortage of stock which will lead us to an optimal stocking level which is a trade-off between the two.

$$\text{Service level (SL)} = C_s/(C_s + C_e),$$

where
C_s = Shortage cost per unit
C_e = Excess cost per unit

Example 5: Sweet cider is delivered weekly to Cindy's bar. The demand varies uniformly between 300 litres and 500 litres per week. Cindy's pays 20 cents per litre for the cider and charges 80 cents per litre for it. Unsold cider has no salvage value and cannot be carried over into the next week due to spoilage. Find the optimal stocking level and its stock-out risk for that quantity.

$$\begin{aligned} C_e &= \text{Cost per unit} - \text{Salvage per unit} \\ &= \$0.20 - \$0 \\ &= \$0.20 \text{ per unit} \\ C_s &= \text{Revenue per unit} - \text{Cost per unit} \\ &= \$0.80 - \$0.20 \\ &= \$0.60 \text{ per unit} \\ \text{SL} &= C_s/(C_s + C_e) = 0.60/(0.60 + 0.20) = 0.75 \end{aligned}$$

Thus, the optimal stocking level must satisfy the demand 75% of the time. For uniform distribution, this will be at a point equal to the minimum demand plus 75% of the difference between maximum and minimum demands.

$$S_o = 300 + 0.75(500 - 300) = 450 \text{ litres}$$

The stock-out risk = 1 − 0.75 = 0.25.

IMPACT OF UNCERTAINTIES

Uncertainties in supply, process and demand are recognized to have a major impact on the manufacturing function. Uncertainty propagates throughout the network and leads to inefficient processing and non-value-adding activities. The uncertainty arising out of uncertain customer orders that leads to the question—how many and how much stock that business should carry and will the supplier deliver the requested stock on time and as per specifications. But those who can manage the uncertainty better deliver much superior performance.

WALMART OUTPERFORMS ITS COMPETITORS

Walmart successfully manages the uncertainty problems. Table 5.5 shows the difference at various stages in the supply chain between Walmart and other competitors.

TABLE 5.5 Comparison of Walmart and Its Competitors

S. No.	Stage Chain in Supply	Walmart	Competitors
1.	Direct inventory supply from warehouse to retail stores	85%	55–65%
2.	Shipping cost	3% of total expenditure	5% of total expenditure
3.	Replenishment time	Maximum 2 days	Maximum 5 days

Source: Chandran (2003).

CHAPTER SUMMARY

This chapter deals with the core issues which influence the level of inventory to be kept at various stock points to cater to the real-term customer demand. Most of the businesses really do not have any idea about how much money and other resources are locked up in the inventory impacting their business performance. This chapter discusses the methods and processes to bring in efficiency in inventory management by elaborating and analysing the key issues and their consequences very critically. It is better to run the business without any inventory following the JIT principle or 'make to order' policy. But this may not be always possible and businesses will end up holding some inventory at various locations. Inventory normally builds up in business often without the knowledge of the management, and it comes to the knowledge of the management when annual or periodic stock audit is conducted. In some of the businesses like retail operation including organized retail and online retail, inventory management is the most critical operation, and in fact, the whole profit from the business hinges on the effectiveness of the inventory management practices. These issues are analysed and discussed in the chapter. In an integrated SCM, the entire planning for production and inventory including ordering of input materials like raw and packaging material starts from the sales order received from the customer and optimized for resource management as well as for the better performance of the company's operations. The issues concerning the demand management and inventory management and control are discussed. The concepts of cycle inventory and safety inventory are discussed with examples. The importance of efficient inventory management in terms of servicing the customer orders and also avoiding a stock-out situation is critically analysed taking many real-life business situations to understand how inventory can impact business performance. Inventory management goals, objective, types of inventory, classification of inventory, inventory cost and management are also discussed with examples. Inventory control, transaction, rotation and SKUs are explained. The bullwhip effect and reasons thereof and how it can be controlled are also discussed. The impact of excess inventory within a business as well as in trade channels and how those to be managed for optimum performance are discussed. How to work out EOQ and take decisions regarding stock ordering and inventory levels of various SKUs for least cost satisfying the customer demand are also discussed. MRP and master production schedule are also discussed in this chapter. A case study on VMI at Tata Steel is also discussed.

In a dynamic business environment, demand fluctuates and businesses need to cater to the fluctuating demand. There are various reasons for demand uncertainty, and this chapter discusses those reasons with examples and exercises as well as a case to drive the point. How safety stock is calculated to ensure product availability under uncertainty conditions is discussed with examples. How global retailer Walmart manages to outperform its competitors in terms of managing the uncertainty in demand in a dynamic and fluctuating business environment is briefly discussed.

DISCUSSION QUESTIONS

1. Why do we need inventory? What are the important goals and objectives of inventory management?
2. How does inventory impact business performance? Discuss different approaches to classify the inventory. For efficient and responsive supply chain operations, how should the inventory of various types be analysed?
3. What constitute inventory cost? Discuss the tools and techniques of effective inventory management.
4. What is the bullwhip effect and what causes it? How does it impact the supply chain performance?
5. How can businesses reduce the impact of the bullwhip effect? Discuss the possible responses of businesses to a stock-out situation.
6. Discuss the TPOP system for inventory management. What is EOQ and how is it determined?
7. Discuss the core concept of MRP. How is it differentiated from the order point system?
8. Discuss the min–max replenishment system of inventory management. How do you calculate the total cost of inventory?
9. What is VMI? Discuss how VMI helps in managing the inventory better taking the example of Tata Steel.

REFERENCES

Ballou, R. H. 2004. *Business Logistics: Supply Chain Management*, 339. 5th ed. New Jersey: Pearson Education.

Chakraborty, Mayukh, and Sukanta Chandra Swain. 2011. 'A Study of Vendor Managed Inventory with Reference to Tata Steel'. *Anvesha* 4 (1, January–June): 12–21.

Chandran, P. Mohan. 2003. 'Wal-Mart's Supply Chain Management Practice'. Research Paper OPER-020. Hyderabad: ICFAI Center for Management Research.

Crowther, John E. 1964. 'Rationale for Quantity Discounts'. *Harvard Business Review* (March–April): 121–127.
Maxwell, William L., and John A. Muckstadt. 1985. 'Establishing Consistent and Realistic Reorder Intervals in Production: Distribution Systems'. *Operations Research* 33 (6): 1316–1341.

BIBLIOGRAPHY

Lee, Hau L., and Corey Billington. 1992. 'Managing Supply Chain Inventories'. *Sloan Management Review* (Spring): 65–73.
Love, S. 1979. *Inventory Control*. New York, NY: McGraw-Hill.
Silver, Edward A., David Pyke, and Rein Petersen. 1998. *Inventory Management and Production Planning and Scheduling*. New York, NY: John Wiley & Sons.
Vrat, P. 2014. *Materials Management: An Integrated Systems Approach*. India: Springer.
Zipkin, Paul H. 2000. *Foundations of Inventory Management*. Boston, MA: Irwin/McGraw-Hill.

6

Transportation

LEARNING OBJECTIVES

Section I: Transportation in an Integrated Supply Chain

- Understand the role of transportation in supply chain and logistics management
- Learn about the types and modes of transportation and decision criteria on the selection of mode of transport system for business
- Know about the global transportation network and challenges of ocean shipping
- Appreciate the role of infrastructure on transportation and its impact on a supply chain
- Familiarize with the global shipping lines and alliances and competition
- Recognize the key drivers of sustainable transportation in global trade

Section II: Packaging Issues in Transportation

- Appreciate the importance of packaging in transportation of goods
- Address the packaging issues in transportation and get clarity about the role of packaging
- Get acquainted with the packaging of hazardous goods and regulations

SECTION I
TRANSPORTATION IN AN INTEGRATED SUPPLY CHAIN

INTRODUCTION

The transport sector is considered as the most vital sector of any economy. Goods and services move faster with well-developed road, port and rail infrastructures, incurring lesser cost. If roads are wide and good, suitable for the movement of heavy transport vehicles, freight cost will come down making the economy more competitive. Transportation is therefore vital for growth and development of any economy and society. The supply chain performance of any corporation is linked with the status of the transport sector in that environment. One of the elements of the cost of logistics operations is transport or shipping cost. There is therefore a need for businesses to study this transport system, infrastructure as well as regulation related to the movement of their goods and services from the point of production to the point of consumption. Freight cost for both bringing the input material to the production site and taking the output material to the consumption point contributes lot to the cost of the product. In a typical situation and market structure that prevails in India which is highly complex, transportation cost is much higher in comparison to the developed countries of the world. Finding out better and more cost-effective options on mode of transport is a big challenge to the logistic manager. Managing transportation effectively helps businesses to have some competitive advantage over others. Manufacturing in-house against out-house options also hinges on savings that can be derived by such decisions on sourcing of products and services.

ROLE OF TRANSPORTATION

Transportation is an essential service and is the nerve centre of any economy. The economy will come to a grinding halt if the transportation service is disrupted and no system can tolerate such situations. This can even create civil unrest if essential goods and services do not reach the locations in time where these are needed. In that sense, the transportation industry plays a very useful role in the economy. The products are produced and stored in one location but they are consumed in different locations. And invariably, products are to be delivered in consuming centres and buyers are spread all over in a geographical area to be covered by a company. Transportation is thus a very important driver of the supply chain as products are hardly consumed where these are produced. There was a time when logistics was almost synonymous with transportation, but the transportation industry is really huge. India's logistics industry which is synonymous with transportation is worth about US$160 billion growing at the compound annual growth rate (CAGR) of 10.5%, and with the implementation of GST, total logistics industry is likely to touch US$215 billion by 2020 as per the Economic Survey of 2017–2018. Indian logistics industry has grown at a CAGR of 7.8% during 2012–2017, and it provides employment to 22 million people. In terms of global ranking of World Bank's LPI, India's rank improved to 35th in 2016 from the earlier ranking of 54th in 2014, indicative of the fact that India has improved in terms of global LPI.

To a large extent, the logistics sector in India remains unorganized. The industry is facing challenges of high cost of logistics, impacting its competitiveness in both domestic and international markets. Other factors responsible for higher costs of logistics are poor physical infrastructure, lack of use of technology for material handing, fragmented warehousing and lack of seamless movement of goods across modes. In order to develop this sector for integrated logistics management, it is important to focus on new technology, higher investment in the sector, skilling and removal of bottlenecks, improvement of intermodal transportation, automation, single window clearance and simplifying processes, which are the key imperatives.

Freight cost is a significant element of cost in the supply chain, and managing transportation effectively is a key determinant of success criteria for the business. In a developing country like

India, because of poor infrastructure, logistics cost is much higher. While in India logistics cost is about 15% of the selling price, in the USA it is about 8% and hence they are more competitive. Because of poor road conditions, it takes much longer for trucks to travel from one place to another for carrying the goods. The truck capacity is also lower because the roads are narrow in many places. Besides, we also use slow-moving vehicles and traditional transport system such as auto-rickshaws, cycle-rickshaws, bullock carts, horse and camel carts and even human beings carrying stock as headload for last-mile connectivity. The last-mile connectivity adds not only cost but also complexity to the whole transport system. Before the implementation of GST, there were checkpoints at the entry of every state, which further delayed vehicle movement and added to both cost and complexity. E-commerce players like e-retailers use courier service to deliver the product to individual customers either sourcing it directly from the manufacturer-marketers or sourcing it from the company's strategic stock point where the inventory of some of the high-demand product categories is always maintained. Because of the limitation of the reach of the courier service in a country like India as well as the complexity of tax compliance in addition to penetration of the internet, e-commerce services have not yet been able to reach their natural potential. Things, however, are now improving.

In global trade, freight is an important consideration of competitiveness. The supply chain performance of some of the global companies such as Walmart and IKEA depends upon the logistics cost as these companies source from low-cost countries and then sell their products throughout the world. Transportation is therefore an important element of consideration. Large format stores and global supply chain network help them to improve the cost effectiveness. Their stocks are normally carried by large shipping lines. The shipper in this case is the company like Walmart itself, as they are the party that requires movement of the product between sourcing point and delivery point of the supply chain, and the carrier is the party that moves or transports the product and in this case that could be shipping lines like Maersk Line or DSV.

The world's economic development is closely associated with the development of transport infrastructure. Transport logistics helps sustain global economic growth and accelerate the globalization of productive activities and markets. The continued growth of geographical infrastructure is critical for the persistence of transport logistics within the global economy. International transport has evolved from its original relationships between ships, airport and other transport vehicles to physically making cargoes between geographical points to match the supply and demand requirement.

FUNCTIONS OF TRANSPORT

Transportation helps in the growth of the business in FMCG by quickly replenishing the goods at numerous stock points and retail outlets. An efficient transportation system is a prerequisite for achieving the growth target in a competitive business. Some products are consumed fast, and if quickly replenished, the incremental demand can be generated. For some products, the sale is lost permanently due to non-availability of stock. Thus, transportation also helps in increasing the demand for the product.

Transport helps in creating both time and space utilities by taking goods from production centres located even in remote locations where there is no local demand to places where demand exists, and also by moving goods and services faster from one location to another. Transport helps consumers to enjoy quality goods produced in distant locations including overseas locations. Without efficient transport, this would not have been possible. Consumers need not have to consume only what is produced locally. They get products produced and manufactured in distant locations as well. Transport makes that distance short.

If the transport system is not efficient and effective, there will be scarcity of stocks in certain locations resulting in price rise. Transport, thus, helps in terms of stabilizing the price of the goods. For essential goods, an efficient transport system is a must. Transport thus ensures even flow of commodities in the hands of consumers throughout the period of consumption.

Transport also provides a competitive edge to the business by transporting large stocks at preferential rates to remain competitive in comparison to local suppliers of a similar or same product.

And lastly, transport increases the mobility of capital and labour from one location to another, which is vital for economic growth. Labours migrate from one location to another in search of jobs. Capital equipment are sourced and transported from various locations even from overseas for setting up large projects, creating new opportunities. New projects would not be possible to set up without having an efficient transport system in place to take the goods to sell where customers exist or even to transport the plant and equipment to site for setting up the project.

MODE OF TRANSPORTATION AND CRITERIA OF DECISION

Mode of transportation largely depends on whether it is a domestic cargo or an international cargo. All international cargoes also involve transportation to the domestic area after the cargo reaches the port of destination. In a typical supply chain, the following modes of transportation are used to ensure movement of goods from the point of origin to the point of consumption. They are also used in combination wherever required. For a domestic cargo, trucks and rails are the most widely used mode of transportation.

- Rail
- Truck
- Air
- Water
- Pipelines
- Package carriers
- Intermodal

An international cargo is taken either by air or water. However, in Europe it is largely surface transport as small countries are all connected through excellent high-speed motorable roads. Rail connectivity is also good. Broadly, several modes of transport can be reclassified as follows:

1. Road transport
2. Water transport
3. Air transport

ROAD TRANSPORT

If we consider the typical transport system that still prevails in a country like India, we can have the following:

- **Pathways:** Goods are also transported as headloads or on animal cart or even on animal backloads. In remote villages and forest areas including hilly areas, this is still an important mode of transport where vehicles cannot reach. In Gomukh from where the holy Ganges emerges and Topovan which is about 18 km from Gangotri or similar such places in the Himalayan region, goods are transported by human beings in headloads or on animals' backs, as road transport is possible only up to Gangotri. Goods reach such areas in animal transport mode. Animals such as horses, ponies, donkeys, asses, buffaloes, camels, elephants, yaks and sheep are used to transport goods in remote areas in hills, forests and deserts.
- **Roadways:** It is used for both vehicular and non-vehicular transport. Road transport is one of the most important modes of transport in the commercial world. There is a significant improvement. Vehicular transport cars, trucks, buses, lorries, auto-rickshaws, bullock carts, tongas, hand carts and so on, and non-vehicular transport such as hamals and animals such as camels, dogs, elephants, horses and mules are seen to be in use for carrying goods. In developed countries like the USA and European Union (EU) countries, majority of the stock moves in heavy-duty, fast-moving trucks, trailers and other fast-moving transport vehicles. Because of an excellent road network connecting most of the countries, road transport is a preferred mode of transport. Even in India, large part of the stock still moves by truckers. Roadways thus facilitate the movement of a major portion of the goods (Mover DB.com 2016).
- **Tramways:** Tramway is one of the cheaper, longer, quicker and safer modes of land transport which is suitable only in large cities where it still exists. But in many cities, it has been phased out. It has many limitations as it is considered a slow-moving, high-cost as well as inflexible in nature mode, covering a limited area, and is hardly used for goods transport even in local areas.
- **Railways:** Railway has been one of the most preferred modes of transport in many countries. It has helped in the growth of commercial and industrial development of various countries. Until the introduction of motor transport, railway had the monopoly over the land transport. In India, it is the principal means of transport. It carries over 80% of goods traffic and over 70% of passenger traffic. It covers more than 60,000 km of distance in India. Railway includes both passenger and goods trains and is much cheaper and hence preferred for bulk goods carrier for essential goods.

WATER TRANSPORT

Water transport is the cheapest and oldest mode of transport for large and bulky cargoes. An international cargo mostly moves by a ship as an ocean cargo. In Kerala, a large part of trade within the state is carried out by water transport. Boats carry stock through rivers and canals, taking stock from one part to another selling the stock of goods en route. This is cheap, environment friendly and also economical. Accordingly, inland water transport can thus be divided into river transport and canal transport. River transport is suitable for small boats and steamers. It was highly developed in the pre-railway days. But with the development of railways, river transport was neglected and decayed gradually. Canals are the artificial waterways constructed for the purpose of navigation as well as irrigation. It is therefore limited to certain areas. A plan has been drawn up to develop some of these river transport for commercial movement of cargo. In northeastern areas again, the idea of water transport has been mooted and a plan has been drawn up for the purpose.

Ocean Transport

Ocean transport or shipping may be subdivided into various sub-categories based on their scope and services offered to the logistics operator:

- **Coastal shipping:** Coastal shipping is a cheaper, speedy, flexible and economical form of transport for the movement of bulky and heavy cargoes. Usually, coastal shipping trade is reserved for the national shipping. In India also, from 1951 onwards, coastal shipping trade is extremely reserved for the national ships. The government has taken initiatives to connect waterways through rivers which can reduce the cost of shipping. In places like Kerala, normal trade is also done carrying goods through canals and local rivers.
- **Overseas shipping:** On the basis of their working, overseas shipping may be divided into the following: liners (those ships which follow defined routes with fixed places and fixed timetables), tramps (those ships which have no set routes or fixed timetables) and oil tankers (special sea carriers of crude oil in very large quantity). Liners may again be subdivided into passenger liners and cargo liners. Major global carriers include Maersk Line, DSV, American President Lines (APL), Evergreen Group, Hanjin Shipping Company and so on. In India, we have Shipping Corporation of India—a public sector company acting as a major shipping line from India. The Great Eastern Shipping Company Ltd is the India's largest private shipping company, which mainly transports liquid, gas and solid bulk products. In global trade, water transport is the most dominant mode of transport for all kinds of products and merchandise such as cars, food, grains and garments. Considering the quantities shipped and long distances involved, the recent trend is in the growth of the container shipment which has led to the demand of much larger in size, faster and specialized vessels to improve the economy of the container transport.

Vessels used in ocean shipping, as mentioned above, thus include the following:

- **Bulk service:** It is engaged in the transfer of dry bulk commodities from rail or truck to deck.
- **Liner service:** It is engaged in a service that operates within a schedule and has a fixed port rotation.
- **Tramp service:** It is engaged in a service that operates within a schedule and has a fixed port rotation.

AIR TRANSPORT

It is the latest mode of transport started in the 20th century. The first air service started between London and Paris in 1919, and it became a regular mode of transport during the First World War (1914–1918), and thereafter it gradually increased and started giving competition to railways.

Like railways, air transport also has two components: passenger and cargo. Air transport is considered for costly cargoes such as defence cargo and urgent cargo, which are required to reach the destination urgently. For example, during any disaster management situation or a war time situation, air cargo is preferred as cost is not that much of an important consideration during those situations.

Air freight is available to and from most countries including the developing world. Forty per cent of the world's manufactured products travel by air. Items that are of high value or are high in size tend to travel by air. Also, items that need to be moved on a short notice need to travel by air and as such defence services and their logistics need to be transported by air.

Considerations for Selecting a Mode of Transport

There are many considerations to be taken into account for taking a decision regarding the mode of transportation to be used in a particular case. These include the following:

- Transit time
- Cost
- Predictability
- Non-economic factors

The non-economic factors could be safety, reliability, past experience and even environmental and sustainability factors.

PACKAGE CARRIERS

Package carriers are actually transportation companies including FedEx, UPS, DHL, Blue Dart, postal service and many such courier companies which take small parcels and courier packets for transporting all over the world. Given the small size of packages and multiple delivery points, consolidation of shipment is a key consideration in terms of increasing the utilization and reducing the cost for package carriers. They make use of trucks for local deliveries as well as for picking up of the packages. They also have collection points and delivery and pick-up boys to manage the huge task of collection and deliveries from multiple locations. Packages so collected are taken to large sorting centres from where these are delivered by road, rail or air, as the case may be, to various destinations. Key issues in this industry are location-specific challenges, the capacity of delivery points and information flow for tracking the package en route till delivered. This mode of transport is preferred for online businesses which handle customers in remote and multiple locations, and as such, with the growth of online businesses, this industry has demonstrated significant growth.

PIPELINE

Pipelines are normally used to transport water by the municipal corporation or crude petroleum oil or gas from the port terminal to the refineries located in the mainland. This requires dedicated pipeline installations involving huge capital investment. However, all refineries have their own network of pipelines to carry crude to the refineries. The pipelines are designed to utilize the full installed capacity. They also face security and pilferage issues and even disputes which they need to resolve.

INTERMODAL

Intermodal transportation is when more than one mode of transport are used to carry the goods from the point of origin to the point of consumption. A variety of intermodal transport is possible, for example, trucks and rails. As container shipping volume has increased in global trade, intermodal transport has also increased as containers are easy to transport from one mode to another and as such, containerized freight often uses truck, water and rail combinations in global trade. Door-to-door deliverers of cargoes in global trade invariably use intermodal transport of water, rail and truck to make the best use of the transport infrastructure available in a given situation. The key issue involved in intermodal transport is exchange of information flow to facilitate the shipment on real-time basis when goods are moving from one mode to another, as these transfers often result in delays in delivery and thus also the performance.

MAJOR MODES OF TRANSPORTATION

Major modes of transportation are thus road, rail (surface transport), sea and air. The selection of the mode depends on cost, urgency and destination, and also on the material to be transported. In global logistics, the most preferred modes of transport are air and sea. However, sometimes special facilities like cold chain or refrigerated containers are required for the shipment of frozen goods like frozen marine products that go from India to major European, Japanese as well US destinations. In domestic transport, road is the most preferred; next to road is railways.

In Europe, both road and railways as surface transport are most important because of the most efficient surface transport network. European cargo movement is somewhat similar to domestic cargo movement in countries like the USA and India. In a domestic cargo, surface transport is the major driver for the delivery of the cargo. However, if waterways are available and efficient, that would be the least costly mode of transportation.

TRANSPORTATION INFRASTRUCTURE

In any business, an important consideration is that how the goods and services required for bringing the input material into the production or manufacturing facilities and also for taking the finished goods to the consumption points, where customers are located, are to be chosen. The management and more particularly the logistics manager must familiarize themselves with the typical issues that determine the most optimum methods of shipping goods out from manufacturing locations as well as bringing goods into the manufacturing plants for processing. A lot of options need to be carefully evaluated before taking such crucial decisions. Some companies manage the task of transportation themselves, using their own transport vehicle which is feasible if the organization is relatively small and their customers are located close by. Some organizations manage the function themselves using transport services of third parties selected from a wide choice available. There are even organizations which have completely outsourced some of their distribution and freight-forwarding activities. For example, Hero Honda has outsourced their distribution activities including international sales. Based on customer orders received, the products are picked up by third-party service providers from the factory gate premises. To take such important decisions, the management needs to consider the following from a strategic point of view:

- A firm's logistics platform is determined by a location's ease and convenience of market reach under favourable cost circumstances.
- Public sector investment priorities, safety regulations, tax incentives and transport policies, each has major effects on the international logistics decisions of the firm.
- The logistics manager must learn about existing and planned infrastructures abroad and at home and factor them into the firm's strategy.

KEY CONSIDERATIONS ON DECISION ON TYPE OF TRANSPORT TO BE USED

The cost of logistics is the primary consideration. The choice depends on the urgency of the customers and the cost of transport. In India, infrastructure is not yet fully developed and logistics cost is high. Transportation cost rises with high motor fuel price and the state of transport infrastructure. In India, global transportation takes place on a larger account and mostly by sea. Only a small volume travels by air, and also fresh and perishables go by air.

FACTORS IMPACTING ROAD TRANSPORT COST

There are several factors that impact the road transport cost which is high in India when compared with that of developed countries. These factors include the following:

- Road condition and network
- Number of traffic signals and crossings on the road to cross
- Type of road and its width
- Type of transport vehicles used for goods transport and their condition
- Loading capacity of the transport vehicle used
- Regulation and policy on surface transport
- Interstate controls and documentation
- Need for transhipment
- Loading/unloading facilities and mechanization
- Monitoring and control system
- Arrangement of stock in transport vehicle
- Communication network
- Driver's personal efficiency and training
- Cost of motor fuel used (petrol, diesel, CNG)
- Last-mile connectivity

All these factors determine the travel time and also travel cost. In India, from the northeastern part to south, the time taken is more than the time taken for a çargo to move from Mumbai to a European destination.

MODE OF TRANSPORTATION: INDIA

DOMESTIC CARGO

This refers to all goods and merchandise required to be transported within the geographical territories of the country. Following are its features:

- Air cargo accounts for less than 1% of total cargo movement.
- Railways contribute 35%.
- Roads contribute 39%.
- Sea contributes 24% (8,000 km of coastline).
- Surface transport (road and rail) takes care of the largest load.
- Rail is cheaper, and for certain categories of goods including bulk commodities it is the best option.

INTERNATIONAL TRANSPORTATION

However, for an international cargo, port-to-port movement is all by sea. From the destination port to the customer location, a cargo follows domestic cargo movement facilities of that country again. An international cargo, therefore, involves multiple agencies and channel partners. Communication and information flow is, therefore, very critical to the efficiency and cost of transport.

HAZARDS IN TRANSPORTATION

Transportation is associated with a lot of hazards and risks, which need to be managed well. Also, there are international regulations and safety standards to be complied with. There are reasons for such hazards. Some of those could be as follows:

- Air hazards are caused by variations and changes in temperature and pressure.
- Sea hazards are due to water damage, corrosive atmosphere, wave impact and hostile storage conditions.
- Road/rail hazards are caused by shock, vibration, careless handling, impact breakage and transhipment.
- Cargo overloading is also a cause of hazards in all forms of transport.
- Hazardous chemicals and inflammable goods also increase hazards in transportation.
- Security issues increase with value of the consignment.

HAZARDS AND RISKS

All kinds of hazards lead to risk, and reducing hazards by taking adequate safety measures increases cost. Risk is directly proportional to unknown travel conditions, particularly handling, transhipment and last-mile connectivity. Risk in business needs to be covered through adequate insurance against risk. And insurance will depend on risk assessment, which in turn will depend on the quality of the cargo and cargo types, geographical location, mode of transport and delivery schedule. Risk is also associated with a specific ocean route. There has to be a trade-off between all these risk variables and cost, but nothing can be made absolutely risk-free. To manage hazards in transport, therefore, experience and gut feeling will come handy in taking such decisions. However, the most important factor is the reputation of the ocean liners in terms of their past performance as well as dispute settlement mechanism in place.

WHAT IS RISK?

Risk actually arises out of unknown and is also directly proportional to the degree of unknown. Nothing meaningful can be possible without taking some element of risk. A dictionary definition of risk is 'the possibility of loss or injury'. Risk involves the understanding of the potential problems that might occur and how they might impede the cargo and logistics movement. Risk management is like a form of insurance and, therefore, it is an investment. Risk utility or risk tolerance is the amount of satisfaction or pleasure received from a potential pay-off. Utility rises at a decreasing rate for a person who is risk-averse. Those who are risk-seeking have a higher tolerance for risk, and their satisfaction increases when more pay-off is at stake. The risk-neutral approach achieves a balance between risk and pay-off.

STATE OF OCEAN TRANSPORT

International transport of cargo is highly competitive. Too many ships chase the same volume of cargo. Large vessels are replacing smaller cargo vessels. A very large mega ship requires huge volume of cargo to be economical. Slow and fluctuating growth of global trade is triggered by occasional recession in many economies. Global ocean liners' losses are mounting—especially by operators in Asia–Europe sector and that includes many global ocean transporters and ocean liners. There are changing times requiring meticulous planning and execution.

HIGHLY FLUCTUATING BUSINESS

The ocean transport industry is thus a highly fluctuating business. The importance of port and ranking of the ocean liners changes depending on cargo volume, and that results in fluctuating business for logistics companies. Constant changes in ranking of port and shipping lines keep the shipping lines on their toes to explore continuously the ways and means to remain competitive. That forces many acquisitions and global alliances. Cargo volume depends on global economic conditions and macroeconomic environment including sociopolitical and geopolitical issues. Dependency on few key customers makes many shipping lines very vulnerable. Effective strategies and meticulous planning are the key to grow and survive the turbulent and volatile as well as highly competitive environment. Ultimately, those who can service better at a lower cost will be able to run a sustainable business. Reducing cost which can impact service quality will not work. Shipping lines globally are working to eliminate non-value-adding activities and keeping critical functions in-house and outsourcing the rest by identifying reliable partners through networking globally by forging strategic alignments and alliances to remain competitive.

Let us look at the top 10 container carriers and how they have been performing over a period of time (Tables 6.1–6.3).

TABLE 6.1 Top 10 Container Carriers

Rank	1996	2010
1	APM-Maersk	APM-Maersk
2	Evergreen	MSC
3	Nedlloyd	CMA CGM
4	SeaLand	APL
5	COSCO	Evergreen
6	Hanjin	Hapag-Lloyd
7	MSC	COSCO
8	NYK	CSAV
9	Mitsui	CSCL
10	Hyundai	Hanjin

Source: *Packing and Labelling Dangerous Goods For Transport.* Safety & Emergency Management, Thomson Rivers University, 2016.

TABLE 6.2 Top 10 North American Ports

Rank	2000	2011
1	Long Beach	Los Angeles
2	Los Angeles	Long Beach
3	New York/New Jersey	New York/New Jersey
4	Charleston	Savannah
5	Oakland	Vancouver
6	Seattle	Oakland
7	Norfolk	Seattle
8	Houston	Virginia
9	Savannah	Houston
10	Tacoma	Manzanillo

Source: *Packing and Labelling Dangerous Goods For Transport.* Safety & Emergency Management, Thomson Rivers University, 2016.

TABLE 6.3 Top 10 Container Ports

Rank	1980	2011
1	New York/New Jersey	Shanghai
2	Rotterdam	Singapore
3	Hong Kong	Hong Kong
4	Kaohsiung	Shenzhen
5	Singapore	Busan
6	Hamburg	Ningbo
7	Oakland	Guangzhou
8	Seattle	Qingdao
9	Kobe	Dubai
10	Antwerp	Rotterdam

Source: *Packing and Labelling Dangerous Goods For Transport.* Safety & Emergency Management, Thomson Rivers University, 2016.

It can be seen from these tables that the fortune and ranking of the global carriers and container ports are changing over the period of time. The reason being that global businesses are becoming more competitive. With trade shifting from one location of importance to another, the services to those locations are also shifting, making difference to their ranking in global trade.

LARGE SHIPPING LINES AND GLOBAL ALLIANCES

Larger ships and larger air carriers are now introduced by the industry to become more cost competitive, which can carry huge volume of cargoes such as mega ships and aircraft carriers. But they come with associated problems. Big players are looking for cargo volume, and smaller operators are finding it difficult to sustain in such an environment. The issues these large ships are facing include the following:

1. **Megas (Express Three or Triple E):** Their capacity is up to 18,000+ TEU now, against 1,000 TEU in 1970, and they have an advantage of lower operating costs. However, their problems include the following:
   - How will ships be filled? Getting that big a volume of cargo within the scheduled commitment will not be that easy.
   - Which ports will handle them? All ports are not even geared to handle such big or mega ships.
   - These mega ships also require huge investment which most of the operators are not in a position to mobilize on their own.
2. Besides, there are other operating bottlenecks.

All mega express ships thus have their associated problems and challenges to be managed effectively. They are big and come with bigger problems. The large players are trying to corner the business by aligning themselves with other carriers and forming a network.

P3 NETWORK: GLOBAL POLITICS

There are global politics to dominate the ocean transport industry, resulting in the formation of networks to get control over the cargo transport in global trade. There are alliances and networks among logistics operators to overcome the hurdles in global ocean transport. For example,

1. On 18 June 2013, Maersk Line, Mediterranean Shipping Company S.A. (MSC) and CMA CGM-Western Trade announced their intention to establish a long-term operational vessel-sharing agreement on East–West trades called the P3 Network.
2. On 24 March 2014, US Federal Maritime Commission (FMC) decided to allow the P3 Network agreement to become effective in the USA.
3. On June 24 2014 (three months later), Chinese Ministry of Commerce announced that they did not approve the P3 Network.

In spite of the fact that the Chinese Ministry of Commece has not approved the P3 Network, it is still a dominant network.

The P3 Network consists of three largest container carriers—Maersk, MSC and CMA CGM. They formed an alliance to control the market. They used big ships with hubs and ports with an objective to control the market share. FMC, USA, EU and also China reviewed their agreement.

But P3 is still a dominant force and has the following market share in various regions:

1. 44% Asia to Europe
2. 24% in the Trans-Pacific
3. 42% in the Trans-Atlantic Trade

The average vessel size of P3 vessel for Asia–Europe increased from 9,300 TEU to 14,200 by the end of 2015. Maersk's largest vessels surpassed MSC and CMA CGM when all megas delivered. When vessel size increases, the cost of operation reduces provided the volume of cargo available. Smaller operators are facing challenges for survival. P3 Network has forced other operators globally to rethink their strategies, and there is a domino effect because others have to follow for survival. The other alliances that came into existence are discussed further.

The G6 Alliance

The G6 Alliance members are as follows:

- APL
- Hapag-Lloyd
- Hyundai Merchant Marine
- NYK Line
- Mitsui (MOL)
- Orient Overseas Container Line (OOCL)

It is a vessel-sharing agreement that allows container lines to achieve economies of scale.

The CKYH Alliance

The partners in this alliance are as follows:

- COSCO
- Hanjin
- K Line
- Yang Ming
- Evergreen

These alliances were created for survival in the competitive ocean cargo carrier industry where big players have made deliberate attempts to corner the larger chunk of the business volume for their own survival. P3 Alliance has forced formation of other alliances such as G6 and CKYH for their survival. P3 took away a larger chunk of the business because of their strength, resources and capabilities. Further, realignment and takeover of the shipping lines are a distinct possibility. Such realignments are already happening.

NEW GLOBAL ALLIANCES IN OCEAN TRANSPORT

NEW OCEAN ALLIANCE

- The new Ocean Alliance will consist of Evergreen Line, CMA CGM, Cosco Shipping, and OOCL.
- In addition to the Ocean Alliance, there are two other alliances: 2M and The Alliance. While the Ocean Alliance will represent 37% of all the Asia–Europe trades' container capacity, 2M will represent 34% and The Alliance 29%, making the Ocean Alliance the largest for Asian–European trade.
- The Ocean Alliance will deploy around 350 container vessels with an estimated total carrying capacity of 3.5 million TEUs, and represent 38% of the entire global trade.
- There are going to be six services connected to Asia and Europe per week in total. The Ocean Alliance will call 18 ports directly in Asia and 13 ports directly in Europe.
- From this year on, the Ocean Alliance will also call ports directly in the Baltic Sea area. One of them is the Port of Gdansk in Poland, which will open up the possibility for the alliance to also extend the feeder network further in the Baltic Sea area. (source: https://blog.greencarrier.com/new-ocean-alliance-will-be-the-largest-for-asian-european-trade/.)

SHIPPING ROUTE AND COMPETITION

The Panama Canal and Suez Canal are long-time rivals within the container shipping industry as both canals support the flow of global trade by shortening historical trade routes. Container ships continued to grow in size and the canals noticed the need for expansion projects in order to keep pace with the industry. Below we compare the two canals' history, expansion projects, individual market share and future. The original Suez Canal opened almost 150 years ago, linking the Mediterranean Sea with the Red Sea. The canal took almost 10 years to dredge and was opened for navigation in 1869. Vessels were then able to bypass the long route around the southern tip of Africa by transiting the 101-mile Egyptian waterway.

The Panama Canal expansion project started in 2007 and was completed in 2016. A new, third set of locks created an additional lane to accommodate larger container ships. After the completion of the project, the canal can now handle 13,000 TEU capacity vessels, more than two times its previous capacity.

The Suez Canal Authority recognized that it would need to compete with the expanding Panama Canal. Therefore, the canal authority announced its plan in August 2014 to deepen the canal and create a new 45-mile parallel lane to enable two-way traffic.

Previously, the Suez Canal only permitted one-way convoys which created delays for ships moving through the waterway. The expansion project shortened the transit time from 18 hours to 11 hours. The wait time to transit the canal also dropped from about 11 hours to around 3 hours (http://blog.ascentgl.com/the-panama-canal-vs-the-suez-canal, accessed on 16 April 2019).

THE FUTURE OF THE CANALS

At the conclusion of the Panama Canal expansion, ultra-large mega ships (capacity of 14,501 TEU and higher) will not be able to transit the canal. Therefore, the Panama Canal Authority is contemplating yet another expansion project which would allow the canal to handle vessels as large as 20,000 TEUs.

Both the Panama Canal and the Suez Canal will likely continue expansion projects into the foreseeable future as mega vessels continue to be introduced on carrier service strings. The anticipated construction of vessels with capacity of 20,000 TEUs will continue to affect the canals and industry as a whole (http://blog.ascentgl.com/the-panama-canal-vs.-the-suez-canal).

Not only will the canals be forced to accommodate the introduction of these ultra-large mega ships, but they will also have a significant impact on infrastructure and terminal berthing around the world.

SUEZ AND PANAMA CANALS

Suez canal connecting Atlantic to Indian ocean and Panama Canal connecting Pacific to Atlantic ocean have played an important role in global trade by reducing the distance for the cargo to travel. Their features have been discussed as follows:

1. The Suez route (Atlantic to Indian Ocean) is well supplied with coaling stations and so on as there are plenty of islands and other points of call. The Panama route (Pacific and Atlantic Oceans) suffers for want of enough islands and halting stations as the Pacific is a dreary ocean with little commerce.
2. Coal is easily and cheaply available on the Suez route, especially as coal occurs in many of the areas served by the Suez route.
3. The Panama route serves regions which are deficient in coal. It has, however, considerable amount of oil.

4. The Suez route serves some of the most thickly populated areas and carries, therefore, a much larger traffic than the Panama route which generally serves poor mountainous or desert regions like those on the east coast of North America or South America.
5. The Suez Canal is longer, has no locks and has cost less than the Panama Canal. It is not so deep; however, the practice of tying up, so annoying in the case of the Suez, is not necessary in the case of the Panama Canal.
6. The Suez Canal dues are higher than those of the Panama Canal.

OTHER IMPORTANT SHIP CANALS

Other important ship canals of the world are as follows: the Sault Sainte Marie Canal (called Soo), the Manchester Ship Canal, the Kiel Canal, the North Sea Canal between Amsterdam and the North Sea, and the New Waterway between Rotterdam and the North Sea.

CURRENT CONCERNS

The current concerns are as follows:

1. Supply of ships and container space exceeds demand
2. Pricing and rates—flat and somewhat low
3. Unhealthy competition
4. Shipping lines reporting losses

SHAKE-OUT AHEAD

Many large shipping lines are incurring losses. For example, Hanjin's operating loss was US$225 million in 2017. Mergers and acquisitions are seen to be happening in this global logistics sector. A possibility exists for CSAV/Hapag-Lloyd joining the P3 Network.

THE NEXT FEW YEARS

As big ships are spread around globally, more rate volatility in more trade lanes is expected. Besides, scheduled/service vagaries and dropped weekly sailings and fewer carriers in global business are expected as a major shake-out, resulting in the emergence of new business models, and realignment and diversification are a distinct possibility. Other signals that are emerging include the following:

1. Alliances, slot exchanges and vessel sharing—created and changed
2. Shipping routes—added and revised
3. Sailing schedules—made and reworked
4. 'Slow steaming'—ongoing practice
5. Irregular performance
6. Lack of service reliability
7. Potential changes as to ports to handle ships

These might result into SCM performance because of increased uncertainty for planning that will undermine inventory yield maximization, resulting in more inventories and more capital tied up in the system.

GLOBAL TRENDS IN TRANSPORTATION AND LOGISTICS

A lot of things are happening in the logistics and transport industry, and the reasons are as follows:

- There are country-specific developments.
- Global market forces are triggering changes.
- Every year the logistics industry is facing new challenges.
- Regulatory and environmental requirements are changing.
- Logistics is the new focus of global industry for competitiveness.
- Security concerns have increased.

BRINGING PRODUCTION LOCATION CLOSER TO THE END CUSTOMERS

To reduce the cost of logistics, businesses and more particularly global businesses are seen to bring the production centres closer to the end users or customers, which has helped in reduction in both labour and transportation costs. This was necessary to offset the increased cost of labour as well as transportation and also due to increased competition. More and more European producers have realized that they can maintain the same level of cost and high quality of the product irrespective of the fact that they produce in their offshore manufacturing plants in Asian countries or even nearby countries in Europe, as bringing the production centres closer to the end users results in lesser transportations, shorter lead times and better planning of the logistics flows in addition to making corrections much easier on the transportation and shipping plans as and when required. As a result, we can now see that some of the production plants are shifting to East European locations from China and other locations for the reason that the market for the company's products is now closer and these European countries are now seen to be more cost effective when compared with their counterparts in other countries located far from the customer locations taking increased logistics and transportation costs into consideration. The logistics issues are now increasingly influencing crucial and critical decisions related to global production and manufacturing locations.

INVESTMENTS IN LARGER VESSELS CREATED OVERCAPACITY IN CONTAINER SHIPPING

Large global shipping companies have invested in larger container vessels in order to reduce the increased operational costs to remain competitive. Larger vessels are expected to reduce the carrying cost of cargo per container unit. However, large shipping companies acquiring larger vessels have also created a situation of overcapacity. The capacity is now more than the demand and that is expected to keep the freight rates low till the time the increased demand in terms of cargo volume can balance the overcapacity so created by the industry.

SUSTAINABILITY AND COMPLIANCE BECOMING IMPORTANT ISSUES IN THE GLOBAL TRANSPORT INDUSTRY

There is an increased global awareness of and concern about environmental impact of transportation sector and guidelines to be complied with. People, in general, are more aware and committed to take care of our planet. Transport industry is blamed for much of the emissions of carbon dioxide and nitrogen oxide and it is, therefore, the key imperative on businesses to take care of the level of emissions and become responsible for such actions. In the global transport industry, there is therefore a continued focus on sustainability and compliance with regard to the environmental issues and CSR. The more you are responsible for causing the damage to the environment, the more CSR you will have. The customers who are reputed and well-meaning will also distance themselves from you under public pressure, resulting in loss of business. In an environment where industries are forced to take care of their own waste, the players in the end-to-end logistics value chain are only interested to work with those companies which can offer sustainable transport solutions supported by good working conditions. This can be traced by compliance requirement of stricter laws and regulations on a global level. The developed countries such as the USA, UK and Germany are now working hard to prevent corruption through new laws that will be applicable globally.

MAJOR ACQUISITIONS IN THE GLOBAL LOGISTICS INDUSTRY

Of late, we have been witnessing many large acquisitions in the global logistics and transport industry. The economic climate has not been that favourable in recent years from a European perspective. However, the solution in Asia could be an acquisition. Other factors such as customer demand and better service at a lower cost to enable them to be competitive in the marketplace, logistics and transport industry, are the opportunities of acquisition to eliminate competition and become more cost effective. We have seen this trend even in North America and the trend is accelerating. The postal service in Japan is one such example which has made great investment in the industry. The Indian post and telegraph industry has been going through also a transformation. Slovenia Postal Service seems to have transformed into becoming the largest logistics company in the country, although they still have to make the company profitable.

HOW ACQUISITION HELPS GLOBAL LOGISTICS COMPANIES

Acquiring a business has many advantages. Some of them are as follows:

- Helps getting critical mass and only after getting critical mass accelerated growth is possible
- Increases market share
- Eliminates a potential competition
- Can eliminate your immediate competitor
- Financial leverage
- Can emerge as a significant global player overnight

- Can draw on a synergistic association
- Is a better way to enter a new geographical area

Many a time an acquisition is made just to destroy a formidable competition. However, an acquisition also comes with its own challenges such as:

- Managing the merger of acquired entity post acquisition
- Cultural diversity
- Value and ethics in two different entities in an acquisition
- Integration challenges
- HRM issues—duplicate workforce and the question arising which one to retain
- Sometimes companies acquired become more of a dominant force than the company which has acquired

GREEN TRANSPORT SOLUTIONS PREFERRED OVER AIR FREIGHT

The Trans-Siberian Railway has been given a boost, as more and more players are interested to invest in eco-friendly transport solutions to and from Asia, and this trend has shifted cargo from air freight to rail transport. For high-value goods, there is a significant increase in rail transport. Although air freight is the fastest shipping method, looking at the entire logistics chain from Asia to Europe, the rail transport seems to be extremely competitive for both economic and environmental reasons. The global companies are increasingly concerned about protecting environment and are thus trying to reduce large parts of their transportation costs by choosing rail transport instead of air freight.

MAJOR SHIFT TO SURFACE TRANSPORT

Rail transport is likely to get significant boost as it does not add to traffic congestion on road. Less pollution, cost-effectiveness, and its schedule do not get impacted, and therefore it runs on schedule. Road transport also will get increasing support as it can provide end-to-end services and is efficient. Also, it is a major mode of transport in any case now. Other reasons are as follows: faster movement, technology shift, fast-moving rail and road transport, and lesser cost. Air transport, as it is costly and has its associated constraints, will thus suffer for cargo movement. Air transport is increasingly becoming costlier with rise in aviation fuel cost. Bunker fuel is also coming under increasing regulatory pressure on environmental issues and as a result surface transport such as rail and road is becoming more preferred. In Europe, a large part of the cargo movement takes place by road and rail. This is a major shift that is now being witnessed.

IMPACT OF GROWING E-COMMERCE ON THE SUPPLY CHAIN

Consumers are increasingly buying goods and merchandise online instead of buying from the physical bricks-and-mortar stores. This new trend in shopping has brought in the following challenges in a supply chain:

- There is a growth in home deliveries commensurate with the growth of e-commerce industry, which in turn increases the complexity and challenges last-mile connectivity.
- For postal services, volume of letters is constantly falling, whereas packages and parcel deliveries are increasing.

The impact of these can be seen in a supply chain in the sense that logistics companies are required to optimize their supply chain and have to find out newer ways of providing last-mile delivery services. This would mean developing a cost-effective mode of transportation to private persons and individuals or to the nearest distribution points. This has helped growth in courier service business in India. This, in fact, is a new type of logistics chain than what we have been doing so far historically.

The fastest-growing segment in China and India is Internet shopping, which is pushing the logistics systems to cope with a booming number of deliveries to individual homes as well as offices.

It is also being experienced that an increasing number of customers who have traditionally moved their production centres from the home countries, for example, Scandinavian countries, to China are then importing back from China to their home markets. These companies have now started to sell even in China and Asia, which requires local SCM infrastructure.

These impacts require a change in the supply chain and there could be several solutions for such a situation. Each solution has to be customer and situation specific, and no one solution can fit all.

NEW GEOGRAPHIES WILL PROVIDE THE ECONOMIC GROWTH

So far, China has had a rapid economic growth and served as a growth engine for increasing global trade. But now we will be seeing the growth coming from other geographic regions including India. Africa is expected to become the next big market and that would mean a big challenge for the logistics operators, given the poor infrastructure, ageing road and seaports, and underdeveloped transportation systems. Exploiting this tremendous growth opportunity of the continent and figuring out how to overcome those challenges are of great interest for all players in the logistics chain. The African countries have to investigate how they can maintain the expected and potential growth to help the economy on a positive development track. If the African market opens up, then European logistics companies will have a distinctive advantage because of their geographical proximity. India is another country to watch, as it is also on a high growth trajectory.

GROWING DEMAND ON CONTAINERIZATION

Containerization is very crucial for the development of global trade as we have seen over the years for various reasons:

- Standardized containers have made it possible to ship increasing volumes of goods around the globe in the most cost-effective manner.
- The demand for containerized transport is thus constantly increasing because it helps in better space utilization and better protection of the cargo.
- The future of transport industry seems to be now going in that direction for some of these inherent advantages.

REASON FOR CONTAINERIZATION

Global Shift in Trade Pattern

With manufacturing moving to new locations such as India and East European countries, industries are adapting to containerization. For example, the paper industry is changing the size of the paper to fit the container. There is a tug of war between containers and roll-on/roll-off (RORO). But containers are much more flexible and becoming cost effective. It is primarily from general cargo that containerized shipment has been gaining. It is believed that in 10 years' time, about 90% general cargo segment will be shipped in containers. There is further potential of containerization of timber. Majority of cargo will now be moving in containers instead of break bulk. Slovenia is an important port for timber trade. Almost certainly, the structural changes that container shipping is undergoing will provide large economies of scale, and the demand and supply ratio will continue to put pressure on container freight rates. This will increase the attractiveness of container shipping (Levinson 2006).

RORO AND BREAK BULK

RORO (or **ro-ro**) ships are vessels designed to carry wheeled cargoes, such as cars, trucks, semi-trailer trucks, trailers and railroad cars, that are driven on and off the ship on their own wheels or using a platform vehicle, such as a self-propelled modular transporter. This can be seen in all major ports around the world. Even in a small port in Slovenia, Luka Koper Port, this practice can be seen.

Break bulk cargoes are defined as general cargoes or goods that do not fit in or utilize standard shipping containers or cargo bins. Cargoes are moved from one mode of transport to another when required.

CUSTOMS-BONDED WAREHOUSE

CUSTOMS-BONDED WAREHOUSING SOLUTIONS TO SHORTEN LEAD TIMES

A typical challenge for exporters in the Nordics is that some of their competing producers are located in China or Asia, and the long lead time from the Nordics makes them less competitive.

Establishing customs-bonded warehousing solutions in, for example, Shanghai, Shenzhen and Hong Kong will cut lead times from order to delivery with more than two months.

BUYER'S CONSOLIDATION SERVICE AND E-SOLUTIONS TO KEEP TRACK OF THE GOODS

Yet another Nordic importer buys vast amounts of small-quantity orders from a large number of suppliers and has problems keeping track of shipments. The solution is buyer's consolidation service, provided at the main ports of China, together with e-solutions to keep track of the goods.

This can minimize administration and lower the costs for customer and can make their everyday operations more efficient.

FUTURE OF GREEN CARRIER AND THE LOGISTICS AND TRANSPORT MARKET IN CHINA

As the environment is an important consideration, some customers take train service from China to the Nordics. It would make a less impact on the environment—the cost is higher, but it saves on the transit time in addition to lowering the pollution. As the cost of pollution management will rise, the increased cost of rail transport for long distance will somewhat get compensated.

THE GLOBAL SHIPPING INDUSTRY WILL FACE NEW SULPHUR REGULATIONS

The International Maritime Organization (IMO) is on the cusp of implementing new sulphur regulations which will have significant impact on the global shipping industry. On 1 January 2020, IMO will enforce a ban on ships using fuel that has a sulphur content of 0.5% and above. Ships will have the option to buy 'scrubbers' to reduce the emissions from the use of a higher sulphur-containing fuel. But the increment will be to the tune of US$1 million–10 million per ship and, therefore, it is not surprising that less than 3% of global ships have made this investment so far. The new regulations are part of the IMO's effort to reduce the greenhouse gas emissions by 50% from the level of 2008 by 2050. IMO is determined to set a new global standard of shipping fuel with exception of the stricter sulphur limit of 0.1% of the existing Emission Control Areas in North America, the Caribbean, the Baltic and the North Sea.

As the global shipping industry is not ready for this change in regulations that are forthcoming, they will be under a very difficult, disruptive and turbulent transition in 2019. The implications of this is likely to go far beyond the shipping industry. With every passing month, the prices of a range of fuel including high and low sulphur-containing bunker fuel, diesel and jet fuel will become more volatile as the refiners and the fuel purchasers will pursue a pricing advantage before the deadline of 1 January 2020. The ship owners are already sounding the alarm bell about the fuel scarcity and an estimated increment of US$60 billion in fuel bills which is almost equal to the total fuel bill of the industry in the year 2016. Some of the largest crude oil tankers could foresee a 25% increase in the shipping cost arising out of a higher fuel cost itself. This will have a cascading effect, and the prices of companies as well as of household goods are also likely to go up by the end of 2019, and the whole drama will continue to unfold by the year 2020 (A.T. Kearney Analysis, based on data from US Energy Information Administration, www.energyfromshale.org.2011).

OCEAN FREIGHT

Ocean freight or sea freight is normally the preferred mode of transportation in global trade when the volume of cargo to be shipped is relatively high. While this is the longest mode of transportation, it is an ideal one when bulk volume has to be transported across geographical regions at regular intervals such as coal, oils and minerals. It is suitable for products with longer lead time in large volumes as it is affordable as well as economical. However, this mode of transportation is also relatively slow and is subjected to custom restrictions and can lead to the product getting damaged due to environmental hazards and movements if the goods are not packed properly. Ocean transport can also lead to multiple handling and transhipment, and packaging therefore needs to be ocean freight worthy. To optimize on cost, it is crucial that you optimize the container load as well to ensure that you are reducing not only the shipping expenses but also the potential for damage during transport. Non-optimized loads would lead to having unused space within the container, allowing the goods loaded enough room to shift and move against each other during the transport. To optimize, it is recommended to follow the following simple steps:

Inspect the container first before loading: It can happen that the container you are loading might have been used earlier for transporting goods, which can become a source of contamination and even hazards for your goods. The container that you are going to use to transport your goods thus needs to be inspected carefully before loading anything. Close attention needs to be paid for any contamination or residue left on the floor which can have a negative reaction with your cargo.

Load heavier materials first: Large and heavy items need to be loaded first on the floor and against the container's front wall, and then lighter materials should be placed at the top. If the shipment is a part load, it is necessary to check what other materials will be packed in the same container and if it is acceptable and compatible with your cargo to avoid any problems later on. For example, food materials cannot be loaded with other materials like chemicals.

Distribute the weight across the containers for balancing: If your container is loaded to the maximum capacity, then it is important that the cargo weight is evenly distributed across the entire floor area. You should plan ahead of loading for the advanced tools and software programs that use values such as package weight, dimension, volume and restrictions in order to help you reach an optimal container load. The packaging should be able to withstand the vibration and shock and even scuffing during ocean freight.

AIR FREIGHT

Companies working with short lead times requiring their packages to be transported as quickly as possible often decide to send goods by air freight. Also, very valuable cargoes, urgent cargoes, defence cargoes and emergency cargoes such as medicines and food during natural calamities are normally transported by air. This is a relatively safer mode of transport and also helps reducing the supplier's lead times and at the same time also improves overall service level. It can also take cargoes to difficult and not easily accessible areas. However, only certain types of goods are suitable for air transport. This expensive mode of transport often comes with airport taxes, custom and excise restrictions, and other regulatory requirements.

Hazards of Air Transport

If you decide to transport your cargo by air freight, there are certain associated hazards which you need to know and take care of by choosing the right packaging system, for example, high and low atmospheric pressures while air transport can have significant impact on certain packages. Also, humidity changes can result in condensation or even corrosion of the products and that could affect your cargo if not taken care of by using an appropriate packaging system. Shocks occur during transport and handling as a result of the impacts with containers, racks, floors and other shipments. Adequate cushioning of the package will reduce the consequential damages resulting from such shocks. Most products will require some type of shock protection in order to prevent such damages during transportation and handling.

In transport movement, your packages are liable to shift and move from their original place. From acceleration and take-off to in-flight dropping and pitching in turbulent weather damage can be caused to your cargo, and as such your package needs to be able to withstand any unexpected pitching or jarring.

ROAD TRANSPORT

Almost all packages and cargoes are subjected to road transport to a certain degree. While domestic cargoes can move on road, international cargoes also after reaching the destination port have to be transported by road to be delivered to the ultimate customers. Road transport is ideal and cost-effective for perishables for short distances. It is easy to monitor the movement of goods on road, but your package can get damaged by mishandling or careless driving or even by multiple handling, transhipment and loading–unloading shocks. Hence, if you choose to use road transport, it is important to prepare for potential delays, including traffic, truck breakdown and bad weather.

If you are shipping your products by road transport, it is also important that you choose the right packaging design. Appropriate cushioning can be designed for protection against vibration. Depending on the thickness and the load-bearing area of the cushion, it should be designed in a way that it does not get impacted by input vibration or isolates the product from the vibration, and the right design will make all the difference in how well the cushion will protect your product from damage due to vibration.

RAIL TRANSPORT

Rail is a very important and cost-effective mode of transport and thus provides a great solution for both domestic and international transport, especially for heavy cargoes. It is a safe and reliable mode of transport, which offers deliveries at affordable price points, and it is also an environmentally safe and friendly mode of transport when compared with other alternatives such as air, ocean and road transport.

However, unfortunately, rail transport is not an ideal mode of transport and comes with many inherent disadvantages. All packaging systems need to be prepared to protect goods from damage due to shunting and vibrations. Use of a right packaging system can reduce the negative impact of vibration during transport. The other disadvantages are that rail transport is available to limited routes with inflexible timetables. It only takes goods to the closest railway station, and if you are not located near a rail freight depot, you also have to take care of the transport by road to deliver the goods to the cargo booking depot.

CASE STUDY: MAERSK LINE

Maersk Line is a flagship company of A.P. Moller–Maersk group, a diversified Danish group and a global leader in the shipping industry. A.P. Moller–Maersk group had a revenue of US$60 billion in 2011, which grew to over US$70 billion in 2016. This revenue was contributed by business divisions including Maersk US$27 billion or 45%, oil and gas US$12.6 billion or 21%, and retail and banking US$20.4 billion or 34% of the group's combined revenue.

A.P. Moller–Maersk group employs 115,000 people worldwide, out of which Maersk Line employs about 16,900 and have their presence in 167 countries. The founding family trusts control 58% of the total share capital and 76% of the voting rights. The company thus is family owned and controlled. Although this family is not known for their explicit commitment to environmental issues, however, the reputation of the company worldwide is extremely important for business and it is positive.

Maersk Line is the world's biggest container shipping company, having 660 either owned or chartered vessels representing about 17% of the industry operating fleet. Its vessel make over 70,000 port calls per year. Maersk ships are 8 years old in average, whereas competitors have 12–15-year-old vessels.

Maersk Line has over 100,000 customers and with most of these customers (50%), they have long-term contracts and remaining 50% are market spot price customers. About 25% of the customers are key customers such as Walmart, Nike and Tesco, 15% are key freight forwarders and remaining 60% are small customers and other freight forwarders. Maersk Line has 7,600 seafarers and has about 500 representative offices globally spread in over 167 countries.

Maersk's Business Strategy

Maersk has three fundamental challenges to differentiate itself from the rest of the industry. These are as follows:

1. Unreliability
2. Complexity (hard-to-do business)
3. Environmental Impact

Reliability

Maersk Line's goal is to become the industry leader and keep their leadership position. They are already leader in on-time delivery up to 80% of the time, but the new goal is to improve upon further to help customers to reduce their inventory level to reach 'just-in-case inventory'. Daily Maersk Asia–Europe route achieves 95% on-time goal requiring 70 new vessels. All service ports operate entirely as planned, and on other routes they work with terminal partners to reduce time in port by 30% and have already achieved 10% reduction.

Simplicity

To reduce immense paperwork, Maersk Line has streamlined and digitized much of the paperwork. They have implemented order and follow cargo online, simplified documentation process and also implemented cargo tracking online and automatic notification to the customers updating the status through appropriate IT systems interface and improved customer service.

Environment Sustainable Strategy

Environment is a major concern in the global logistics industry. Ships' exhaust emission from bunker fuel is considered a large source of greenhouse gas emissions, and this has become a major concern of the industry as clients are exerting pressure on the vessel operators. Earlier it was thought that climate change is occurring because of greenhouse gas emissions from human activity, but maritime shipping accounts for 3.3% of global emissions and bunker fuel releases 2,000 times more sulphur than diesel fuel. A.P. Moller–Maersk group has given considerable importance to the environmental impact, and sustainability has become a key differentiator. The four key themes around this key strategic driver or key differentiator are as follows:

1. Environment and climate change
2. Health and safety, which also includes piracy
3. Social responsibility
4. Responsible business practices (similar to Sarbanes–Oxley Act of 2002 [SOX], Foreign Corrupt Practices Act [FCPA] and Dodd–Frank): Dodd–Frank is a consumer protection Act.

This strategy will be executed through a number of initiatives including technology intervention, route optimization, fleet type and sizes, and market integration as shown in Figure 6.1.

FIGURE 6.1 Business Strategy Initiatives of Maersk Line

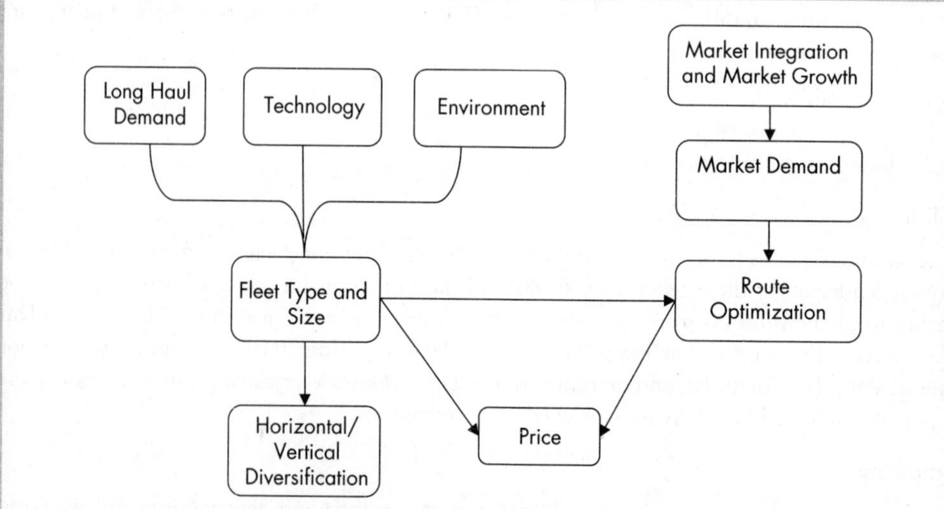

The environmental goal of Maersk Line is to become the global leader in low carbon shipping by having a greater focus on environment and sustainability with an objective to lead the industry towards zero SOX emissions by reducing its impact on marine environment. Achieving these goals would meet the group's environmental sustainability initiative.

Maersk Line intends differentiating from other competing global players on the following lines:

1. Focus on sustainability
2. Customer satisfaction and on-time delivery schedule
3. From order booking to 24 × 7 online tracking of consignment
4. Covering more destination than others
5. More focus on key customers who are long-term associates
6. Delivering incremental value

The competitors such as CMA CGM and Hapag-Lloyd had CO_2 calculators to measure the carbon footprint of shipments journey, but APL had been named the sustainable shipping operator of the year for 2010. Maersk Line is concerned and will not allow competition to score better in this score.

Financial Performance

Due to difficult and volatile market conditions, the financial performance of Maersk Line had witnessed fluctuation during 2015 and 2016.

The highlights of the financial performance of 2015 and 2016 are as follows:

- **Maersk Line** made a profit of US$1.3 billion (US$2.3 billion) and a return on capital invested (ROCI) of 6.5% (11.6%). The underlying profit declined to US$1.3 billion (US$2.2 billion) due to poor market conditions, leading to significantly lower freight rates, particularly in the second half of the year, only partially offset by lower bunker prices, USD appreciation and cost efficiencies.
- Maersk Line placed three new building orders for a total of 27 vessels with a total capacity of 367,000 TEU. Further, investments were postponed due to the weak market conditions.
- During the first part of 2015, the implementation of the Vessel Sharing Agreement with MSC on the East–West network was completed successfully with the phase-in of 193 vessels.
- **Maersk Line** expected an underlying result significantly below the last year (US$1.3 billion) as a consequence of the significantly lower freight rates going into 2016 and the continued low growth with expected global demand for seaborne container transportation to increase by 1%–3%.
- The underlying profit was US$711 million (US$3.1 billion), within the latest guidance, negatively impacted by a loss in Maersk Line.
- Lower container rates and weak market growth severely impacted earnings in Maersk Line during the year, but with a positive underlying trend recognized through the fourth quarter.

- Stabilization of oil prices in the second half of 2016 combined with cost and production efficiencies led to positive earnings growth in Maersk Oil.
- Maersk experienced a negative result due to impairments totalling US$2.8 billion after tax primarily related to Maersk Drilling and Maersk Supply Service.
- Free cash flow was negative US$29 million (US$1.6 billion excluding the sale of the Danske Bank shares).
- Cash flow from operating activities decreased to US$4.3 billion (US$8 billion), including a one-off dispute settlement in Maersk Oil.
- Gross cash flow used for capital expenditure was US$5 billion (US$7.2 billion) mainly related to the TCB acquisition and development of the Culzean and Johan Sverdrup oil fields.

Making Loss in a Decade

- The Board of Directors have proposed a dividend of DKK150 per share approved at the Annual General Meeting on 28 March 2017.
- A.P. Moller unveiled one of the biggest losses in Danish corporate history as the conglomerate suffered from a weak container shipping industry and massive write-downs on its oil businesses in 2016.
- Shares in Maersk fell as much as 7% as it reported only its second annual loss in seven decades and halved its dividend to try to protect its investment grade credit rating.
- Maersk recorded a net loss of US$1.9 billion for 2016, compared with analysts' expectations of a US$960 million profit, as it booked impairments of US$2.7 billion on its oil rig and supply services units.
- Maersk Line suffered a tough end to 2016, slipping to a loss in the fourth quarter and for the year as a whole in spite of a rebound in freight rates from record lows. It made a loss of US$376 million in 2016 compared with a profit of US$1.3 billion one year earlier.

Performance in 2017

- Due to gradual improvements in container rates, **Maersk Line** expected an improvement in excess of US$1 billion in underlying profit compared to 2016 (loss of US$384 million).
- Global demand for seaborne container transportation was expected to increase by 2–4%.
- Maersk Line reported a profit of US$339 million after four consecutive loss-making quarters, resulting in an ROCI of 6.7%.
- Market fundamentals continued to improve as demand outgrew nominal supply growth for the third consecutive quarter and further industry consolidation was announced.
- Revenue increased by 8.4% mainly driven by higher revenue in Maersk Line and Maersk Oil, partly offset by Maersk Drilling and APM Terminals.
- Profit declined to US$264 million, negatively impacted by impairments amounting to US$732 million in APM Terminals, Svitzer and Maersk Tankers.

Market Share Price Movement

It can be seen that the stock price of Maersk Line was fluctuating during 2016 and 2017. The company's performance was much better in earlier years during 2014 and 2015, but in 2016 the company suffered a setback but did not skip the dividend. The company expected a significant turnaround in the year 2017, and their new business strategy was expected to deliver better results.

FIGURE 6.2 Share Price Movement of Maersk Line

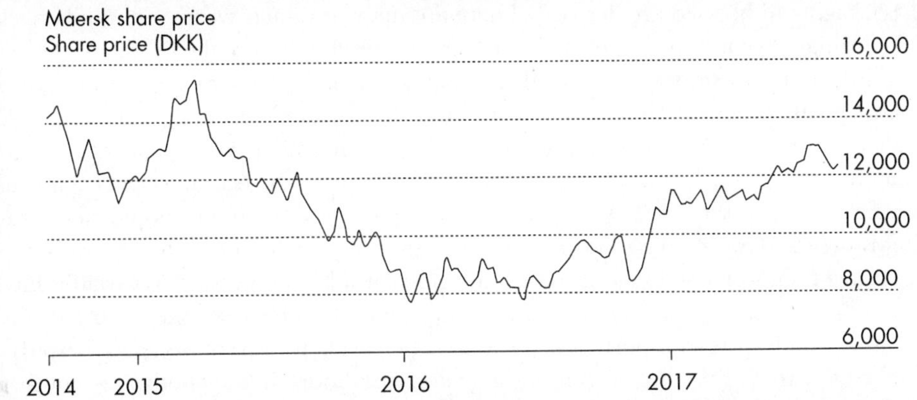

Source: https://investor.maresk.com/static files/maersk strategy and performance (accessed on 17 November 2018).

From the share price movement from 2015 to 2018 (Figure 6.2), it can be seen that share price was high at 15,000 DKK in 2015, and then due to recession, it started declining and came down to as low as 8,000 DKK in 2016 eroding almost 50% of the market value of the company and then started gradually going up again during 2017 showing a turnaround in the company's performance.

Case Questions

1. Discuss the ownership and capital structure of the company.
2. What are the various business verticals the company has, and what is their contribution in terms of revenue and profit?
3. What are the key competitive advantages of the Maersk Line. How are they doing to keep the leadership on those differentiators?
4. Explain the reasons of a sudden drop in profit in 2016.
5. What was the projected performance for 2017?
6. Who are the key competitors of Maersk Line, and from what considerations you have identified them as Maersk Line's competitors.

SECTION II
PACKAGING ISSUES IN TRANSPORTATION

INTRODUCTION

Consumers first get exposed to the packaging before getting to know about the product. The way product is packaged therefore helps to create the first impression about the product kept inside. Depending on the product category as well the distance it has to travel and the type of transportation to be used at various levels till it reaches its destination, packaging design as well as types of packaging to be used are decided. There are many products where a multiple packaging system like primary, secondary and tertiary packaging is used to ensure the products' security and integrity till they are consumed. Tertiary packaging is normally the shipping cartons which also has to comply with various requirements of size and shape as well as configuration. In addition, there is also a concern about cost and impact on the environment. While packaging has many other functions and roles to play for the success of the product, transport packaging has the primary role to ensure the integrity of the products packed throughout its journey. Transport packaging is designed to protect goods that are in transit, especially products that are shipped by truck or train or ship or combination of all. In global trade, the product invariably has to go through multiple types of transport and many transhipment. However, the supply chain often includes other modes of transportation as well. Therefore, transport packaging needs to be designed for both the local conditions and the export conditions if the goods are sent from one country to another. Any international cargo travels through both the international cargo route and the domestic cargo route, both within the country and the destination country, till the goods reaches the end customer. Some of these travel and transport infrastructure conditions are not really known to both senders and cargo operators. The packaging system designed and the type of packaging material used have to withstand these unknown travel conditions and keep the product quality and integrity intact throughout its journey till the product is consumed by the end consumers. Packaging therefore has a very distinct role to play.

IMPORTANCE OF PACKAGING IN TRANSPORTATION

The goods and merchandise need to be packed well to sustain the vagaries of transportation. In global transport, sellers are not always aware of the physical transport infrastructure that are available in transporting goods to the ultimate customers and consumers, but sellers have to ensure that the product is safe and fit for the consumption or use as the case may be till it is consumed by the end customer. Transportation, therefore, is a very important parameter to be designed and developed by the manufacturers and marketers. In some countries, and that include India and Africa, the secondary and tertiary transport conditions to take the product and merchandise to the ultimate destination from the port are very difficult and involve multiple agencies and people; the task of packaging design and type is to be very judiciously selected so that it preserves the integrity of the product and ensures delivery of performance at reasonable, affordable and competitive costs, failing which even the best products in the world will be useless if you cannot get them where they need to be at a competitive price, and in that respect, from making transportation possible to protecting goods during transit, logistics packaging is a vital part of the supply chain delivery process.

Sending something for delivery, or supplying to retailers, involves far more than simply putting the goods into a shipping carton and/or box. If enough thought and care are not taken for designing the packaging system, it can prove to be a disaster.

INTERNATIONAL PACKAGING ISSUES

For international cargo movement, packaging is most important to secure the cargo from damages during transit and also for retaining the quality and integrity of the cargo intact. This can be done by strictly following the regulations according the cargo types and mode of transport. Following points are to be noted:

- Packaging is instrumental in getting the merchandise to the destination in a safe, presentable condition.
- Because of the added stress of international shipping, packaging that is adequate for domestic shipping may be inadequate for international shipping.
- Packaging considerations that should be taken into account are environmental conditions and weight.
- One solution to the packaging problem has been the development of intermodal containers.
- Cost attention must be paid to international packaging.

Reckitt & Colman introduced Mortein, a popular household insecticide brand and a new product in the market, but did not carry out the transportation trial thinking that they have wealth of experience in consumer product marketing globally. But when the product reached down south in Tamil Nadu for launch at many distribution points, it was found on the days before the product launch that the products reached distributors warehouse all broken inside which was a shock to everyone after making all preparations for the product launch. This was a huge cost forcing the company to postpone the launch date by about a month. This delay also had several associated problems that the company faced such as cancelling the release of media launch and advertisement which had its impact on the business. Every product thus has to go through as marketed transportation test before clearing the primary packaging as well as secondary and transport packaging design and quality agreed and implemented.

FUNCTIONS OF PACKAGING

Without adequate packaging, transportation is thus just not possible. The right **transport packaging** makes it possible to get products out into the world. In the case of smaller products, packaging allows to deliver large quantities in a convenient and cost-effective way. There are many other functions that packaging serves.

PACKAGING PROTECTS GOODS

This is the primary function of packaging as it has to keep and preserve the integrity, quality, taste, flavour, colour, texture and so on intact during the useful life of the product till the product is declared unfit for consumption and/or use. Goods that are damaged upon arrival can cause major problems as explained above with an example. Not only does one lose the cost of the original item and shipping it in the first place, but he/she may also have to send replacements at an additional cost. Besides, there can even be claims from the buyers for non-performance of the contract and in addition such failures also bring in disrepute to the manufacturer of the product which can even cause permanent loss of business. Several cases and compensation related to packaging failure have come to our knowledge. For inflammable products like aerosol, defective packaging can even cause a costly accident during use. It is therefore the responsibility of the business to ensure safe and secured packaging at an affordable cost. Broken or marked items can upset customers and retailers, souring relationships and giving the company a bad reputation. **Logistics packaging** thus keeps all items safe, so they arrive at their destination in a perfect condition.

PACKAGING PROVIDES INFORMATION ABOUT THE PRODUCT

Packaging carries many information regarding the product related to its contents, ingredients used, type of use or how it has to be used, special declaration for safe use and so on, including the statutory information such as name and address of the manufacturer, country of origin, date of production and date of expiry as the case may be, license number, weight or volume, and special declaration on promotion and scheme. There can be a lot of important information that distributors need to know about the product. The **transport packaging** is the perfect place to display these information. For example, the transport packaging also carries the identification mark. A lot of different things can be printed on the boxes. It could be something simple, like which way up the packages need to stored, stacked and kept, or that the contents are fragile and require handling with care. One can also specify more detailed handling instructions, such as a particular temperature range the products need to be stored at or any other special storing conditions.

FACILITATES STORAGE AND WAREHOUSING

Transport packaging system needs to be designed to facilitate the storage requirement so that space utilization is maximum in **both warehouse** and **container shipping. Odd size packaging configuration has to be avoided. It will make handling the** kinds of products easy to store. No matter what shape, or how fragile, the right packaging allows them to be stacked, placed onto pallets, or otherwise arranged for convenience.

PACKAGING IS INDICATIVE OF QUALITY OF THE PRODUCT PACKED

For consumer products and more importantly for FMCG products, packaging is extremely important and also serves for promotion of the product. A good, attractive and also convenient packaging indicates that the products packed are of good quality and thus influences the customer to buy and try the product. It thus helps in selling and promoting the products. If one chooses retail-ready packaging, the products can be displayed on the shelves in their own custom display. By choosing an appropriate packaging system featuring the brand colours, product details and other relevant sales information, one increases their chances of catching the eye of their target market. Getting the right packaging makes a big difference to one's products, if they want logistics packaging that keeps their product safe, displays key information and assists with storage. An attractive packaging gets the attention of the buyers, leading to trials, and if they like some of them, they may even become permanent customers.

ENSURE THE RIGHT TRANSPORT PACKAGING SOLUTION

When shipping products for distribution, the transport packaging solution and design are key decisions that should be taken with all seriousness. Transport packaging works to protect goods while they are in transit, and because most shipments are subject to more than one mode of transportation throughout their journey, packaging needs to be designed to stand up to both local and export conditions. Let us discuss the four major modes of transportation and the challenges of packaging system and the solution needed.

PACKAGING AND SAFETY REGULATIONS FOR HAZARDOUS GOODS

Hazardous and dangerous goods require special packaging as per regulation. In global trade, they also need special labelling following the regulation of International Maritime Institute (IMI). Depending on the products and their conditions, they are classified under various categories as given in Table 6.4. Dangerous and hazardous goods like crude oil or gas require bulk transport and normally do not carry any other types of goods. The packaging, labelling and transportation of these types of goods need to follow the prescribed standards to be acceptable to the transporters and freight forwarders as well as carriers (Thompson Rivers University 2016).

TABLE 6.4 Classification of Dangerous Goods

Class	Division	Characteristics
1 Explosives (Sections 2.9–2.12)	1.1	A substance or article with a mass explosion hazard.
	1.2	A substance with a projection hazard but not a mass explosion hazard.
	1.3	A substance or article with a fire hazard and either a minor blast hazard or a minor projection hazard, or both, but not a mass explosion hazard.
	1.4	A substance or article which presents no significant hazard beyond the package in the event of ignition or initiation during transport.
	1.5	A very insensitive substance with a mass explosion hazard.
	1.6	An extremely insensitive article with no mass explosion hazard.

(Table 6.4 Continued)

(Table 6.4 Continued)

Class	Division	Characteristics
2 Gases (Sections 2.13–2.17)	2.1	A flammable gas which is easily ignited and burns.
	2.2	A non-flammable, non-toxic, non-corrosive gas.
	2.3	A toxic gas.
3 Flammable Liquids (Sections 2.18–2.22)	None	A flammable liquid with a closed-cup flash point less than or equal to 60°C.
4 Flammable Solids (Sections 2.20–2.22)	4.1	A flammable solid which is readily combustible and may cause fire through friction or from heat retained from manufacturing.
	4.2	A spontaneously combustible substance that ignites when exposed to air.
	4.3	A water-reactive substance which emits flammable gas when it comes in contact of water.
5 Oxidizing Substances, Organic Peroxides (Sections 2.37–2.39)	5.1	An oxidizing substance which may yield oxygen and contribute to the combustion of other materials.
	5.2	An organic peroxide which releases oxygen readily and may be liable to explosive decomposition, or sensitive to heat, shock or friction.
6 Toxic and Infectious Substances (Sections 2.26–2.36)	6.1	A toxic substance that is liable to cause harm to human health.
	6.2	An infectious substance.
7 Radioactive Materials (Sections 2.37–2.39)	None	Radioactive materials as defined in the Packaging and Transport of Nuclear Substances Regulations.
8 Corrosive Substances (Sections 2.40–2.42)	None	Solids or liquids like acids or alkali materials that cause destruction of the skin or corrode metals.
9 Miscellaneous Products, Substances or Organisms	None	A regulated substance that cannot be assigned to any other class. It includes genetically modified organisms, marine pollutants and substances transported at elevated temperatures.

Source: Thomson Rivers University. 2016. *Packing and Labelling Dangerous Goods for Transport*. Kamloops: Safety & Emergency Management, Thomson Rivers University.

Also, some dangerous goods from each group are assigned packing classes. These classes are determined by physical and chemical testing described in Part 2 of the Transportation of Dangerous Goods Act & Regulations (TDGR). Table 6.5 briefly outlines the packing classes used by Transport Canada to classify materials.

TABLE 6.5 Packing Groups for Hazardous Items

Packing Group	Level of Hazard
I	Very hazardous substance
II	Hazardous substance
III	Moderately hazardous substance

PACKAGING REGULATIONS

As per TDGR, shipping of some dangerous goods above certain specified quantities is prohibited in the absence of a developed emergency response assistance plan (ERAP). Consulting the *TDG Handbook* helps determine if shipments fall under or are in excess of the value published in Column 7 of Schedule 1. If an ERAP is required, consultation with Thompson Rivers University (TRU)'s Office of Safety and Emergency Management (OSEM) is required.

Means of transport determine the packaging that is required for the shipment to be in compliance with TDGR. Packages shipped exclusively via terrestrial means must meet the packaging instructions as stated in the TDG Clear Language Regulation and Transport Canada Standard: 'Small containers for Transport of Dangerous Goods, Classes 3, 4, 5, 6.1, 8, and 9'.

If transporting by air, the packaging must meet International Air Transport Association's (IATA) requirements which can be purchased from IATA. OSEM can also be contacted to obtain the correct information.

If transporting via marine means, if solely domestic, the TDGR are adequate guidance for shipping and receiving dangerous goods. On the other hand, if the package is to be shipped internationally, the International Maritime Dangerous Goods (IMDG) Code must also be followed.

Importantly, the OSEM at TRU can always be contacted to obtain the required information, depending on the shipping circumstances and concerns (Thompson Rivers University 2016).

CASE STUDY: CONTAINER CORPORATION OF INDIA LTD

Container Corporation of India Ltd (CONCOR) is a Navratna (nine jewel) public sector undertaking under the Ministry of Railways, Government of India. Incorporated in March 1988, CONCOR commenced operations in November 1989, taking over an existing network of seven inland container depots (ICDs) from Indian Railways.

Four decades ago, importing and exporting of goods were really difficult and cumbersome tasks. A truck or lorry had to carry the stock from the factory gate to the port and unload it in a warehouse from where goods were loaded into the cargo ship piece by piece. Malcolm McLean was a transport entrepreneur who developed the modern intermodal shipping container which revolutionized transport and international trade in the second half of the 20th century. His idea of containerization changed the cargo transport by standardizing the dimensions of the container to hold the cargo which changed the industry dramatically. Containerization has also improved the productivity and cost. In future, international cargo will be only in containers.

From its humble beginning, it is now an undisputed market leader having the largest network of 7 ICDs and 83 terminals in India. In addition to providing inland transport by rail for containers, it has expanded to cover management of ports and air cargo complexes and establish a cold chain. It has played the key role of promoting containerization of cargo movement in India by virtue of its modern rail wagon fleet, customer-friendly commercial practices and extensively used IT. The company has developed multimodal logistics support for India's international and domestic containerization and trade. Though rail is the main stay of CONCOR's transportation plan, road services are also provided to cater to the need of door-to-door services, in their International or Domestic business.

CONCOR achieved highest-ever throughput of 3.83 million TEUs and 43.5 MMT of containerized cargo by rail in FY 2018–2019. With 7 ICDs to 83 terminals to date, CONCOR is diversifying into other logistics businesses such as distribution logistics, coastal shipping and cargo handling at airports. CONCOR has decided not to increase tariff up to 31 March 2020 and by starting vertical integration in logistics by providing warehousing and first-mile/last-mile transportation to their customers.

Main Functions of CONCOR

CONCOR's core business is characterized by three distinct activities, that of a carrier, a terminal operator and a warehouse operator.

Carrier

Rail is the mainstay of CONCOR's transportation plans and strategies. Majority of CONCOR terminals are rail-linked, with rail as the main carrier for haulage.

Terminal and CFS Operator

CONCOR started operations in November 1989 with seven ICDs. They have since extended the network to a total of 83 terminals, of which 18 are export–import (EXIM) container depots, 13 are exclusive domestic container depots and as many as 50 terminals perform the combined role of domestic as well as international terminals.

Warehouse Operator

CONCOR offers a comprehensive warehouse service for their customers in international trade, for example, transit warehousing for import and export cargo. CONCOR provides bonded warehousing, enabling importers to store cargo and take partial deliveries, thereby deferring duty payment. Warehousing service is also provided for less than container load (LCL) consolidation and reworking of LCL cargo at nominated hubs as well as air cargo clearance using bonded trucking.

The total warehousing space available for CONCOR's EXIM business is presently approximately 150,000 sq. m with facilities for handling bonded cargo, multi stacking, consolidation of LCL cargo, air cargo handling and so on, besides conventional transit warehousing. CONCOR also provides value-added services such as palletization/fumigation of cargo and repacking/strapping of cargo at all its terminals.

The global trend is that 70–80% of containerized cargo moves directly between the hinterland customers and the seaports in containers. Of total containers handled at Indian ports, CONCOR at present moves 30%. There is therefore intrinsic potential for further growth in CONCOR business apart from the push given by the increase in foreign trade. In the decades of its existence, the throughput growth of the company's EXIM business has been almost 20% per annum.

CONCOR Containers

CONCOR has a wide range of containers for its containerized cargo movement and service. Although there are some differences in the dimensions between containers produced by various manufacturers broadly, CONCOR has the following:

Conventional Dry Cargo Containers

20/40 ft conventional end open containers: These are usually built to ISO standards and are used for the movement of conventional dry cargo. For domestic movement, CONCOR has inducted a fleet of approx 12,000 such 20 ft containers either under direct ownership or on lease for internal movements within the country.

20/40 ft high cube containers: These containers offer the added advantage of extra volumetric capacity due to their additional height and are especially useful for movement of light but bulky cargo.

20 ft side access containers: These containers are used exclusively for domestic traffic movements within the country. They offer the advantage of having doors on the side panels, and this makes it convenient for use in locations where chassis stuffing operations have to be used. CONCOR currently has about 3,300 such self-owned domestic side access containers in its fleet.

22 ft high cube domestic containers: These containers have also been exclusively introduced by CONCOR for the purpose of carrying cargo that requires greater volumetric capacity or container length. CONCOR currently has about 2,000 such company-owned domestic 22 ft containers in its fleet.

Specialty Containers

20/40 ft high cube refrigerated containers: These are containers that can be used for the movement of refrigerated/perishable cargo where controlled temperature is a requirement. Special facilities such as the availability of plug points, portable clip on generators for trailer movements and power packs for train movements are required for moving cargo in these containers. It must, therefore, be ascertained whether such facilities are available at the handling terminals before planning such movements.

20/40 ft collapsible flat rack and platform containers: These containers are especially useful for carrying over dimensional cargo or fully packed machines, equipment and so on. Since most of the movement of containers on CONCOR's network is through rail, special permission must be obtained for movement of over dimensional consignments to ensure that these do not infringe upon the standard moving dimensions of the Indian rail network.

20/40 ft open top containers: These containers are used mostly for cargo that needs to be handled with cranes and cannot be easily loaded from the front doors of the containers. Open tops can also be used for carrying over dimensional cargo of certain types. Such containers have also been inducted for domestic service and can be supplied on demand if such cargo is offered. CONCOR currently has about 100 such self-owned domestic open top containers in its fleet.

20 ft tank containers: These containers are especially designed for the movement of liquid cargo of different types. Such containers have also been inducted for domestic service and can be supplied on demand if such cargo is offered. CONCOR currently has about 300 such self-owned tank containers in its fleet.

At the end of the financial year 2018–2019, the company had a fleet of around 26,000 containers for domestic business 82, 342 own rakes, 82 RSTs and 16 gantry cranes.

Terminal Network in India

CONCOR has a nationwide network of terminals to provide service to any part of the country for both domestic and international cargo movement. At present, the company has the following terminals spread over various regions:

Northern region: Babarpur (Panipat); Ballabhgarh; DCT Okhla, Dhappar; Garhi Harsaru; Gotan; ICD-DDL (Ludhiana); ICD Moradabad; ICD Tughlakabad (Delhi); Jaipur; Jodhpur; Kharia Khangar; Moga; Panipat; Phillaur; Rewari; Sonepat

Western region: CFS Dronagiri–Concor DRT (Navi Mumbai); CFS Mulund (West)-Exports (Mumbai); DCT Turbhe (Navi Mumbai); ICD Chinchwad (Pune); ICD Miraj; ICD New Mulund (Mumbai); ICD Pithampur (Indore); ICD Ratlam; Jawaharlal Nehru Port; Mumbai Port Trust

Eastern region: Balasore; CONCOR Terminal KoPT Coal Dock Road; Durgapur; Fatuha; Haldia; ICD Amingaon; Kolkata Port; Raxaul; Shalimar Terminal; Tata Nagar Terminal

Southern region: Container Freight Station Milavittan (Tuticorin); Container Freight Station Tondiarpet; Domestic Container Terminal Salem Market; HAL/CONCOR/MSIL/JWG; ICD Kudalnagar (Madurai); ICD Whitefield; ICD Irugur; ICD Tirupur; Port Side Container Terminal Harbour of Chennai; Port Side Container Terminal, Vallarpadam; Rail Side Container Terminal, Cochin

Central region: Bhusawal; Daulatabad (Aurangabad); ICD Nagpur; Mandideep Container Terminal; Raipur

South Central region: DCT Guntur; ICD Desur (Belgaum); ICD Visakhapatnam; ICD Sanathnagar (Hyderabad)

Northwestern region: CFS Gandhidham; ICD Sabarmati (Ahmedabad); ICD Ankleshwar; ICD Khodiyar (Ahmedabad); Mundra; Pipavav; RCT Vadodara

North Central region: Agra; Dadri; Kanpur; Madhosingh (Mirzapur); Malanpur (Gwalior); Rawtha Road, Kota (RDT)

Hub and Spoke Services of CONCOR

One of the areas in which CONCOR faces competition in the transportation of goods is from truck operators offering transportation by road. Competition with such operators is primarily on the basis of price and dependability. The objective of hub and spoke transportation is to provide seamless door-to-door service.

The company believes that it competes favourably with road transportation on the basis of price on movement of heavier cargoes over longer distances, although the truck operators may offer, among other things, greater flexibility with respect to the timing of shipments. Volvo trucks, with vastly reduced transit times as compared to conventional trucks, are challenging the rail transit times of CONCOR and are set to heighten competition.

In the domestic arena as well, hub and spoke movements allow for a better utilization of transport potential and allow for long lead services to be generated on the basis of short lead traffic collections using road and rail shuttle services. This service can be especially useful for big corporates for whom production centres are concentrated in a single location but distribution needs are from the whole country. CONCOR has already successfully moved white cement as a commodity using this experiment, whereby the product has been distributed over various locations after being picked up from a single production centre.

Integrated Freight Terminals

As part of the overall strategy for expansion of business and movement towards the provision of complete logistics services, the company is considering the option of moving into operating large railway goods-shed hubs. This will mean managing integrated freight terminals. To achieve this, CONCOR in the long term plans to set up district parks/freight centres/trade development centres and so on at some of its terminals. The focus of providing such services will be on the backward and forward integration of various value-added services with the core business of transport logistics in which the company already has an established foothold.

Coastal Shipping

As part of its overall strategy of expansion and entry into areas of business that would complement its position as a multi-model logistics service provider, coastal shipping is an area of business the company is examining for making an entry. CONCOR's interface with coastal shipping can be easily established by undertaking all port operations for coastal vessels or only taking up the rail interface for such vessels at port terminals and providing hinterland connectivity. For getting into coastal shipping, the company is open to pick up equity stake in sea-going vessels and identify a strategic partner with adequate experience and resources.

Cold Chains and Reefers

A key business area with high potential for growth is the provision of cold chains. This involves providing transportation to perishable products from source to end user while maintaining a certain temperature along the route. Today, 85% of the cold storages are in the private sector, and not a single complete cold chain solution provider is available in the market. Absence of reefer container linkages and high and increasing power costs are proving to be major impediments. CONCOR is already providing basic rail-based reefer services between Delhi and Mumbai and could get into providing cold chains by making a few arrangements that would expand its market presence. These would mainly include the following:

- Tie up with an international major, preferably with developing country experience with both technology and equity commitment for bringing in the basic equipment.
- Organize terminal-to-factory transport, refrigerated warehouses, where needed, and delivery, while maintaining both temperature-controlled environments and transit commitments.
- Identify viable corridors for specific products. This will require tying up with producers and consumers independently or tying up with a food-processing major to distribute its products. Return trips wherever possible make cold chain operations more profitable and viable and as such desirable. Otherwise, the operation sometimes leads to break-even or even loss.

Total Logistic Service Providers

CONCOR offers most comprehensive logistics service under one roof. The infrastructure that they have built over time makes them a dominant player in Indian logistics service.

Logistics signifies the integration of two or more activities for the purpose of planning, implementing and controlling efficient flow of raw materials, in-process inventory and finished goods from the point of origin to the point of consumption. Transportation is often the single largest cost in the logistics process. Logistics is a source of value addition. By streamlining transport, storage and handling operations, by reducing inventories (and the corresponding financial and storage costs) and by making the most cost-efficient use of available assets, logistics reduces the overall cost of the delivered goods while increasing their time and space utilities (delivering in right time and at right place).

Handling Hazardous Cargo

Transportation of hazardous cargo in containers by rail is subject to the statutory provisions of the IRCA Red Tariff. Railways have also accorded provisional permission for carriage of dangerous/hazardous/offensive goods which fall under the IMDG Code in containers, subject to their packing and stuffing being as per specifications of the IMDG Code.

The following is the procedure that shall be followed by CONCOR in booking of hazardous cargo in containers:

1. When a container is laden with a commodity classified as hazardous in IRCA Red Tariff or IMDG Code, CONCOR shall accept it for rail booking only on a pink forwarding note and collect the prescribed additional surcharges.
2. There should be no restriction in acceptance of containers laden with commodities not classified as hazardous as per both IMDG Code and IRCA Red Tariff.
3. In case lines offer containers containing some commodities with apparent dangerous/hazardous characteristics and if such commodities do not find any reference in either IRCA Red Tariff or IRCA Goods Tariff or IMDG Code, then such containers will be accepted for booking by rail after taking a specific undertaking from the shipping line that the cargo loaded in the containers is not hazardous.

Information Systems

A primary component of CONCOR's overall business strategy has been the development of an advanced IS. A container and cargo logistics IS went online at company's ICD at Tughlakabad in 1994, and most other facilities have been equipped with computer systems to monitor traffic movement and maintain inventory records.

CONCOR is using various online applications such as Export/Import Terminal Management System (ETMS), Domestic Terminal Management System (DTMS), Oracle Financials ERP and HR Payroll System, which are based on centralized architecture deployed through Citrix environment and running over a VSAT-based hybrid network.

CONCOR has been certified to ISO/IEC 27001:2005 standard for establishing and maintaining an information security management system (ISMS) for its IT functionality.

CONCOR has been awarded for its project titled 'Web based Integrated Container/Terminal Management System' which has been adjudged by AFACT (Asia Pacific Counsil for Trade Facilitation & Electronic Business) as winner for e-ASIA 2009 award for the category 'Electronic Business in Public Sector'.

Company Performance

CONCOR has delivered an improved performance during 2018–19 in which it gained market share and moved on the path of long-term sustainable growth. During the year it has handled 3.83 million TEUs and transported 43.50 million tonnes of cargo volume by rail which is an increase of 8.42% and 8.83% respectively over the previous year. There was 8.11% and 10.23% growth in the physical volumes of both EXIM and domestic segments respectively. The gross turnover also has increased by 11.71% to ₹72.160 billion and the net profit for the year was ₹12.15 billion showing a healthy growth of 16.37% over the previous year. The net worth of the company, thus, has increased from ₹93.74 billion to ₹103.68 billion during this period.

Case Questions

1. What are the main functions of CONCOR?
2. Discuss the comprehensive service that CONCOR offers for its customers.
3. What are the different types of containers that CONCOR has?
4. What does CONCOR have for better online customer service?
5. Discuss the service that CONCOR offers for hazardous cargo as well as reefer cargo.
6. Why are cargo movements globally now containerized?

CHAPTER SUMMARY

This chapter deals with the most important function in logistics and integrated SCM which is transportation. Transportation is the most vital sector of any nation's economy. The growth and performance of any economy get reflected from the status of their transport industry. Goods and services need to be carried from the point of production to the point of consumption by several modes of transport system. If the transport system collapses, whole economy will collapse. On the other hand, an efficient transport system can help making an economy vibrant. There are multiple modes of transport vehicles and systems that are used in the industry to manage supply chain and operations including logistics which are discussed in this chapter. Different modes of transportation used in both domestic and international cargo handling are discussed with their relative advantages and disadvantages and also the costs thereof. The latest trends in global ship or ocean transport citing competitive issues are taken up for discussion, giving examples of couple of global ocean lines. Recent collaborations and acquisitions of very large vessels to be more economic and cost-effective are also discussed. Global ocean liners' strategies and performance to be sustainable shipping lines of preference are also discussed. Within large countries such as India and the USA as well as in regions like EU, most of the stocks and goods are moved on surface; the issues concerning those and competition between rail and road transport are discussed in detail. The challenges of new regulations and also environmental stipulations impacting the cargo movement are also discussed in this chapter including recent trends in transportation in global trade. In global trade, more and more collaboration and collective bargaining to get critical mass and bargaining power to retain the customer accounts are widely witnessed. These recent alliances in global transportation are discussed. Finally, key concerns in energy sectors relating to cost, environment, ecosystem and sustainability issues are discussed, along with how the logistics industry around the world is addressing those issues for its own survival and growth.

DISCUSSION QUESTIONS

1. Why is surface transport going to rise in preference to air transport?
2. Discuss the reasons why containerization is going to rise and 90% of break bulk cargo will be containerized.
3. What are the reasons for alliances and joint ventures in international cargo movement?
4. What kind of changes will be triggered by increased environmental and regulatory factors? And how will those be tackled?
5. Discuss if high-speed trains can make any difference to international cargo transport.
6. Discuss how customs-bonded warehouses help in cost reduction in international logistics.
7. Write a short note on the new Ocean Alliance.
8. What are the various modes of transportation available for international cargo movement and what are the key considerations for taking a decision on the mode of transport?
9. Discuss the transportation system for movement of cargo in EU countries. Compare the efficiency of various modes of transport for their functional efficiency.
10. Discuss the container shipment scenario after large vessels have come into the market. What were the typical problems faced by large container liners?
11. What are the various joint ventures that were formed to leverage the collective strength in international cargo movement business? Discuss their relative strength and current scenario?
12. How did Suez Canal and Panama Canal change the dynamics of global ocean transport? Discuss their relative importance?
13. Discuss the functions and importance of packaging in transportation.
14. How does packaging add value in the business?

15. Discuss the packaging issues and regulations for transporting hazardous goods in global trade.
16. Discuss the information and their relevance that need to be provided on the package for transportation of goods.
17. Discuss the packaging configuration issues in container loading for optimum space utilization.

REFERENCES

Levinson, Marc. 2006. *The Box: How the Shipping Container Made the World Smaller and the World Economy Bigger.* Princeton, NJ: Princeton University Press.

Mover DB.com. 2016, March. 'Top 10 International Container Shipping Companies'. Available at: https://moverdb.com/shipping companies (accessed on 30 May 2019).

The Economic Times. 2017. 'India's Transport Infra Growth to Gain Pace over 5 Years: Report'. Available at: https://economictimes.indiatimes.com/news/economy/infrastructure/indias-transport-infra-growth-to-gain-pace-over-5-years-report/articleshow/57652534.cms?from=mdr (accessed on 2 June 2019).

Thomson Rivers University. 2016. *Packing and Labelling Dangerous Goods for Transport.* Kamloops: Safety & Emergency Management, Thomson Rivers University.

BIBLIOGRAPHY

Ballou, Ronald H. 1999. *Business Logistics Management.* Upper Saddle River, NJ: Prentice Hall.

Eno Transportation Foundation. 1988. *Transportation in America.* Washington, DC: Eno Transportation Foundation.

Hammond, Janice H., and John E. P. Morrison. 1988. 'Note on the US Freight Transportation Industry'. Harvard Business School Note 688080. Boston, MA: Harvard Business School.

Robenson, James F., and William C. Copacino. 1994. *The Logistics Handbook.* New York, NY: The Free Press.

Tyworth, John E., Joseph L. Cavinato, and C. John Langley Jr. 1991. *Traffic Management: Planning, Operations, and Control.* Prospect Heights, IL: Waveland Press. www.transsiberianexpress.net

The World Bank. *Transportation in India.* http://web.worldbank.org/archive/website01291/WEB/0__CO-21.HTM

7

Total Logistics Cost Management for Competitive Advantage

LEARNING OBJECTIVES

Section I: Total Logistics Cost

- Define total cost in logistics
- Explain TLC and their components
- Realize implications of each cost element on the TLC
- Manage each element of the TLC for better performance
- Derive competitive advantage in business by containing the TLC
- Understand benchmarking parameters and practices to improve SCM performance

Section II: Sustainable Transport Logistics and Supply Chain

- Realize the importance of sustainability in supply chain
- Identify challenges of sustainability issues in business and supply chain
- Define the key dimensions of sustainability supply chain and their implications
- Understand how to manage sustainability issues for better public image and performance of the business

SECTION I
TOTAL LOGISTICS COST

INTRODUCTION

Logistics costs quite significantly impact business performance in a country. In the least developed as well as in less developed countries, logistics cost as a percentage of total cost of goods and services is much higher than that in developed countries, where logistics infrastructure is well developed. Analysis of the total cost offers insight and a key to managing the logistics function for optimum performance. Management should strive to reduce the total cost of logistics by carefully analysing each cost component to understand the opportunity available to better manage that cost element. To manage a business better, logistics must be viewed as an integrated system. The need to view the logistics function as an integrated system is paramount because reduction in one cost element may even lead to increase in the cost of other components. Therefore, understanding interrelationships among various cost elements will be useful in order to take an integrated view and manage the total cost. Effective management and real cost savings can be accomplished only by viewing logistics as an integrated system and minimizing its total cost, keeping the firm's customer service objectives in focus. Businesses are exploring ways and means to reduce the logistics cost to become more competitive. With rising fuel costs, TLC has also been increasing. Besides, there are regulations relating to sustainability and environment forcing logistics companies to strategize to contain the freight and other related costs. Businesses are also evaluating the various options on sourcing the products from logistics cost and convenience point of view. Logistics cost management has thus assumed increased significance in business.

ORGANIZATIONS ARE HUGE COST CENTRES

Businesses are normally managed to create wealth for the shareholders. Although businesses are managed as profit centres or SBUs, but everything we do inside the business is all costs. Organizations are therefore huge cost centres. Profit actually lies outside the business, and it comes by transacting your cost with a margin of profit. Today's customers are very discerning and are not willing to pay for organizational inefficiencies. Cost management, therefore, is very important for businesses. Managing costs better would ensure higher profits and more competitiveness. Excess cost is like excess fat; once you acquire, it becomes very difficult to lose. Better way to manage cost is to not allow it to increase in the first place. Added cost is very difficult to shed. Non-value-adding costs are required to be eliminated. As it is difficult to shed a cost once added into the system, it is better that we start allocating resources, including human resources, less than desirable; only after experiencing the performances, we should be deciding if extra resources are required. The objective of cost management is to eliminate avoidable and non-value-adding costs. Logistics costs provide opportunities for cost reduction.

THE LAW OF LOWEST TOTAL COST

The law states, 'The total cost of producing and delivering product is usually larger than the sum of the lowest functional costs of each element in the supply chain.'

Individual functions or interconnected or interrelated functions and activities will incur a cost to perform, but when a series of such activities are to be performed, the experience will be that total cost to produce end result is always higher than the individual cost of each element for the reason that there is always an additional cost of integration of activities. The focus, therefore, should be on the total cost management.

LOGISTICS COST: BRIEF HISTORY

Since 1974, Establish Davis Database conducts annual surveys and contains data related to logistics costs (transportation, warehousing, customer service, administration and inventory carrying cost) and service performance level for many industries/groups. This database can serve as guidelines to see how such costs vary in a typical organizational setup. This database offers a standard guideline, but it will vary from country to country as well as from company to company in a given country. The database also helps in budgetary process for resource allocations and for the improvement of budget and targets.

Logistics cost for the average company in the database is 9.34% of sales and US$69.74 per hundred weight shipped. Logistics costs increased by 11% from 2013 to 2014. Transportation cost is driving the increase. Companies with higher product values continue to have lower logistics costs. Smaller companies continue to have higher logistics costs. Service performance levels have improved since 2014.

ELEMENTS OF LOGISTICS COST

The various components of logistics costs can be classified as given below:

- Transportation costs
- Warehousing costs
- Order processing costs
- Inventory carrying costs
- Information and communication costs
- Administrative costs
- Customer servicing cost

LOGISTICS COST ACCOUNTING SYSTEM

It is not possible to improve anything if not measured properly. Measuring the existing logistics cost incurred by the business is therefore the primary task. The more the details available, the better it will be to manage the logistics cost of each element. It is a managerial task to decide in what format, and what details, these costs are to be recorded for the study to find out where improvement is possible. There are three major cost elements, namely fixed cost, variable cost and process cost, that impact product cost and pricing.

Broadly, there are two approaches followed in the business to determine the logistics cost:

- The financial accounting system
- The managerial accounting system

Every company should have their TLC budget to control the total cost. For initiating any improvement on logistics cost budget, organizations must generate management reporting system. Businesses normally generate both financial accounting statement as well as management accounting statement.

FINANCIAL ACCOUNTING

Financial accounting system provides reports such as balance sheet, income statements like profit and loss statement, and cash flow statements which are required by outside stakeholders such as investors and stockholders as well as statutory authorities. But this system may fail to meet the needs of managers of the organization. To manage the company's performance, the managerial accounting system serves the purpose better. For all companies, monthly and other periodical reviews are conducted by generating various reports to serve internal needs of the company and manage its resources and profits better.

In this system, the logistics cost often gets merged with other operating costs of the business and loses focus, as logistics cost elements are not differentiated and isolated to draw managerial attention to understand the reason why, and therefore, the system may fail to meet the needs of the managers.

MANAGEMENT ACCOUNTING

The logistics accounting system is a type of managerial accounting system which addresses the typical parameters and more particularly various cost parameters of logistics activities within the company and compares those with the budgeted numbers as well as determines the variance against previous year's actuals costs incurred, giving reason thereof. In addition, periodically these figures are also compared with the industry standards as well as with the best practices and best performer in the same category of the business. It can help managers to plan, implement and control logistics system. Logistics accounting information is useful for budgeting, which is an important part of the logistics planning process. It also helps in the allocation of resources for implementing the plans. Logistics accounting statements are not standardized like financial accounting statements because the integrated information needs of one manager often differ from those of another. Logistics accounting system generally allows the user to analyse decisions, based on logistical costing.

Managerial accounting system can be prepared for the logistics manager's needs and focus, depending on which additional element-specific costs data can be generated to pay focused attention to the specific problem areas to rectify or improve the scenario from the current level. It can help managers to plan, implement and control logistics system. Logistics accounting information is useful for budgeting, which is an important part of the logistics planning process.

LOGISTICS COST MANAGEMENT MODELS

There are various approaches employed for the management of logistics cost. They are as follows:

- Activity-based costing or ABC
- Total cost of ownership

- Supply chain costing
- Total cost of relationship
- Total cost/value analysis
- Cost-to-serve method

LOGISTICS IS OMNIPRESENT

Across functions in a business, logistics plays a crucial role and therefore it is omnipresent. Improving logistics functions can help improve business performance in multiple ways. Logistics function is there not only in sales, marketing, customer service as well as in manufacturing, procurement and production but also in R&D, and finance and administration (Figure 7.1).

LOGISTICS IMPROVES BUSINESS PERFORMANCE

Logistics cost in many ways impacts performance and therefore ROI. The impact of logistics costs can get reflected in many ways in different business functions and processes as can be seen in Figure 7.2. For example, better logistics management can impact the quality of customer service and hence the customer satisfaction positively, which can help in increased sales and revenue. Improved logistics performance can help reduce the inventory holding, and thereby reduce the working capital requirement in the business. Logistics management can also reduce debtors and stock return as well as stock expiry. The collective impact of all these is higher profit for the business and higher ROI (as depicted in Figure 7.2).

FIGURE 7.1 Logistics Is Omnipresent: Encompasses All Functions in Business

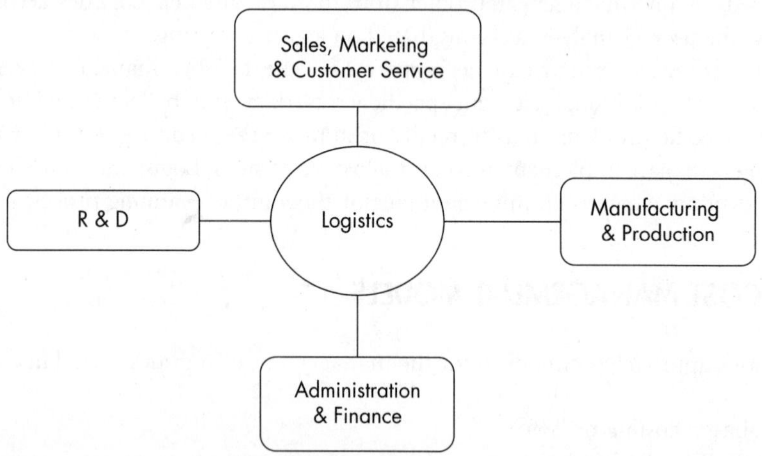

FIGURE 7.2 How Logistics Cost Impacts ROI

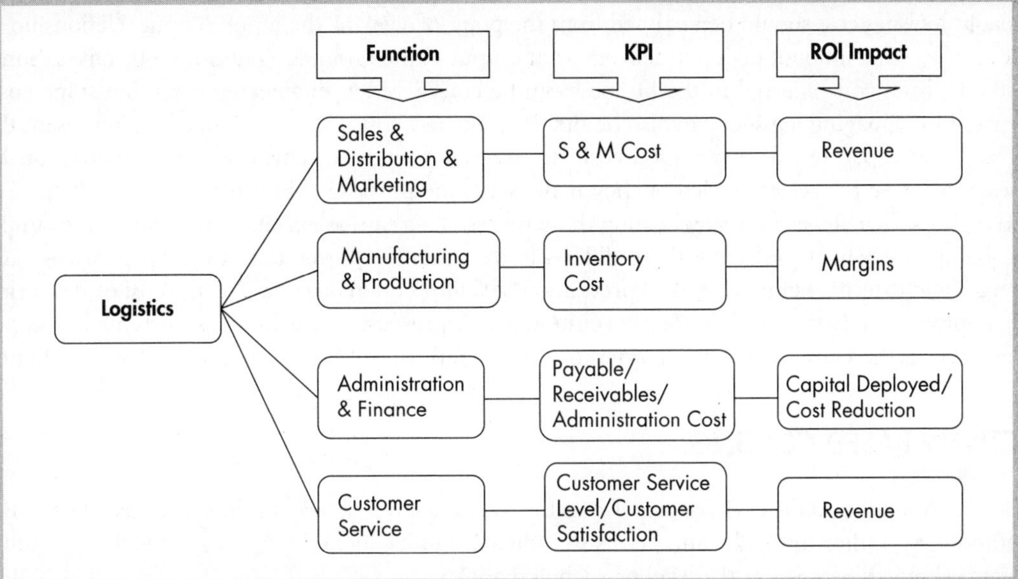

DIFFICULTY IN ESTIMATING LOGISTICS COST

Problems with traditional cost accounting as related to logistics (Christopher 1998) are as follows:

- The true costs of servicing different customer types, channels and market segments are poorly understood.
- Costs are captured at too high at a level of aggregation.
- Costing is functionally oriented at the expense of output.
- The emphasis on full cost allocation of products ignores customer costs.

As a result, either the customer is loaded with full cost (unjustifiably) or not apportioned the cost specific to them (under recovery).

Traditional costing methods have many inherent disadvantages such as:

- Assumption that all cost is volume-related
- Departmental focus, not process focus
- Focus on costs incurred, not cause of costs

Logistics cost can be better represented from the perspective of engineered costs and discretionary costs as has been shown in Figure 8.3. This way, logistics cost management programme can be better managed.

ANALYSIS OF LOGISTICS COST

Broadly, logistics cost should be analysed from the point of view of the input–output relationship in a sense that what amount of input delivers what output in the business against the objectives. Some of the logistics cost incurred in the business can be considered as engineered costs, but some costs incurred in managing logistics can also be the discretionary cost. Hence, it is better to represent the logistics cost separately as engineered cost and discretionary cost. This discretionary cost can be assessed if these are really needed or they really serve the purpose. ABC costing is often helpful to find such issues if those are really helping the business. This can be explained by taking an example of quality cost which has really three different costs, namely prevention cost, appraisal cost and internal and external failure cost. And prevention of failures often takes care of the cost of delivering the improved or better quality for the customers. Representing the logistics costs in its proper perspective is therefore important in order to manage and control the logistics cost in business better.

ACTIVITY-BASED COSTING

ABC represents a radical departure from the traditional cost accounting systems. The ABC methodology, rather than allocating costs to individual units, identifies the activities that consume resources, matching costs to the level of such activities.

The key aspect of this methodology is the development of models that represent a logical and quantifiable relationship between the utilization of resources, the performance of activities and the products or services that they provide. With these models, one can simultaneously mirror the flow of orders and products along the logistic chain, capturing the costs at a level of desegregation that enables the analysis of profit by the type of client, market segment and distribution channel. This application of ABC costing to a logistic operator illustrates its main difficulties and benefits. ABC approach helps businesses to understand if there are any redundant or non-value-adding activities that are undertaken in the end-to-end logistics value chain so that those can be eliminated to get significant improvement in the logistics cost and performance.

WHEN ABC METHOD IS MORE USEFUL

Large diversified global corporations should undertake ABC costing methods and cost audit. In general, companies having high overheads, product diversity or multiple products, customer diversity, service diversity, and multiple location integrated logistics are better placed to undertake ABC method. Let us examine in detail the components of various items constituting logistics cost.

TOTAL LOGISTICS COST

Logistics cost for the average company is given in the Davis database. This cost is increasing and transportation cost which is 37% of the total cost is driving the increase. Transportation cost is again driven by the fuel or energy cost. Good rail and road infrastructure and energy efficient high-speed transport carrier can help logistics cost in handling domestic cargo. The Establish Davis

TABLE 7.1 Logistics Cost Breakup

Items	% Sales (%)	S/C WT (US$)
Transportation	4.43	36.42
Warehousing	1.99	16.16
Customer Service	0.41	1.92
Administration	0.30	1.15
Inventory Carrying	2.22	14.09
Total Logistics Cost	9.34	69.74

Source: The Establish Davis Logistics Cost and Service Database 2014.

Logistics Cost and Service Database is an ongoing annual survey that manufacturers, distributors and retailers participate to receive indicators of logistics cost elements (Table 7.1). Companies with higher product values continue to have lower logistics costs. Smaller companies continue to have higher logistics costs. Service performance levels have improved since 2014. The Establish Davis Logistics Cost and Service Database is an ongoing annual survey that manufacturers, distributors and retailers participate in to receive indicators of logistics cost elements.

Poor logistics performance will reduce the company's profitability by locking up increased amount of capital in working capital management which is basically the difference between current assets and current liabilities. Current asset would include the stock levels coverage for raw material, packaging material, finished goods, inventories in transit and WIP. Poor logistics management performance will eventually raise the level of stocks in the system.

TOTAL COST APPROACH IN LOGISTICS

In a competitive marketplace, businesses are constantly striving to deliver higher value to their identified and target customers to avoid the immediate competition. This is tantamount to the fact that the businesses are trying to make customer happy by improving service delivery. Customers have many alternatives and options to choose from, and losing a customer thus is suicidal for many businesses. It takes time and resources to create a new customer, and therefore it makes immense sense for businesses to try and retain an existing customer by constantly improving service quality. Businesses exist because of customers; hence, customer service level and quality cannot be undermined or compromised even if it has to be met at a higher cost. As rightly said, customer is the king; at whatever cost, the customer must be satisfied. Thus, the importance of customer service assumes additional significance in a business.

A dissatisfied customer can easily spread a negative image of the company while a satisfied customer can help create new customers by spreading positive word-of-mouth publicity. This can be explained by taking an example of a customer who received a damaged product which needs to be returned. Returning the goods can upset his/her production or marketing plans and affect the performance of his/her business. This customer is likely to remain a onetime customer and will soon switch over to another supplier. The dissatisfied customer can also become a source of negative publicity for the concerned manufacturer damaging its reputation. On the other hand, a satisfied and happy customer would recommend a particular product and/or manufacturer and can even give unsolicited testimonials to the prospective customers. Thus, it is important to keep the customers satisfied by ensuring high level of customer service which would also mean having an up-to-date logistics system. The logistics operator therefore plays a vital role in terms of promoting the suppliers market reputation by ensuring timely delivery as well as keeping the goods free from any damage and other forms of abuse. To make the customers happy and to improve the service level, logistics performance management has a great role to play which would also entail investment into the company's logistics system which may require huge investments. The capital costs of logistics is quite significant if businesses intend to improve on logistics performance and cost.

HOLISTIC VIEW OF TOTAL LOGISTIC COST

It is imperative that a holistic view is essential to reduce the logistics cost and as such total cost analysis is the key to managing the logistics function. The management has to strive for reduction of TLC rather than the cost of each activities, which would mean that logistics function should be viewed as an integrated system rather than the individual system because sometimes reduction of cost of one activity may even give rise to the increase in cost of other logistics activity. As such effective management and real cost savings can only be accomplished by taking an integrated view covering all sub-elements and components of logistics cost as mentioned above, with an objective that customers service level will never be compromised.

The TLC will thus depend on the customer service levels that the marketers would like to maintain and that can include various costs discussed here.

INVENTORY COST

All businesses are required to carry certain level of inventory of input material such as raw and packaging material, standard spares, etc., as well as of finished goods and work in progress to manage the business. This is necessary to service the customers' order. Company's production programmes need to be planned keeping this objective in mind. The level of inventory to be maintained depends on many factors, including lead time of ordering and for receiving the input materials, mode of transport, the number of warehouses planned, the levels of inventory to be maintained to ensure a certain level of service, safety stock and so on. The inventory cost is the money locked up in the cost of goods, insurance, occupation of space, pilferages, losses, damages and so on, as well as the maintenance of inventory. Inventory costs are directly affected by such factors as the mode of transport, number of warehouses planned and the levels of inventory maintained to ensure certain level of service. These costs are increased by the cost of the obsolescence of a product over a period of time, especially when the company makes rapid changes in product models or when products are perishable. As and when a new product is introduced or an existing model is replaced with a new one, some stocks of both input material and of finished goods become redundant and obsolete in spite of having best plan for the transition. This obsolete inventory also adds up to the total inventory cost not only for the cost of material but also for the space occupied. When the manufacturer is unable to produce goods because of lack of raw material or is unable to supply goods because of inadequate stock of finished products, he loses particular sales. Therefore, it is necessary to examine both low and high inventory issues in relation to their impact in the business.

WAREHOUSING COST

Goods have to be stored for some time after production, however small that time interval may be. This is done either at the production centres or in the marketing area or somewhere in between or at all the three locations. Raw materials as well as other input materials are kept closer to the manufacturing locations, whereas the finished goods' warehouses are strategically located closer to the customer locations. The warehousing of raw materials either steps up the cost of their supply or of the cost of distribution of finished products. As a manufacturer wishes to approach the objective of zero stock of the finished products or zero loss of production, adequate warehousing capacity becomes essential; and this pushes the firm in higher fixed and operating costs of warehousing. Also, to improve customer service to certain levels, it becomes necessary to increase the number of warehouses. Accordingly, the company management has to arrive at the optimum number of warehouses which is consistent with the minimum total cost of distribution, taking into account the effect on the other elements of cost in the total logistical system.

PRODUCTION AND SUPPLY COST

Production cost per unit tends to decrease with an increase in the volume of production with higher capacity utilization. Also, these costs vary between various production points. If a manufacturer has several manufacturing plants producing the same product, company has to make a decision to vary the supplies or production from certain plants, based on both the cost of production in that particular plant and the customer demand that is planned to be satisfied from the goods produced from that particular plant. This move of shifting production from one plant to another is taken for these considerations, which inevitably affects the cost of production as well as the cost of transit times, warehousing and inventory. The decision related to produce 'in-house' vs 'out-house' is taken from the considerations of cost, quality and flexibility to manage dynamic business environment today.

CHANNEL DISTRIBUTION COSTS

Various alternatives for distribution are available to a manufacturer or marketer. Distribution channels are decided upon various considerations, including product types and distribution objectives and target markets and customers to be served which we have discussed in Chapter 3. Which channel to be opted for depends on numerous criteria, including channel effectiveness and costs. This distribution may be through a sole selling agent at the national level or through regional distributors or through wholesale dealers or by direct supplies to dealers and retailers and even to customer as in the case of e-retailers. Mail order sales or catalogue sales at different retail outlets of a manufacturer are direct sales to the customer, which automatically involves decisions on establishing stockists, storage points or warehouses in strategic locations. In the traditional marketing concept, the manufacturer is interested in scaling down the discounts to the distributor to reduce the total cost. But if the distributor's discount is low, he may either not, perhaps because of his low profit margin, distribute the goods in sufficient volume or not render satisfactory level of customer services. This may bring about a loss of present and future sales to the manufacturer. Similarly, changes in the distribution system may take place by alternative usage of space, say, for inventory or marketing or production centre. This may also affect customer service in one way or the other. Therefore, a company has to carefully select channels of distribution since it affects decisions relating ultimately to customer service and satisfaction. Whatever channel of distribution company has decided to follow, there is a cost involved with it. The channel distributions costs will typically include the following cost elements such as channel partners margin, freight and insurance, trade inventory holding cost, frequency of servicing and also trade debtors. The more frequent the service, the less the trade inventory; the less the trade inventory, the less the debtors. In addition, the possibility of out of warrant or expiry stock and goods return will also come down.

TOTAL DISTRIBUTION COST

Perhaps the most important research concerning logistics is going on in designing efficient and cost-effective distribution systems. For this, an understanding of total distribution cost is essential, so that proper trade-offs can be applied as a basis for the planning and reassessment of distribution systems. The urgency of dealing with transportation cost was highlighted by Thomas and Griffin (1996), who argued that since transportation cost accounts for more than half of the TLC, more active research is needed in the area. To optimize the distribution costs, it is essential to measure the individual cost element and their impact on the customer service. Sometimes a judicious trade-off can be encouraged which can result into more effective and efficient distribution system

SUPPLY CHAIN AND LOGISTICS COST

The efficiency of a supply chain can be assessed using the TLC—a financial measure. It is necessary to assess the financial impact of broad-level strategies and practices that contribute to the flow of products in a supply chain. Since logistics cut across functional boundaries, care must be taken to assess the impact of actions to influence costs in one area with reference to their impact on costs associated with other areas (Cavinato 1992). For example, a change in the capacity has a major effect on the cost associated with inventory and order processing.

COST ASSOCIATED WITH ASSETS AND ROI

Supply chain assets include accounts receivable, plant, property and equipment, and inventories. With increasing inflation and decreased liquidity, pressure is on the firms to improve the productivity of capital—to make the assets sweat. In this regard, it is essential to determine how the cost associated with each asset, combined with its turnover, affects total cash flow time. One way to address this is by expressing it as average days required to turn cash invested in assets employed into cash collected from a customer (Stewart 1995). Thus, total cash flow time can be regarded as a metric to determine the productivity of assets in a supply chain. Once the total cash flow time is determined, this can be readily combined with profit to provide insight into the rate of ROI. This determines the performance by the top management in terms of earnings on the total capital invested in a business.

With customer service requirements constantly increasing, effective management of inventory in the supply chain is crucial (Slack et al. 1995). In a supply chain, the total cost associated with inventory can be broken down into the following: opportunity cost, consisting of warehousing, capital and storage; cost associated with inventory at the incoming stock level and WIP; service costs, consisting of cost associated with stock management and insurance; cost of finished goods, including those in transit; risk costs, consisting of cost associated with pilferage, deterioration and damage; cost associated with scrap and rework; and cost associated with too little inventory accounting for lost sales/lost production (Lee and Billington 1992; Levy 1997; Slack et at. 1995).

INFORMATION PROCESSING COST

Information processing cost includes costs associated with order entry, order follow-up/updating, discounts and invoicing. On the basis of survey results from various industries, Stewart (1995) identified information processing cost as the largest contributor to TLC. The role of IT is shifting from a general passive management enabler through databases to a highly advanced process controller that can monitor activities and decide upon an appropriate route for information. Modern IT, through its power to provide timely, accurate and reliable information, has led to a greater integration of modern supply chains than anything possible by any other means (Benjamin and Wigand 1995; Naim 1997).

COMMUNICATION AND DATA PROCESSING COSTS

An effective distribution system requires optimum management and control related to order processing, inventory control, accounts receivable, dispatches, communications and so on. An increased number of distribution points would certainly improve customer service, but it would make processing of information more cumbersome and expensive. At the same time, if the time taken to process the information is decreased, it is likely to lead better customer services. A manufacturer has to decide about the speed and convenience with which information may be processed. One of the ways is the use of computers with advance software. The communication and data processing now has changed with technology and automation. A lot of improvement has been seen across manufacturing sector to help reduce this cost. Many large global corporations have also outsourced these activities to provide much faster service and 24×7 communication and information to its customers. This is particularly necessary for global companies working in different time zones.

ADMINISTRATIVE COSTS

For providing the efficient logistic service to improve the customer satisfaction, the marketer does not only need adequate facilities and infrastructure and investment in technology and software and in material-handling equipment, but operating the trained manpower is also required. To improve the efficiency in the whole system, there will be some administrative expenses which is also a part of the administration costs. Administrative cost also includes documentation and record keeping cost.

TRANSPORTATION COSTS

The cost of transportation varies generally with the speed with which goods are transported as well as with the mode of transportation and distance to be covered. Water transport is the cheapest, while air transport is the most expensive one. Rail transport is cheaper than road transport, beyond a certain distance. Both rail and road transport stand somewhere in between water and air in terms of the cost of transportation. Transportation cost is a significant part of the TLC. Businesses decide on various modes of transportation based on the infrastructure available within the given geographical area. For international trade, bulk of the transportation takes place by ocean; in domestic trade, bulk of the transportation takes place by road or rail. Certain categories of goods require special model of transportation like refrigerated containers for the frozen goods which are quite costly. The cost of transportation would also vary on the loading factor of the vehicle/ container used. Appropriate packaging design can help improve the loading factor of the product in a typical transport vehicle or container.

MATERIAL-HANDLING COSTS

A suitable material-handling system should be designed to reduce the cost of material-handling to the minimum. Material-handling equipment is required both within production plant and inside the warehouse. Also, a significant cost will be involved in the investment on material-handling equipment, but there will be savings on operation cost as well as on labour. Although one time capital investment will be high, the recurring cost will be less. This would require the consideration of several possible combinations of manual and mechanized handling of the goods and materials. But material-handling operations have an impact on other distribution aspects such as the cost of packaging as well as damages and losses that results from material-handling. The design of the material-handling system and the consideration of its cost also affect the selection of the mode of transportation, and hence the cost of transportation gets affected.

PACKAGING COSTS

Decisions on packaging are affected by decisions on factors such as type of product, the mode of transportation and type of material-handling equipment used. A total cost approach would make it necessary for us to select packaging version, which takes into account other distribution factors as well. Thus, it would not be sufficient merely to reduce the cost of packaging to the minimum. Packaging has many functions including protecting the integrity and quality of the product until it is consumed. Packaging can be of various types, including primary, secondary and tertiary or shipping cartons; each of these has specific roles to play. Packaging has many functions in addition to its primary function of protecting the product integrity and quality to make it survive the hazards of transportation, multiple handing and adverse storage conditions which are not always under the control of the manufacturers and marketers. The other functions of packaging are as follows:

- It provides all product information, identity of product with its distinctive characteristics as well as all statutory information including messages such as how the product has to be used and/or consumed and how the product has to be stored until consumed, and so on.
- Packaging also serves as a primary advertisement for the product and its manufacturers, and for that, packaging also has a merchandizing display value. For this purpose, it needs to be made attractive to radiate the value of the product. And its quality and cost will also be commensurate to these criteria.

CUSTOMER SERVICE COSTS

If the service level as well as the service frequency increases, customer satisfaction improves, but the cost of service also increases. This needs to be viewed against reduction on trade inventory, and a decision can be taken on the frequency of service. Companies such as HUL and P&G have significantly increased the service, thereby reducing the distributors and retailers inventory level, making them happier as the channel partners' investment on stock reduces and ROI increases at the same time. If the manufacturer or supplier guarantees the satisfaction with goods and agrees to give a refund on returned goods or exchange the returned goods, he must arrange for the movement of defective or returned goods from the customer (or retailer) back to the supply warehouse or manufacturing centre. For higher level of customer satisfaction, if the marketers guarantees 100% return, if not satisfied, there is a cost attached with this. Complaints of defects or deficiencies pointed out by customers in the goods that are returned may therefore be utilized as management feedback to improve the quality of the service/product. Incidentally, with such a guaranteed service, the manufacturer would win the customer's loyalty on a permanent basis. Guaranteed customer service, therefore, involves certain costs to the organization, but it also leads to certain benefits in the long run. It increases the value of the company in the market. As servicing customers and ensuring their satisfaction are the primary tasks of a business for growth, survival and sustainability, there is always a cost attached to the higher level of customer satisfaction. As we understand, customer service is a process of providing a business competitive advantage over others and adding benefits to the supply chain in order to maximize the total value to the end consumer.

There can be three levels of products that marketers may try to promote. First, the core benefit or service, which constitutes what end-consumer expect. Second, the tangible product, or the physical product or service itself. Third, the augmented product, which includes benefits that are secondary, but an integral enhancement, to the tangible product the customer is purchasing. Logistical customer service, installation warranties and after-sale service are examples of augmented product features.

Having the right product at the right time in the right quantity without any damage or loss for the right customer is an underlying principle of logistics system that recognizes the importance of customer service.

Another aspect of customer service that deserves mention is the growing consumer awareness of the price/quality ratio and the special needs of today's consumers, who are time conscious and demand flexibility.

EXAMPLES OF CUSTOMER SERVICE

Customer service can be improved by resorting to various kinds of extra services, including supports and incentives, that are not part of the marketers' obligation. These can include the following:

- Revamping a billing procedure to accommodate a customer's request
- Providing financial and credit terms
- Guaranteeing delivery within specified time periods
- Providing prompt and congenial sales representatives
- Extending the option to sell on consignment
- Providing material to aid in a customer's sales presentation
- Installing product
- Maintaining satisfactory spare parts inventories

These services are extended by the marketers to customers in order to gain loyal customers by helping them. At the same time, it also helps them become more competitive in the market and earn better margin.

LEVELS OF CUSTOMER SERVICE

In a competitive market environment, a business has to deliver superior service to its target customers. To some extent, providing customer service is also a legal requirement and contractual obligation in all sales agreements. But this one is the lowest level which can be considered as an activity or simple function. To be competitive in the marketplace, customer service has to graduate from a simple function to a level where it is ingrained in the company's mission and philosophy of existence and survival. And this should be done by focusing on a higher level of customer service to retain customers and derive life-long value. A brief description of customer service is as follows:

- **Customer service as an activity:** This level treats customer service as a particular task that a firm must accomplish to satisfy the customer's needs. Order processing, billing and invoicing, product returns and claims handling are all typical examples of this level of customer service. This is the basic level of customer service that all manufacturers and marketers have to perform and adhere to, failing which they cannot exist nor will have any reason to exist.
- **Customer service as performance measures:** This level emphasizes customer service in terms of specific performance measures, such as the percentage of orders delivered on time and the number of orders processed within acceptable time limits. At this level,

manufacturers and marketers keep the track of performance and also have a measurement of performance determined by occasional customer satisfaction surveys, and they try to improve upon those criteria to eventually improve the business performance itself.

- **Customer service as a philosophy:** This level elevates customer service to a firm-wide commitment for providing customer satisfaction through superior performance by delighting the customer at every interface. They manage the business with an objective of always providing customers a higher level of performance, and therefore they redefine the customer satisfaction criteria and levels and always strive to adhere to them. In these type of corporations, customer service is managed as a philosophy.

ELEMENTS OF CUSTOMER SERVICE

Customer service has multifunctional interest for a company, but from the point of view of the logistics function, we can view customer service as having four traditional dimensions:

1. **Time:** The time factor is usually order fulfilment cycle time, particularly from the perspective of the seller looking at customer service. On the other hand, the buyer usually refers to the time dimension as the lead time or replenishment time.
2. **Dependability:** Dependability can be more important than lead time. The customer can minimize its inventory level if lead time is fixed.
3. **Cost:** Providing service within a well-defined cost as percentage of sales.
4. **Quality:** Delivering the quality of product and service every time as per agreed standards.

COST AUDIT

Regular or periodic cost audit will reveal the following:

- Variance against company's own standard and budgeted cost heads
- Variance report against last year actual and also against budgeted is generated
- Variance against industry standard

Undertaking regular or even periodic cost audit can help organizations to perform better.

BENCHMARKING LOGISTICS COST AND PERFORMANCE

Organizations should periodically benchmark their logistics costs and performance to better manage and improve upon the cost and performance of select criteria which will help them:

- To identify opportunities and trend cost and service performance drivers in their logistics cost
- To know where to focus next to improve company's logistics network from the perspectives of cost and service
- To benchmark with the best in competition as well as the best in class to serve as objective

CASE STUDY

Dry Ice Inc. is a manufacturer of air conditioners in the USA that has seen its demand grow significantly. Also, the demand is coming from various regions of the country. Nationwide demand will have significant cost on logistics. The company, therefore, is considering setting up production plants close to customer's centres in different regions in order to optimize on the logistics costs. They anticipate nationwide demand for the year 2001 to be 180,000 units in the South, 120,000 units in the Midwest, 110,000 units in the East and 100,000 units in the West. Managers at Dry Ice Inc. are designing the manufacturing network and have selected four potential plant manufacturing sites that are New York, Atlanta, Chicago and San Diego. From the consideration of capital cost in production, the capacity of the plants could be either 200,000 or 400,000 units. Along with the cost of producing and shipping air conditioners to each of the four markets, the annual fixed cost at the four locations are as follows: US$6 million for New York, US$5.5 million for Atlanta, US$5.6 million for Chicago and US$6.1 million for San Diego.

Source: https://www.chegg.com (accessed on 4 September 2019).

Case Questions

1. Where should Dry Ice Inc. build its factories to cater to the increased demand of its air conditioners?
2. How large should the manufacturing plants be in terms of capacity?
3. Discuss the logistics costs with decentralized production system against one central location to cater to the demand from all regions.

OUTSOURCING LOGISTICS SERVICES

In recent years, with increasing competition, specialization in logistics function is growing. With the growing specialization, accompanied by the rapid development of e-commerce, many companies choose to outsource their logistics requirements, which has helped in accelerating the development of logistics companies. The rapid development of the logistics industry did not only accelerate the delivery speed of goods and capital flow but also improved the rate of economic growth. In order to maintain the rapid and healthy development of the logistics industry, many countries, like say China, introduced a number of incentive measures and policies. Like India's, China's logistics industry has also started relatively late. When compared to American and European logistics industry, there is considerable room of development for China's and India's logistics industry. In these countries, the technical level of the logistics industry is not high and the hardware is not good.

REASON WHY LOGISTICS COST MANAGEMENT PROGRAMME IS NOT ALWAYS EFFECTIVE

Surveys have indicated that profit margins of domestic logistics player are less when compared with that of international logistics companies. It has been seen that domestic logistics companies not only have the higher cost but they are also seen to be slower in terms of implementing logistics cost reduction programme.

Another reason resulting into high logistics costs is that many logistics companies work in isolation and will not consider a company's supply chain operations analysis into account in order to provide an integrated service to improve the overall performance of the total supply chain. Taking isolated view does not really deliver expected results.

The services of logistics companies cannot be cost-effective by remaining in the middle of the supply chain cost control, including warehousing costs and shipping costs. Throughout the supply chain, logistics companies did not use the best way to arrange for the delivery process, which resulted in short positions departure, detour traffic, repeated situation, delivery and the resulting increase in cost.

The fact that supply chain is very complex and logistics has many links within the supply chain and therefore without seamless integration, it will not be easy to achieve the desired or targeted level of cost reduction.

Customer service level is directly linked with the performance of logistics companies as logistics failure can stop business in supply chain leading to failure in customer demand and even losing a client.

The other reasons for cost reduction programme not being very effective is that many corporate managers cannot fully understand the importance and logistics cost control which has not yet formed the part of the core concept of modern logistics and as such there is a lack of comprehensive understanding in this regard. Company executives do not pay sufficient attention to the concept of logistics cost control and fail to form awareness of modern logistics. However, great opportunity exists for reducing the logistics cost without compromising the quality and service levels which can be a key to providing the competitive advantage of business in a keenly contested global market.

KEY TASKS TO IMPROVE THE LOGISTICS COST

To bring about improvement in logistics costs, businesses need to engage better trained and qualified people in the function and not to manage the logistics activities in the traditional mode of storage and transport. These managers not only have to be trained and qualified but also must have very clear understanding of the needs of the business and implications of various cost parameters on the overall performance of the business as well as the industry standards. With a detail analysis of logistics of the performance data and with a clear focus on the objective, areas of improvement can be identified and implemented. The team members who are better trained can achieve the cost reduction objective better. It is therefore better if the managers in logistics operations are trained earlier to enable them to understand the processes better to find where opportunities are there. Early training in all sectors of the operations can help in maximizing the use of company information in the supply chain software which are currently being used.

Through coordination with the network technology and computer systems, an integrated view can be taken for the supply chain logistics system covering the various departments of the company. Team leaders can play an exemplary role with active participation and cooperation in all aspects of the implementation, as long as all team members carry out their duties and closely cooperate in order to implement the logistics cost control measures effectively.

The core concept of the formation of integrated supply chain cost control would mean that logistics companies are required not only to implement cost control programme in the business of their own but also to help to control the external environment in relevant companies through cooperation to get advantage of collective gains. By forming the space and time effect, the goal of cost control is positioned as the lowest total cost of logistics, so to maximize the value of logistics services. Logistics companies want to achieve the goal of cost control, balance the relationship between the cost of logistics and get maximum of logistics performance. It should be on the integration of the company's various logistics resources, choose the way the whole process of logistics costs in the supply chain from the point on the control and manageability.

Depending on the logistics company's specific circumstances, the nature of the company and the scale of operations, they will have different supply chain processes, and thus have a different supply chain strategic objectives, using different costing methods.

ABC, as discussed earlier, can help in finding the avenues of cost control which facilitates more focussed analysis of a company-wide cost control programme for better result and performance, and hence should be implemented.

Logistics companies should reduce their own costs and should have close contact with all companies in the supply chain, partnership, mutual assistance, mutual benefit and reciprocity to benefit from each others knowledge and experience. It can also be an effective control and supervision of the entire total cost of logistics, covering the entire chain.

CASE STUDY: MARUTI SUZUKI—HOW THEY REDUCED THEIR LOGISTICS COST

In the early 2000s, Maruti Suzuki was the largest car manufacturer in India, with over 50% market share. It relied on 400 major suppliers located across India, with some almost 2,500 km distant from its main plant in Manesar, Gurugram. Its TLCs were well above its wage bill (up to four times as high). It had to carry large buffer stocks and deal with substantial freight costs. In 2013, there was a turnaround and those costs were slashed by requiring almost all suppliers to build a warehouse within a few hours radius of the plant. Today, approximately 80% of suppliers are located within a 100km of the plant. Its buffer stocks are now down to zero, and it is running lean production processes. Maruti Suzuki is the leading automotive manufacturer in India and is an acknowledged industry category leader. Being a market leader with over 50% of the passenger cars, Maruti Suzuki could command their approved vendors and suppliers to move closer to the factory location, to be flexible and more responsive in terms of meeting the manufacturing schedule of the company. The number of vendors and suppliers were also rationalized on the basis of their performance and ability. These vendors not only shifted their manufacturing location close to the factory but also helped the company to reduce the inventory significantly. Company also implemented VMI which helped reducing the input material inventory drastically, making the company more competitive in the marketplace. Vendors and suppliers are dependent on the Maruti Suzuki for their survival and growth, as most of those vendors are actually dedicated suppliers to Maruti Suzuki. The company has helped their well-performing vendors to deliver the expected ROI, many of those are quite big and public companies. Because of the dependence, it was much easier for Maruti Suzuki to implement a drastic logistics cost reduction programme by leveraging their relationship and dependency of the vendors on the company for their survival and growth as well as performance.

Source: https://www.ibef.org/download/Gujarat-March-2018.pdf (accessed on 4 September 2019).

Case Questions

1. What factors forced Maruti Suzuki to optimize logistics cost?
2. How did the company go about dealing with logistics cost reduction programme?
3. What factors helped the company to implement their decision and to what consequences?
4. What are the key challenges of implementing company-wide logistics cost management programme?

SECTION II
SUSTAINABLE TRANSPORT LOGISTICS AND SUPPLY CHAIN

SUPPLY CHAIN SUSTAINABILITY

Sustainability in supply chain is a key concern of businesses now which in turn are forcing corporations to decide on the logistics network keeping SECH ratings in mind. For example, in July 2009, the US-based Walmart announced its intentions to create a global sustainability index that would rate products according to the environmental and social impact made while the products were manufactured and distributed. The sustainability rating index is intended to create environmental accountability in Walmart's supply chain, and provide the motivation and infrastructure for other retail industry companies to do the same (Karen, 2012). The Dodd–Frank Wall Street Reform and Consumer Protection Act, signed into law by President Obama in July 2010, contained a supply chain sustainability provision in the form of the Conflict Minerals Law. This law requires SEC-regulated companies to conduct third-party audits of the company's supply chains, determine whether any tin, tantalum, tungsten or gold (together referred to as conflict minerals) is made of ore mined/sourced from the Democratic Republic of the Congo (DRC), and create a report (available to the general public and SEC) detailing the supply chain with due diligence efforts undertaken and the results of the audit (Karen, 2012). Of course, the chain of suppliers/vendors to these reporting companies will be expected to provide appropriate supporting information. Due to regulatory challenges as well as increased awareness of customers, sustainability parameters are increasingly seen to be more important in terms of preserving the public image of the large corporation. It is therefore very common for these companies to report on sustainability parameters in their annual report for information of their shareholders in particular and general public in general.

DEFINING SUSTAINABILITY

There is no universally accepted definition of sustainability, sustainable development or sustainable transport (Beatley 1995).

Some of the popular definitions are as follows:

- Sustainable development 'meets the needs of the present without compromising the ability of future generations to meet their own needs'. (Brundtland Commission 1987)
- 'Sustainable development is the achievement of continued economic development without detriment to the environmental and natural resources.' (Themes Sustainable Development 2004)
- 'The goal of sustainable transportation is to ensure that environment, social and economic considerations are factored into decisions affecting transportation activity.' (MOST 1999)
- 'Sustainability is not about threat analysis; sustainability is about systems analysis. Specifically, it is about how environmental, economic, and social systems interact to their mutual advantage or disadvantage at various space-based scales of operation.' (Transportation Research Board 1997)
- Sustainability is 'the capacity for continuance into the long term future'. Anything that can go on being done on an indefinite basis is sustainable. Anything that cannot go on being done indefinitely is unsustainable. (Center for Sustainability 2004)

TRANSPORTATION IMPACTS ON SUSTAINABILITY

Transportation facilities and activities have significant sustainability impacts, including those listed in Table 7.2.

TABLE 7.2 Transportation Impacts on Sustainability

Economic	Social	Environmental
Traffic congestion	Inequity of impacts	Air and water pollution
Mobility barriers	Mobility disadvantaged	Habitat loss
Accident damages	Human health impacts	Hydrologic impact
Facility costs	Community interaction	DNPR
Consumer costs	Community liveability	
DNPR	Aesthetics	

Source: Developing Indicators for Comprehensive and Sustainable Transport Planning, Todd Litman, Director Victoria Transport Policy Institute, 4 February 2011, p. 5.
Note: DNPR—Depletion of non-renewable resources.

SIMPLE SUSTAINABILITY INDICATORS

To facilitate sustainable transportation analysis, some evaluations use a relatively simple set of indicators using relatively easily available data. Followings are a few examples:

- Transportation fossil fuel consumption and CO_2 emissions: less is better
- Vehicle pollution emissions: less is better
- Per capita motor vehicle mileage: less is better
- Mode split: higher transit ridership is better
- Traffic crash injuries and deaths: less is better
- Transport land consumption: less is better
- Roadway aesthetic conditions (people tend to be more inclined to care for environment that they consider beautiful and meaningful)

SUSTAINABLE TRANSPORT IN GLOBAL TRADE

The sustainable development should emerge in more regulatory and controlled fashion in global logistics. And we may need different ways of transporting and delivering goods, as the current set of transport and logistics in many sectors is 'unsustainable' due to their energy consumption and resulting pollution. Transport logistics is evolving on a global scale. Global inter shipping firms are working jointly to fast shipping alliances.

ECONOMIC BENEFITS OF SUSTAINABLE TRANSPORTATION

The economic benefits of sustainable transportation are as follows:

- **Attractive new business opportunity:** Sustainable transportation can open up other opportunities in business. For example, rail stations in London, Brussels, Philadelphia and Washington DC have been renovated into vibrant commercial complex with offices, restaurants and shops.
- **Help generate incremental sales:** Motor bike is a more fuel-efficient vehicle. In Toronto area itself, consumers spent over US$56 million on bike accessories and repairs in 1991.
- **Encourage local circulation of money:** To encourage public transport in Los Angeles, 80 cents of every US$1 spent on public transport gets recirculated in the same region which translates into US$3.80 in goods and services or, in other words, 85 of every US$1 spent on gas leaves the region.
- **Promote other types of cost effective services:** When focus is on sustainability, other types of cost-effective services are introduced. For example, 'Cops on Bikes' programmes offer cost-effective police services for many areas with much lower cost and greater flexibility and faster service when compared with policing in automobiles.
- **Development of real estate around metro and rapid transit rails:** Real estate development takes place in high-value area in close vicinity of metro stations. In Atlanta,

US$70 billion in apartments, offices and other services have been spent near rapid transit lines. Around Washington DC, 40% of new building spaces in the 1980s, worth US$3 billion, were built within walking distance of a Metro shop. Similar developments have also been observed near metro and rapid metro in NCR regions and more particularly in Gurgaon, India.

- **Improves productivity:** Sustainable transport helps in increasing the labour productivity. A study on the impact on worker productivity due to US government spending estimated that US$100 billion increase in public transport spending in a course of 10 years would boost worker output by US$521 billion, compared with US$237 billion for the same spending on highways.
- **Reduction in the transportation costs:** Sustainable transport can lead to reduction in costs. For example, as per the business plan for a video conferencing network at British Columbia (BC), Ministry of Transportation projects that an investment of US$977,000 is expected to recover US$2,241,500 in travel costs itself over a period of two years.
- **Helps growth in economic development:** Sustainable development is desirable. A study in Montgomery County found that if growth continued in the usual pattern, economic development would be stifled by the traffic congestion. Whereas in contrast, if growth is focused preferentially in pedestrian and bike-friendly clusters along the expanded transit system and subsidies were revised to discourage car use, jobs and households would double in the County without any traffic congestion.
- **Reduction in infrastructure costs:** For building urban expressways, the cost would be much higher. For example, cost of creating new expressways can be US$100 million per mile, while rail and bike facilities cost can come down to on average of US$15 million and US$0.1 million respectively.
- **Helps creating jobs:** Sustainable transportation offers possibilities of job creation in services, design, high technology construction, manufacturing, maintenance as well as in education and research.

KEY ISSUES IN SUSTAINABLE TRANSPORTATION

The key issues in sustainable transportation are as follows:

- **Access, not mobility:** We move in order to gain access to people, places and things we need. But in car-oriented cities and towns, activities tend to spread out which forces people to travel further and further for the same level of accessibility as before. What we need is access and not mobility.
- **Moving people, not cars:** Focus has to be on moving people and goods and not vehicles. In densely populated cities, dependence on public transport saves the valuable space and energy compared to private transport and can be profitable. But to achieve that, cities have to give preference to public transport on the road over the cars. If public transport like buses always get caught in traffic then the vicious cycle starts in the sense that people abandon public transport and shifts to private vehicles, adding to the traffic jams.
- **Reclaim city space for walking and pedalled vehicles:** The healthiest and most sustainable modes of transport are walking and cycling. In the capital city of Denmark, Copenhagen, one can see only cyclists on main roads and city centres. The effective public

transport depends on people being able to walk comfortably to stations and shops and also to their work places. But walking and cycling are vulnerable to the impacts of traffic. Many rapidly motorizing Asian cities are quickly losing their walking spaces. In Bangkok, only 14% of all trips are on foot or bicycle compared to a whopping 45% in the enormous Tokyo metropolitan area. It requires planning by the city planners to create space for cyclists and pedestrians to walk or cycle safe.

SUSTAINABILITY HELPS BUSINESS

A McKinsey report (https://www.mckinsey.com/business-functions/sustainability/our-insights/greenhouse-gas-abatement-cost-curves, accessed on 22 August 2019), focusing on the greenhouse gas emissions, reported 'Almost forty percent of greenhouse gas abatement could be achieved at a negative marginal costs which means that investing in these options would generate positive cash flows and hence the economic returns over their life cycle'.

Walmart started its focus on sustainability as a defensive move given the negative criticism they were receiving from environmental activists. The company, however, has seen many benefits to its bottom line after they had taken several such initiatives. For example, installing LED lights had significantly reduced their energy bill (Walmart 2013).

Starbucks (2013) is another example of a company that has focused on sustainability for significant business reasons. The company started its Coffee and Farmer Equity Initiative (CAFE) and that evaluates the sustainable production of coffee along four dimensions: product quality, economic accountability, social responsibility and environmental leadership (Stewart 1995).

S. C. Johnson, an FMCG major in household goods, has reported that between 1990 and 1999 the company used eco-efficiency efforts to cut more than 410 million pounds of waste and saved US$125 million.

Recycling boiler flue gas to recover Carbon dioxide to be used again in the product for carbonization as well as heat recovery from boiler flue gases is a common practice in carbonated soft beverages manufacturing plants like Coca Cola.

CASE STUDY: VOLVO'S STRATEGY FOR SUSTAINABILITY

Corporate Overview

AB Volvo, at year-end 1998, was the largest industrial group in Scandinavia, with over 79,000 employees and 55 production plants in 26 countries. Sales in 1998 were SEK 212,936 million (US$25 billion). The Volvo Group's products include cars, large trucks, buses, aircraft engines, construction equipment, and drive systems for marine and industrial applications. About 88% of Volvo sales are outside Sweden, primarily in Western Europe and North America.

To students of management, Volvo gained recognition over 20 years ago for challenging the traditional approach to assembly line production processes by designing production work around intact teams with 'whole tasks'. Volvo's innovative work redesign, which considered the 'social system' in addition to the technical system, set the standard for creating self-managing work teams and improving 'Quality of Work life'.

In the last decade, this strength in high-performance work teams has been augmented by an impressive implementation of lean production methods such as JIT manufacturing, waste reduction, flexible manufacturing, and concurrent engineering, to shorten time-to-market. Volvo now manufactures using a 'pull' production system and produces cars to individual customer specifications, and has inventory turns of about four hours in its car assembly plants.

To this powerful production capability and team synergy—driven by market demand, legislative requirements and a visionary strategy—Volvo has added a rigorous effort to reduce the negative environmental impact of its products. Based on a deep understanding of the entire life-cycle impacts of the automotive and transport industries, Volvo has integrated its value for 'Environmental Care' into design of products and services, production process design and management, product end-of-life handling, customer and employee education, supplier management, and new business services and products.

Volvo's strategy for sustainable development is an integral part of their wider competitive business strategy, and environment has been added as one of three core underlying values of the company.

There is alignment on environmental strategies and objectives, and their relevance to the business, from the board of directors to the shop floor.

By 31 December 1998, over 49,000 employees, suppliers and dealers were supposed to be educated about the basic functioning of nature and conditions of life, the key environmental issues facing our society today (e.g., climate change, ozone depletion, loss of biodiversity), the environmental aspects and impacts of energy and transportation, and the company's environmental objectives and programmes.

About 350 people from almost 60 European suppliers have received environmental education and clear performance expectations regarding establishment of an environment management system, environmental impact improvements, data exchange for life-cycle assessments, 'black lists' and 'grey lists' of chemicals, optimized handling of waste and packaging, and materials recyclability.

Improvements have been made in production processes, where emissions (particularly from solvents) have been reduced substantially with the result that Volvo estimates it is achieving a savings of US$2.50 per car directly to the bottom line simply from its improvements in waste sorting.

Volvo has implemented product design changes. For example,

1. Design changes focus on the reduction of environmental impact 'in use' by providing greater fuel efficiency; buses as alternative modes of transportation (one-third of the Volvo buses sold in Sweden in 1996 were designed to burn alternative fuels, and 21 natural gas buses were supplied to the UK in 1997); mobile data communication systems; and products with alternative fuels such as natural gas, biofuel, alcohol and electricity.
2. The degree of recycled materials in cars is increasing, with rising levels of economic viability. Today, the average recycling percentage of cars is around 75% and of heavy trucks over 90% (by weight higher than cars, given the higher metal content).

Volvo has developed a new company, 'Volvo Mobility Systems' (VMS), to provide products and solutions for the design of safer and more environmentally benign transportation systems globally. For example, Volvo has partnered in developing a more sustainable transportation system based on bus systems which provide service and environmental impact equivalent to light rail systems—at a 1/100th of the cost.

Volvo's platform car S80 (May 1998) is the first car in the world with an 'Environmental Product Declaration', certified by a third party and based on life-cycle assessment.

Sustainable business practices are the foundation for the current and future successes in the era of new challenges arising out of increased concerns on environmental as well as ecological issues. Any company planning to be a profitable company fifty years from now needs to be building sustainability into their strategic thinking. As such successful companies in next millennium will be those that understand and practice sustainability.

Companies committed to integrating the sustainability agenda into their businesses tend to display the following:

- A clear and focused strategic perspective on how sustainability relates to the company, its value chains, markets, products and operations
- Management systems that enable the company to monitor and manage environmental and social issues and integrate them into core business decisions
- Stakeholder dialogue processes that ensure that internal and external concerns are heard and addressed effectively
- Product development processes that integrate triple-bottom-line thinking into the design process and account for impacts throughout the life-cycle of the product
- Open, transparent, quantified and verified communication of the triple bottom-line performance, with growing numbers of companies signing up to the Global Reporting Initiative following the reporting guidelines
- Innovative SCM approaches, where the environmental and social performance of a company's suppliers is seen as an important part of that company's overall performance
- A toolbox that includes life-cycle assessment, design for the environment and life-cycle costing methodologies that internalize what were previously external environmental costs
- And a range of tailored communications activities designed to carry the message through to key market actors, particularly consumers and customers (in terms of performance and quality messages) and financial markets.
- Volvo added environment to its core values of quality and safety and views it as an integral part of company strategy for competitive advantage. Changes were targeted at three areas of highest leverage: (a) product design based on reducing environmental impact over the entire product life-cycle; (b) business development—for example, market access in Asia and a new company VMS aimed at providing products and solutions for the design of safer and more environmentally benign transportation systems; and (c) tough procurement standards for suppliers regarding environmental management and materials. All of this has been supported by clear messages from the boardroom to the shop floor regarding the business relevance of environmental issues, and by extensive education of engineers, employees, suppliers, customers and stakeholders and various measures of ROI.

Sustainability as a Central Strategic Issue

- What critical insights can guide managers and governments as they make strategic decisions to position for the emerging economy?

- What will be the business context of the next decade?
- What innovations in business design and technology will redefine the future competitive landscape?
- What shifts in market demand will drive new requirements and expectations for winning customer loyalty?
- How can corporate policies and strategies be translated and implemented in multinational companies with very diverse product lines?
- What competences and practices from leading global companies and governments could inform our business strategies and practices?
- What is the key to achieving sustainable competitive advantage and value?
- By what measure should we determine success?

The principles of sustainability—perspectives and processes for redesigning our industrial system and practices and our social culture and metabolism (industrial throughput) to achieve sustainable development—offer critical insights for developing the answers to these strategic questions. The organizations are using sustainability in forming strategic plans to:

- Position for the new economy
- Anticipate critical elements of the emerging business context
- Meet shifting customer requirements
- Build customer loyalty and brand introduction
- Stimulate innovations in business design and technology
- Develop new competences
- Achieve competitive advantage
- Increase value
- Redefine measures of corporate, community and national success

Key Drivers of Sustainability Strategies

Volvo's evolution towards sustainability has been influenced by a number of key market drivers: increasing customer demand, competitive pressures, stringent regulatory requirements and new business opportunities. Additionally, Volvo's high-integrity, holistic, life-cycle approach to understanding customer requirement.

Market demand: Volvo is experiencing increasing market demand in certain segments in many countries. Industrial customers, fleet owners, leasing customers, 'authorities' and community sectors (e.g., city transport, airports) are intensifying their purchasing requirements, information requests and concerns about the environmental impact of their transportation choices. The ripple effect that is cascading through the supply chain, especially in Northern Europe, is affecting Volvo. As any one corporation seeks to improve its environmental profile, it of course looks to lessen the negative impacts within its supply chain and transportation activities. So, for example, as Baxter Europe or Eastman Kodak communicated their environmental improvement expectations and goals to their transport company, ASG, this spurred ASG to be more selective in its choice of transport vehicles. Volvo's work in the development of fuel-efficient trucks, alternative fuels and other environmental performance attributes positioned it well for this business. There is a growing demand for efficient and environmentally friendly transport solutions.

Legislative Pressures

The transport industry faces increasingly rigorous legislative standards regarding emissions (led by California's 2003 zero emissions law, and a plethora of EU emissions standards for cars, trucks and buses which were introduced in 2000), recycling (e.g., Sweden's June 1996 legislation which established producer responsibility for scrap cars, mandating that, by 2002, 85% of the vehicle weight must be recovered for re-use, material recycling or energy recovery), waste handling, reduction of noise and traffic congestion, and packaging (e.g., the 1994 legislation in Sweden establishing producer liability for packaging requiring that manufacturers facilitate the sorting and re-use, recycling or energy recovery of all packaging made of glass, corrugated board, paper or cardboard, metal and plastic). More stringent controls on diesel-powered buses and trucks are on the docket in the USA (1998), Japan (2000) and the EU (2001). Many of the regulations have parallels in other countries, and the overall expectation is that these provisions will continue to be tightened in the future. For example, in July 1999, the EU approved 'End-of-Life Vehicle' (ELV) legislation requiring takeback for new cars from 2001 and for all cars by 2006. By 2015 many EU countries achieved the recycling of up to 85% of the vehicle weight (https://en.wikipedia.org/wiki/End_of_Life_Vehicle_Directive). Volvo is working actively to promote harmonization of regulations at an international level. (Overall, there has been exponential growth in the number of legislative restrictions on industry, and the expectation is that this trend will continue.) Legislative requirements related to environment facing the automotive and transport equipment industry are summarized below:

- California has the toughest emissions legislation, where the mandate for a 'zero emission vehicle' was expected to come into force in 2003. EU standards on car, truck and bus emissions tightened in 2000, 2005 and 2008.
- Greenhouse gas reduction goals in Europe required 25% reduction of 1995 levels of carbon dioxide emissions by 2008.
- Sweden legally requires producer liability for ELVs as of 1998, and at least 85% by weight of a vehicle should have been recovered for re-use, recycling or energy recovery, increasing to 95% by 2015.
- The EU has approved a similar measure on ELVs (awaiting ratification by the European Parliament) which would have required manufacturers to take back new cars for recycling and re-use by 2001 and all cars by 2006.

Life-cycle Perspective

Another key driver of Volvo's journey towards sustainability stems from approaching strategy and decisions from its high-integrity, holistic, integrated life-cycle perspective, which stimulates powerful insights into customer requirements, generating and managing value, and reducing environmental impacts and effects. A holistic, life-cycle perspective based on facts and data has permeated Volvo's planning and decision-making at all levels within the organization, from strategic planning efforts that examine Volvo's strategic positioning within the value chain to improvements in design and production to attain environmental efficiencies. Volvo managers have remarked that life-cycle thinking is a natural consequence of focusing on the environment, and that it has been dramatically reflected in priority-setting moving to a product (rather than production process) focus. Life-cycle analysis is now part of the basic public dialogue internally in Volvo, within its value stream, and in Europe more generally.

Genuine Caring

Volvo managers are quick to point out that their interest in environment is not only externally driven. Since 1927, a deeply held concern for people has been a central underpinning of the Volvo company culture, so current efforts towards sustainability are not 'trendy', ancillary or superficial. Rather, it builds on a long-standing tradition in Volvo of commitment to supporting human safety in transport.

New Business

Volvo has identified its strategic strengths and capabilities within the context of more environmentally sustainable industrial practices. It is well positioned to take advantage of emerging business opportunities created by the need for more sustainable transport systems through their action programmes of supplying natural gas and biogas buses; providing integrated rapid transit system design services; addressing concern about pollution levels and emissions in emerging markets; assuring production facilities have strong environmental management systems; and providing transport and logistics information services. In some cases, these competences already existed; in others, Volvo is investing heavily in technology, process and human resource development to build them.

A major signal that a company is moving towards sustainable development is its willingness to fundamentally incorporate different products, services and business designs. The theoretical underpinning of this redesign is often a move towards dematerialization. Industry, overall, is moving towards becoming solution suppliers rather than simply product suppliers. Volvo is actively working to be part of this. Although the company's primary focus is certainly still on production of transportation equipment, it is taking initial steps to lay the groundwork for an alternative business design as a provider of transportation system technology products and services rather than simply manufacturing. A major success for Volvo in this area involves its collaboration with the city of Curitiba, Brazil, to develop an attractive, cost-effective, environmentally sensitive mass transport system. The system is based on buses, and was implemented quickly at significantly lower costs than light rail alternatives. Based on value creation opportunities revealed by Volvo's experience in assisting Curitiba and other cities design transportation systems, Volvo established VMS as a new company in 1998. The history behind the Executive Committee's deliberations in forming VMS, and its vision for the company, is intended to 'Create value by providing efficient, clean, and safe mobility systems for goods and people to demanding customers, primarily in metropolitan areas'.

VMS guidelines are:

- Work with and supply the development of environmentally sensitive mobility solutions.
- Develop alternative power sources and fuels.
- Actively develop sustainable transportation system.
- Operate in the forefront of mobility systems, thus becoming known as credible partner.
- Assist the development of inter-modal transport system that managed the seamless transition between different modes of transport.
- Leverage information technology to support transport.

Volvo's Curitiba Story

Volvo used innovative but simple technology to support the Brazilian city of Curitiba in creating a bus line that rivals the efficiency of light rail or subways, at a fraction of the construction cost and disturbance. Typically, a 12m bus normally carries 1,000 passengers per day. By incorporating double-articulated buses each with a capacity of 270, exclusive bus lanes, timed traffic signals for peak times, and tube stations for prepaid fares, these larger buses can each carry 4,000 passengers per day along the main busway.

The 900 km network transports 23,000 passengers per peak hour, approximately the same number as on the Rio de Janeiro Metro. The double-articulated buses operate at 20kmh, only 5–12 kmh slower than the New York City Subway. Although subways and light rail systems have a slight advantage if they have been previously established, Curitiba's transit system presents many advantages for cities that have not yet developed rail systems. The primary advantage is cost: Volvo's Curitiba system costs $200,000 per km, only

This unsubsidized system carrying 800,000 passengers per day has been proven effective by those using it. Although Curitiba has the highest rate of car ownership in Brazil (one in three), it also has the highest rate of use of public transit: 75% of all commuters take the bus. In addition, 28% of car owners regularly take the bus. As a result, fuel consumption per capita is 30% less than in other Brazilian cities. Traffic has declined by 30% since 1974, while population has doubled.

Source: Rowledge et al. (2017). Included with permission from the publisher.

Case Questions

1. What is the Volvo's strategy for sustainability?
2. Discuss the key insights of the sustainability as central strategic issues.
3. What are key strategic drivers for evolving a sustainable development strategy?
4. Discuss key lessons from Volvo's Curitiba story.

CHAPTER SUMMARY

The component of logistics and their influence on total logistics in global business environment has been discussed here along with what are the implications and on what criteria those costs will depend and how they can be improved further. How some of these costs are better managed in a collaborative networked environment with direct real-time information exchange is also discussed. Different approaches to determine the logistics costs in a business and how customer service level costs are determined are also discussed. Large logistics businesses are increasingly seen to be outsourcing some of the key components, and activities for managing end-to-end logistics for better performance were discussed with some case examples. Logistics management strategies in global trade and commerce and how companies are deriving competitive advantages by reducing cost of operations and unlocking incremental value have been discussed taking the case of a global logistics company. The logistics challenges in e-commerce trade and how large e-retailers like

Amazon were addressing those challenges to create competitive advantages were also discussed. How international logistics management companies are developing relationship with other operators in both domestic and international players to be more effective were discussed with cases. How better and effective logistics management can deliver competitive advantage to marketers were also discussed taking examples. Sustainable transportation is the new challenge to the global logistics operators. How these are being addressed in global transportation and the impact on economic development are also discussed. Finally, a Volvo case study on sustainable transport and technology development programme within the company deriving the strategic direction for the business is discussed.

DISCUSSION QUESTIONS

1. Explain the role of different cost approach in logistics.
2. What are the different costs involved in logistics?
3. How is the total cost approach relevant in the case of global logistics cost management in business?
4. How can businesses organize themselves to benchmark their performance?
5. Explain the role of different cost approaches in logistics.
6. How can an efficient SCM create shareholders' value?

REFERENCES

Beatley, T. 1995. 'Environmental Ethics and Planning Theory'. *Journal of Planning Literature* 4 (1):1–32.

Benjamin, R., and R. Wigand. 1995. 'Electronic Markets and Virtual Value Chains on the Information Super High Way'. *Sloan Management Review* 36 (2): 67–72.

Cavinato, Joseph L. 1992. 'A Total Cost/Value Model for Supply Chain Competitiveness'. *Journal of Business Logistics* 13 (2): 285–291.

Christopher, M. G. (1998). *Logistics and Supply Chain Management, Strategies for reducing cost and improving services.* London: Pitman Publishing.

Karen E. Woody. 2012. 'Conflicts Minerals Legislation: The SECs New Role as Diplomatic and Humanitarian Watchdog'. *Fordhan Law Review* 81 (3): 1315–1351.

Lee, H. L., and C. Billington. 1992. 'Managing Supply Chain Inventory: Pitfalls and Opportunities'. *Sloan Management Review* 33 (3): 65–73.

Levy, D. L. 1997. 'Lean Production in an International Supply Chain'. *Sloan Management Review* 38 (2): 94–102.

Naim, M. M. 1997. 'The Book That Changed the World'. *Manufacturing Engineer* 76 (1): 67–72.

Rowledge, Lorinda R., Russell Barton, Kevin Brady, James Fava, Cynthia Figge, Konrad Saur, and Steven Young. 2017. *Mapping the Journey, Case Studies in Strategy and Actions towards Sustainable Development.* Routledge.

Slack, N., S. Chambers, C. Harland, A. Harrison, and R. Johnston. 1995. *Supply Chain Operations Management.* London: Pitman Publishing.

Starbucks. 2013. Starbucks Global Responsibility Report: Goals and Progress 2013.

Stewart, G. 1995. 'Supply Chain Performance Benchmarking Study Reveals Keys to Supply Chain Excellence'. *Logistics Information Management* 8 (2): 38–44

The Establish Davis Logistics Cost and Service Database. 2014. Available at https://www.establishinc.com/establish-davis-database (accessed on 22 August 2019).

Thomas, D. J., and P. M. Griffin. 1996. 'Co-ordinate Supply Chain Management'. *European Journal of Operational Research* 94 (3): 1–15.

Walmart. 2013. *Walmart 2013 Global Responsibility Report.* Available at https://cdn.corporate.walmart.com/39/97/81c4b26546b3913979b260ea0a74/updated-2013-global-responsibility-report_130113953638624649.pdf (accessed on 16 April 2019).

World Commission on Environment and Development—Our Common Future (1987). Oxford University Press.

BIBLIOGRAPHY

Andrew C. Revkin. 2007. 'Poor Nations to Bear Brunt as World Warms'. *The New York Times*, April 1.

Beyond the Green Corporation. 2007. *Bloomberg Businessweek*, January 29.

Rushton, Alan, Peter Baker, and Phil Croucher. Ed. 1989. *The Handbook of Logistics and Distribution Management: Understanding the Supply Chain.* London: Kogan Page Publishers.

Stepien, Marcin, Sylwia Legowik-Swiacik, Wioletta Skibinska, and Izabela Turek. 2016. 'Identification and Measurement of Logistics Cost Parameters in the Company'. *Transportation Research Procedia* 16: 490–497.

Story, Louise. 2007. 'Lead Paint Prompts Mattel to Recall 967,000 Toys'. *The New York Times*, August 2.

Toyli, J. 2008. 'Logistics and Financial Performance: An Analysis of 424 Finish Small- and Medium-sized Enterprises'. *International Journal of Physical Distribution and Logistics Management* 38 (1): 57–80.

Xian-min ZOU. 2005. 'Management and Control of Logistics Coast in Enterprises'. *Industrial Engineering Journal* 4: 3.

8

Global Logistics Value Chain Management

LEARNING OBJECTIVES

Section I: Integration of Global Value Chain Components

- Define international logistics and key drivers of its evolution and tools that facilitated global logistics
- Identify logistics value chain linkages and integration of value chain components
- Recognize international logistics challenges and barriers to global logistics
- Identify complexity in global logistics and source of competitive advantage
- Classify features of international trade and impact of globalization on international logistics
- Know the global operating levels of logistics companies
- Recognize security issues and environmental concerns in global logistics management

Section II: Sourcing Decisions in Global SCM

- Understand global sourcing challenges and strategies
- Link global sourcing and supply chain sustainability
- Identify global sourcing models and frameworks
- Realize global trends in sourcing
- Identify CSFs in global sourcing and future factories

SECTION I
INTEGRATION OF GLOBAL VALUE CHAIN COMPONENTS

INTRODUCTION

By value, it would normally mean a chain of activities that a firm of a specific industry performs to deliver valuable products or services for the market (first introduced by Michael Porter in 1985). Value is created by unlocking the hidden value and also by removing non-value-adding activities from business processes. The value so created needs to be captured to be delivered for offering better cost-value benefit to the customers to succeed in the marketplace. Value chain matrix would suggest the areas of improvement. In a competitive environment, businesses must have a better understanding of their consumers and are also required to deliver the customer requirement better in comparison to their immediate competitors. Projecting and delivering superior values hold the key to success, and for doing so, businesses need to constantly upgrade the product and services to remain aligned with the technology. Speed of action and delivery as well as delivering the product where customer wants are also the key requirements for success. A business has to deliver its normal profits as returns to the shareholders. The normal profit is generated from pricing and costing of the product and services. But incremental profit for the business can only be generated by managing the business processes better. One way of improving the value or performance is reducing cost or improving cost management and resorting to eliminating non-value-adding and redundant processes in the business. Another way of reducing costs is by resorting to better working capital management such as reducing the average inventory holding or increasing the average settlement period of debtors and also the average settlement period of creditors.

Businesses have multiple objectives for their existence in addition to making profit for which any economic activity is undertaken first of all. A business also has to deliver growth by increasing market share and expanding geographical territory. Besides, businesses also have to deliver a larger responsibility for the society by creating social value. Shareholder's value is normally measured by financial parameters such as ROI, PAT, EVA, and so on, and these can be increased by managing logistics more effectively, which can also help in delivering incremental financial performance. The logistics cost can significantly impact ROI in any business. Although the significant cost of logistics is arising out of transportation function, logistics competency is achieved by coordinating the various functions and logistics activities including network design, information, transportation, inventory, warehousing, material-handling and packaging.

INTERNATIONAL LOGISTICS

International logistics is the design and management of a system that controls the forward and reverse-flow of materials, services, information into, through and out of international corporation and international geographic boundaries. This flow of goods and services happens through an international logistics channel. International logistics is a multidisciplinary function and covers a wide variety of disciplines and management functions.

Therefore, international logistic channel means the optimal routes created purposefully and in a systematic way, most often within the confines of the already existing international logistic networks (although in emergency, logistics networks may be created individually, for example, temporary landing sites or warehouses) to the recipient along with accompanying information.

The physical network: It begins with the supplier and ends with the ultimate client and embraces all aspects related to product development, purchase, manufacturing, physical distribution, after-sales service and the circulation of information.

KEY DRIVERS FOR EVOLUTION OF INTERNATIONAL LOGISTICS

FIRST: GLOBAL SOURCING OF COMPONENTS

In international logistic channels, the subjects are linked by the physical movement of goods and information. A good example may be the Singer sewing machine. The basic components of these machines are produced in three continents: the housing in the USA, the drive shafts in Italy, and the motors in Brazil. The final product is assembled in Taiwan, while the customers are spread all over the world. The supply-, manufacturing- and distribution-related functions between subjects located in various parts of the world is a huge challenge, which needs to unite and integrate the system.

SECOND: NEW PRODUCT DEVELOPMENT—GLOBAL EXPERTISE

International logistic channel is a network of companies established to develop a new product, exchange resources, gain advantages through its size, reduce costs, increase a competitive advantage and so on. They could be either horizontal and vertical. The horizontal networks are established by manufacturers of similar or same goods. And the vertical networks are represented by a set of companies connected with one another in a 'supplier–receiver' relationship.

THIRD: MINING COMPANIES DRIVING THE PROCESS

The subject structure of international logistic channels is created by mining companies, suppliers of materials and components, manufacturers, service providers, transport companies, warehouses and logistics centres, distributors and all the relationships between them.

FOURTH: HIGH LEVEL OF CUSTOMER SATISFACTION

An international logistic channel is a quick, flexible and interconnected system, driven by the mechanism of the customers' choice, aiming to achieve a high level of customer satisfaction as well as to gain the highest possible profit by the companies within this channel.

FIFTH: HIGH DEGREE OF PROCESS ORIENTATION

Increased focus and process orientation for standardization of business processes across countries in the network served as key drivers of global logistics operations. The international logistic channel can be described by means of the following characteristics: the process (the subject of the flow), the structure (the entity structure) and the objectives (the scope of action and the areas of cooperation of participating entities).

SIXTH: DRIVEN BY COST QUALITY CONSIDERATIONS

The range of international logistics channel consists of raw materials, auxiliary materials and cooperating elements, purchased on the supply market according to the need, passed on to the production process and finished products submitted for sale and delivered to the customer. The cost and quality consideration has driven the global logistics business.

SEVENTH: CHANNEL LINKED TO EXPERTISE IN THE AREAS

Depending on the configuration of the international logistic channel, its links may consist of different kinds of mining, processing, service and trading companies. Their position within the channel results from the division of work in the next stages of production and sales of goods. Because of their role as senders and receivers of loads, as well as the accompanying information and finance streams, their basic role in the functioning of the international logistic channel is unquestionable.

METHODS AND TOOLS FACILITATING INTERNATIONAL LOGISTICS

Tools facilitate international logistics so that International logistics may function effectively and efficiently. If we effectively manage all participants and processes that constitute logistic channels businesses can become more competitive and cost-effective.

Modern logistics management in reality is a decision-making process related to the synchronization of the physical, informational and financial supply and demand streams flowing between its participants, so as they would gain competitive advantage and create added value with benefits for all its elements, customers and other stakeholders.

In supply international logistic chain management, many methods and devices are used, which have been and still are applied in effective economic systems management. To this group, we may include the following:

- **Lean management:** This concept is about the elimination of all actions that do not create any added value, that is, such actions, for which the customer would not pay. Or perceived value of the service will not improve.
- **Agile management:** Agile management, in contrast to lean management, takes place under conditions of constant and unpredictable changes within the supply chain. Such cases may be evoked with emergency situations (a temporarily organized supply chain in case of fires, floods, technical disasters, etc.) or unplanned customer order.
- **Efficient consumer response:** It is a supply chain, including the Euro-logistic one, that is customer-oriented. It is a modern strategy, the foundation of which lies in the partnership of its participants—a synchronized supply management. It is a strategy to increase the level of services to consumers through close cooperation with retailers, wholesalers and distributors.

- **Total quality management:** The American Society for Quality has defined quality in the form of interdependent dimensions, as the characteristic features of a product or service that have impact on its ability to satisfy customer's specification as per contract, every time at all interfaces.
- **Business process re-engineering:** It is the process of eliminating the non-value-adding and redundant services/activities from the end-to-end value chain.
- **Theory of constraints and queues:** Constraints in any business process limit or dictate the performance and eliminate the constraints to improve performance. It has been observed that the 0.1% constraints can dictate 99.9% performance.
- **Time-based management (TBM):** Time-based management is an aspect of lean production. It is a general approach that recognizes the importance of time and seeks to reduce the level of wasted time in the production processes of a business.
- **Just in time:** In this, production lines up and delivers just when it is needed. It has driven global logistics business for improved performance and acted as a key driver. Sales order processing and ERP helped logistics operators to perform better.
- **Supply Chain Operation Reference (SCOR) Model:** In 1966, the Supply Chain Council (SCC), the organization standardizing supply support systems, published the SCOR Model, which is used for description and comprehensive analysis of the supply chain. This model is continuously updated; the latest version of SCOR bears a number, was published in May 2008 and has been successfully applied in Euro-logistics.
- **VMI:** Cost-reduction, shortening the time of reaction to the customer's needs and the optimization of inventory level in the supplier–customer relation are the main areas of interest and management in Euro-logistic channels.

STORAGE FACILITY

Storage facility is generally referred to the stationery period involved with respect to merchandise because inventory is stored in the warehouse. The location decisions, addresses as well as how many distribution centres to have and where to locate them depend on various factors, including cost, customer location and cluster of customers, availability of the infrastructure as well as service quality and frequency. The storage facilities abroad can differ in availability and quality which need to be carefully assessed. The logistician should analyse international product sales and then rank order products according to warehousing needs. The storage facilities can be of various types and sizes depending on the purpose and quantity of the stock kept in those facilities. These facilities can be called logistics centres.

LOGISTICS CENTRES (NODAL POINTS)

The function of logistics centres is to ensure the efficient movement of products within the region. Euro-logistics has nodal points of nodal logistics network, which in practice, depending on the time of formation, classification, purpose and strategy, would be called as the following:

- Storage building
- Storage centre
- Logistic services centre
- Distribution centre
- Logistics park
- Logistics hub

DECENTRALIZED LOGISTICS SYSTEM

When a firm serves many diverse international markets, total centralization might leave the firm unresponsive to local adaptation needs. If each subsidiary makes a profit centre in itself, each one carries the full responsibility for its performance. Once products are within a specific market, increased input from local logistics operation should be expected and encouraged. When the market to be serviced is too wide and spread out, centralized management of logistics will not be cost effective and easy to control. The local logistics industry also performs and practices their own methods based on the available logistics infrastructure and business practices which a local logistics company can perform with much higher effectiveness. Decentralization of logistics functions and system makes good sense in terms of managing global logistics value chain.

OUTSOURCING LOGISTICS SERVICES

The systematic outsourcing of logistics capabilities is the third option. Outsourcing logistics function is a very common practice in the industry. This saves a lot of resources and also reduces complexity. By collaborating with transportation firms, private warehouses or other specialists, corporate resources can be concentrated on the firm's core products and functions. For example, a company like Hero Moto Corp. Ltd, formerly Hero Honda, is an Indian motorcycle and scooter manufacturer based in New Delhi, India. The company is the largest two-wheeler manufacturer in the world, and also in India, where it has a market share of about 46% in the two-wheeler category. The company has outsourced its logistics services to the third party that collects goods ex-factory and manages the transportation, distribution and delivery functions both for domestic and the international markets. Operating at arms-length with TPL company is advantageous in the sense that cost is less, there are flexibility and it prevents blocking of corporate resources.

LOGISTICS AND ENVIRONMENT

Since environmental laws and regulations differ across the globe, the firm's efforts need to be responsive to a wide variety of requirements. Reverse distribution systems are instrumental in ensuring that the firm does not only deliver the product to the market but also can retrieve it from the market for subsequent recycling or disposal. Companies need to learn how to simultaneously achieve both environmental and economic goals.

FIRM'S VALUE CHAIN

The generic value chain of any firm is as shown in Figure 8.1, consisting of some primary functions of the business and supported by some support functions. The support functions help the business to perform their primary functions well.

In firm's value chain, the company's activities are divided into the technologically and economically distinct activities that the company performs in doing business. 'Value activities' are nine generic activities (split into two categories: primary and support) that value the amount that buyers are willing to pay for a product or service. 'Primary activities' are those involved in the physical creation of the product or service. 'Support activities' provide the inputs and infrastructure that allow the primary activity to take place.

A company's value chain is a system of interdependent activities. A value chain for a company in a particular industry is embedded in a larger stream of activities that is called 'value system'. The various elements of the logistics value chain covering logistics and value-added services along the entire supply chain would include raw material procurement and inbound logistics, production and operations and outbound logistics and warehousing, and distribution and return logistics to bring back the goods not needed or returned for any reasons.

TRANSFORMING THE VALUE CHAIN

Businesses have both primary activities and support activities, and logistics is all pervasive. Value chain can be transformed by improving the business processes as well as using relevant and appropriate technology. For example, firm's administrative infrastructure can be improved by

FIGURE 8.1 **Firm's Value Chain**

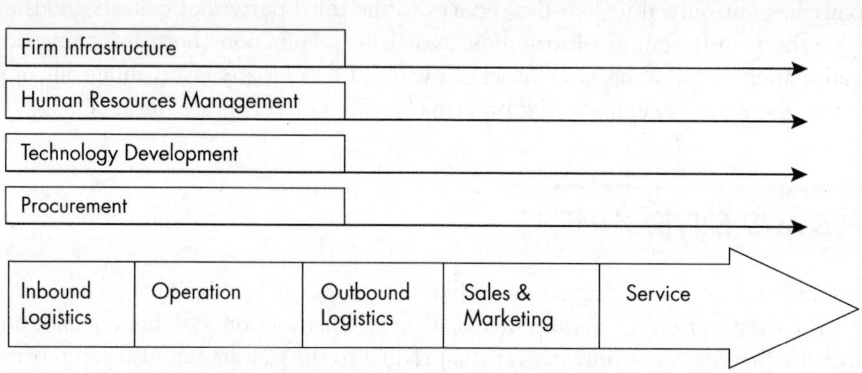

Source: Porter (1985).

implementing office automation system. Similarly, HRM function can be outsourced as well as can be improved by workforce planning system. Procurement function these days is remarkably improved and is technology driven. EDI can help improve procurement function, and accordingly designing and technology can be transformed by the use of CAD/CAM in the business. These are all support activities in the business.

In terms of primary activities, inbound logistics can be transformed by implementing automated warehousing whereas outbound logistics can be transformed by implementing WMS and automated shipment scheduling. Computerized ordering and ERP as well CRM can significantly improve the value in the areas of sales, marketing and customer service. Even process changes can bring in significant improvements and transform the firm's value chain in the areas of sales, marketing and customer service. In the operations and manufacturing or production function, infusion of technology such as computer controlled and programmed machines, robotics and artificial intelligence can greatly transform and unlock hidden value in the business.

LINKAGES WITHIN VALUE CHAIN

Same function can be performed in different ways, for example, conformance to specifications can be achieved through high-quality purchase input, specifying close tolerances in manufacturing process or even 100% inspection of finished goods. Cost or performance of direct activities is improved by greater efforts in indirect activities, for example, better scheduling (an indirect activity) reduces sales force travel time or delivery vehicle time (direct activities) or better maintenance improves tolerances achieved by machines. Activities performed inside a firm reduce the need to demonstrate, explain or service a product in the field, for example, 100% inspection can substantially reduce service costs in the field but will significantly increase the inspection cost and time. An enterprise value chain is linked and interconnected with its suppliers value chain, channel and distribution partners value chain as well buyers value chain. Linkage among activities does not only connect value activities inside a company but also creates interdependence between its value chain and those of its suppliers and channel partners. Businesses need to manage the buyers and suppliers value chain effectively to create incremental value in the business.

Corporations that are operating on a global scale also need a global logistics management strategy from the considerations of business objective and how those objectives would be measured from the perspectives of shareholders as well as customers to align the key organizational processes to achieve the stated goals. In that strategic roadmap, organization's logistics performance and costs indicators are also required to be analysed and measured. The key organizational processes have to be synchronized across all regional markets. The logistics function has to be managed to ensure the movement and distribution of product to ensure product availability in all markets at the least cost of delivery. This has been shown schematically in Figure 8.2.

Businesses have to be managed for support functions to ensure performance of primary functions as indicated in the firm's value chain for optimum performance. Many businesses are focused on volume performance by preferentially focusing on the primary functions instead of the results in terms of incremental value created in the business. To help create value in the business, functional activities in the value chain need to be closely monitored for results, and for that, financial control, profit and cost control, and value-based management are required.

FIGURE 8.2 Global Logistics Strategy Drivers

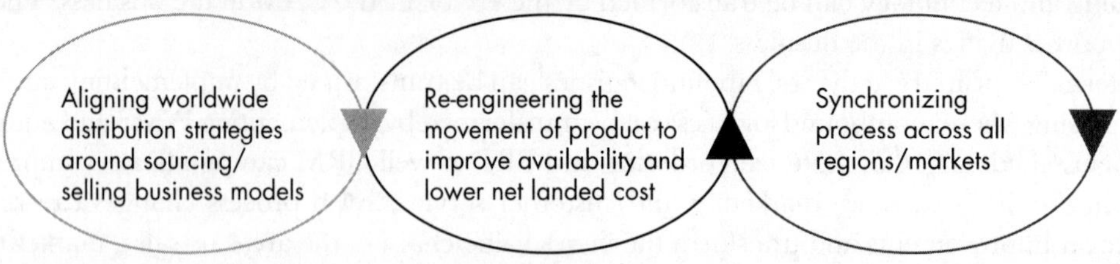

Key Requirements	Key Performance Measures	Key Organizational Process
Centralized management/ worldwide integration	<u>Shareholder Measurements</u>	<u>Planning and control</u>
Customer service option	Inventory turns	Configuration and scheduling
Sourcing initiatives and alliances	Asset utilization	Demand management and communication
Procurement/supplier integration	Operating costs	Sourcing strategy
Global network optimization	Customer satisfaction	Manufacturing strategy
Process driver information systems.	Loss management (asset protection)	Supply chain integration
	<u>Customer Measurements</u>	Product life cycle
	Product availability	<u>Support</u>
	Flexibility	Infrastructure
	On-time performance	Information and technology
	Speed	Key performance indicators
	Responsiveness	
	Consistency	
	Quality	

INTERNATIONAL BUSINESS

International trade is in reality an extension of domestic trade. International trade would thus mean the import and export activities carried out by any nation with another nation or by any company in one country with a company in another country. For Example, Japan is a highly industrialized country. The country exports high-quality machineries and imports agricultural products from Malaysia. Other examples of international trade are as follows:

- The exchange of services or goods between different countries
- When the residents or businesses of two or more different countries do the transactions of sale and purchase of goods or services

FEATURES OF INTERNATIONAL TRADE

International trade is controlled and guided by various regulations which can be both country-specific and global trade practices and as per guidelines of World Trade Organization (WTO) signed by 164 countries. The WTO is an inter-governmental organization created to regulate global trade between the nations. The key features of international trade include the following:

- **Involvement of different monetary units:** Each country has its own currency for domestic trade, but for international trade only globally tradable and accepted currency is used. For example, USD and Euro.
- **Imposition of restrictions in import and export by various countries:** To protect the domestic manufacturers and trade, each country normally puts some restrictions on both imports into and exports out of the country.
- **Imposition of restrictions on release of foreign currencies:** Depending on the foreign exchange reserve of the country which has to be used for essential imports like oil or other essential goods, the foreign exchange is regulated in each country.
- **Existence of multiple regulations:** There exist both global and country-specific regulations that govern the global trade, making it more complex for the operators.
- **Legal practices and rules in different countries:** Although there are regulations that govern international trade, legal framework of each country in global trade would be different and one has to be familiar with the local legal requirement, processes and practices for doing business in that country.

INTERNATIONAL LOGISTICS CHALLENGES

There are numerous challenges that global logistics players have to face to deliver performance. While effective logistic system is important for domestic operations, it is also absolutely critical for global manufacturing and marketing. Domestic logistics focuses on performing value-added services in a relatively controlled environment. It is imperative that global logistics operations must accommodate all domestic requirements and also deal with growing uncertainties associated with distance, demand, diversity and documentation. In global trade, the customers are demanding in terms of quality, lead time and order fulfilment criteria. The marketers need to have clear understanding of changing customer needs and expectations. The firms must be more and more flexible and proactive to anticipate and to adapt to such changes. The quest for flexibility and reactivity affects the conception and the management of firms and more generally their logistic systems, and contributes to the development of partnership relations to the emergence of mergers or strategic alliances between companies. As a result, a firm can no longer be considered an isolated entity but a component of a wider supply chain network.

Operating challenges faced by global logistics systems vary significantly within operating regions. North American logistics vision is one of the open geographies with extensive demand for land-based transportation and limited need for cross-border documentation. European logistics views operations from a perspective characterized by relatively compact geography, involving numerous political, cultural, regulatory and language barriers. Pacific Rim logistics has an inland perspective that requires extensive water or air shipment to transcend vast distances. In past, enterprises could survive and also could achieve substantial success with a unique North American, European or Pacific Rim logistics regional capability. This is still true for some firms. Those who intend to grow regional capabilities are required to extend service zones. For global scale operations and economies, enterprises are developing global logistic expertise.

Logistics principle is same domestically and globally; operating environments are more complex and costly. Cost and complexity are represented by four D's: distance (longer), documents (extensive), diversity in culture (wide variation with cultural difference) and demand of customers (variable and fluctuating demand). Developing appropriate strategies and tactics to respond to these four D's is a challenge for logistics management.

BARRIERS TO GLOBAL LOGISTICS

While many forces facilitate borderless operations, some significant barriers continue to impede global logistics. Every country is concerned about balance of trade which has a reflection on country's economy. Three significant barriers are as follows:

- Markets and competition
- Financial barriers
- Distribution channels

Market and competition will cover entry restrictions, availability of information (market size, demographics, competition, infrastructure) and pricing, competition law, transfer pricing and anti-dumping law. Entry restrictions limit market access by placing legal and physical barriers on import.

Protection of domestic industry by favourable tax structure and unfavourable import duty also acts as barriers in global trade. In addition, complex duty structure and compliance issues add to the barriers and challenges. Financial barriers normally result from forecasting and institutional infrastructures. Difficulty in forecasting is due to global environment considering customer trends, seasonality and competitive action. As such barriers to global trade can be broadly classified as: trade barriers which are normally in terms of custom duties and non-trade barriers which will be due to operational hurdles and constraints.

In global environment, forecasting becomes difficult compounded by custom laws, government policies and complexities as well as facilitating intermediaries such as banks, insurance firms, legal counsellors and transport carriers. Logistics manager must allow for additional inventory, transportation lead time and financial resources to operate globally.

Distribution channel difference, infrastructure and trade agreements also act as barriers confronting global logistics managers. Difference in transportation and material-handling equipment, warehouse and port facilities and communication systems are other such barriers.

Recently, efforts have been made to improve standardization with respect to containerization. However, major differences still exist with respect to transportation equipment, vehicle dimension, capacity, weight, rail gauge and so on. When infrastructure is not standardized, it is necessary for the products to be unloaded and reloaded into different vehicles or containers as they cross national boundaries, resulting in increased cost and time.

IMPACT OF GLOBALIZATION ON INTERNATIONAL LOGISTICS

Globalization brings homogenization of consumer needs, liberalization of trade and competitive advantages of operating in global markets. Companies are forced to think and act globally in order to survive in such a dynamic environment. All these elements have a deep impact on the development and the positioning of companies on international marketplaces where competition is cruel.

ROLE OF GLOBAL LOGISTICS

Globalization has helped in doing businesses beyond the national boundaries. Internet has made it easier, and world has become really a global village. Cargo movement is done physically using available options: physical movement of cargo, intermediaries, freight forwarders, custom house indispensable. Knowledge, connectivity and documentation are crucial areas. Global operations of a business increase complexity. Decrease in control over movement of goods is a challenge in global logistics operations.

SUPPLY CHAIN AND THE INTERNET

Because of the internet, firms are able to conduct many more global comparisons among suppliers and select from a wider variety of choices. When a customer has the ability to access a company must be prepared for 24 hours order-taking and customer service. For all countries, but particularly in less developed nations, the issue of universal access to the Internet is crucial.

GLOBAL LOGISTICS CAPABILITIES

Global logistics capabilities must include international transportation, cultural diversity, multilanguage capability and extended supply chain operations. Global operations increase logistics cost and complexity. As complexity, operational uncertainty increases in global logistics, control capability decreases. Control problems result from extensive use of intermediaries, coupled with government intervention in customs requirement and trade restrictions and control.

GLOBAL OPERATING LEVELS OF LOGISTICS COMPANIES

There are five levels of enterprise evolution from domestic logistics operation to becoming global logistics operator:

- Level 1: Arm's length
- Level 2: Internal export
- Level 3: Internal operations
- Level 4: Insider business practices
- Level 5: Denationalized operations

Arm's Length

It is a preferred method of operation for the players with limited international experience. In this mode, companies either sell or consign their goods to the international specialists who accept the responsibility of ordering, providing international transportation, documentation as well as market coordination, inventory management, invoicing and product support. Advantage is that it reduces the risk substantially, but the disadvantage is the loss of control on product and logistics operations.

Internal Export

When players develop the expertise to coordinate and manage international transportation and documentation, they graduate to this mode of operation. However, local agents and distributors are retained to provide marketing, inventory management, invoicing and product support. The advantage is that margins are improved because of part control, but complete benefits are still not derived. The disadvantage is that it reduces the sensitivity to local requirements for not being involved in sales, distribution and marketing for international market.

Internal Operations

At this level, companies would have local market presence in foreign countries, and internal operations would include marketing, sales, production and distribution. Companies would engage parent company employees and not local employees and follow parent company practices for better control and low-risk internal operations. Advantage is that at relatively lower level of risk there will be further increase in control and sensitivity. However, the disadvantage is that it still relies heavily on home country values, practices, policies, procedures and operations.

Insider Business Practices

This is a level up from the earlier level of operations in the sense that this further internalizes international operations and follows local business practices by hiring host country management, marketing and sales organizations and even local business system and practices, and, as it grows, a separate host country business philosophy emerges. The advantage is still further increase in control and sensitivity at manageable risk. However, the disadvantage is that home country business practices and philosophy will still be dominant, and home country expectations and standards will still be applicable.

DENATIONALIZED OPERATIONS

This level operates and maintains foreign country operations and develops regional headquarters to oversee the coordination of operations in the area. At this stage of development, enterprise is stateless and policies and practices are not specific to home country. Local marketing and sales organizations are supported by world-class manufacturing and logistics operations. Also, product sourcing and marketing decisions are made across a wide range of global alternatives and systems; processes are designed to meet individual country requirement and aggregated to share knowledge and financial reporting; and the company is acting as truly international or global company.

GLOBAL OPERATIONS LEVEL

Most of the organizations involved in global logistics are actually operating at Levels 2, 3 and 4. But a truly international firm must focus on Level 5 or denationalized operations. Organizations at any other levels will retain a home country perspective. Denationalizing operations require a significant level of management trust across countries, involving diverse culture which would be possible when managers and staffs of the organization are hired from other cultures as well. As the global operational levels progress, there is an increasing dependency on system and also on the process of integration.

STAGES OF REGIONAL INTEGRATION

Free Trade Agreement

FTA normally is signed between friendly countries to facilitate the trade which eliminates tariff on trade between countries in a region. This helps when the participants in the free-trade area expect to gain by specializing in the production of goods and services in which it has a comparative advantages and by importing such products and services from other countries in agreement in which it faces comparative disadvantages. In such a situation, trades among countries give them less expensive access to a number of goods. FTA as such may either stimulate or reduce international trade, and it can also reduce the access of the firms to more efficient producers or markets outside their region. FTA must ensure the complementarity. India has such FTA with countries in the Association of Southeast Asian Nations (ASEAN).

Customs Union

This eliminates the tariff between member countries and establishes external tariff structure towards other regions and non-member countries. Advantage accrued to the member countries in customs union is that none of the member nations can position themselves to gain a tariff advantage at the expense of other countries. Member countries under this agreement are required to give some control over the economic policies to the group.

Common Market

The tariff policy in common market is similar to that of customs union. Besides, the common market allows factors of production such as labour and capital as well as goods and people to move freely between member countries as dictated by the market conditions. This has considerable impact on the local economy of the countries working in a common market because people move generally and relatively from a weaker economy country to a stronger economy country.

Economic Union

This is the most advanced stage of development and it implies harmonization of economic policies which is beyond the common market. Under this arrangement, member countries standardize the monetary and fiscal policies, and although not essential but normally economic union is likely to include common currency and harmonized tax structure. Here, goods and production factories can also move freely according to market conditions and demands, and no major fluctuations in monetary exchange and interest rates will occur as we can see happening in EU.

COMPLEXITY OF LOGISTICS MANAGEMENT

End-to-end logistics management covers delivering input material to industry and then taking output to end consumer at the least cost. This would entail the following:

- Trade inventory—low
- Delivery time—fastest and timely
- Efficient system
- Failure rate—low
- Order fill rate and pack fill rate—accurate

Efficient service delivery at a lower cost provides competitive advantage to businesses. Logistics cost in typical distribution of FMCG products in India would be anything up to 10–15% of the end selling price, including freight, insurance and warehousing but excluding channel margins. Managing it effectively obviously provides competitive advantage to the business in terms of distinctive cost advantage.

ENTRY OF GLOBAL RETAILERS IN INDIAN MARKET

Global retailers such as Walmart, Tesco and others have already entered the Indian market, competing with local retailers such as Big Bazar, More, Reliance and so on. Global wholesalers (cash and carry format) such as Booker, Metro (Macro), and so on also are operating in Indian market competing with local wholesalers such as Reliance and Bharti Retail. Global online retailers such as Amazon.com and e-bay also entered India and are competing with local e-retailers such as Flipkart.com and Snapdeal.com. Overall retail market is of about US$300 billion, growing at the rate of 6% every year. Together they only control about 4% of the total market. Rest is still covered in traditional mode of distribution.

If we look at the retail density, it is at a high with 13 million retail outlets, 95% mom and pop stores. On the other hand, organized retailing has only 4–5% share. Channel intermediaries which are large in numbers—C&F agents, wholesalers, semi-wholesalers, consignment agents, super-stockists, distributors, retailers make the distribution and logistics tasks very complex to be managed.

Even large global companies such as P&G, Unilever, Nestle and Phillips that are operating in Indian soil for over several decades can reach about 1–2 million retailers through their own network. Smaller players will not have the reach of more than 0.5 million. The remaining market has to be covered through redistribution route. Traditional channels have limited reach. Innovation in channel management holds the key. Global logistics companies such as DHL and FedEx are also operating in India, competing with local players such as GATI, Safe Express and many more. The 3P logistics providers offer only point-to-point service in B2B mode. The entire spectrum of the chain was never covered. Logistics industry has large, medium, small and tiny operators offering connectivity and control at various levels. Last mile connectivity is always a challenge.

No single model will work for all markets. Some markets are reached through the wholesale route. Some markets are covered through the organized retail route; some markets through dealer distribution network; and some through super-stockists/consignment agents/C&F agent. No one model will work for all markets.

LOGISTICS: A SOURCE OF COMPETITIVE ADVANTAGE

Procurement effectiveness of all these players is more or less the same. Success will depend on competitive advantage from efficient SCM, mainly logistics. Competitive advantage will have to be derived from the following:

- Time to deliver goods to the customer
- Reducing inventory in the system without losing out on delivery commitment
- Logistics cost which is the only source of competitive advantage is smart management of logistics

Supply chain delays and uncertainty are major constraints to manufacturing growth and competitiveness. According to a World Bank report, halving the delays due to road blocks, tolls and other stoppages could cut freight times by 20–30% and logistics costs by 30–40%. This alone can boost the manufacturing sectors by 3–4% of net sales. There are around 650 check points at 29 state and 7 union territory borders across India. Regulatory checks to the movement of goods across these borders raise truck transit times by as much as 25%.

VALUE CHAIN IN SALES

Sales value chain will cover and include all service processes from receiving the sales order to processing, executing as well as servicing the sales order. When customer places an order, it needs to be processed and executed as per customers requirement as stipulated in the order. And post execution of the order, customer has to be serviced as per commitment which may include installation of the unit or equipment, demonstration and grievance redressing or attending to the complaints of the customer. Each stage of the processes, starting from receiving the order to services, has to conform to the contract and has to be competitive. The following parameters have to be continuously improved by benchmarking with the competition and industry practices:

- Sales order receiving
- Sales order processing
- Sales order executing
- Sales order servicing

As international trade continues to grow, imperatives on improving logistics would be as follows:

- Customers are more knowledgeable and demand higher quality, lower costs and better service.
- Competition is getting fiercer, and organizations must look at every opportunity to remain competitive.
- There is changing power in the supply chain. Very large retail chains demand customized logistics from their suppliers.
- Other changes in retail markets include the growth of 24-hour opening, home deliveries, out-of-town malls, retail parks, telephone and online shopping.
- Organizations are introducing new types of operation, such as JIT, flexible manufacturing, and so on.
- Some organizations are turning from a product focus to a process focus. This encourages improvement to operations, including logistics.

- There have been considerable improvements in communication.
- Organizations are increasing cooperation through alliances, partnerships and other arrangements.
- Managers are recognizing the strategic importance of the supply chain.
- Attitudes towards transport are changing, because of increased congestion on roads, concerns about air quality and pollution, broader environmental issues and so on.

INTEGRATED SUPPLY CHAIN AND LOGISTICS VALUE CHAIN

MANAGEMENT CHALLENGES FOR INTEGRATED SUPPLY CHAIN

Management challenges and complexities with respect to integrated supply chain will increase with the number of links within a business process, which can range from low to high (Ellram and Cooper 1990; Houlihan 1985) and thus adding more management components or levels of each component can lead to an increase in the level of integration. Existing literature in BPR and SCM suggests various components requiring management attention. Lambert and Cooper (2000) have identified the following:

- Planning and control
- Work structure
- Organization structure
- Product flow facility structure
- Information flow facility structure
- Management methods
- Power and leadership structure
- Risk and reward structure
- Culture and attitude

But a more careful study needs to be done on previously identified supply chain business processes to understand what kind of relationship the components might have which are related to suppliers and customers.

OPTIMIZING THE END-TO-END VALUE CHAIN THROUGH AN INTEGRATED SOLUTION

Well-managed supply chain processes are an important differentiator in the highly competitive environment of commoditized markets. Supply chain transparency is the key and companies are increasingly developing one-stop-shops for supply chain information and reporting.

Integrated performance management in supply chain and operations focuses on the following:

- A common understanding of supply chain objectives and disciplined target-setting
- Goal-oriented information on target achievements to all relevant stakeholders and the addressing of key messages to executives, managers and professionals
- Supply chain transparency by considering and aligning supply chain processes and technology with the organizational structure
- Aligned and agreed-upon supply chain metrics covering all perspectives in SCM and also process performance indicators to enable root cause analyses in the event of deviations

- Integrated technical solutions for the gathering of information and the distribution of reports covering the full cycle from planning to reporting to intervention
- A flexible enterprise data warehouse and the adaptability of metrics, reports and layouts

MULTIFACETED ANALYTICAL FUNCTIONS

To understand the impact of issues arising out of say, the delivery failure or delay in servicing a customer order resulting in rescheduling or even in disruption in the total SCM function, supply chain performance management (SCPM) must have multifaceted analytical functionality. In such a situation, SCPM can help by comparing real term demand, actual stock in transit, physical inventories in the system as well as consumption that can become a valuable input to materials management and planning. This would help the business to achieve an overall optimization between logistics and transport cost, ensuring on-site inventories at lowest level while ensuring the requirement of production and supply. To achieve this optimization, every individual step has to be digitalized and added to the integrated software services of SCPM which would include the evaluation of the suppliers as well as carriers delivery performance, analyses of inventory as well as of demand, transport costs, comparison on various targets against actual performance and so on to the level of relating to components or parts.

INTEGRATED LOGISTICS SYSTEM

Integrated logistics system is an iterative process for developing the support strategy that optimizes and leverages existing resources. An integrated system will help the businesses in the following ways:

- Integrated logistics system on strategic level is to minimize the logistics cost by concentration on core business processes and the transaction costs by getting the best relationship and cooperation between the parties involved.
- To reduce logistic costs, focus on core business processes is necessary. Core business of the company could be both primary and support. It is also required to eliminate non-value-adding processes to reduce logistic costs.

INTEGRATION OF LOGISTICS WITH THE ORGANIZATION

The real-time customer demand can be met through the appropriate planning, control and implementation of the effective movement and storage information of goods and services from the point of origin to destination if logistics system is integrated with various functions within the organization.

- Integrating logistics within an organization has all the related activities working together as a single function.
- This is responsible for all storage and movement of materials throughout the organization. It tackles problems from the viewpoint of the whole organization, and looks for the greatest overall benefit.
- In practice, it is difficult to integrate all the logistics within an organization.
- The supply chain consists of many different activities, with different types of operation, using different systems and is geographically dispersed.

STAGES OF INTEGRATION

The entire process of integration happens through stages of development of logistics function as part of the overall supply chain. There is increased consideration of how logistics will impact customer service, procurement and manufacturing to achieve productivity enhancements and cost reduction through competitive benchmarking and continuous improvement. This can be achieved through:

- Separate logistics activities, those are not given much attention or considered important.
- Recognizing that the separate activities of logistics are important for the success of the organization.
- Making improvements in the separate functions, making sure that each is as efficient as possible.
- *Internal integration.* Recognizing the benefits of internal cooperation and combining the separate functions into one.
- Developing a logistics strategy, to set the long-term direction of logistics.
- *Benchmarking.* Comparing logistics' performance with other organizations, learning from their experiences, identifying areas that need improvement and finding ways of achieving this.
- *Continuous improvement.* Accepting that further changes are inevitable and always searching for better ways of organizing logistics.

BENEFITS OF INTEGRATION

The benefits of integration are as follows:

- **Genuine cooperation** between all parts of the supply chain, with shared information and resources.
- **Lower costs:** Due to balanced operations, lower stocks, less expediting, economies of scale, elimination of activities that waste time or do not add value.
- **Improved performance:** Due to more accurate forecasts, better planning, higher productivity of resources, rational priorities and so on.
- **Improved material flow,** with coordination giving faster and more reliable movements.
- **Better customer service,** with shorter lead times, faster deliveries and more customization.
- **More flexibility,** with organizations reacting faster to changing conditions.
- **Standardized procedures,** becoming routine and well-practiced with less duplication of effort, information, planning and so on.
- **Reliable quality and fewer inspections,** with integrated quality management programmes.
- Integration can be difficult and involve major changes. There are, however, many benefits, and most companies have moved in the direction of internal integration.
- There are also the benefits of **extending integration to more organizations in the supply chain.** There are several ways of organizing this external integration, ranging from informal agreements to vertical integration. The most popular has some form of strategic alliance or partnership.
- First step is to achieve internal integration and then attempt external integration.

LOGISTICS AND SECURITY

Logistics systems and modern transportation systems are often the targets of attacks. The need to institute new safeguards for international shipments will affect a firm's ability to efficiently plan their international shipment.

LOGISTICS SECURITY ISSUE

- Traditional security issues are as follows:
  - Pilferage
  - Burglary
  - Theft
  - Cargo contents—tampering
- Since the terrorist attacks of September 2011, security has taken increasingly more significant role in the global supply chain.
- Manufacturing, transporting and delivering goods safely and securely is as important and as complex.
- Credential of participants in the supply chain need to be verified.
- Screening and validation of contents of the cargo being shipped.
- Advance notification of the contents to the destination country.
- Ensuring the security of cargo while in transit—use of locks and tamper-proof seals.
- Inspecting cargo on entry.
- Security of cargo is always a big challenge.
- In ocean cargo, nuclear bombs, radioactive material and explosive weapons or even terrorists operatives can be concealed in marine containers.
- The speed at which today's supply chain operates, it can be very difficult to reconcile with the security measures.
- Air transportation system has clearly been the mode of choice for terrorists; so air cargo is of special concern.
- Air cargo is vulnerable to a number of potential terrorist actions—a bomb placed in cargo carried on a passenger plane could lead to a mass casualty event.
- A stowaway in a cargo freighter could hijack the place and use it as a weapon.

SUPPLY CHAIN SECURITY INITIATIVES IN THE USA

Supply chains face a broad range of threats, ranging from physical threats to cyber security threats. The physical threats are perhaps the more blatant and obvious ones that can occur at various points along the supply chain. Think of terrorists disrupting a supply chain by attacking oil infrastructure. Supply chain terrorism is, in fact, a great concern for many countries. The supply chain security initiatives that are adopted in USA are as follows:

- The Customs Trade Partnership against Terrorism (C-TPAT), a voluntary compliance programme for companies to improve the security of their corporate supply chains.
- The World Customs Organization (WCO) adopted the Framework of Standards to Secure and Facilitate Global Trade in 2005, which consists of supply chain security standards for customs administrations, including Authorized Economic Operator programmes.

- The Container Security Initiative, a programme led by the USA. Customs and Border Protection in the Department of Homeland Security focused on screening containers at foreign ports.
- The Global Container Control Programme, a joint United Nations Office on Drugs and Crime (UNODC) and WCO initiative working to establish effective container controls at select ports across the globe with the aim to prevent trafficking of drugs, chemicals and other contraband and to facilitate trade by strengthening cooperation between the customs, trade and enforcement communities.
- The Global Trade Exchange, a DHS data-mining programme designed to collect financial information about shipments, with the objective of determining safety of cargo shipments are safe.
- Efforts for countries around the world to implement and enforce the International Ship and Port Facility Security Code, an agreement of 148 countries that are members of IMO.
- Pilot initiatives by companies in the private sector to track and monitor the integrity of cargo containers moving around the world using technologies such as RFID and GPS.
- The International Organization for Standardization has released a series of standards for the establishment and management of supply chain security. ISO/PAS 28000 Specification for Security Management Systems for the Supply Chain offers public and private enterprises an international high-level management standard that enables organizations to utilize a globally consistent management approach for applying supply chain security initiatives.

TECHNOLOGY TO TACKLE SECURITY

Creation of open Smart manufacturing platform and network-based information technologies, block chain technology, scanning, etc., can greatly help in tackling the security concern. For example:

- A Boston-based company has developed a scanning technology that breaks down every item in a cargo container and provides make up to the cargo within. This tool could be a game changer.
- Cooperation among supply chain partners (including shippers, intermediaries, carriers, ports and government agencies) along with active data exchange, proper funding for security initiatives and effective technologies are all needed to secure the global supply chain.

LOGISTICS INDUSTRY IN INDIA

A glimpse into various industrial sectors highlights the anticipated upsurge in trade and commerce and the consequent growth in the need for a strong logistics industry:

- Indian Logistics sector is 13% of its GDP. This is both significant and inefficient.
- India's nominal GDP could grow from US$2.37 trillion currently to US$3.6 trillion by 2020 at an annual growth rate of 7%.
- By 2030, India's crude steel production is expected to increase by a factor of 4.
- The demand for cement in the country is expected to double by 2030.

- Agricultural output, although reduced in size as a percentage of the economy, is expected to increase from 207 MMT to 295 MMT by 2020.
- The Indian textiles industry is expected to triple from US$78 billion currently to US$220 billion by 2020.
- The share of organized retail is expected to increase from 5% currently to 24% by 2020.
- India's industrial energy consumption is expected to double by 2020. In this scenario, the country will need to mine 2 billion tonnes of coal by 2030 and transport 75% of it. Further, around 30% of total transported coal will have to be imported through ports.
- Overall EXIM cargo at Indian ports is projected to increase to around 2,800 MMT by 2020 from approximately 890 MMT currently.
- Finished consumer goods, both imported and those produced in India, will have to be transported to the country's middle-class consumers, which, by 2030, are expected to increase fourfold from the current middle-class population of 160 million.
- Because of the constraints and bottlenecks in the logistics infrastructure and more particularly in the road transport infrastructure, there is a negative impact on the India's GDP growth (Table 8.1).

TABLE 8.1 Comparison on Key Parameters: India vs Global

Logistics Efficiency Indicators	India	Global
Road Transportation		
Average truck speed (in kmph)	30–40	60–80 (China)
Four lane road length (in km)	7,000	34,000 (China)
National highway length (in km)	66,540	190,000
Average surface freight (in cents/km)	~7	3.7 (Japan)
Average distance travelled by a truck per day (in km)	200	400
Air Transportation		
Airport waiting time – Exports (in hours)	50	12
Airport waiting time – Imports (in hours)	182	24
Aviation turbine fuel as a % of operating cost	35–40%	20–25%
Ports & Sea Transportation		
Turnaround time at ports (in hours)	84	7
Annual container handling capacity	8.4 mm TEUs	60 mm TEUs
Containers handled per ship, per hour (maximum)	15	25–30
Throughout density (maximum)	45,000 TEUs/hectare	17,000–220,000 TEUs
Warehousing		
Average inventory days	33	24 (China)
Others		
3 PL share of logistics	9–10%	57% (USA)

- A comparison of logistics Performance Index based on the data of 2014 between India, China and Germany has been shown in Figure 8.3 to indicate that India is well below in terms of global ranking.

FIGURE 8.3 LPI of India, China and Germany on Select Parameters

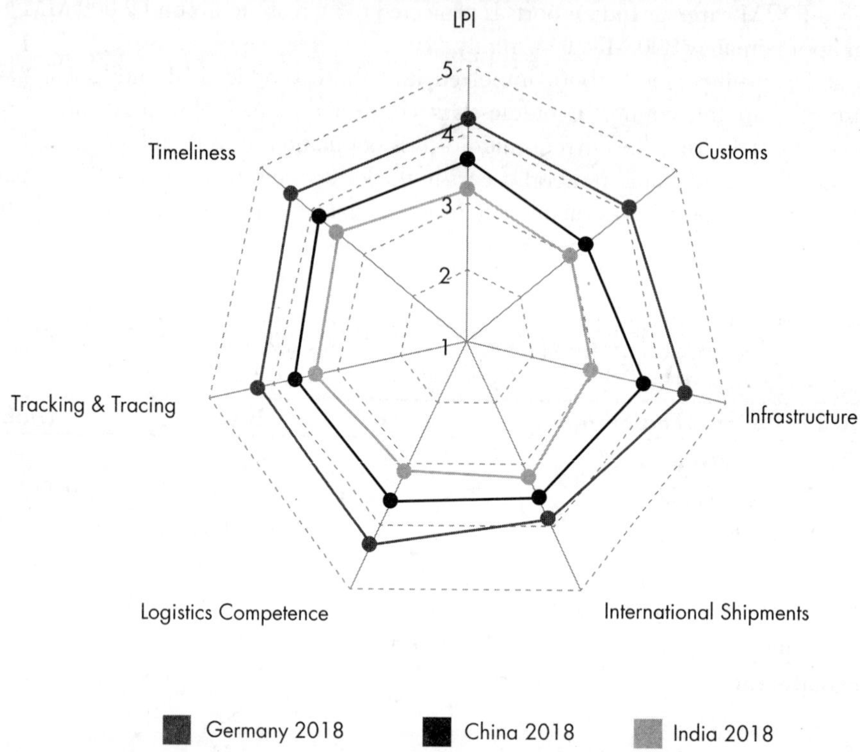

Country Parameter	Germany	China	India
LPI rank	1	26	44
Customs	1	31	40
Infrastructure	1	20	52
International shipments	4	18	44
Logistics competence	1	27	42
Tracking & tracing	2	27	38
Timeliness	3	27	52

Source: https://lpi.worldbank.org/

CASE STUDY: ANAND MILK UNION LIMITED (AMUL)

Amul means priceless in Sanskrit, *amoolya*. Brand name managed by an apex cooperative organization—Gujarat Cooperative Milk Marketing Federation (GCMMF)—producer of the World's biggest vegetarian cheese brand, world's largest pouched milk brand. Amul is also the largest food brand in India that spurred the white revolution. It has accreditation with ISO 9001 and has a HACCP certification by QAS, Australia.

Amul is a cooperative dairy founded in 1946, having annual revenue ₹292.25 billion or US$4.1 billion in 2017–2018. Amul is the world's largest milk producer. To make the largest milk producing entity, more than 15 million milk producers pour their milk in 144,500 dairy co-operative societies across the country. A total of 184 district cooperative unions are marketed by 22 state marketing federation and 18,544 village societies. Total milk handling capacity of Amul is 32 million litre per day. Amul manufactures wide range of milk, milk powder, health beverages, cheese, ghee, butter, ice cream and traditional Indian sweets and milk products as well as chocolates. It operates through 56 sales offices, having 10,000 dealers and servicing 1 million retail outlets directly (Figure 8.4).

FIGURE 8.4 **AMUL Value Chain**

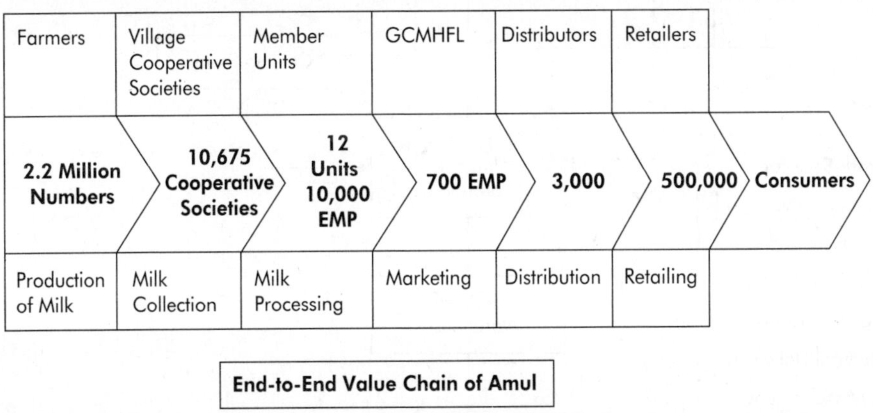

End-to-End Value Chain of Amul

Logistics Challenge of AMUL

Procurement Logistics

- Handling of 32 million litre of milk per day
- About 18,544 separate village cooperative societies

- Approximately 15 million milk producing members
- 144,500 dairy co-operative societies across the country; 184 district cooperative unions marketed by 22 state marketing federation; and 18,544 village societies.

Logistics/Coordination

- Storing and transportation of the milk from collection centres to production centres and then to consumers.
- Distributing the milk and milk products through 10,000 distributors and more than 1 million retailers.

Supply Chain Network of Amul

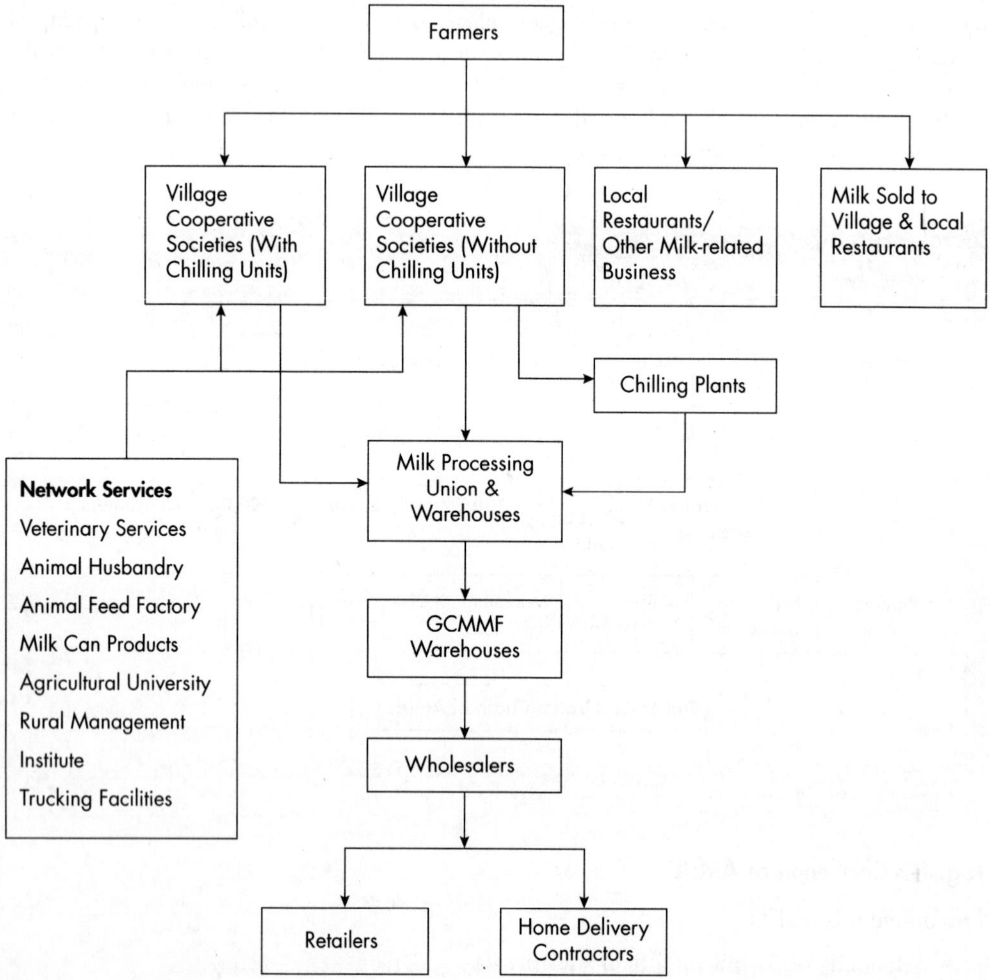

Decentralized Organization Structure of AMUL at Different Levels

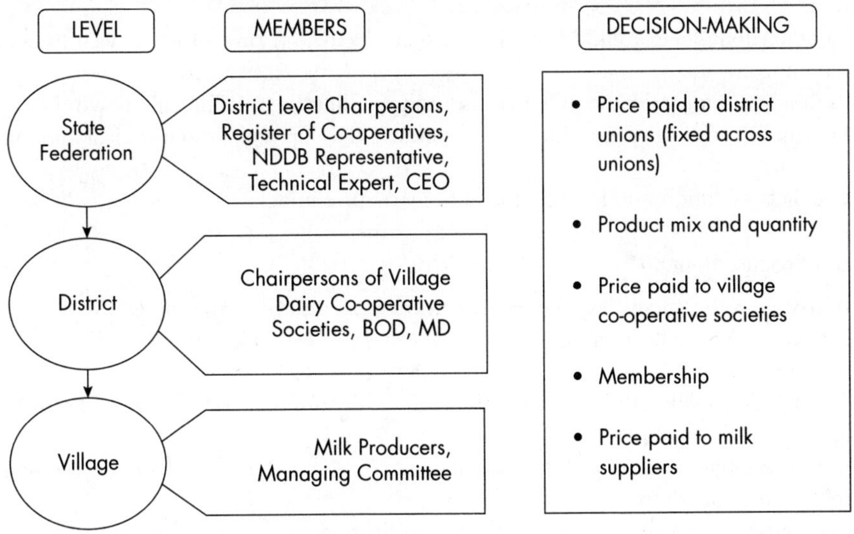

Coordination Between Participating Entities

The participating entities on the inbound side are as follows:

- Village Dairy Cooperative Society (DCS)
- State Cooperative Milk Federation

Main Functions of DCS

- Collection of surplus milk and payment on the basis on quality and quantity
- Providing support services to the members
- Selling liquid milk for local consumers of the village
- Supplying milk to the district milk union

State Cooperative Milk Federation

- Marketing of milk and milk products processed/manufactured by milk unions
- Establish a distribution network for marketing of milk and milk products
- Arranging transportation of milk and milk products from the milk unions to the market
- Creating and maintaining a brand for marketing of milk and milk products
- Providing support services such as technical inputs, management support and advisory services to the milk unions and members
- Pooling surplus milk from the milk unions and supplying it to deficit milk unions
- Establish feeder-balancing dairy plants for processing the surplus milk of the milk unions
- Arranging for common purchase of raw materials used in manufacture/packaging of milk products
- Decide on the prices of milk and milk products to be paid to milk unions

- Decide on the products to be manufactured at milk unions and capacity required for the same
- Conduct long-term milk production, procurement and processing as well as marketing planning
- Arranging finance for the milk unions and providing them technical know-how
- Designing and providing training in cooperative development, and technical and marketing functions
- Conflict resolution and keeping the entire structure intact

Upstream Procurement

- Activities at the village level comprised developing and servicing the DCSs.
- Increasing milk collection, procuring milk and transporting it to the chilling and processing units twice a day.
- The DCSs provided the farmers with good quality animal feed, fodder and other services like veterinary first aid.
- On an average, around a thousand farmers come to sell milk at their local co-operative milk collection centre.
- Each farmer is given a plastic card for identification.
- At the milk collection counter, the farmer drops the card into a box and the identification number is transmitted to a computer attached to the machine.
- The milk is then weighed and the fat content of the milk is measured by an electronic fat testing machine.
- Both these details are recorded in the computer. The computer then calculates the amount due to farmer on the basis of the fat content.
- The value of the milk is then printed out on a slip and handed over to the farmer who collects the payment at the adjacent window. Now farmers get direct credit to their account and get paid for their milk supplies. Payment information comes on their mobile.

Cold Storage Network

- Chillers in proximity of villages
- Prompt transport to district facilities for further dispatch to consumers/processing units
- Chilled trucks to transport processed products
- Delivery to local chillers by insulated rail tankers and chilled trucks
- Refrigerators and freezers with retailers and departmental stores to retain freshness

Distribution Downstream

- GCMMF coordinated with various unions to get a regular supply of milk and dairy products.
- The processed milk and dairy products were procured from district dairy unions and distributed through third-party distributors.
- To ensure quality and timely deliveries, GCMMF and the district unions had several mechanisms in place.
- The unions monitored the supplies of milk and the distribution of finished products.

Complexity of Distribution Operation

- First leg: Manufacturing units to company depots using 9 and 18 MT trucks
- Frozen food below −18°C, Dairy wet below 0–4°C
- Second leg: Depots to WDs (wet dealers), transport through insulated 3 and 5 MT TATA 407s
- Third leg: WDs to retailers, transport through rickshaws according to the beat plan

Technology to the Rescue

- Amul started implementation of ERP in phases.
- Automatic milk collection system (AMCS) units at village society were installed in the first phase to automate milk production logistics.
- AMCS facilities to capture member information, milk fat content, volume collected and amount payable to each member electronically.

Automatic Milk Collection System

The benefits of the AMCS system are as follows:

- Time reduction
- Reduction of pilferage
- Reduced human errors
- On the spot payments for farmers
- Wastage is reduced
- Transparency of operation
- Operational integration

Transformation

- Radical changes in business processes—eliminating middlemen.
- Improved delivery mechanisms and transparency of business operations.
- Due to this process, AMUL is able to collect six million litres of milk per day.
- Huge reduction in processing time for effecting payments to the farmers from a week to couple of minutes.
- Processing of 10 million payments daily, amounting to transactions worth US$3.78 million.
- Amul also connected its zonal offices, regional offices and member's dairies through very small aperture terminals (VSATs).
- The customized ERP-EIAS has been implemented across the organization integrating various operational departments.
- Amul is also using Geographic Information Systems (GIS) for business planning and optimization of collection processes.
- Indian Institute of Management Ahmedabad supplemented Amul's IT strategy by providing an application software—Dairy Information System Kiosk (DISK)—to facilitate data analysis and decision support in improving milk collection.
- The kiosk would also contain an extensive database on the history of cattle owned by the farmers, medical history of the cattle, reproductive cycle and history of diseases.

- Farmers can have access to information related to milk production, including best practices in breeding and rearing cattle.
- As a large amount of detailed history on milk production is available in the database, the system can be used to forecast milk collection and monitor the produce from individual sellers.
- Movement of 5,000 trucks to 200 dairy processing plants twice a day in a most optimum manner.
- Practising JIT SCM with six sigma accuracy.
- Online order placements of Amul products.
- Distributors can place their orders on the website.
- Amul exports products worth around US$25 million to countries in West Asia, Africa and USA. Amul also has a franchised operation in USA supplying Amul products to locals in USA.

Source: The data presented in this case is sourced from various published data and AMUL website.

Case Questions

1. Discuss the complexity of the logistics task in the corporation.
2. How did management attempt to find unorthodox solution to the problems?
3. What are the various operational constraints in managing the logistics task?
4. What are the KPIs which you find have improved?
5. What are failure risks that organization is taking and what are their consequences?
6. What are the possible improvement areas?

SECTION II
SOURCING DECISIONS IN GLOBAL SCM

SOURCING CHALLENGES AND STRATEGIES

Companies can source their products and services from their company-owned manufacturing plants. They also have the option to get the product manufactured by third parties through contract manufacturing route. Which option to be accepted would be governed by various factors. It can also be a mixed sourcing in the sense that it will be sourced from contract manufacturers partly and a part of the requirement is taken care of by the company-owned manufacturing plant.

In the 1980s and 1990s, companies were manufacturing the products themselves. When competitive pressure increased, they started outsourcing manufacturing to reduce cost as major sourcing strategies. We have seen that many corporations are closing down their production plants or even giving those plants on lease to contract manufacturers and focusing on the core functions of the business such as sales and marketing. Managing a product or manufacturing facilities does not only involve lot of fixed capital but also requires working capital to run the day-to-day production operations. Additionally, there are numerous issues and challenges in terms of managing industrial workers. These challenges can be overcome going through contract manufacturing route. In some cases, workers are even seen as highly volatile, creating industrial relation issues to be tackled by the management. If there are proprietary technology to be safeguarded, it is better to have your own manufacturing plant. For capital goods and automobiles, most of the organizations and players opt for their own manufacturing plants. But if the same product has to be manufactured for global supply, companies will have the assembly line owned by themselves and rest of the components are sourced from where it is cheap and best in quality. For FMCG, it is now widely outsourced through contract manufacturing route. Global supply chain is highly complex and competitive, and components need to be sourced from global suppliers for specific markets.

Contract manufacturers play a vital role in the following:

- Reducing cost of production
- Reducing cost of distribution and logistics
- Providing much needed flexibility in business
- Improving response time for variable customer needs
- Allowing bigger players to focus on their core competency
- Providing competitive advantage to the business

Small but efficient contract manufacturers can be cost-effective for large companies and can provide support to the flexible market demand in dynamic business environment. Small is therefore beautiful. Small but efficient contract manufacturers also play a vital role in logistics management.

FUTURE FACTORIES

There are two distinct possibilities that can emerge for global manufacturing and production operations. The future factories could be:

- Smaller
- More flexible
- Closer to the customers
- More cost-effective
- Use latest technology
- Be competitive

Or will it be large global focused factories? It is economy of scale against flexibility and productivity. Or both have to co-exist? Global players are getting product and services manufactured in low cost countries such as China and India. But there are other logistics cost that can force the global players to shift the production locations to even European locations. East European countries are seen to be cost- effective and closer to the market and therefore can emerge as preferred location for global production and supply requirement. The logistics cost of taking products and merchandises to European markets from China will be high and the inventory holding will also be high, which makes a valid case for production closer to the customer locations with more flexibility and higher productivity.

GLOBAL SOURCING CHALLENGE AND SUSTAINABILITY OF SUPPLY CHAIN

In the past, there have been considerable concerns among academics, businesses and government and also among non-governmental organizations about the so-called global sourcing and logistics 'carbon footprint' of supply chain. Although only recently this debate has really taken off, and there is a growing realization that the days are not too far that organizations and even individuals will probably have to pay for the carbon impact of the activities of the organizations. The penalty can be in the form of additional taxes, levies or even capping of allowable emissions under carbon trading regime. This incremental cost may raise questions regarding the commercial viability of the operations of certain organizations.

From the organization's perspective, it is not just the carbon impact of in-company activities but also the total carbon effect of end-to-end supply chain that needs to be clearly understood. With the current trend of global sourcing the implications of total carbon impact can be very significant. Understand the total carbon impact for any product clearly will require conducting the 'Life Cycle Analysis' of the emissions at each stage from cradle to grave, in the sense that what is the total environmental cost starting from sourcing raw material through manufacturing and selling and distribution and final disposal.

The decisions that businesses are now taking with regard to manufacturing and sourcing locations have a bearing on the impact of carbon footprint in the context of their supply chain performance from the point of view of environmental concerns. The sourcing of products from low-cost countries in the last 10 years or so has transformed the shape of many supply chains through the creation of longer and more transport-intensive pipelines. As a result, in some cases, it can so happen that the true cost of global sourcing might be much more than what companies realize as their cost. It is not simply the logistics cost that the companies have to bear but also, in the broader context, the external cost in the form of often-enlarged carbon footprint. In view of the fact that transport represents a large proportion of the worldwide greenhouse gas emissions, which is about 20% and still growing, it is inevitable that supply chains will increasingly be under scrutiny in the future which would otherwise mean that organizations will be in search for the ways to make their supply chains less transport intensive.

MODELS AND FRAMEWORKS FOR SOURCING

Meixell and Gargeya did a comprehensive literature review of global supply chain design models and summarized that models developed prior to 1990 focus on the problems of location of the plants. But models developed during 1990–1995 continue to put emphasis on plant location issues and also pay attention to transportation issues as well as infrastructure, lead time, currency fluctuation and selection criteria for vendors. Whereas models developed during 1996–2000 consider price as a variable and reconsider the plant location issue, but the models developed since 2000 took global sourcing as part of the organization's sourcing strategy and is linked with marketing and concluded that global supply chain models need to address the supply chain design problems from the consideration of both internal manufacturing and external supplier locations. These can be summarized as follows:

- Global supply chain models have to be more comprehensive in design, with emphasis on multiple production and distribution tiers in the supply chain.

- The performance measurement in global supply chain models has to be more broadened in definition to address alternative objectives.
- And finally more numbers of the industries in various categories need to be investigated in the context of global supply design.

These authors have concluded that most of the models have aimed to solve a difficult problem related to globalization. However, only a few of them were able to address the practical issues of global supply chain in more comprehensive manner. Jin (2004) attempted to find an ideal point to minimize cost/agility trade-off, meaning a mix of domestic and global sourcing strategy. Vestring, Rouse and Reinert (2005) proposed the spreading of foreign operation and outsourcing relationships over a broad, well-balanced mix of regions and countries to reduce the risk and increase the potential reward.

These models have identified comprehensive lists of factors to consider when the companies opt for global sourcing of goods and services. In risk management literature, some more comprehensive models dealing with the sourcing process can also be found. However, Cousins, Lamming and Bowen (2004) argue that the literature is still weak when it comes to environmental supply chain initiatives and practices where risk identification needs to be more comprehensive to manage the risk arising out of environmental issues.

CHARACTERISTICS OF SUCCESSFUL GLOBAL SOURCING

Based on a survey among companies using global sourcing, Trent and Monczka (2003) identify a number of CSFs, which are summarized below:

- Personnel with required knowledge, skills and abilities
- Availability of required information
- Awareness of potential global suppliers
- Time for personnel to develop global strategies
- Availability of suppliers with global capabilities/suppliers interested in global contracts
- Ability to identify common requirements across buying units
- Operations and manufacturing support/internal customer buy-in
- Direct site visits to suppliers

Based on the same survey presented in Trent and Monczka (2003), and additional case studies on 15 companies, Trent and Monczka (2005) list the following sets of characteristics for companies with successful global sourcing:

- Commitment at an executive level to global sourcing
- Rigorous and well-defined processes
- Availability of needed resources
- Integration through IT
- Supportive organizational design
- Structured approaches to communication

GLOBAL SOURCING AND LOGISTICS

The potential savings that can be accrued through global sourcing strategies will depend on various factors as discussed by Fagan (1991) which includes commitment of top management and total cost, not simply the direct cost. To derive the total advantage, the relationships with foreign suppliers should be developed on the basis of trust and respect. Monitoring and controlling through technology should also be used in addition to the ways of handling business risks. A contingency plan should be developed.

GLOBAL SOURCING TRENDS

Global sourcing is being practised in international trade for centuries, although the types of sourcing that we practice now are qualitatively different from the century-old practices for both technical and social reasons. Earlier, trade used to be mostly carried out on raw materials or final finished products and seldom in intermediate products such as components and services. Besides, unlike today, buyers–suppliers coordination and co-operations were not crucial, and all communications were limited to order processing. In addition, we have plethora of rules, regulations, control and risks associated with the global trade.

A comprehensive global sourcing strategy will refer to the issues related to the following:

- Logistics to identify the production units and locations which will serve the particular identified market(s) and how input material and components will be supplied for manufacturing.
- The coordination and interfaces among manufacturing, R&D and marketing on a global basis.

The primary objective of global sourcing for the firm is to exploit both its own and suppliers' competitive advantages as well as comparative locational advantages of various countries in global competition. From the contractual point of view, the global sourcing of intermediate products of components and services takes place in two ways; these are as follows:

- From the parent or their foreign subsidiaries on intra 'firm basis', that is, in-sourcing.
- From independent suppliers on 'contractual' basis, that is, outsourcing.

Similarly, from a locational point of view, multinational firms can procure goods and services either (a) domestically (i.e., onshoring) or (b) from abroad (i.e., offshoring).

The new waves of global sourcing were observed during last few decades. The first one was in mid-1980s, which was focused primarily on global sourcing of manufacturing activities, and research work during that era was also focused on manufacturing firms. Kotabe and Omura (1989) did some study on global sourcing. During that period, large manufacturing firms set up their operation globally and started to use suppliers from many countries to exploit opportunities for best-in-class sourcing (Quinn and Hilmer 1994). As a result, supply chain became more complex and global, with manufacturing firms sourcing from many suppliers in many countries for input materials, intermediates and also final product. We have discussed these taking cases earlier.

We have witnessed in early 1990s the second wave of global sourcing when firms started outsourcing IT services and companies abandoned in-house development of a new IS, and we have seen the emergence of specialist providers such as EDS and Accenture. Global sourcing is labour-intensive and involves standardized programming that can easily be sourced from countries like India. The rising commercial applications for a wide range of firm activities helped the introduction of ERP systems. All organizations were seen implementing ERP to optimize on the suppliers and vendors to make business operations more competitive.

The third wave was characterized by the offshoring in the recent years since 2000. During this stage, we have witnessed the rise in business process outsourcing that extends beyond IT services and covers a wide range of other services relating to HRM, finance and account, sales and after sales assistance provided by call centres. In this regard, India is still a primary source country for producing the business process software by the companies like Infosys, TCS and Wipro and many more. However, competition is also now seen from other countries for such services.

In this regard, it has been observed by many that the foreign business process suppliers may be moving up the knowledge chain more rapidly than expected by the sourcing firms. Such knowledge transfer could in the long run undermine sourcing firms' ability to differentiate themselves from their foreign suppliers, and these concerns have previously been raised by many authors (Bettis, Bradley, and Hamel 1992; Kotabe 1998; Markides and Berg 1988). The technology is therefore redefining the business processes which is increasingly being witnessed now in Industry 4.0 environment. The new technologies such as AI, block chain technology, robotics and digitization are redefining the supply chain and logistics management processes. The experience so far on these recent waves of global sourcing is summarized in Table 8.2.

TABLE 8.2 Recent Waves in Global Sourcing

Time Period	First Wave (Since 1980s)	Second Wave (Since Early 1990s)	Third Wave (Since Early 2000s)
Type of activity	Manufacturing	Information Technology	Business processes
Destinations	China, Central and Eastern Europe, Mexico and others	India, Ireland and others	India, Pakistan, South Africa and others
Type of firms	Manufacturing	Manufacturing, banks and others	Financial services, services more generally
Primary motives	Reduction in labour costs	Obtaining enough skilled programmers and cost reduction	Reduction in labour costs and round-the-clock service provision

Source: Kotabe and Murray (2018).

GLOBAL SOURCING AND BUSINESS PERFORMANCE

One of the key drivers of global sourcing is to improve the business performance by achieving cost-effectiveness (Trent and Monczka 2003). Companies located in OECD countries often find that the labour costs are too high when compared to the value that they add to the products and services they produce. Developing countries like India lag behind in terms of productivity, but a part of the loss from lower productivity is compensated by lower hourly labour costs. The labour-intensive activities like garment manufacturing in India and China could be more attractive and cost competitive. In some cases like bicycle components, the production cost differences are so large that it is not economically viable to use domestic sourcing, especially when the labour costs represent a substantial part of overall production costs.

On the other extreme, some global sourcing is driven by knowledge concerns. For example, inputs like say aircraft parts and technical expertise or some critical technology and knowledge may be available in OECD countries, and global sourcing in this case is not a choice but an imperative. When some raw materials are just not available in domestically, they have to be sourced from the producing countries. Also, sometimes intermediate products are sourced from locations near the source of raw materials.

Another factor in favour of global sourcing is that it is more cost effective to produce the products closer to customer markets, which enables easier access to customers. This also has many logistics advantages. For example, Japanese auto manufacturers have succeeded in replicating supply chains in North America and Europe to operate closer to these markets, which has enabled them to improve their product offerings and enhanced customer service. Global sourcing also helps in terms of pooling the demand from the various regions and thus achieving maximum scale and bargaining power through single sourcing from a foreign supplier.

The major problems and constraints in global sourcing arise out of cultural barriers between various countries. These barriers include their value system coupled with the issues related to language that can create communication problems and misunderstandings which can even lead to quality problems in addition to those caused by differences in technical standards or expectations. The other concerns related to global sourcing is long lead time and supply chain uncertainty (Swamidas and Kotabe 1993). Finally, foreign suppliers may be able to integrate forward into the buyer's market by inventing around patents or ignoring them altogether.

Regarding long-term sustainability of firm's core competencies, there are two opposing views on long-term implications of international sourcing. One school of thought argues that many successful companies have developed a dynamic organizational network through increasing cross-border joint ventures, subcontracting and licensing activities (Miles and Snow 1986). This flexible network system, also known as supply chain alliances, allows each participant to pursue its particular competence with each network participant complementing rather than competing against the other participants for the common goals. Such alliances are often formed by competing companies in pursuit of complementary abilities (e.g., new technologies or skills) from one another, thus helping the sourcing firm to acquire a competitive advantage by sourcing major components that involve high asset specificity from its alliance partners (Murray 2001).

The other school of thought argues that while a firm may gain short-term advantages, there could also be negative long-term consequences. As the firm becomes more reliant on its independent suppliers, it may not be able to keep abreast of constantly evolving design and engineering technologies without engaging in those developmental activities (Kotabe 1998). Consequently, the firm encounters the inherent difficulty in sustaining its long-term competitive advantages. In other words, over time, a firm's technical expertise and capability surplus vis-à-vis its foreign suppliers may diminish to the point that its value added is limited, and it may become more like a trading company. An example of this is the development of Emerson Electronics which turned into a trading company from an electronics producer and then into nothing more than a brand that changed owners several times (see Kotabe, Mol, and Ketkar 2008).

The advantages and disadvantages of global sourcing is summarized in Table 8.3.

TABLE 8.3 Advantages and Disadvantages of Global Sourcing

Possible Advantages	Possible Disadvantages
Increases size of potential supply base	Having to deal with foreign institutions such as legal differences
Lower production costs, especially for labour intensive production and services	Having to deal with a foreign culture which could affect communication
Increased technical expertise, especially for high-tech products from specialized locations	Having to deal with a foreign language which could affect communication
More flexibility to switch between supply sources, whether internal or external	Need to pay import duties where applicable
Source closer to sales markets, experience in sourcing may be translated into sales	Transportation costs and supply chain uncertainty
Achieve scale economies through use of one global supply source	Forward integration by foreign suppliers, patent infractions possible
Source of intermediate products closer to source of raw materials	Quality problems
Raw materials only available from foreign sources	Can affect employee commitment and public relations
Focus on core competencies	Dependence on independent suppliers, and decreased ability to keep abreast of emerging technical requirements

Source: Jean (2008, 266).

DEGREE OF OUTSOURCING AND FIRM'S PERFORMANCE

There is a relationship between the degree of outsourcing and firm's performance, and therefore a balanced approach can deliver better performance. Kotabe and Mol (2004, 2006) examined the relationship between the degree of a firm's outsourcing across all activities and its performance.

Their underlying argument is that firms that outsource all of their activities run into a multitude of problems such as a lack of innovation and bargaining power and an inability to be distinct in the eyes of the customer.

If, however, firms decide only to insource, they are likely to fail to use the powerful incentives supplied by markets and will tend to become bureaucratic and inefficient. Thus, outsourcing some parts but not all activities is the best solution. There is always an optimal degree of outsourcing. If some activities and functions in a business are outsourced, there is always a positive impact on the performance of the business. Hence, there is a negative curvilinear (inverted U-shaped) relationship between the degree of outsourcing and firm performance. Likewise, Leiblein, Reuer and Dalsace (2002) empirically found that deviations from the optimal form of sourcing, as dictated by transactional attributes associated with various contracting hazards, may have a negative effect on the performance of the business.

Williamson (1985) distinguished between production and transaction costs. The former refers to the costs of producing a good or service while transaction costs represent all the costs incurred, as the product moves from one supply chain partner to the next. On one hand, when firms use offshoring by procuring from foreign suppliers, it may help reduce their production costs, while in some instances, a local supplier's production costs may be lower than those of foreign suppliers. This is often the exception rather than the rule. Transaction costs, on the other hand, tend to be higher for offshoring as there are many types of institutional, cultural and language-related barriers that must be overcome. Rangan (2000) discussed this situation in terms of the costs of 'search and evaluation'. Searching for supply sources abroad, whether internal or external, is somewhat more expensive than searching for local supply sources. Evaluating those foreign supply sources is much more expensive because the evaluation costs are strongly related to the familiarity that decision-makers have with the other party. Since firms are likely to be less familiar with foreign supply sources and decision-makers may not be able to draw on their networks in helping them evaluate these sources, this situation induces substantial evaluation costs. Rangan (2000) used this argument to explain why buying firms are much more likely to choose a domestic than a foreign supplier even when the physical distance between the buyer and each of these suppliers is the same. There should be a 'balancing' act between production and transaction costs, and firms need to find the proper balance between domestic and foreign sources if they wish to be located on the top of the curve and deliver highest possible performance.

We argue that offshoring is a 'balancing' act between production and transaction costs. Firms need to find the proper balance between domestic and foreign supply sources (i.e., using onshoring and offshoring), if they wish to locate on the top of the curve and obtain the highest possible performance. They can achieve this goal by using foreign sources for part but not all of their sourcing. Sourcing everything from abroad gives poor performance results because the disadvantages of offshoring, like the hollowing-out argument, become too large. Focusing all efforts on onshoring, however, is a serious form of myopia with equally disastrous effects for firm performance, primarily because the firm is not capitalizing on important opportunities to improve competitiveness.

Some activities are best outsourced globally while others ought to be integrated (from a performance perspective). Optimal performance is reached when all activities are correctly outsourced and/or integrated. Deviations from the optimum are costly and in such a way that the farther from the optimum, the more costly these deviations become.

KEY ISSUES IN GLOBAL SOURCING

Despite its inherent advantages, many firms have been seen to be highly dissatisfied with their performance. This is because firms have failed in terms of evaluating the global sourcing strategy—performance relationship in proper perspective—and have taken over-generalized view of the sourcing benefits. The environment is a key constructs for understanding the organization's behaviour and performance. It has been seen that 'the appropriateness of different strategies depends on the competitive settings of businesses' (Prescott 1986, 765). For manufacturing, Murray, Kotabe and Wildt (1995) concluded that the financial performance advantage of global insourcing over global outsourcing of non-standardized components improved with increased product innovations, process innovations and asset specificity.

TECHNOLOGICAL PERFORMANCE AND SOURCING DECISIONS

Using foreign firms manufacturing in China as subjects of the study, Murray, Kotabe and Zhou (2005) found that global outsourcing of major components (in the form of strategic alliance-based sourcing) did not have an effect on market performance. Instead, product innovativeness and technological uncertainty moderated such a relationship. Specifically, at low levels of product innovativeness/technological uncertainty, the use of strategic alliance sourcing of major components by the sourcing firm is positively related to market performance. However, at higher levels of product innovativeness/technological uncertainty, the sourcing–performance relationships become negative.

Similarly, findings by Leiblein et al. (2002) in the manufacturing context concur with the above conclusions. In refuting the popular arguments that insourcing or outsourcing will lead to superior technological performance, they found that sourcing strategy per se did not significantly affect technological performance. Instead, the sourcing strategy–performance relationship was driven by factors underlying sourcing strategy choice. They further cautioned against the universalistic normative implications for firms deciding on whether or not to insource or outsource their value chain activities and stressed the value of contingency-based theoretical approaches.

FACTORS INFLUENCING OUTSOURCING

The global sourcing of services did not take place until the second wave of global sourcing so that the extant literature on global sourcing of services is limited when compared to that in global sourcing of manufactured goods. Consistent with previous studies of the global sourcing of manufactured goods, transaction cost analysis, involving asset specificity, transaction frequency and business uncertainty, offers a useful framework in studying the sourcing of services. Asset specificity refers to investments made in specific (non-marketable) resources. When these investments are made, a supplier and a buyer are 'locked into' the transaction because the assets are specialized to that transaction and have limited or no value outside that transaction (Williamson 1985). Murray and Kotabe (1999) found that, similar to components and finished goods sourcing, supplementary services were sourced globally either by insourcing or outsourcing. In addition, the relationship between asset specificity and insourcing of supplementary services was moderated by the level of inseparability and transaction frequency. Their empirical findings showed that firms tended to rely more on global insourcing for inseparable supplementary services with high asset specificity. Furthermore, the higher the asset specificity and the lower the transaction frequency of the supplementary services, the higher these firms would use global insourcing. Finally, insourcing and offshoring of supplementary services were negatively related to a service's market performance.

There is a range of contingency factors such as capital intensity, degree of service inseparability, market uncertainty, transaction frequency at the transaction, firm and context levels. These factors determine how much global outsourcing ought to take place from a performance perspective. These contingency factors also explain how much global outsourcing actually takes place in practice. If a company matches an outsourcing decision to the relevant contingency factors, the resulting strategic fit helps achieve superior performance. Table 8.4 summarizes the contingency factors in global sourcing decisions.

It is important to note that these perspectives operate at three different levels: the transaction, the firm and the context. Taken together, they represent almost all the contingency factors that the academic literature has produced to date. Which of these perspectives matters most is, to an extent, determined by the empirical context in which outsourcing is investigated? Some of the perspectives have been more prominent than others in recent academic studies of outsourcing. Transaction-cost economics and the resource-based view may reflect their actual importance in practice, the scholarly knowledge production process or other factors. However, all of these perspectives have some bearing on global outsourcing. Global sourcing decisions are based on many complex and dynamic issues and require frequent review from cost, availability, flexibility and performance. In addition, there are numerous industry-specific issues. In this chapter, two such industry sectors are covered from the perspective of global sourcing head.

TABLE 8.4 Perspectives on Global Outsourcing

	Firm Level	Context Level	Transaction Level
Past	Resource-based view	Social networks	
Present	Costly contracting	Industrial organization	Transaction-cost economics
	Microeconomics Core competences	Institutional voids	Agency
Future	Real options		
	Relations and learning		

Source: Masaaki et al. (2008).

CASE STUDY A: INDUSTRY SECTOR—RETAIL

Global Sourcing Strategy: Perspective of Global Sourcing Director

Company A (a leading retail group in the UK) believes that they are a driver in leading change; their global sourcing strategy reflects this, which is largely driven by its customers. Their sourcing portfolio is changing rapidly because the global marketplace has evolved so much over the last few years. However, in some product areas, they are now sourcing more from Europe rather than the Far East because of emerging markets and changes in consumer behaviour. On the other hand, it is exploring new sources in the Far East, that is, Vietnam, Madagascar, Shanghai and so on, where capabilities are stronger. The sourcing strategy is determined by the product category, for example, quick response items are sourced primarily from Turkey, but new opportunities are arising from Bulgaria and Romania as they enter the EU. For other categories, 95% items are sourced from China. In case of some categories, it is planned to source them from Britain to promote local businesses.

Positive factors

Spreading risks:

- Range of factories that can produce the same products at varying lead times and costs
- Increased number of options to source from
- Direct sourcing

Negative factors

- Do not have a panoramic view of the supply base, and have not always found the right supplier
- Large number of suppliers, hence, supply base is being consolidated
- Maintaining control of factories
- Communication with suppliers, lack of visibility: 'If you get it wrong direct sourcing could go very wrong'

Main mode of transport

- Mainly sea freight, depending where products are procured from
- Quick turnaround products are moved by road
- Airfreight is used for strategic products only, and this is only 0.1% of everything moved

Key priorities of global sourcing strategy

- Reliability of product
- Shipment on time
- Right product
- Delivered on time

Supply chain risk management tools and techniques

- Risk management is an integral part of the global sourcing decision-making.
- Supply management programme is a standard toolkit and enables decision-makers to identify how to best deal with the capabilities from the supply base and how to document performance.
- KPIs enable Company A to analyse key suppliers' performance. The risk review is completed every 3–6 months and supplier scorecards are developed to assess the performance.

Major risks identified in global sourcing decisions

- Factories are ethical and not breaking civil law
- Communication with global supply base: Do they truly understand company philosophy and product requirements?
- Missed opportunities that competitors can exploit
- Lack of visibility

Environment and infrastructure considerations

- Aiming to reduce CO_2 emissions by 60% by 2010
- Sponsoring sourcing locally and closer, that is, European Initiatives such as reducing the price of energy bulbs
- Not enough choice for transportation; UK rail network is poor and unreliable

CASE STUDY B: INDUSTRY SECTOR— FMCG FOOD AND DRINK

Global Sourcing Strategy: Perspective of Global Head of Procurement

Company B is again a major FMCG food and drink player based out of the UK. The input is given by their global sourcing director. The sourcing strategy is based on balancing cost and customer service. The sourcing strategy is determined by the type of products: bulky products (e.g., detergents, paper, etc.) are sourced locally to reduce logistics costs; small high-value products are produced in a few factories and then distributed around the world.

To make the sourcing decisions, the company looks at sales projections and service level requirements from different regions, then they look at local supply availability and import tariffs and duties, and finally at the capital costs involved. Find a balance between cost and service levels.

- A total of 90% products come from the EU. In the future, Eastern Europe is more likely to develop.
- Contracts and supplier relationships vary in length. Tend to use short-term contracts (and relationships) for commodities and long-term for strategic supplies.

Positives factors

Optimizing total delivered cost (logistics and manufacturing)

Negative factors

Difficult trade-off between cost and service

Main mode of transport

- Roadways is the dominant source of transport (95%). Railways takes the rest.
- Railways is not used for delivering to customer because of long lead times and poor reliability.

Key priorities

- Customer service
- Cost
- Quality

Supply chain risk management tools and techniques

- There is a health and safety organization focused on looking at risks at the plants.
- There is a business continuity plan for every plant, which the plant engineer is responsible for. This includes risks at suppliers.
- Business continuity planning and health and safety analysis are used to assess risks.
- Generally use dual sourcing or multiple sourcing to mitigate supply risks. For most of the products, they have several plants so that they can source from another one in case of a disruption.

Major risk identified in global sourcing decisions

- Since most of the products come from EU, the company finds that there is not much risk of global sourcing.

Environment and infrastructure considerations

- Environmental issues are in line with the company's economic necessities, and the company aims to minimize transport as much as possible.
- The company looks for a high vehicle utilization (over 90%). The network is designed to minimize transport and achieve high utilization.
- Life-cycle analysis is conducted when designing new products. They try to design new products to have the minimum environmental impact.
- The company primarily use road, and road congestion is a big issue. Rail is not always appropriate, firstly because rail is not as flexible as road, but also because it is not as reliable and not always more cost effective. All of our plants have rail connections, but they are not fully utilized.

Case Questions

1. How and why key priorities of global sourcing criteria in two different industry sectors differ?
2. Discuss the positives and negatives of the global sourcing strategy.
3. What are the key motivation factors for global sourcing?
4. Discuss the risks involved in global sourcing as perceived by Company A and Company B.

Source: Christopher et al. (2007).

CHAPTER SUMMARY

Value chain is another name of end-to-end supply chain. In global business environment large companies are managing their supply chain in a networked environment. They are sourcing input materials from many countries wherever those are available at best price meeting the quality and delivery schedule criteria, and transporting these input materials yet to another country for production and or manufacturing or assembling for least cost and capturing the value at each stage of the interface through effective logistics management. These issues are elaborately discussed in the chapter. Key drivers as well as tools and methods that are facilitating international logistics were discussed. Current scenario with respect to international trade and how companies are going for acquisitions to acquire critical mass and competitive edge in terms of managing international logistics challenges is also discussed. Several terminologies used in international logistics trade are defined with examples. Logistics management and cargo-handling efficiency issues are also discussed. The value chain analyses and strategies for competitive advantage have been covered in detail.

Logistics industry in India and its status and ranking in the world logistics industry as well as logistics security issues are covered in this chapter; global operating levels of the logistics companies are also discussed. The chapter also deals with the issues of managing the challenges of integrated supply chain and logistics management, including a discussion on stages of integration and benefits of integration.

The case of Amul has been discussed to explain how they are addressing the very complex supply chain and logistics issues in the business and also how successfully they are able to integrate the functions.

Key advantages and disadvantages of outsourcing and also the stages of evolution of global outsourcing have been discussed in brief. Global sourcing strategy and factors influencing global sourcing are discussed in detail in this chapter along with two cases from retail and FMCG sectors to show what are the key factors these businesses consider in order to take global sourcing decisions. We have also discussed the recent trends in outsourcing.

DISCUSSION QUESTIONS

1. Discuss the tools and processes that have facilitated international logistics.
2. Discuss the logistic value chain and sources of competitive advantage.
3. Discuss the key drivers of global logistics management strategy formulation.
4. Take five logistics companies and five manufacturing marketing companies in India and Europe and determine their operating level giving reasons.
5. Discuss four stages of regional integration. Indicate tasks of logistic companies under those stages. Under which stage do EU (Schengen countries) and India fall and why?
6. Discuss the challenges and barriers of global logistics operation.
7. What role can global logistics companies play and what are the capabilities that they can display?
8. Discuss the benefits of supply chain integration.
9. Discuss the key drivers of outsourcing. What are the advantages and disadvantages of global outsourcing?

10. How international logistics channel got evolved over the decades of continued international trade? Discuss.
11. Discuss the recent trends in global outsourcing and the factors behind that.

REFERENCES

Bettis, R., S. Bradley, and G. Hamel. 1992. 'Outsourcing and Industrial Decline'. *Academy of Management Executive* 6 (1): 7–16.

Byoungho Jin. 2004. 'Achieving an Optimal Global versus Domestic Sourcing Balance Under Demand Uncertainty'. *International Journal of Operation & Production Management* 24 (12): 1292–1305.

Christopher, M., Fu Jia, Omera Khan, Charlos Mena, and A. Palmer. 2007. *Global Sourcing Logistics*. Technical report, Cranfield University. https://www.researchgate.net/publication/308402707

Cousins, P. D., R. C. Lamming, and F. Bowen. 2004. 'The Role of Risk in Environment-related Suppliers Initiatives'. *International Journal of Operation & Production Management* 24 (6): 554–565.

Cross, J. 1995. 'IT Outsourcing: British Petrol'. *Harvard Business Review* 73 (3): 94–102.

Dunning, J. H. 1993. *Multinational Enterprises and the Global Economy*. Addison-Wesley.

Ellaram, Lisa M., and Martha C. Cooper. 1990. 'Supply Chain Management Partnership, and the Shipper-Third Party Relationship'. *International Journal of Logistics Management* 1 (2): 1–10.

Fagan, M. L. 1991. 'A Guide to Global Sourcing'. *The Journal of Business Strategy* 12 (2): 21.

Jean, B. 2008. *Advantages and Disadvantages of Global Sourcing* (14 edition). Bingley: Emerald Group publishing.

John B. Houlihan. 1985. 'International Supply Chain Management'. *International Journal of Physical Distribution & Materials Management* 15 (1): 22–38.

Kotabe, M. 1998. 'Efficiency vs Effectiveness Orientation of Global Sourcing Strategy: A Comparison of US and Japanese Multinational Companies'. *Academy of Management Executive* 12 (4): 107–119.

Kotabe, M., and G. S. Omura. 1989. 'Sourcing Strategies of European and Japanese Multinationals: A Comparison'. *Journal of International Business Studies* 20 (1): 113–130.

Kotabe, M., and J. Y. Murray. 2018. 'Global Sourcing Strategy: An Evolution in Global Production and Sourcing Rationalization'. In *Advances in Global Marketing*, edited by L. Leonidou, C. Katsikeas, S. Samiee, and B. Aykol, 365–384. Cham, Switzerland: Springer.

Kotabe, M., and M. J. Mol. 2004. 'A New Perspective on Outsourcing and the Performance of the Firm. In *Global Corporate Evolution: Looking Inward or Looking Outward*, edited by M. Trick, 331–340. Pittsburgh, PA: Carnegie Mellon University Press.

———. 2006. 'International Sourcing: Redressing the Balance. In *Handbook of Global Supply Chain Management*, edited by J. T. Mentzer, M. M. Myers, and T. P. Stank, 393–408. London: SAGE Publication.

Kotabe, M., M. J. Mol, and S. Ketkar. 2008. 'An Evolutionary Stage Model of Outsourcing and Competence Destruction: A Comparison of the Consumer Electronics Industry'. *Management International Review* 48 (1): 65–93.

Lambert, Douglas M., and Martha C. Cooper. 2000. 'Issues in Supply Chain Management'. *Industrial Engineering Management* 29 (1): 65–83.

Leiblein, M. J., J. J. Reuer, and F. Dalsace. 2002. 'Do Make or Buy Decisions Matter? The influence of Organizational Governance on Technological Performance'. *Strategic Management Journal* 23 (9): 817–833.

Loh, L., and N. Venkatraman. 1992. 'Determinants of Information Technology Outsourcing: A Cross-Sectional Analysis'. *Journal of Management Information Systems* 9 (1): 7–16.

Markides, C. C., and N. Berg. 1988. 'Manufacturing Offshore is Bad Business'. *Harvard Business Review* 66 (5): 113–120.

Kotabe, Masaaki, Janet Y Murray and Michael J. Mol. 2008. 'Global Sourcing Strategy and Performance: A "Fit" Versus "Balance" perspective'. *Research in Global Strategic Management* 14 (5, June): 259–277.

Miles, R. E., and C. C. Snow. 1986. 'Organizations: New Concepts for New Firms'. *California Management Review* 28 (Spring): 62–73.

Murray, J. Y. 2001. 'Strategic Alliance-Based Global Sourcing Strategy for Competitive Advantage: A Conceptual Framework and Research Propositions'. *Journal of International Marketing* 9 (4): 30–58.

Murray, J. Y., M. Kotabe, and A. R. Wildt. 1995. 'Strategic and Financial Implications of Global Sourcing Strategy: A Contingency Analysis. *Journal of International Business Studies* 26 (1): 181–202.

Murray, J. Y., M. Kotabe, and J. N. Zhou. 2005. 'Strategic Alliance-based Sourcing and Market Performance: Evidence from Foreign Firms Operating in China'. *Journal of International Business Studies* 36 (2): 187–208.

Porter, Michael E. 1985. *Competitive Advantage*. New York: The Free Press.

Prescott, J. E. 1986. 'Environments as Moderators of the Relationship Between Strategy and Performance. *Academy of Management Journal* 29 (2): 329–346.

Quinn, J. B., and F. G. Hilmer. 1994. 'Strategic Sourcing'. *Sloan Management Review* 35 (4): 43–55.

Rangan, S. 2000. 'The Problem of Search and Deliberation in International Exchange: Micro Foundations to Some Macro Patterns'. *Journal of International Business Studies* 31 (2): 205–222.

Swamidas, P. M., and M. Kotabe. 1993. 'Component Sourcing Strategies of Multinational: An Empirical Study of European and Japanese Multinationals'. *Journal of International Business Studies* 24 (1): 81–99.

Trent, R. J., and R. M. Monczka. 2003. 'International Purchasing and Global Sourcing: What are the Differences?' *Journal of Supply Chain Management* 39 (4): 26–37.

———. 2005. 'Achieving Excellence in Global Sourcing'. *MIT Sloan Management Review* 47 (1): 24.

Vestring, T., T. Rouse, and M. Reinert. 2005. 'Hedge Your Off Shorting Bets'. *MIT Sloan Management Review* 46 (3): 27–29.

Williamson, O. E. 1985. *The Economic Institutions of Capitalism*. New York: Free Press.

BIBLIOGRAPHY

Baufield, Emiko. 1999. *Harnessing Value in Supply Chain: Strategic Sourcing in Action*. New York: Wiley.

Biullington, Corey, and Jager Francois. 2008. 'Procurement: The Missing Link in Innovation'. *Supply Chain Management Review* 12 (1): 22–28.

Cachon, Gerald P., and Martin A. Larivieve. 2001. 'Turning the Supply Chain into a Revenue Chain'. *Harvard Business Review* 79 (3): 20–21.

Cavimato, Joseph L., and Ralph G. Kauffman. 2000. *The Purchasing Handbook: A Guide for the Purchasing and Supply Chain Professional*. New York: McGraw Hill.

Coyle, J. J., C. J. Langley, R. A. Novade, and B. Gibson. 2016. 'Supply Chain Management: a Logistics Perspective'. *Journal of Business Logistics* 28 (1): 1–24

Dekhne, Ashutosh, Xin Huang, and Apratim Sarkar. 2012. 'Bridging the Procurement–Supply Chain Divide'. *Supply Chain Management Review* (Sept–Oct): 36–42.

Ferreira, John, and Len Prokopets. 2009. 'Does Offshoring still Makes Sense?' *Supply Chain Management Review* (Jan–Feb): 20–27.

Goel, Ajay, Nazgol Moussavi, and Vats N. Srivatsan. 2008. 'Time to Rethink Offshoring?' *McKinsey Quarterly* 14 (Winter): 32–35.

Larsen, P. D., R. F. Poist, and A. Hallorsson. 2007. 'Perspective on Logistics Vs Supply Chain Management'. *Journal of Business Logistics* 28 (1): 1–24.

Remko I. van Hoek. 'Measuring the Unmeasurable and Improving the Performance in the Supply Chain'. *Supply Chain Management: An International Journal* 3 (4): 187–193.

9

Supply Chain Performance Management

LEARNING OBJECTIVES

Section I: Performance Management in Supply Chain

- Understand why achieving strategic fit of supply chain capabilities with business objective is critical to a company's overall success and how a company achieves strategic fit between its supply chain strategy and competitive strategy
- Get insights into major challenges that need to be managed successfully for better performance
- Realize key performance criteria of supply chain and how those have to be derived and measured within the system
- Get clarity on how to start a company-wide performance management programme to succeed and create competitive advantage
- To be exposed to a framework of performance management programme that can be applied in a given situation
- Recognize supply chain maturity levels and models and their implications in business

Section II: Benchmarking Supply Chain Performance

- Understand the importance and scope of supply chain benchmarking
- Decide on supply chain performance metrics
- Initiate benchmarking exercise within the company and standard benchmarking process
- Understand the importance of identifying companies to be benchmarked
- Gain clarity on some common misconception on benchmarking

SECTION I
PERFORMANCE MANAGEMENT IN SUPPLY CHAIN

INTRODUCTION

SCM has been a major component of competitive strategy to enhance organizational productivity and profitability. The literature on SCM that deals with strategies and technologies to effectively manage a supply chain is quite vast. In recent years, organizational performance measurement and metrics have received much attention from researchers and practitioners. The role of these measures and metrics in the success of an organization cannot be overstated because they affect strategic, tactical and operational planning and control. Performance measurement and metrics have an important role to play in setting objectives, evaluating performance and determining future courses of actions of any organization. There are frameworks to promote a better understanding of the importance of SCM performance measurement and metrics (Ramakrishna et al. 2010).

In ultimate analysis, better SCM has to result into improved financial performance. The SCM objective primarily has to be achieving company's strategic business objective. Businesses achieve financial goals, pursuing a few key strategic drivers developed through careful analysis of the competitive environment and business opportunity and also key competitive advantage of the corporation. The strategic drivers of growth and performance of companies operating in a category will thus be different for different corporations. The methods of distributions and product pricing will also be different for companies operating in a typical business vertical, derived from their target market and strategies to reach and service those identified markets. A company's supply chain thus has to be managed to support its business strategy and therefore has to have an ideal fitment of supply chain strategy with the business strategy.

Achieving the strategic fitment of supply chain with the company's value chain, strategic goal and key drivers to achieve that goal is essential and that will ensure the consistency between customer priorities that the competitive strategy of the corporation intend to satisfy and the supply chain capabilities that the supply chain strategy aims to build. To achieve that, different functions in the company must follow the appropriate and approved structure and processes, and resources should be able to execute these strategies successfully. Also the design of the overall supply chain and the role of each stage must be aligned to support the supply chain strategy. If this does not happen, company may even fail either because of a lack of strategic fit or because its overall supply chain design, processes and resources do not provide the capabilities to support the desired strategic fit. Most importantly, supply chain strategies and capabilities will be required to support the company's sales and marketing strategies.

For example, if company stands for immediate delivery on receipt of the order, supply chain has to ensure stock availability at all times at the stock delivery points and do not resort to delaying the delivery for achieving other objectives like economy in transport operations.

Another example that can be cited is of Dell. The competitive strategy of Dell is to provide a large number of options to the customer by providing customizable products with their unique customer-specific configuration at a reasonable and competitive price. As their focus was on customization, Dell's supply chain was designed to be responsive by ensuring that assembly units owned by Dell were not only strategically located but also flexible and capable to easily handle the variety of customer-specific product specification. A facility focused on low cost and efficiency derived from producing large numbers of the same specification would not have been appropriate for the Dell's business strategy.

SSCM performance then will be analysed if the business strategy has been supported well by the supply chain capabilities and strategies to deliver the corporation's business goals and objectives.

SCM PERFORMANCE CRITERIA

Several studies have indicated that there is a strong relationship of the largest number of suppliers and customer integration with market share and profitability. This would mean that taking advantage of supplier capabilities and emphasizing a long-term supply chain perspective in customer relationships can be correlated with firm's performance in terms of growth and profit. The growth can be measured in terms of both business volume growth and increased market share. As logistics competency becomes a more critical factor in creating and maintaining competitive advantage, logistics measurement becomes increasingly important because the difference between profitable and unprofitable operations becomes narrower. Firm's logistics management needs to be integrated with SCM in order to ensure improved customer service and satisfaction.

Power (2005) noted that firms engaging in comprehensive performance measurement realized improvements in overall productivity. According to experts, internal measures collected and analysed by the firm would generally include the following performance criteria:

- Cost
- Customer service
- Productivity measures
- Asset measurement
- Quality

In addition to the internal performance criteria as mentioned above, there can even be company-specific additional criteria that are normally derived from the company's past performance indicators and typical issues and problems that company experiences in their supply chain. For example, vendor's performance and ratings can greatly influence supply chain performance of a corporation. Typically, it may be required to track and rate the performance of key vendors.

External performance measurement is examined through customer perception measures and benchmarking the 'best practice' as well as 'best-in-class' as mentioned below:

- Customer perception measurement
- Benchmarking with best practice

THE KEY ELEMENTS OF SCM

Supply chains comprise the flow of products, information and money. How they are managed greatly affects an organization's competitiveness and profitability. Proper alignment with the business strategy is essential to ensure strong overall performance.

SCPM is a unified approach to improving the effectiveness and efficiency of all supply chain processes. Key elements that need to be considered are as follows:

- Supply chain strategy
- Organization
- Planning
- Management
- Control activities

The combination of these elements fills the gap between the business's decision-makers and IT systems for performance measurement with data structures and reporting tools.

In a nutshell, they create a bridge between strategic directives and successful execution by using available information to steer supply chains from an end-to-end perspective.

The foundation is aligned metrics that drive intended behaviour at the management and operational levels. Ultimately, this will create value for both shareholders and customers.

SCPM IN INDUSTRY 4.0

When companies look beyond the horizon of their daily business operations and begin to think about Industry 4.0 and Smart Factory (or self-managed production), they soon realize that a stable supply chain and a reliable forecast of quantities and dates are prerequisites for Industry 4.0. With its wide range of functions, SCPM plays a key role by delivering the required information and data for an optimal production supply. Managing supply chain for better performance is a pre-requisite to operate in Industry 4.0 environment when technologies including AI and robotics will redefine the way businesses would be conducted and thus it will serve as a basis for entering the new era of Industry 4.0.

DIGITALIZATION OF SUPPLY CHAIN CHANGING TODAY'S PERFORMANCE MANAGEMENT

Shortened product life-cycle, product complexity, increased customer focus, increasing digitalization and closer cooperation between partners in business are increasing the demand on performance management in supply chain. The main drivers behind these developments are customer demands and new technology which have already reshaped the traditional supply chain. The results are the customization of products and services, real-time transparency, cost competition in global scale and increased efforts in sustainability. Digital transformation in supply chain and big data in SCM are disrupting many large organizations. Sensors and other types of connected devices are increasingly deployed for tracking deliveries and monitoring assets. New technologies encourage process automation as well as precision in execution. While with the help of analytics some insight derived from analyses of huge volume of data to achieve better management of conflicting supply chain objectives and trade-offs. As a result, access to analytical insights is now given to operations manager and supply chain executives and not kept limited to leaders in supply chain.

There are two sides to trade-offs. On one hand, with the help of new technologies, companies can coordinate and manage their entire network better and more efficiently. Analysing value chain activities to identify performance deviations and irregularities has become easier and is based on more information than in the past.

On the other hand, real-life use cases and the increasing application of Industry 4.0 technologies are transforming supply chains across multiple industries towards digital supply networks. The technology is already there and has hit the ground. It affects all areas of the value chain, the established supply chain and operations processes and the metrics a company utilizes.

In summary, proven approaches to SCPM need to be rethought to cope with increasing customer requirements, technological advancements and ongoing challenges in supply chain complexity as well as pressure to increase revenues and profit margins.

CURRENT STATE OF SCPM

The purpose of a successful performance management approach is to give a complete and well-balanced view of all relevant supply chain information and underlying activities. KPIs are intended to structure the desired information in different dimensions such as customer service, costs and assets. Ideally, KPIs are aligned across the reporting hierarchy levels and are available as required. Further, supporting metrics allow deep dives into root causes to identify irregularities. However, for most companies the reality is different.

Many companies have implemented supply chain performance measurement systems solely focusing on a limited number of considerations. Most systems are isolated, static and with metrics that are backward looking and often not holistic. Root cause analyses are limited by data aggregation, with the loss of full details, or are simply not possible due to the lack of information. An end-to-end perspective has often not been considered, and an integrated performance measurement concept has not been implemented.

Supply chain leaders and the business often face complex reporting landscapes with numerous options to measure and calculate performance. Different KPI definitions as well as specifics in the corporate structure and business processes make it difficult to compare overall supply chain outcomes.

Among the reasons, there may be country-specific regulations or a unique business/supply chain steering logic. This complicates informed decision-making and in some cases results in significant cost to fulfil reporting requirements.

Balanced reporting ensures that trade-offs are transparent and properly managed. KPIs should cascade from strategy to tactics and to the operational level. Successful organizations enable employees to understand the performance levers they influence and how they affect the overall performance.

Standardized processes and metrics are prerequisites for realizing such advanced integration. These include the following:

- Planning details throughout the entire sales and operations planning (S&OP) process
- Customer service levels
- Accuracy of current inventories
- Transparency of supply chain costs

Leading performance management solutions utilize joint metrics to ensure the integration of all functions. For example, finished goods inventory is shared between production and sales. KPIs might be communicated to key supply chain partners using an overall perspective to optimize the end-to-end value chain and to manage trade-offs. Advanced solutions with dashboards exist that visualize a comprehensive suite of supply chain information at a single glance.

IMPLEMENTING ROBUST PERFORMANCE MANAGEMENT SYSTEM

Many companies have already implemented a robust SCPM and are steadily improving their capabilities. New technologies that drive supply chain digitalization are being used increasingly and allow for ad-hoc analyses and predictive analytics as well as improving report visualization. However, the maturity of these SCPM solutions varies. Leading companies differentiate in four areas.

1. Supply chain strategy
   - Steering focus and related supply chain processes
   - Characteristic measurements and metrics
2. End-to-end processes
   - Integrated business planning and customer centricity
   - Transparency on inventory and SCM costs
3. Organizational alignment
   - Individual employees who react are proactive to supply chain challenges
   - Continuous improvement is encouraged
4. Integrated technology
   - Single source of 'clean' supply chain and financial data
   - Supply chain KPIs are calculated and distributed automatically

KEY DIFFERENTIATORS IN IMPLEMENTATION

Supply Chain Strategy Sets the Direction and Defines the Steering Focus

The foundation for performance management is a company's supply chain strategy with its unique value proposition to customers, the derived steering focus and related supply chain processes. Regardless of whether supply chains are response-oriented or configured for efficiency, the strategy defines what and where to measure. Companies that have mastered the challenge of measuring the right areas in their supply chain and that have the right metrics in place can say why those measurements and steering are important for the execution of strategy.

End-to-End Processes Paired with Transparency of Inventories and Supply Chain Cost

Integrated business planning drives the alignment of sales, operations and finance towards the highest possible state. Planning information is coherent and always up-to-date. Supply chain end-to-end processes have been identified, globally harmonized and sustainably implemented. ERP systems act as the backbone of SCM processes and their outcome, and the performance of the process in execution is accurately measured.

Customer centricity is the key to delivering exceptional performance. KPIs such as perfect order rate, delivery reliability or delivery capability might be proper metrics for measuring customer service. Naturally, different service levels and business-specifics are considered when overall supply chain performance is evaluated.

Accurate inventory levels, including details on specific batches/serial items, are pivotal for taking meaningful decisions about supply and demand as well as managing working capital. Seamlessly integrated inventory data allows the swift identification of stock level variances and enable detailed root cause analyses in material flow movements.

Supply chain cost might be aggregated and should be available at a cost component level. The focus is often on production, warehousing, freight and inventories, as these are typically the largest cost components. Leading companies utilize a total landed cost perspective and challenge their actual SCM cost. For example, logistics rebates agreed by sales are verified by operations and are objected to if rebate conditions and prerequisites are not met.

Organizational Alignment and Clear Accountability for Metrics

Leading companies structure their organization according to the principle of customer centricity. The objectives of supply chain organization are clearly defined. By using an established set of SCM KPIs, individual employees are proactively reacting to supply chain challenges and risks.

The complete set of supply chain KPIs, including additional metrics such as process indicators, needs to reflect all relevant performance attributes and should be available to the whole organization. Cascading metrics permit a deep dive into single process measurements and enable more detailed analyses to identify irregularities. Reasonable targets and established thresholds cover all dimensions of supply chain performance. Continuous improvement is encouraged by a performance evaluation process and recurring (cross-functional) feedbacks.

The ownership of performance management systems is typically with the CFO, who forms partnerships with business functions such as sales and operations to achieve transparency of the company's performance.

Integrated Technology and Adaptive Reporting

Technology is a key enabler of world-class supply chain reporting and performance management. Successful companies operate an enterprise data warehouse that serves as single source of 'clean' data for analyses. Source systems ensure consistent data provision in close to real-time with sufficient details to fulfil reporting needs and allow for ad-hoc analyses. External data is collected as required and seamlessly integrated with in-house supply chain information.

Reporting can be described as a centralized data highway with a uniform reporting language which is integrated, cross-functional and adaptive. A supply chain dashboard application creates a single point of entry and provides an overview of the relevant supply chain metrics over multiple dimensions such as brands, products, locations, customers and segments.

A robust reporting governance process ensures continuous and automated monitoring. Supply chain KPIs and related process performance indicators are measured and distributed proactively to relevant stakeholders. Predictive algorithms are used for advanced business intelligence and to determine timely corrective actions along the end-to-end supply chain.

FURTHER DEVELOPMENT OF PERFORMANCE MANAGEMENT IN SCM

Many companies are evaluating the opportunities of new technologies offered by Industry 4.0 and are conducting pilot use cases. Information transparency and the inter-operability of machines and people are the key drivers that take supply chains and their performance to the next level.

As a result, SCPM is gradually evolving, due to faster access to information and new ways of gaining insights. Trends with significant impact on how supply chains are managed include the following:

- Ongoing digitalization of supply chains and resulting exponential growth in data from connected devices, for example, fleet assets, containers, deliveries and in-use products
- A shift to real-time data enabled by sensors covering geographic locations and conditions such as temperature and pressure
- New ways of visualizing SCM insights and increasing the use of predictive methods to forecast sales evaluate maintenance requirements or detect product quality issues early enough for a proactive mitigation management
- Easier linking of internal supply chain data with external data sources, for example, traffic and meteorological data for navigating trucks, the status of outsourced processes for enabling full supply chain transparency or financial information about suppliers for improved supply chain risk management
- Improved analytics capabilities using cloud technologies and in-memory data storage that allow for fast analyses and the processing of large amounts of data. In order to capitalize on trends and improved reporting possibilities, performance management frameworks and reporting systems should be investigated and updated. Given the changes in SCM and in customer behaviour, it is essential to maintain the right focus on what and where to measure.

TRENDS IN MANAGEMENT REPORTING ON SUPPLY CHAIN PERFORMANCE

In an information-enabled supply chain organization, more and more data are available. Deloitte predicts that reporting will advance towards finding the most relevant information in the data jungle by using web mining to quickly react to new events, predictive analytics with sound 'what if?' scenarios, and preselected content using artificial intelligence.

Managers' new working styles will shift reporting towards an always-on state with 24×7 availability. Reporting systems prospectively provide a personalized view and enable target groups of one. When designing reports, neuroscience insights will be increasingly incorporated and design will be no longer based on matters of taste. Automation frees up human time and robotics are being increasingly applied. Logistics companies around the world offer 24×7 real-time information about the cargo movement. Well-performing corporations in a highly competitive environment as well as some MNCs review their SCM performance on identified and critical criteria at regular intervals and compare those with the budgeted target and last year's actual to enable them to take corrective actions. Management reporting helps the businesses to compare their own performance also with the competition and industry standards to remain relevant as well as competitive to the category of industry that they represent.

Organizational boundaries are gradually being removed through flexible teams, communities and virtual organizations. This will affect the decision-making process that accelerates through collaboration, interactive discussions in 'war rooms' and a shared performance culture.

SIGNALS FOR BUSINESSES TO IMPROVE SCM PERFORMANCE

Any time is right to initiate implementation of company-wide SCM performance management system to be more competitive and also more productive. However, there can be situations when company has to seriously consider improvement of their SCM performance.

Such indications are when customer expectations and new technologies are transforming SCM faster than ever. Signs of concern are sub-optimal overall supply chain performance, inefficient resource allocation, individual targets that are not aligned with strategic objectives, operational managers without clear accountability or reporting analyses efforts that fail to highlight potential issues in a timely manner.

If one of these symptoms is present, it is time to rethink your company's performance management capabilities and the approach to measuring and managing supply chains.

Businesses have initiated strategies and supports for companies to drive large-scale transformation initiatives in their supply chains, helps to institutionalize performance management and enables the organization to steer their value chain activities towards exceptional performance. With state-of-the-art SCPM from strategy to processes to technology, a company's performance management should be covering a full range of services as a discipline and in managing value chains from an end-to-end perspective with an objective to increase the overall performance of the business in a highly competitive environment.

PERFORMANCE MEASUREMENTS AND METRICS IN SCM

Performance measurement can be initiated at strategic, operational and tactical levels in any organization.

The metrics and measures can be discussed in the context of the supply chain activities and/or processes such as plan, source, make or assemble and delivery and customer service (Gunasekaran et al. 2001; Stewart 1995).

ORDER ENTRY METHOD

This method determines the way and extent to which customer specifications are converted into information exchanged along the supply chain.

ORDER LEAD TIME

The total order cycle time, called order-to-delivery cycle time, refers to the time elapsed in between the receipt of customer order until the delivery of finished goods. The reduction in order cycle time leads to reduction in supply chain response time, and as such is an important performance measure and source of competitive advantage (Christopher 1992), it directly interacts with customer service in determining competitiveness.

THE CUSTOMER ORDER PATH

The path that an order traverses is another important measure whereby the time spent in different channels can be determined. By analysing the customer order path, non-value-adding activities can be identified so that suitable steps can be taken to eliminate them.

EVALUATION OF SUPPLY LINK

Traditionally, supplier performance measures were based on price variation, rejects on receipt and on-time delivery. For many years, the selection of suppliers and product choice were mainly based on price competition with less attention afforded to other criteria such as quality, reliability and so on. More recently, the whole approach to evaluating suppliers has undergone drastic change.

EVALUATION OF SUPPLIERS

The evaluation of suppliers in the context of the supply chain (efficiency, flow, integration, responsiveness and customer satisfaction) involves measures important at the strategic, operational and tactical level.

Strategic-level measures include lead time against industry norm, quality level, cost saving initiatives and supplier pricing against market.

Operational level measures include ability in day-to-day technical representation, adherence to developed schedule, ability to avoid complaints and achievement of defect-free deliveries.

Tactical level measures include the efficiency of purchase order cycle time, booking in procedures, cash flow, quality assurance methodology and capacity flexibility.

Supply chain partnership is a collaborative relationship between a buyer and a seller, which recognizes some degree of interdependence and co-operation on a specific project or for a specific purchase agreement (Ellram 1991; van Hoek 2001). Such a partnership emphasizes direct, long-term association, encouraging mutual planning and problem-solving efforts (Maloni and Benton 1997). Supplier partnerships have attracted the attention of practitioners and researchers (Ellram 1991; Graham, Dougherty and Dudley 1994; Macbeth and Ferguson 1994). All have contended that partnership formation is vital in supply chain operations and as such for efficient and effective sourcing.

The parameters that need to be considered in the evaluation of partnerships are the ones that promote and strengthen them. For example, the level of assistance in mutual problem-solving is indicative of the strength of supplier partnerships. Partnership evaluation based on such criteria will result in win–win partnerships, leading to more efficient and more thoroughly integrated supply chains.

PERFORMANCE MEASURES AT PRODUCTION LEVEL

Performance measures at production sites have major impact on product quality, cost and speed of delivery as well as delivery reliability and flexibility (Mapes, New and Szwejczewski 1997; Slack et al. 1995) and thus constitute an important part of the supply chain, and therefore production function needs to be measured and continuously improved. Some measures of production levels are as follows:

Product range and services: According to Mapes et al. (1997), a plant that manufactures a broad product range is likely to introduce new products more slowly than plants with a narrow product range. Plants that can manufacture a wide range of products are likely to perform less well in the areas of value added per employee, speed and delivery reliability. This clearly suggests that product range affects supply chain performance.

Capacity utilization: According to Slack et al. (1995), of the many aspects of production performance, capacity utilization directly affects the speed of response to customer demand through its impact on flexibility, lead time and deliverability.

EFFECTIVENESS OF SCHEDULING TECHNIQUES

Scheduling refers to the time or date on or by which activities are to be undertaken. Such fixing determines the manner in which resources will flow in an operating system, the effectiveness of which has an important impact on production and thus supply chain performance. For example, scheduling techniques such as JIT, MRP and ERP have implications on purchasing, throughput time and batch size. In case of the supply chain, since scheduling depends heavily on customer demands and supplier performance, the scheduling tools should be viewed in that context (Little et al. 1995).

EVALUATION OF DELIVERY LINK

The link in a supply chain that directly affects customers is delivery. It is a primary determinant of customer satisfaction; hence, measuring and improving delivery is always desirable to increase competitiveness. Delivery by its very nature takes place in a dynamic and ever-changing environment, making the study and subsequent improvement of a distribution system difficult. It should be noted that it is not an easy matter to anticipate how changes to one of the major elements within a distribution structure will affect the system as a whole (Rushton and Oxley 1989).

MEASURES FOR DELIVERY PERFORMANCE EVALUATION

According to Stewart (1995), an increase in delivery performance is possible through a reduction in lead-time attributes. Another important aspect of delivery performance is on-time delivery. On-time delivery reflects whether perfect delivery has taken place or otherwise and is also a measure of customer service level. A similar concept, *on time order fill*, was used by Christopher (1992), describing it as a combination of delivery reliability and order completeness. Another aspect of delivery is the percentage of finished goods in transit, which, if high, signifies low inventory turns, leading to unnecessary increases in tied up capital. Various factors that can influence delivery speed include vehicle speed, driver reliability, frequency of delivery and location of depots. An increase in efficiency in these areas can lead to a decrease in the inventory levels (Novich 1990).

NUMBER OF FAULTLESS NOTES INVOICED

An invoice shows the delivery date, time and condition under which goods were received. By comparing these with the previously made agreement, it can be determined whether perfect delivery has taken place or not, and areas of discrepancy can be identified so that improvements can be made.

FLEXIBILITY OF DELIVERY SYSTEMS TO MEET PARTICULAR CUSTOMER NEEDS

This refers to flexibility in meeting a particular customer delivery requirement at an agreed place, agreed mode of delivery and with agreed upon customized packaging. This type of flexibility can influence the decision of customers to place orders, and thus can be regarded as important in enchanting and retaining customers (Novich 1990).

Of the factors by which supply chains compete, flexibility can be rightly regarded as a critical one. Being flexible means having the capability to provide products/services that meet the individual demands of customers in a dynamic market environment. Some flexibility measures include (a) product development cycle time, (b) machine/tool set up time, (c) economies of scope (Christopher 1992), which refers to the production of small quantities of wider range (e.g., JIT lot size) and (d) number of inventory turns.

MEASURING CUSTOMER SERVICE AND SATISFACTION

Measuring customer service is critical to the business survival and has therefore to be undertaken at regular interval and with utmost care. Without achieving the customer satisfaction, the whole exercise of performance management in supply chain will become useless. As such, Lee and Billington (1992) and van Hoek et al. (2001) emphasized that to assess supply chain performance, supply chain metrics must centre on customer satisfaction.

CUSTOMER QUERY TIME

Customer query time relates to the time it takes for a firm to respond to a customer query with the required information. It is not unusual for a customer to enquire about the status of order, potential problems on stock availability or delivery. A fast and accurate response to those requests is essential in keeping customers satisfied.

POST-TRANSACTION MEASURES OF CUSTOMER SERVICE

The function of a supply chain does not end when goods are provided to the customer. Post-transaction activities play an important role in customer service and provide valuable feedback that can be used to further improve supply chain performance.

STARTING PERFORMANCE MANAGEMENT PROGRAMME IN THE ORGANIZATION

The goal of this approach is to identify the necessary steps for a successful visibility programme that improves supply chain productivity, responsiveness and reliability. Companies must evolve through three levels of maturity when seeking operational improvement and financial value from visibility technology. In the first level (shipment tracking), the system provides shipment tracking to locate the product. This information improves customer satisfaction and helps internal operations planning. In the second level (supply chain disruption management), disruption management is notified proactively if shipments deviate from planned milestones and assists in problem resolution. This information improves the on-time delivery performance and lowers expediting costs. The greatest financial value comes in the third level (supply chain improvement), when visibility information helps identify and eliminate root causes of delays. Effectiveness at this level has a positive impact on lead time, inventory investment and freight cost.

The successful implementation of such a supply chain visibility technology requires five critical steps. First, it is important to devise a visibility strategy. Since visibility develops over time, the strategy should focus on the highest problem areas first and then expand from there. The creation of an 'as is' assessment of key metrics, targeted for improvement, is part of the strategy process. Key metrics should include both cross-functional and department-based metrics, such as cycle times, on-time delivery performance or safety stock levels. The definition of the visibility strategy also includes the identification of responsibilities for the improvement of each metric and the establishment of a cross-functional team with an executive sponsor. Second, the company has to select a visibility technology that meets their requirements. There are different visibility technologies available. These can be classified into three categories: internally developed systems, systems provided by logistics providers and systems from commercial technology vendors. The most important aspect of a visibility project is the creation of a rollout plan, described in step three. The project team has to determine which areas of the supply chain to concentrate on first. This requires the identification of small, simple projects. Depending on the company, this can mean concentrating on certain regions, shipments for key customers or certain product lines, perhaps those with the highest value or time sensitivity. Assessing the availability of quality status data is another consideration for determining the scope. Therefore, it is beneficial to start with the smallest dataset possible that still drives value. Successful pilot programmes often focus on areas in which better visibility will lead to significant improvements in lead times and on-time delivery performance. The fourth step deals with the improvement of disruption management. Many commercial visibility systems now include functionality to not only serve as a problem detector but also to provide resolution insights and support. If necessary, these features help decide what actions should be taken if the actual status deviates from the planned status. As a result, resolution functionality can help enforce corporate policies for expediting, rerouting, reallocating inventory and so on. This has positive effects on customer service capabilities and delivery performance. Driving structural supply chain improvement, however, requires analytical discipline, as described in step five. Using visibility data to measure actual lead times across the supply chain network is one quick opportunity to update the inventory and customer service system with these times. Identifying bottlenecks and recurring points of variability, analysing their underlying causes and taking corrective actions, on the other hand, helps companies achieve the highest value from visibility technology.

The conceptual background of the model describes the maturity of supply chain transparency with a special focus on the flow of goods. It therefore addresses the topics relevant for the organization. First, the goal of this approach is to create transparency throughout the entire supply chain to increase customer satisfaction and improve the supply chain performance sustainably. Second, on-time delivery performance and lead time represent two very important parameters for measuring and improving supply chain performance. Third, the roadmap to supply chain visibility provides an appropriate project approach.

The supply chain visibility roadmap provides an appropriate project approach, especially by describing the necessary steps of defining a visibility strategy and creating the rollout plan. According to the visibility roadmap, the following elements are important when defining a strategy that aims to create transparency:

- Focusing on the main problem areas first and then expanding from there
- Creating 'as is' assessment of key metrics, targeted for improvement
- Including both cross-functional and department-based metrics
- Establishing a cross-functional team with an executive sponsor when creating the roll-out plan

It is recommended that we start with a small project to create a visible result and then extend to other areas of performance management in order of importance. Therefore, we need to start by doing the following:

- Determining which areas of the supply chain to concentrate on first
- Identifying small, simple projects
- Assessing the availability of quality status data

Starting with the smallest dataset possible that still drives value-specific maturity models, use different supply chain views to analyse the process performance of each viewpoint. This is especially important since the SCM processes are cross-functional. The SCM Process Maturity Model uses the SCOR Model as a conceptual basis to describe the process maturity of the supply chain activities plan, source, make and deliver.

The SCOR model is a management tool used to address, improve and communicate SCM decisions within a company and with suppliers and customers of a company. The model describes the business processes required to satisfy a customer's demands. The SCOR Model also represents the conceptual framework for measuring the SCM performance. However, this mainly represents the internal perspective on SCM performance. It is also important to consider other viewpoints, such as those presented in the customer relationship management. For instance, assesses performance in terms of meeting the customers' expectations. According to the SCM definition, all SCM activities focus on the needs and expectations of customers. Therefore, the customer's viewpoint is indispensable to find out how SCM performance is perceived and how they measure their supplier's SCM performance.

Performance measurement systems represent an important viewpoint, since they determine the performance metrics to measure the enterprise's performance regarding processes, functions and employees. Some of the maturity models considered already emphasize the importance of direct process performance measures, such as delivery performance and lead times. This chapter aims to analyse the importance of performance measures and metrics in each of the four basic supply chain processes (plan, source, make and deliver).

The following four aspects are crucial for effective performance measurement and improvement:

- First, measurement goals must represent organizational goals. This allows measuring the achievement of those targets and evaluating the effectiveness of the strategy employed.
- Second, selected metrics should reflect a balance between financial and non-financial measures. Financial performance measurements are important for strategic decisions and external reporting, whereas non-financial measures support the day-to-day control of manufacturing and distribution operations.
- Third, metrics should be related to strategic, tactical and operational levels of decision-making and control. The decisions of top-level management are based on the strategic level and, thus, mainly on financial measures. The tactical-level measures deal with the allocation of resources and the achievement of the results specified at the strategic level. Operational-level measurements and metrics assess the results of the decisions of low-level managers in order to achieve the tactical objectives.
- Finally, performance assessment can be better addressed by using a few performance measures that are critical to success and truly capture the essence of organizational performance.

Gunasekaran, Patel and McGaughey (2004) reviewed the literature on SCM performance measurements and metrics in the context of the following activities/processes: (a) plan, (b) source, (c) make/assemble and (d) delivery/customer.

PLANNING PERFORMANCE EVALUATION METRICS

This section deals with financial and non-financial strategic-level performance measures. The importance of these parameters needs to be established by taking customer responses to determine the importance of performance measures from customers' perspectives which can be further categorized on the basis of their importance such as highly important, moderately important and less important. The approach can be like the one in the methodology used in ABC inventory (inventory item's annual cost is stated as percentage of total inventory costs) to prioritize inventory management decisions (item cost percentages sorted in descending order and grouped into A—most important; B—moderate importance; and C—less important on the basis of their contribution to total costs). However, it should be noted that categorizing a measure as less important does not mean it is unimportant, but rather it seems less important compared to others in the measurement group taking customer service perspective in view. A similar approach could be used by managers in setting priorities in the development of a measurement system for supply chain performance. A more rigorous study to validate the framework should employ better data and more rigorous statistical techniques. The first set of measures can include 4–5 non-financial and 3–4 financial measures that pertain to planning, but more specifically to strategic planning.

This clearly indicates that customer satisfaction is of the utmost importance in increasing competitiveness. The measures considered within the moderately important category include three financial and three non-financial measures, which reflect the importance of a balance between financial and non-financial measures in strategic planning. Variances against budget represent the highest-rated financial metric, whereas order lead time represents the highest-rated non-financial metric. At the order planning level, the customer query time is highly important, whereas the product development cycle time is moderately important. Both metrics are related to meeting customer needs by performing in a timely fashion, which again emphasizes the importance of customer service. At the bottom line, customer satisfaction and service are most important at the planning level.

SOURCING PERFORMANCE EVALUATION METRICS

The sourcing process includes purchasing and supplier management activities. Suppliers and vendors play a great role in terms of improving SCM performance of any organization. Vendors need to be determined and selected following a rigorous rating criterion. The most important criterion for sourcing performance can be delivery performance, which is directly linked with production performance. The other criteria can be the lead time against the established industry norms, pricing, flexibility, quality and so on.

PRODUCTION PERFORMANCE EVALUATION METRICS

In this section, supply chain production link metrics/measures are rated in importance. The performance measures for the production link can include percentage of defects (a measure of product quality), cost per operation hour, capacity utilization, range of product and services and utilization of EOQ. Depending on the product category, the degree of importance of these production performance parameters could change. For example, percentage defect can emerge as the most important criterion than others. But two others, cost per operation hour and capacity utilization, were also highly important. Percentage defect can directly affect customer satisfaction level. But the latter two are essentially measures of the efficiency with which resources are used in manufacturing or production plant (produce/assemble), and good performance in these two areas translates into lower cost per unit to manufacture products/provide services. Efficiency of operations is important for all supply chain partners, if the elusive goal of supply chain optimization is to be achieved. Note that the percentage importance of each of these three clearly sets them apart from the moderately important and less important measures.

The other measures can include range of products and services. As noted in the literature, a broader range of products tend result in fewer new products being introduced, and a narrower range is associated with greater product innovation. For this reason, the measure does seem worthy of the attention of managers, especially in making decisions about the breadth and depth of product lines. EOQ could also be a measure but customer survey may not recognize that as an important measure, as revealed in some surveys. It was the only measure rated less important.

It may be that the participants, in assigning their ratings, regarded the use of EOQ as a means to an end rather than an end in itself. In short, quality and efficiency seem to be more important considerations in evaluating production performance.

DELIVERY PERFORMANCE EVALUATION METRICS

Similarly to the production performance metrics, there are three delivery performance metrics that are highly important. The first two measures, quality of delivered goods and on-time delivery of goods, have nearly the same rating. Flexibility of service systems to meet customer needs represents the third highly important metric. It is important to provide the customer with a quality product in a timely fashion, and maintaining customer satisfaction with a service system designed to flexibly respond to customer needs are key in producing value for the customer.

A framework to promote a better understanding of the importance of SCM performance measures and metrics that help organizations in developing a performance measurement programme for SCM (Gunasekaran et al. 2004) has been shown in Table 9.1. The framework considers the four major supply chain activities (plan, source, make/assemble and deliver) as well as the three management levels (strategic, tactical and operational).

It seems that customer satisfaction is of paramount importance in increasing competitiveness, especially for the planning and delivery activities: each first-mentioned metric, at least on the tactical or strategic level, in some ways deals with meeting the customers' needs. Companies can use this framework to identify the supply chain activity to be measured, the appropriate metric and the level of management to which the measure should be applied. However, not all supply chains are identical, and the company will certainly have individual performance measurement needs that reflect the unique operations of their business. In terms of the practical example, it is necessary to first devise a strategy and create a rollout plan to determine which areas of the supply chain to focus on. This allows for the selection of performance measures reflecting the operations of the respective supply chain areas.

A FRAMEWORK FOR PERFORMANCE MEASUREMENT IN A SUPPLY CHAIN

A framework for performance measures and metrics is presented (Table 9.1) considering the four major supply chain activities/processes (plan, source, make/assemble and deliver). These metrics were classified as strategic, tactical and operational to clarify the appropriate level of management authority and responsibility for performance. This framework is a part of a theoretical framework discussed by Gunasekaran et al. (2001). Measures are grouped in cells at the intersection of the supply chain activity and planning level. For example, supplier delivery performance can be found at the intersection of the source activity and tactical planning level indicating that it pertains to sourcing activities (source) and the tactical planning level. Supplier delivery performance would thus be a measure useful in analysing the performance of mid-level managers—who are generally the ones responsible for tactical decisions—as they undertake sourcing activities. More details could be added to fix personal responsibility for measures with individual managers, or management positions.

TABLE 9.1 Framework of Supply Chain Performance Matrix

Supply Chain Activity/ Process	Strategic	Tactical	Operational
Plan	Level of customer perceived value of product Variances against budget Order lead time Information processing cost Net profit vs productivity ratio Total cycle time Total cash flow time Product development cycle time	Customer query time Product development cycle time Accuracy of forecasting techniques Planning process cycle time Order entry methods Human resource productivity	Order entry methods Human resource productivity
Source	Technological capability of supply source Ability to develop alternative material Constant upgradation on cost and quality parameters	Supplier delivery performance Supplier lead time against industry norm Supplier pricing against market Efficiency of purchase order cycle time Efficiency of cash flow method Supplier booking in procedures	Efficiency of purchase order cycle time Supplier pricing against market
Make/ Assemble	Range of products and services Manufacturing in-house vs out-house	Percentage of defects Cost per operation hour Capacity utilization Utilization of EOQ	Percentage of defects Cost per operation hour Human resource productivity index

Supply Chain Activity/ Process	Strategic	Tactical	Operational
Deliver	Flexibility of service system to meet customer needs Effectiveness of enterprise distribution planning schedule	Flexibility of service system to meet customer needs Effectiveness of enterprise distribution planning schedule Effectiveness of delivery invoice methods Percentage of finished goods in transit Delivery reliability performance	Quality of delivered goods On-time delivery of goods Effectiveness of delivery invoice methods Number of faultless delivery notes invoiced Percentage of urgent deliveries Information richness in carrying out delivery Delivery reliability performance

Source: Gunasekaran et al. (2001).

This framework should be regarded as a starting point for an assessment of the need for supply chain performance measurement. It is likewise important to understand that the rated importance of metrics in this framework is based on a relatively small sample, and thus, care should be taken in generalizing results to all supply chains. The importance of individual metrics presented herein might not apply to all supply chains in all industries. Again, the framework is only a starting point. It is hoped that this framework will assist practitioners in their efforts to assess supply chain performance.

MATURITY MODELS TO MEASURE SUPPLY CHAIN PERFORMANCE

Essentially, maturity models are intended to describe the typical behaviour exhibited by a company at a number of levels of 'maturity'. This allows companies to codify what might be considered good practice (and, conversely, bad practice). In addition, there are some intermediate or transitional stages. The concept applies to a range of activities, including quality management, software development, supplier relationships and many more, both as a means of assessment and as part of a framework for improvement. One of the earliest maturity approaches was Crosby's Quality Management Maturity Grid (QMMG). For this reason, most of the following approaches have their roots in the field of quality management. QMMG expects companies to evolve through five levels of maturity before ascending to quality management excellence, namely uncertainty, awakening, enlightenment, wisdom and certainty.

At each level, the performance of a number of key activities is described. For this purpose, the approach provides a descriptive text for the characteristic traits of performance for each level. The Capability Maturity Model (CMM) for Software, developed by the Software Engineering Institute at Carnegie Mellon, is perhaps the best-known derivative from this line of work. CMM for Software provides software organizations with guidance on how to gain control of their processes for developing and maintaining software and how to evolve towards a culture of software engineering and management excellence. CMM for software provides a framework consisting of five maturity levels that define the extent to which a specific process is defined, managed, measured, controlled and effective which is widely accepted and implemented. The fundamental assumption of this approach is that quality can be cultivated through control. Therefore, companies at higher maturity levels are better managed, have less risk and are more likely to deliver a quality product that meets the budget and schedule. CMM for Software inspired the development of other frameworks, such as the CMM for Systems Engineering (SE-CMM) and the CMM for Integrated Product and Process Development (IPD-CMM). The most recent attempt to consolidate the multiple models is the Integrated CMM (CMM-I), which has motivated the development of similar frameworks in other disciplines.

During the various stages of development in terms of maturity models of SCM practices, the corporation progresses from some initial state to more advanced state. Some do it faster than others and with fewer detours, but fast or slow, every company that gets to world-class must evolve through theses stages to get there. Therefore, no stage can be left out. In assessing performance or maturity level, a distinction is made between two types of models: On one hand, there are models in which different activities may be scored at different levels. On the other, there are models in which maturity levels are 'inclusive', where a cumulative number of activities must all be performed. In practice, however, maturity models are not primarily used as absolute measures of performance but rather as part of an improvement process. In this regard, the purpose of using a maturity model is to identify a gap that can be closed by subsequent improvement actions.

OVERVIEW OF SCM MATURITY MODELS

Many of the aforementioned approaches and ideas of maturity have been adapted to supply chains and their management. To analyse the characteristics of maturity models in the field of SCM, Jording and Sucky (2016) developed a design-based characterization of SCM maturity models. The goal of their work is to provide the reader with a purpose-driven design-based catalogue that serves as a guideline for a more efficient construction of maturity models.

The analysis of these models and their shortcomings reveals quality attributes of SCM maturity models, which then provides the basis of the purpose-driven catalogue. This catalogue specifies the essential building blocks of SCM maturity models.

A maturity model can be defined as a construction-based model that consists of an anticipated, limited development path, separated into stages with defined characteristics and dimensions. It has one or more objectives related to the stage evaluation, gap identification and transformation. If a model of this kind focuses on intercorporate collaboration, customer focus, management of flow of goods and/or management of information flow, it is called a SCM maturity model. The examination of the numerous models identified in the literature review reveals that those models differ between the anticipated evolutionary content and the operationalization of the stages.

SCM PROCESS MATURITY MODEL

The SCM Process Maturity Model shows the progression of activities towards effective SCM and process maturity based on five stages. Each of the stages contains characteristics associated with process maturity. These characteristics include predictability, capability, control, effectiveness and efficiency. Due to its process orientation and wide adoption by the supply chain academic and practitioner communities, the SCOR model serves as the basis to conceptualize the SCM Process Maturity Model. The five stages describe the process maturity of four areas: plan, source, make and deliver.

In Stage 1 (ad hoc), the supply chain and its processes are unstructured without any process measures in place. Functional cooperation is low, and the process performance is unpredictable. As a result, customer satisfaction is low.

In Stage 2 (defined), basic SCM processes are defined and documented, and process performance is more predictable. The improvement of functional cooperation requires considerable effort. Targets are defined but still missed most of the time. Customer satisfaction has therefore improved but remains low.

Stage 3 (linked) represents the breakthrough, as broad SCM jobs and structures are put in place, and intra-company functions, vendors and customers are cooperating. Process performance is more predictable, and defined targets are often achieved. Increased customer satisfaction begins to show market improvement.

In Stage 4 (integrated), organizational structures and jobs are based on SCM procedures, and traditional functions begin to disappear. Cooperation between the company, its vendors and suppliers takes place on a process level. Advanced collaboration with customers and suppliers helps process performance become highly predictable. Targets are reliably achieved, SCM costs are dramatically reduced and customer satisfaction becomes a competitive advantage.

In Stage 5 (extended), individual companies are no longer just competing against each other but against entire supply chains. These supply chains represent a horizontal, customer-focused, collaborative culture that shares common processes and goals, as well as joint investments in improving the system.

It is revealed that there is a significant relationship between SCM process maturity and overall SCM performance in an organization. Performance measured by each area of the SCOR Model is the measurement of performance most related to SCM process maturity. An explanation for this result is that the four areas of the SCOR Model provide a clear process context (Table 9.2). Delivery performance and order lead times are also significantly correlated with SCM process maturity.

To achieve the defined enterprise goals, a company needs to successfully manage the following seven supply chain views:

- **SCM and logistics:** Functions, processes, activities and tasks related to the integration, collaboration and development of the suppliers.
- **Production systems:** Functions, processes, activities and tasks regarding the transformation of the product or service.

TABLE 9.2 Maturity Levels of the Supply Chain Maturity Model

Level	Level Name	Description
1	Undefined	Describes a competency area for which the enterprise has no documentation or standardization. The processes are ad hoc, dependent on the person doing the activity and reactive to the environment.
2	Defined	Describes a competency area for which the enterprise has defined the process and procedures. The competency areas are isolated, and there is little forward effort to integrate the many processes.
3	Manageable	Describes a competency area for which the enterprise has defined established procedures that they measure and manage to those measurement. Moreover, the enterprise has taken action to integrate and coordinate the internal processes and systems of the enterprise.
4	Collaborative	Describes a competency are for which the enterprise has established procedures to collaborate with suppliers and customers.
5	Leading	Describes a competency area for which the enterprise has established procedures to collaborate with suppliers and customers; it measures these practices and regularly obtains feedback to improve these practices.

Source: SCOR Model, Supply Chain Council, 7 October 2004.

- **Inventory management:** Actions related to inventory management and control.
- **Customer relationship management:** Actions regarding meeting the customer's needs.
- **Human resource management:** Actions related to the enterprise's employees, their integration into the company and the work environment.
- **ISs and technology management:** Actions linked to the development and implementation of ISs and the technology management process.
- **Performance measurement systems:** To measure the enterprise's performance regarding processes, functions and employees.

SECTION II
BENCHMARKING SUPPLY CHAIN PERFORMANCE

INTRODUCTION

SSCM function covers a wide range of functions of the business, and becoming competitive in that area is a key imperative for all businesses. The performance of supply chain depends on technology deployed and also processes followed. One way of keeping a track if an organization is competitive or not is to benchmark performance periodically with identified competitors or industry leaders.

Benchmarking criteria can be decided by the businesses based on the key differentiators that can make a difference in performance. One such differentiator is, of course, the cost of production, and another key differentiator is customer service level and customer satisfaction. If businesses can upgrade in these two parameters then it can expect to deliver above average performance. This section will deal with the issues concerning benchmarking criteria, and how to go about initiating supply chain performance benchmarking and what precautions are necessary to be taken to get a useful outcome. Benchmarking can also be done by collectively forming a syndicate of a few progressive players in a business category to gain from each other's experience. However, benchmarking is not to be confused with typical syndicated survey that periodically some businesses participate in to find the larger issues and direction a business category players are likely to face in future.

WHAT IS BENCHMARKING?

Benchmarking can somewhat philosophically be defined as follows (APQC 1992):

> Benchmarking is the practice of being humble enough to admit that someone else is better at something, and being wise enough to learn how to match them and even surpass them at it.

This definition captures the essence of benchmarking, namely learning from others. The core of the current interpretation of benchmarking is as follows:

- **Measurement** of own and the benchmarking partners' performance level, both for comparison and for registering improvements
- **Comparison** of performance levels, processes, practices and so on
- **Learning** from the benchmarking partners to introduce improvements in your own organization
- **Improvement** which is the ultimate objective of any benchmarking study

The basic objective of using benchmarking supply chain is to increase the knowledge about the SCM process and to enable the industrial partners to learn from the best practices. This was done through identification and study of other enterprises in Europe and their processes.

To reach this objective, a process benchmarking study needs to be undertaken to compare the processes in this area within or even outside the country where business is located. The purpose was to gain information that could lead to improvements in the areas of vendor management practices, supplier's efficiency and so on, but more importantly to gain an understanding of best practice in this area.

The primary information from the benchmarking activity is flowcharts and process descriptions. It was more important to find 'best practices' than numerical performance data. The collection of data was done by visits to the benchmarking partners. To ensure consistent information from all the benchmarking visits, a questionnaire needs to be developed to be used during the interviews (Andersen and Randmael 1997). The questionnaire should be so designed that it captures all information that need to be understood related to SCM processes and practices.

BENCHMARKING SUPPLY CHAIN PERFORMANCE

Benchmarking of performance is required to be done to find if the company is competitive enough in a given market. After all, everything ultimately can be related to cost, and businesses have to be cost-competitive. Two companies with different cost structure cannot co-exist for a long time; higher cost company has to close down sooner or later. Supply chain of a corporation can be considered as the largest cost centre for the business and, therefore, it is imperative that SCM function is managed for delivering the company's performance objective. And performance objective, therefore, has to be competitive in order to survive in a keenly contested market. One way of knowing if a business is competitive enough is to conduct benchmarking periodically. Benchmarking is normally done against the best in class as well as against the best in the category. This would mean that benchmarking under a given set of parameters should be done against best performer in the same category of the business, for example, an automobile manufacturer should benchmark against the best-known performer in automobile sector itself. Benchmarking can also be done against the best in class. For example, same automobile manufacturer can also benchmark against say Unilever or P&G who are known to be pioneers in their SCM practices.

Supply chain operations in a business should constantly be reviewed to identify possible areas of improvements. One method is to perform a series of benchmarking tests for parameters such as price, quality, design, efficiency and cost effectiveness.

In general, companies perform either benchmarking of results focusing on quantitative performance measures or benchmarking of best practices focusing on how well processes are executed by the competitor. The results of both these approaches of benchmarking are best used together. Benchmarking of results only provides a basis for ranking a company to understand where company stands but does not reveal how that performance has been achieved or what strategies are required to improve its performance. Successful supply chain benchmarking incorporates all of the elements in the global supply chain and focuses on product specifications, operational performance, management practices and software solutions (Peter, 1999). Supply chain benchmarking involves three major components—the supplier, the distributor and the interface of the two. However, primary focus of the business is to improve upon its customer satisfaction index and that should be the primary motivation for establishing a benchmarking programme.

HOW TO START

Companies' benchmarking efforts have to help businesses to become cost-competitive. The supply chain benchmarking can help them achieve this goal. It is therefore a good idea to use benchmarking exercise in conjunction with the companies' improvement initiatives. Benchmarking then offers a performance measurement tool that can measure companies' comparative operating performance, identify best practices and possible improvements, and determine how a business is performing against its potential. Benchmarking can also help businesses assess a variety of costs—the cost of goods, the cost of doing business (including inbound and outbound logistics) and opportunity costs.

But a question that will normally arise is where companies should begin with? Previously created benchmarking data—whether quantitative (performance-based) or qualitative (best practices)—can provide a good starting point. It always helps to engage consulting and research firms with experience to advice how to organize or undertake competitive benchmarking projects. Companies can even first accomplish an internal benchmarking against their own standards of KPIs and then compare those with the identified competitors like best performer or leader in the category or even best in class.

SCOPE OF SUPPLY CHAIN BENCHMARKING

Supply chain performance and process benchmarking provide useful comparisons with other companies. In addition, it can also help organizations to identify the following areas:

- Performance improvements
- Interdependencies and relationships between KPIs
- Better business trade-offs
- Opportunities for cross-industry best practices
- Baseline information for goal setting, prioritization and ongoing performance measurements

Companies need adequate preparation in capturing all data for a meaningful benchmarking exercise. The processes that need to be followed for an effective benchmarking can briefly be summarized as below:

- Determine the scope of the benchmarking exercise covering planning, procurement, manufacturing and logistics
- Decide on a set of KPIs under each identified areas for measurement and comparison
- Zero in on the companies to be benchmarked which can be immediate competitors, best in class and best performers in the category
- Develop reporting templates and formats and frequency of measurement
- Work out a plan of implementation and action
- Identify resources required and data collection plan
- Ensure agreements and involvement of stakeholders on its objective, process and benefits
- Collect and validate the data
- Analyse and interpret data collected
- Compare with companies' own performance and identify the reasons thereof to plan for the future

SUPPLY CHAIN PERFORMANCE METRICS FOR BENCHMARKING

Companies can use performance metrics to perform gap analyses and identify areas requiring improvement. SCM KPIs should generally include the following:

- **Delivery performance metrics:** On-time delivery, performance to commitment, fill rates like stock fill rate, pack fill rate and order fill rate and stock return rates
- **Cycle-time metrics:** Promised lead time, actual lead time and supply chain cycle time

- **Inventory and cash management metrics:** Inventory days of supply, days sales outstanding, days payables outstanding and cash-to-cash conversion
- **Supply chain cost metrics:** Overall supply chain costs, order management costs, inventory carrying costs, supply chain finance and planning costs, supply chain IT costs, procurement department staffing and savings

Specific benchmarking data gained through these metrics are focused on the identification of key capabilities to enable an integrated demand–supply network (IDSN).

SUPPLY CHAIN BENCHMARKS OF STANDARD PROCESSES

Another way to approach supply chain benchmarking is to look deeper into traditional supply chain processes.

Planning (demand management, materials planning and production scheduling). Many planning KPIs are available, but companies must determine the indicators that are truly important to their organization's operational performance. Examples include cash-to-cash cycle time, inventory carrying costs, days inventory outstanding, finished goods inventory turn rate, cost of goods sold as a percentage of revenue, forecast accuracy, number of full-time equivalents (FTEs) for the supply chain planning function per US$1 billion in revenue, production schedule adherence, total expediting of costs to execute the production plan, value-added productivity per employee, and return on assets.

Procurement (sourcing strategy development, supplier selection and contract management, order management, and supplier appraisal and development). Examples of KPIs benchmarked for procurement include total cost of the procurement cycle per purchase order or per US$1,000 in purchases, rate of annual raw material inventory turns, average supplier lead time in days, days payable, number of FTEs for the procurement cycle per US$1 billion in purchases, and the percentage of purchases made via an electronic marketplace.

Manufacturing (production scheduling, production and performing maintenance). Common manufacturing KPIs include finished product first-pass yield (FPY), percentage of defects per million opportunities (DPMO), and scrap and rework costs as a percentage of sales and quantities shipped per employee. Other KPIs benchmarked for product manufacturing are manufacturing cycle time, actual production rate as a percentage of maximum capable production rate, annual WIP inventory turn rate, unplanned machine downtime as a percentage of scheduled run time, warranty costs (i.e., repair and replacement) as a percentage of sales, and labour turnover rate as a percentage of the workforce.

Logistics (logistics strategy, planning for inbound material flow, warehousing, outbound transportation, and managing returns and reverse logistics). Standard KPIs for product delivery include order fill rate, pick-to-ship cycle times for customer orders, total cost of outbound transportation process per US$1,000 in revenue, number of FTEs required to operate outbound transportation per US$1 billion in revenue, the percentage of sales order line items not fulfilled due to stock-outs, the percentage of full-load trailer/container capacity used per shipment, and the percentage of orders expedited. Examples of KPIs for logistics/warehousing as a whole include TLCs as a percentage of revenue, freight costs as a percentage of revenue, the percentage of sales orders delivered on time, the number of FTEs for the logistics function per US$1 billion in revenue, and the ratio of premium freight charges to total freight charges.

IMPORTANCE OF IDENTIFYING RIGHT COMPANIES TO BE BENCHMARKED

Businesses formulate strategies to gain market share and deliver higher level of performance. Competitive business strategies are generally directed against identified competitors. No business considers all players in the category as its competitors. Benchmarking needs to be done only against identified competitors and best-in-class players.

The benchmarking team should also be clear about what it wants to learn before approaching a potential benchmarking peer group. Competitors will also expect learning from exchange of information related to specific KPIs. Both parties should understand and agree on the expected outcome and how the information will be gathered and analysed, who will have access to the data, and how the data will be used.

Best-in-class companies involve suppliers and customers in S&OP process and use customer feedback to ensure a more accurate match of demand and supply. These companies also collaborate with suppliers on inventory management levels and on invoice reconciliation to improve invoice and payment processes. Best-in-class companies offer good learning opportunities from their SCM practices to improve the customer satisfaction and reduce costs.

IMPROVING PERFORMANCE

The ultimate aim of benchmarking is to incorporate the best practices within the company to improve performance and to become more competitive in the marketplace. That is how company can ensure survival and growth. The analysis of the data collected to create meaningful and actionable process improvements plan holds the key. This needs a great care. The best practices can be captured from benchmarking exercise from various partners and then an agreed practice and process to be prepared for implementation considering the other constraints and limitations that a specific business can have. Experience from post-implementation of improved processes can help businesses to even improve further by resorting to eliminating the constraints and limitations. Thereby, continuous improvement in business is possible through such kind of benchmarking and process mapping. Sometimes even some breakthrough improvement is also possible.

Different people will have different interpretations of the numbers, and there may be some organizational resistance to change. A structured approach should be used to coordinate the action plan effort and ensure a meaningful outcome. The focus should be on relationships between the metrics rather than the comparison of individual KPIs to benchmark numbers (e.g., trade-offs between cost and service levels).

SOME COMMON MISCONCEPTIONS IN BENCHMARKING

Participating in an industry survey covering a category of industry on the basis of certain parameters is not benchmarking. This is too general and does not give any actionable standards of performance, and they are too broad. For example, many companies participate in the syndicated research done by established market research agencies periodically. These should not be confused with benchmarking. These survey findings will be difficult to corelate with customers of the company, as they are too general and not specific to the corporation.

Businesses should also be careful about undertaking some action plan based on pre-existing benchmark. A narrow focus on cost parameters overlooking the customer service delivery and satisfaction will only serve as part of the story.

Benchmarking too many companies at the same time should be avoided as it will only complicate the whole exercise and diffuse the focus. The scope of benchmarking should be focused and limited to the identified companies.

Not aligning the business goals with benchmarking criteria will also not be effective and meaningful. After all, the ultimate goal is to improve end-to-end performance of the business.

Not defining clear roles and responsibilities and in the absence of an executive sponsor and a data coordinator can result in data access difficulties, defensiveness, blame and incorrect metrics. The effectiveness of benchmarking efforts is hampered when the details, costs and performance levels of all of the company's processes are not known.

Supply chains, which are a critical determinant of a company's competitiveness, are incredibly difficult to manage because they are cross-functional, covering enterprises from different geographic and political boundaries. To set appropriate goals and identify best practices, an individual company's supply chains should be understood and compared with those of industry peers and best-in-class organizations. Through this process, companies can gain greater understanding of the very latest systems and practices that are crucial for improving the management of their own supply chains.

CASE STUDY: SUPPLY CHAIN PERFORMANCE MEASUREMENT OF AN AUTOMOTIVE INDUSTRY—APPLICABILITY OF SCOR MODEL

SCOR Model as proposed by SCC for performance measurement is easy to understand, practical and suitable for the automotive sector.

Introduction

Over the past 10 years, logistics sector in Morocco went through a strong growth which has been reflected in the improvement of the performance of the LPI, a ranking done annually by the World Bank. Morocco is currently at the 86th place worldwide in logistics performance after being at 94th in 2007. A national strategy has been implemented in Morocco to improve logistics performance and develop the competitiveness of Moroccan businesses. The automotive industry is a highly globalized sector, where there is competition from around the world. Faced with the increase in supply and the strong pressure on prices, reinforced by the power of Asian groups (Toyota, Hyundai, etc.) and the arrival of new players from emerging countries (Geely, Tata Group, etc.), many companies seek to optimize their value chain in order to remain competitive. In the supply chain of the automotive industry, many factories are working together to manufacture a product (car, motor, truck, etc.).

Logistics can be considered a key competitive factor in the automotive industry due to the increasing number of variants and options of the model. With the growing importance of logistics, the evaluation of logistics effectiveness and efficiency is gaining increased attention. There are many continuous improvement tools such as TQM, six sigma, continuous process improvement and others that are available for companies to improve their operations. However, none of these improvements programmes is dedicated to the logistics chain.

In order to improve business systems, the ROI, to deal with competitiveness and optimize the efficiency of their supply chain, some global companies apply the SCOR Model.

SCOR Model

In SCOR, the integrated processes of plan, source, make, deliver, return and enable from the supplier's supplier to the customer's customer represent SCM. Elements of business process engineering, metrics, benchmarking, leading practices and people skills into a single framework are combined with SCOR. The model itself is structured around primary management processes. Using these process definition blocks, SCOR can be used to model supply chains that are very simple or very complex using a common set of definitions in disparate industries. In fact, public and private organizations and companies around the world use the model as a basis for projects to improve the global supply chain.

Basic Approach to Determine Performance

The SCOR Model has three levels of process detail. In practice, Level 1 describes the number of supply chains, how their performance is measured, and necessary competitive requirements. Level 2 presents the configuration of the planning and execution strategies in the material flow, involving standard categories such as 'make-to-stock', 'make-to-order' and 'engineer-to-order'. Level 3 considers the business processes and system functionality used to process sales orders, purchase orders, work orders, return authorizations, replenishment orders and forecasts. Level 4 process details are not contained in SCOR but must be defined to implement improvements and manage processes. Advanced users of the framework have defined process detail as far as Level 5.

Organizations using the SCOR Model performance metrics can compare their performance levels with other organizations in the supply chain using a benchmarking tool called SCORmark. The SCORmark database contains historical data from over 1,000 companies and 2,000 supply chains. The benchmarking process using the SCORmark can be performed through the following steps: (a) defining the supply channels to be compared, (b) measuring the internal and external performances, (c) comparing the performance to relevant industrial companies, (d) establishing competitive demands and (e) calculating the opportunity value of improvement.

- *Superior* is the performance (median value) on a specific indicator attained by 10% of the best classified supply chains (SCs) comparing to the total of the supply chains surveyed.
- *Advantage* is the performance (median value) among the top 10 companies and the median of all the supply chains considered.
- *Parity* is the performance (median value) of all the supply chains considered.

The APICS, an association, announced the launch of the SCOR Model version 12.0. Developed by a panel of international supply chain experts, this latest version of SCOR incorporates Omni-channel, metadata, block chain and other emerging engines that supply chain professionals are using today. SCOR has been the global inter-sectorial standard for supply chain excellence over the last 20 years and, with this update, will continue to support ways to measure, improve and communicate the supply chain's business performance.

APICS is the association for SCM and the leading provider of research, education and certification programmes that elevate supply chain excellence, innovation and resilience.

The company in this case is an international automotive company with more than 45 years of experience in the automotive sector, an annual turnover of approximately 3,300 million EUR and 14,500 employees around the world. For the purpose of evaluation, a combination of workshops across all logistic functions, interviews of key executives, physical documents made available and the data analyses was resorted to. The participants are dispersed across all levels of grading, from operative level up to logistics management of the different sites.

In the beginning, the first series of workshops were conducted with the aim of aligning the logistic objectives found in the literature with those used on the site. From these workshops, the proposed performance indicators as per the model are aligned with those identified by the experts and proposed performance indicators with the ones identified in the experts' workshops. Performance indicators that were not named by the experts, but proposed in standard SCOR, were highlighted and discussed in respect of their added value in a supplement meeting. The subsequent model was aligned in another round of workshops and additional interviews. After changing the detailed definition of the SCOR model and each measure (alignment with data sources, adding responsibilities), the system was implemented and data evaluation started as well as a dashboard allowing performance indicator evaluation launched. Based on that, a quantitative evaluation of each metric was started, which also emphasized initial improvement potentials.

After having implemented the model and finalized its deployment, two brainstorming sessions were conducted to compare the different experiences with this project and to capitalize on it.

Brief Description of the Company

The company already present at Tunisia chose to develop in Morocco in order to accompany its client and to have a base of production of plastic systems and be able to deliver the manufacturers based in Spain. The Sheet Metal workshop has 10 presses having capacity to press 150 to 800 tons of steel and transforms approximately 10,000 tons of steel per year. It issues components for the body-in-white of the vehicles of a carmaker. The plastic factory integrates approximately about 10 press 350 and 2,700 tons, and transforms approximately 3,500 tons of plastic annually. It issues auto components and engines for the two vehicles including components for the equipment suppliers associated with the company.

Supply and Production Control

The trades of the supply model and production control are exerted in the factory where the role of the logistics consists in supplying the raw material, the components sub-contracted and the sub-components necessary for the manufacturing of the components. The trades of handling interns (receipt, shipping, management of the warehouses, etc.) are also part of this model.

Administration of the sales: An administrator is in charge of the receipt of the customer orders, imputation of the prices, the establishment of client base for an article whose finality is the satisfaction of the client in terms of quantity, quality and lead times.

Shipping, receipt, and transport: The trades of this model are exerted on upstream flows of supply raw material, components and sub-contracted components.

Currently, logistics is at the centre of all the activities of the company, divided into four business families that cover all logistics activities: from the supply of raw material to the shipment of the final product. In addition, logistics is one of the services of the company that makes the most use of the computer tool: By following all the flows of the company, by anticipating these flows (forecasts, expression of needs, etc.) and overflowing beyond from the company to suppliers and customers.

For the case, it uses as management tools: (a) SAP (Systems Applications and Products) where the information is centralized, which integrates the different functions of the company (accounting, finance, production, supply, marketing, human resources, quality, maintenance, etc.), (b) EDI for the exchange of various documents internally and externally of the company. It is indeed commercial documents or transport such as invoices. The planning process within the company that were studied is managed by the planner who processes once a week his calculation of net need for finished products via SAP, checks the break dates of each part, and thanks to an Excel file it establishes the planning of all the week as well as the orders of manufacture of the parts to manufacture. These production orders are then issued to the production manager to be distributed to the production items, once the valid and closed planner has been completed and sent to the stock manager as recorded on SAP.

Establishing Performance Metrics

The benchmarking of SCOR Model is done by comparing the indicators of Levels 1, 2 and 3. However, it is not necessary to apply the three performance levels in each axis. That is why it would be better to prioritize these axes in order to put the level indicators 1 for less important axes and up to 3 for the most important. The prioritization of performance axes depends on the type of business and management of the company. SCOR standard set the notations for prioritizing strategic axes of the dashboard that will define for each objective parameters to be fixed for benchmarking. Indeed, the notations S, A and P are used by the SCOR model to prioritize the axes; these are as follows:

S stands for superior: It corresponds to the 90th percentile. This means that it will line up with 10% of the best-performing companies.
A stands for advantage: It corresponds to the 70th percentile. The objective will be to reach the performance of 30% of the best companies.
P stands for parity: It corresponds to the 50th percentile. The objective is to exceed 50% of the best companies.

In order to evaluate the process performance, it will be very interesting to complete the indicators that were already in place by other indicators proposed by the SCOR Model, which correspond to its strategic axes.

According to the baseline with which to compare, there are three types of benchmarking:

- *Comparison on a historical basis.* Monitoring indicator development.
- *Internal benchmarking.* It is the comparison between companies of the same group.
- *External benchmarking.* The comparison is made by external organizations.

The SCOR Model proposes the external benchmarking because the more the reference database will be, the results will be significant. The objective here will be to line up with the best companies in the automotive sector basing on logistics activities. After defining the indicators on the dashboard, the data were collected to calculate their values which were considered depending on the importance as mentioned below:

Reliability: Basic information for these indicators was derived from the history of logistics rates and weekly reports.

Management of assets: This data was collected from the finance department and management control. Most of them are confidential, so they will be expressed as a percentage.

- *Logistics costs.* This information was collected from the accounts department from history.
- *Reactivity.* This indicator corresponds to the lead time or the time required to complete an order.
- *Flexibility.* Only the part of the supply was held in account for this axis because it is the most important component in terms of time.

The next step is the measurement of the performance indicators for the dashboard. Indeed, the formulas for calculating the different KPIs are presented below:

Equations

1. $\text{Service rate (SR)} = \dfrac{\text{Number of processed orders}}{\text{Number of total orders}}$
2. Order fulfilment rate = SR (quantity by reference) × SR (deadline) × SR (accuracy of documents)
3. $\text{Fill rate} = \dfrac{\text{Delivered volume}}{\text{Capacity of the truck}}$
4. Percentage of sales costs (COGS) = Sales – Profits – Administrative cost/sales
5. $\text{Working capital ratio} = \dfrac{\text{Current assets}}{\text{Current liabilities}} = \dfrac{\text{Receivables}}{\text{Payables}}$
6. Financial cycle delay = Delay of customer dept + Number of days of stock – payables delay
7. $\text{Payables delay} = \dfrac{\text{Paybles} \times 365}{\text{Annual sales}}$
8. $\text{Delay of customer debt} = \dfrac{\text{Customer debt} \times 365}{\text{Annual sales}}$
9. $\text{Number of days of available stock} = \dfrac{\text{Stock value} \times 365}{\text{Annual sales}}$
10. $\text{Forecast reliability rate} = \dfrac{\sum_1^n \text{Abs}(\text{sales forecast}(i) - \text{sales}(i))}{\sum_1^n \text{sales forecast}(i)}$

11. Coverage rate $= \dfrac{\sum_1^n \text{Warehouse stock}(i) + \text{Outstanding}(i)}{\text{week average forecast}}$

12. Internal service rate $= \dfrac{\sum_1^n \text{Abs}(\text{planned}(i) - \text{realized}(i))}{\sum_1^n \text{planned}(i)}$

13. Rate of stock variance $= \dfrac{\sum_1^n \text{Abs}(\text{SAP stock}(i) - \text{physical stock}(i))}{\sum_1^n \text{SAP stock}(i)}$

14. Rotation of fixed assets in the supply chain $= \dfrac{\text{Slaes}}{\text{Net fixed assets}}$

15. Customer complain rate $= \dfrac{\text{Number of written complaints}}{\text{Total number of affected deliveries}}$

16. Service supplier rate $= \dfrac{\text{Number of complete delivered orders on time}}{\text{Number of orders to be delivered by suppliers}}$

17. Cost of an out of stock = total costs related to a cessation of customer activity

18. Number of days of available stock $= \dfrac{\text{Total outstanding TTC} \times \text{number of days}}{\text{Total turnover for the period}}$

19. Customer return rate $= \dfrac{\text{Number of returned deliveries from customers}}{\text{Total number of deliveries}}$

20. Supplier return rate $= \dfrac{\text{Number of returned deliveries to suppliers}}{\text{Total number of deliveries}}$

The established scorecard containing the benchmarking values provided by the SCOR standard as well as the improvement objectives for each metric are presented in Table 9.3.

Best Practices Proposed by the SCOR Model

As presented in the dashboard set out in Table 9.3, the difference between the current situation of the company and the value of benchmarking differs from one indicator to another. It is clear that better gap analysis implies good performance improvements. So the first task to do is to know the root causes of these gaps and the processes involved. Regarding the processes mentioned above, the most performing companies have established certain practices that have reported to them tangible benefits. This is a kind of capitalization of experience that the SCOR Model offers through benchmarking. Table 9.4 lists best practices offered by SCOR framework, taking into account the processes previously diagnosed and the anomalies observed.

Table 9.4 shows the best practices according to their difficulty of implementation and the impact they will have on business processes. Priority actions for this project will obviously be those who have the greatest impact and the least difficulty.

TABLE 9.3 The Scorecard Containing Performance Metrics Measured for the Company

Performance Metrics	Criteria	Unit	Maximize/ Minimize	Frequency	Actual Value	Benchmark Class			Company Objective	GAP
						S	A	P		
Service rate (SR)	Reliability	%	Max	Week	92%	100%	90%	80%	S	8%
Order fulfilment rate	Reliability	%	Max	Week	77%	100%	90%	80%	A	13%
Fill rate	Reliability	%	Max	Week	76%	96%	82%	75%	A	6%
% of sales costs (COGS)	Logistics costs	%	Min	Month	5%	3%	8%	13%	S	−3%
Working capital ratio	Management of assets	Ratio	Min	Month	2.2	1.2	1.5	2	A	−0.7
Financial cycle delay	Management of assets	Day	Min	Annual	90	13	42	80	A	−48
Payable delay	Management of assets	Day	Min	Annual	30	—	—	—	—	
Delay of customer debt	Management of assets	Day	Max	Annual	45	—	—	—	—	
Number of days of available stock	Flexibility	Day	Min	Annual	85	13	34	78	A	−55
Forecast reliability rate	Reliability	%	Max	Annual	91%	100%	90%	80%	S	9%
Coverage rate	Flexibility	Ratio	Min	Month	2.5	1	1.4	2	S	−1.5

(Table 9.3 Continued)

(Table 9.3 Continued)

Performance Metrics	Criteria	Unit	Maximize/ Minimize	Frequency	Actual Value	Benchmark Class			Company Objective	GAP
						S	A	P		
Internal service rate	Reliability	%	Max	Week	95%	100%	95%	90%	S	55
The rate of stock variance	Flexibility	%	Max	Week	88%	100%	95%	90%	S	12%
Rotation of fixed assets in the supply chain	Management of assets	—	—	Annual	C^b					
Customer complaints rate	Flexibility	%	Min	Week	6%	0%	2%	5%	A	4%
Service supplier rate	Flexibility	%	Max	Week	95%	100%	95%	90%	S	5%
Cost of an out of stock	Logistics costs	K€	Min	Month	12	0	1	2	A	−12
Number of days of available stock	Logistics costs	Day	Min	Month	15	3	5	7	A	−10
Customer return rate	Logistics costs	%	Min	Week	2%	0%	0.5%	1%	S	−2%
Supplier return rate	Flexibility	%	Min	Week	1%	0%	0.5%	1%	S	−1%

Source: The case is based on the data presented by Radouane Lemghari, Chafik Okar and Driss Sarsri presented at MATEC conference held at Morocco 2018.

TABLE 9.4 The Best Practices Proposed by SCOR Model

Processes	Best Practices
P2 Supply planning	All key participants in the supply chain, including strategic partners, have full visibility of the demand/supply plan VMI CPFR
P2.1 Identify, prioritize product requirements	The demand plan is updated frequently to reflect actual consumption or customer forecast information Maximize data integrity and system accuracy by ensuring over 99% accuracy of BOM configuration, inventory levels and schedule requirements
P2.4 Establish procurement plans	Digital linkage (EDI, XML, etc.) is used to provide real-time demand information and handle routine transactions Maintain data and system integrity by ensuring production data, inventory levels and schedule requirements are over 99% accurate A detailed production model that synchronizes PLAN and MAKE activities in real-time
EP.7 Manages planning configuration	ABC classification
S1.1 to S2.1 Schedule deliveries	Electronic Kanban Pull Signals are used to notify suppliers of the need to deliver product

Conclusion

Being part of a complex and highly competitive field, and in order to evaluate its position in the automotive industries and to implement a benchmarking to improve its performance, the company proposed to model its supply chain. To meet this need, the SCOR Model was opted as a diagnostic tool by the company. The first step was to model its supply chain, according to the SCOR Model, this model aimed to standardize the structure of the process from the existing model. The next step is to develop the dashboard. Based on the results of this benchmarking, represent an opportunity for improvement for the company. A set of best practices were selected that can rectify the weaknesses detected at certain axes. To do this, an action plan was developed to implement these best practices. The key outcome of this performance measurement using SCOR Model adapted to company needs will help the company to integrate proposals for improvements in future projects and logistics department of the annual performance of external benchmarking, in order to validate and renew the strategic direction of the company.

Case Questions

1. What are the advantages and key features of the SCOR Model of supply chain performance measurement?
2. Discuss the methodology adopted to implement the performance measurement system in the company.
3. How are performance measurement criteria determined?
4. What are the key benefits of conducting and implementing such performance measurement model in the company in terms of its long-term objective delivery and strategic direction?

CHAPTER SUMMARY

This chapter deals with the SCPM and also benchmarking supply chain performance. The objective of integrated SCM practice is to improve the overall performance of the company. The chapter discusses in detail the performance criteria of a business and how those are identified and measured against stated objective as well as to deliver above average industry-level performance. While performance measurement of supply chain can be initiated in a business anytime, there are indications or signals for businesses to improve their supply chain performance for their own survival, those signals are discussed in the chapter. The performance criteria can include the general measurement criteria, but most important criteria that impact the customer service and satisfaction have to be included. In this connection, a broad framework of supply chain performance index was discussed in detail. Various tools and techniques used to measure supply chain performance were also discussed in detail. The chapter also discussed the maturity levels of SCM in organization which can be used by enterprises to understand their performance level and compare with their competitors in the industry. This will be a useful tool which will direct businesses regarding where they stand today in terms of SCM practices and what is the way forward for them.

In the second section of the chapter, benchmarking supply chain performance has been discussed in detail, covering the purpose and objective of benchmarking, how to identify the companies to be benchmarked and what are the key performance criteria to be benchmarked. How the conclusions from the benchmarking exercise can be used to improve companies' performance has been covered in detail. Finally some common misconceptions regarding benchmarking have also been discussed.

DISCUSSION QUESTIONS

1. Why is performance management in supply chain so important and how will you go about identifying performance management criteria?
2. Discuss a framework of performance measurement matrix.
3. Discuss how benchmarking performance of supply chain can be helpful to improve the performance and also to get future strategic direction in the business.

4. How will you know at what level a business stands today and if there is a need to initiate performance management programme?
5. Discuss the SCM performance maturity models and stages of evolution.
6. What are the various tools and techniques of conducting performance management in supply chain?
7. How do you determine the benchmarking criteria as well as identify companies with whom a business needs to benchmark? Discuss the basic approach.
8. Discuss the relative advantages of business process benchmarking and benchmarking only the performance.

REFERENCES

APQC. 1992. *American Productivity & Quality Center: Basics of Benchmarking*. Houston, Texas: APQC.

Anderson, B., and Stine Randmael. 1997. 'Questionnaire for the Benchmarking Visits'. SMArTMAN SME Document, Trondheim, Norway.

Christopher, M. 1992. *Logistics and Supply Chain Management*. London: Pitman Publishing.

Ellram, L. M. 1991. 'A Managerial Guide for the Development and Implementation of Purchasing Partnership'. *International Journal of Purchasing and Materials Management* 27 (3): 2–8.

Fisher, L. M. 1997. 'What is the Right Supply Chain for Your Product?' *Harvard Business Review* 75 (2): 105–116.

Graham, T. S., P. J. Dougherty, and W. N. Dudley. 1994. 'The Long-term Strategic Impact of Purchasing Partnerships'. *International Journal of Purchasing and Materials Management* 30 (4): 13–18.

Gunasekaran, A., C. Patel, and E. Tirtiroglu. 2001. 'Performance Measure and Metrics in a Supply Chain Environment'. *International Journal of Operation & Production Management* 21 (1/2): 71–87.

Gunasekaran, A., C. Patel, and R. E. McGaughey. 2004. 'A Framework for Supply Chain Performance Measurement'. *International Journal of Production Economics* 87 (3): 333–347.

Jording, T., and E. Sucky. 2016. 'Improving the Development of Supply Chain Management Maturity Models by Analysing Design Characteristics'. In *Supply Chain Management Research*, 97–119. Wiesbaden: Springer Gabler.

Lee, H. L., and C. Billington. 1992. 'Managing Supply Chain Inventory: Pitfalls and Opportunities'. *Sloan Management Review* 33 (3): 65–73.

Little, D., J. Kenworthy, P. Jarvis, and K. Porter. 1995. 'Scheduling Across the Supply Chain'. *Logistics Information Management* 8 (1): 42–48.

Macbeth, D. K., N. Ferguson. 1994. *Partnership Sourcing: An Integrated Supply Chain Management Approach*. London: Pitman Publishing.

Maloni, M. J., and W. C. Benton. 1997. 'Supply Chain Partnerships: Opportunities for Operations Research'. *European Journal of Operational Research* 101 (3): 419–429.

Mapes, J., C. New, and M. Szwejczewski. 1997. 'Performance Trade-offs in Manufacturing Plants'. *International Journal of Operation & Production Management* 17 (10): 1020–1033.

Novich, N. 1990. 'Distribution Strategy: Are You Thinking Small Enough?' *Sloan Management Review* 31 (1): 71–77.

Peter, Gilmour. 1999. 'Benchmarking Supply Chain Operations'. *Journal of Physical Distribution and Logistics Management* 29 (4): 283–290.

Power, Damien. 2005. 'Supply Chain Management Integration and Implementation: A Literature Review'. *Supply Chain Management* 10 (4): 252–263.

Rushton, A., and J. Oxley. 1989. *Handbook of Logistics and Distribution Management*. London: Kogan Page Ltd.

Slack, N., S. Chambers, C. Harland, A. Harrison, and R. Johnston. 1995. *Supply Chain Operations Management*. London: Pitman Publishing.

Stewart, G. 1995. 'Supply Chain Performance Benchmarking Study Reveals Keys to Supply Chain Excellence'. *Logistics Information Management* 8 (2): 38–44.

Van Hoek, R. I. 2001. 'The Contribution of Performance Measurement to the Expansion of Third Party Logistics Alliances in the Supply Chain'. *International Journal of Operations & Production Management* 21 (1/2): 15–29.

Van Hoek, R. I., A. Harrison, and M. Christopher. 2001. 'Measuring Agile Capabilities in the Supply Chain'. *International Journal of Operations & Production Management* 21 (1/2): 126–147.

BIBLIOGRAPHY

Andersen, Bjørn, and Per-Gaute Pettersen. 1995. *The Benchmarking Handbook: Step-by-Step Instructions*. London, UK: Chapman & Hall.

Benita M. Beamon. 1999. 'Measuring Supply Chain Performance'. *International Journal of Operations & Production Management* 19 (3): 275–292.

Bolstorff, P., and R. Rosenbaum. 2011. *Supply Chain Excellence: A Handbook for Dramatic Improvement Using the SCOR Model, Third Edition*. New York: AMACOM.

Cryts, Jon, Anton Derkach, Scott Nyquist, Ken Ostrowski, and Jack Stephenson. 2007. *Reducing U.S. Greenhouse Gas Emissions: How Much at What Cost?* McKinsey & Company.

Ganga, G. M. D., and L. C. R. Carpinetti. 2011. 'A Fuzzy Logic Approach to Supply Chain Performance Management'. *International Journal of Production Economics* 134 (1): 177–187.

Guide, V. Daniel R., Jr, and Luk N. Van Wassenhove. 2009. 'The Evolution of Closed Loop Supply Chains'. *Operations Research* 57 (1): 10–18.

Lebas, M. J. 1995. 'Performance Measurement and Performance Management'. *International Journal of Production Economics* 41 (1–3): 23–35.

Lee, Hau L. 2010. 'Don't Tweak Your Supply Chain: Rethink It End to End'. *Harvard Business Review* 88 (10): 61–69.

Lima-Junior, F. R., and L. C. R. Carpinetti. 2016. 'Combining SCOR® model and fuzzy TOPSIS for Supplier Evaluation and Management'. *International Journal of Production Economics* 174: 128–141.

World Bank. 2016. *Logistics Performance Index (LPI) Report: The Gap Persists*. Washington, WA: World Bank. http://lpi.worldbank.org/international/global/2016

Mentzer, J. T., J. S. Keebler, N. W. Nix, C. D. Smith, and Z. G. Zacharia. 2001. 'Defining Supply Chain Management'. *Journal of Business Logistics* 22 (2): 1–25.

Min, H., and G. Zhou. 'Supply Chain Modeling: Past, Present and Future'. *Computers & Industrial Engineering* 43 (1–2): 231–249.

Neely, A., M. Bourne, and M. Kennerley 2000. 'Performance Measurement System Design: Developing and Testing a Process Based Approach'. *International Journal of Operations & Production Management* 20 (10): 1119–1145.

Neto, M. S., and S. R. I. Pires. 2012. 'Performance Measurement in Supply Chains: A Study in the Automotive Industry'. *New Advances in Vehicular Technology and Automotive Engineering* 19 (4): 733–746.

Peter, Gilmour. 1999. 'Benchmarking Supply Chain Operations'. *Journal of Physical Distribution and Logistics Management* 29 (4).

Pierreval, H., R. Bruniaux, and C. Caux. 2007. 'A Continuous Simulation Approach for Supply Chains in the Automotive Industry'. *Simulation Modelling Practice and Theory* 15 (2): 185–198.

Plambeck, Erica. 2007. 'Wal-Mart's Sustainable Strategy'. Stanford Graduate School of Business Case OIT–71.

Prokesh, Steven. 2010. 'The Sustainable Supply Chain'. *Harvard Business Review* 88 (10): 70–72.

Ramakrishna, D. S., Ahmed, K. Sabeel, and Kumar, C. D. Ashok. 2010. Proceedings of the National Conference on Advances in Mechanical Engineering, 24–25 September.

Saad, M., and B. Patel. 2006. 'An Investigation of Supply Chain Performance Measurement in the Indian Automotive Sector'. *Benchmarking: An International Journal* 13 (1/2): 36–53.

Sako, M., and S. Helper. 1998. 'The Information Requirements of Trust in Supplier Relations: Evidence from Japan, Europe and the United States'. *Trust and Economic Learning* 23–47.

Supply Chain Council. 2012. *Supply Chain Operations Reference Model (SCOR)*. Available at www.supply-chain.org (accessed on 23 August 2019).

Afterword

FUTURE OF LOGISTICS INDUSTRY IN INDIA

Indian logistics industry is on a growth path. According to the rating agency ICRA, Indian logistics industry is expected to grow at the rate of 8–10% over the medium term, which is a significant growth over the earlier five years' CAGR of 7.8%. The logistics industry in India was estimated to be around US$160 billion, and post-GST implementation, this estimate was revised to about US$215 billion in next two years, according to the Economic Survey 2017–2018. According to the Global Ranking of the World Bank's 2016 LPI, India jumped to the 35th rank in 2016 from the 54th rank in 2014 in terms of overall logistics performance index. The World Bank Survey, in fact, revealed that India's logistics sector has improved its performance in all six parameters: efficiency of the clearance process by border control agencies, including customs; quality of trade- and transport-related infrastructure covering ports, railroads, roads and IT; ease of arranging competitively priced shipments; competence and quality of logistics services (transport operators and customs brokers); ability to track and trace consignments; and timeliness of shipments in reaching destination within the scheduled or expected delivery time.

AIR CARGO SECTOR WITNESSED SIGNIFICANT GROWTH

Indian air cargo sector has witnessed unprecedented growth in the last few years. As per the latest report of CRISIL, India's air cargo segment grew 14–15% in the fiscal year 2018, up from 12% growth in the previous year. With the support of enhanced connectivity, improved infrastructure and regulatory environment, this sector is expected to grow even further in the next five years. The government policy is also supportive, which can be seen from the initiatives taken to boost growth in the sector including the recent National Civil Aviation Policy, which has given a major thrust to boost air cargo business in view of rising e-commerce activities and exports. Besides, Civil Aviation Ministry, Government of India, has set up Air Cargo Logistics Promotion Board with an objective to ensure efficiency, reduce cost and improve inter-ministerial coordination for growth. In addition, significant investment in infrastructure and technology by the government authorities has also supported the growth trajectory.

THE HURDLES STILL TO OVERCOME

Although there are improvements on various parameters, in competitive scenario India has to further improve related to infrastructure and logistics cost and availability of skilled manpower to emerge as a global air cargo hub. The other obstacles include lack of common policies across all sectors of transportation and logistics within India. Also, border control processes in India are still tedious and time-consuming, adding to delays and costs. The cost of logistics to GDP should be about 8%, but in India it is still over 14%. This increases with more regulatory intervention and more touch points in the movement of cargo within the country, although some argue that the cost could be lowered down by increasing the business scale. However, with the enabling policies, entrepreneurs get enthusiastic to invest more in the business activities, which in turn can make business scale bigger.

Many initiatives from the private sector also help in terms of catalysing the growth. For example, all systems must be process-driven without human intervention. Indian logistics players can collaborate with their counterparts in developed countries to develop cost-effective logistics models with infusion of technology to benefit from the projected growth environment in India. The flexible solution in warehousing based on the concept that you pay only when you make use of the facilities as well as leased warehouse avoiding huge investment to start with and implementing effective WMS and automation will help in accelerating the growth process.

INDIAN LOGISTICS INDUSTRY: GOVERNMENT INITIATIVES

Indian logistics industry has really grown during the last five years and GST implementation has also created a positive impact; as a result, more and more corporations are consolidating their operation by moving closer to the consumption centres and thereby driving the demand for the larger warehouse. Leasing activity was primarily driven by the expansion and consolidation of businesses such as e-commerce, TPL, retail, engineering and manufacturing, which together accounted for more than 75% of the leasing reported in recent surveys. The grant of infrastructure status to the logistics and warehousing sector has in fact increased investors' interest, as it has helped developers to gain access to infrastructure lending at easier terms and with enhanced limits. Further, government has also set up National Investment and Infrastructure Fund (NIIF) in partnership with certain domestic and international investors as a quasi-sovereign wealth fund with a corpus of ₹0.4 trillion. Relaxation of FDI norms has further created a positive impact on investment climate in the country's logistics sector. Also, the government has proposed to develop 35 multimodal logistics parks, which will ease the movement of freight and reduce transportation costs to spur further growth in the sector. Another initiative is of increasing the load capacity of heavy vehicles by 20–25% and bringing it at par with global standard which will reduce the logistics cost. The government's plan to develop a National Logistics Information Portal which will be the single online window to link seven ministries including railways and highways under one portal will also be helpful for various stakeholders in the logistics industry.

These initiatives have led to addition of over 20 million sq. ft new supply (both A and B grades) to enter the market by the end of 2019. The entry of various private equity firms and foreign players in the Indian logistics market would boost quality supply, propelling the demand. Cities such as Mumbai, Pune and Chennai have attracted major investments including Delhi-NCR and Bengaluru.

SOME MEGA TRENDS PAVING THE WAY FOR LOGISTICS SECTOR GROWTH

The new trends which will have significant growth in logistics sectors are seen to be the following:

- Demand-driven supply chain
- Robotics increasingly seen to be helping to reduce cost and improve efficiency

- Omni-channel logistics solutions
- Autonomous trucks to take logistics forward
- Blending of logistics and technology services
- Internet of things strengthening the SCM
- Hyper-local supply chains
- Blockchain technology

E-COMMERCE LOGISTICS: DRIVING THE CHANGE

With the robust growth in consumer demand of online purchases, Indian e-commerce industry has emerged as one of the most dynamic and fast-paced growth industry and is at its inflection point. The rapid growth of smartphones and internet connectivity across the country especially in tier-II and tier-III cities has led to the growth of online retailers, and thus direct beneficiary of this is the logistics industry. Whereas many retailers are still losing money, the logistics industry including the courier industry has shown significant positive impact. Developments such as digital payments, analytics-driven customer engagement by the use of artificial intelligence (AI) and machine learning tools, and government-led initiatives have supported the growth of this sector. The biggest challenge, however, in this cycle of supply chain depends on the last-mile delivery. Connect India is committed to design the largest and most robust last-mile distribution e-ecosystem by creating a model through 100,000 bricks-and-mortar stores entrepreneurs, covering up to panchayat level distribution, which will create proximity to the customers in rural India, which is the future of India. However, the challenge here is skilled manpower, higher fuel costs impacting margin due to increased cost and lack of volumes in many rural areas.

INLAND WATERWAYS

The Ministry of Shipping aims to double the share of transportation of cargo through coastal shipping lines and inland water navigation by 2025 under Sagarmala programme. The estimated volume of the total cargo transported by coastal shipping in 2017–2018 is 110 million tonnes. The coastal shipping has also experienced a growth of 9% CAGR over the last three years as against 4.5% CAGR over the preceding three years. The National Waterways Act, 2016, has declared 106 new national waterways in addition to 111 national waterways across 24 states with total navigable network of over 20,000 km of waterways as it exists now.

OCEAN SHIPPING

Shipping lines have experienced consolidation over the last few years. Supply is still high with most services having a higher capacity than demand. The higher capacity and lower demand lead to price competition and rate cutting. Most carriers are expecting larger vessels being delivered during next one to two years and some even placing new orders. The pressure on rates will continue unless demand moves up significantly. The industry is working on digitizing the entire shipping value chain to positively impact the shipper, the consigner and the consignee, and provide much greater control of their shipments by offering instant price quotes and bookings, transparency and tracking, simplified paper work and proactive customer care.

INDIA ROAD TRANSPORT: ADAPTING DIGITIZATION

Indian transportation industry is continually growing at a CAGR of 15%. Over 7 million goods vehicles are moving around the country and the freight volume has reached 1,325 billion tonne km, which is expected to double by the year 2025. India spends about 14% of the GDP on transportation in comparison to 6–8% by developed countries. The industry is still very fragmented, traditional and unorganized. However, the Indian trucking industry has already started accepting digitization in its business, and online truck booking is now common. In the trucking industry, spot market plays a pivotal role in India. Both big and small players have to reach out to the spot market to fulfil their daily transport requirements. Technology-enabled players have taken substantial chunk of the market in last three to four years. Companies are now seen using machinery and AI to predict the kind of volume which would happen at routes and lanes.

THE FUTURE

Some of the researchers suggest that the logistics industry of India which was at ₹6.4 trillion in FY 2017 would grow at a CAGR of 13% over the next three years to get at ₹9.2 trillion by the FY 2020. The government is also extending a lot of support. The Ministry of Commerce and Industry has decided to give a one-time funding of ₹8 million to the sector for building up initial infrastructure and also a phase-wise support of ₹33.9 million in four years to bring down the logistics cost from its current level to 10% in four years' time. This is a significant move to boost the competitiveness of the sector to provide greater impetus for its further growth.

Projects Worth ₹2.35 Trillion under Sagarmala in Maharashtra Alone

The Ministry of Shipping is planning to undertake work worth ₹2.35 trillion under the Sagarmala project in Maharashtra alone. Eight projects entailing an investment of ₹53.84 billion have already been completed, while 45 other projects involving an investment of ₹270 billion are in various stages of implementation. This investment includes ₹1 trillion for waterways development. At least five rivers in the state are included for exploiting potential of water transport in India. An Indian company has forged a joint venture with the Russian firm United Shipbuilding for ethanol-powered 'watercrafts' in the Ganga river.

Port Blair Airport to Get a New Terminal Building

Port Blair airport, which is now known as Veer Savarkar Airport, will have a new terminal building soon. A world-class terminal building is coming up at the airport at an estimated cost of ₹4.17 billion by 2020. The built-up area of the new terminal will be 40,000 sq. m and will be able to handle 1,200 (600 domestic and 600 international) passengers at a time during the peak hours. The new building will have 3 floors, 10 elevators, 6 escalators, 28 check-in counters and an in-line scan system for handling baggage with 3 conveyor belts at the arrival section (2 for domestic and 1 for international). The entire terminal will have 100% natural lighting which will be achieved by skylight along the roof.

Cochin Shipyard Chalks Out Biggest Expansion with ₹17.99 Billion Dry Dock

Cochin Shipyard Ltd is India's biggest state-owned shipbuilder by dock capacity and will start work on a new dry dock at a cost of ₹17.99 billion. The dry dock will generate employment opportunities for 2,000 people, directly or indirectly, in core shipbuilding and ancillary industries. It will also help Cochin in diversifying its product portfolio to build large, complex and technology-intensive vessels such as LNG vessels, jackup rigs, drillships, dredgers and a second indigenous aircraft carrier of much higher capacity than the one it is building for the Indian Navy. The dry dock can accommodate aircraft carriers of 70,000 tonnes docking displacement and tankers and merchant vessels of 55,000 tonnes docking displacement. Larsen & Toubro was awarded the turnkey contract for the new dry dock for ₹12.99 billion, which is expected to be completed by May 2021.

Index